M.A. Leadership for Healthcare

Proven Strategies to Get People to Do What You Want Them to Do

Motivate – Align – Differentiate

WENDY LIPTON-DIBNER, MA

GREENBRANCH
PUBLISHING
Phoenix, Maryland

Published by Greenbranch Publishing, LLC
PO Box 208
Phoenix, MD 21131
Phone: (800) 933-3711
Fax: (410) 329-1510
Email: info@greenbranch.com
Website: www.mpmnetwork.com,
www.soundpractice.net

Requests for permission, information on our multi-copy pricing program, or other information should be addressed to the Permissions Department, Greenbranch Publishing, LLC.

This publication is designed to provide general medical practice management information and is sold with the understanding that neither the author nor the publisher is engaged in rendering legal, accounting, ethical, or clinical advice. If legal or other expert advice is required, the services of a competent professional person should be sought.

Printed in the United States of America by United Book Press, Inc.

PUBLISHER
Nancy Collins

EDITORIAL ASSISTANT
Jennifer Weiss

BOOK DESIGNER
Laura Carter
Carter Publishing Studio

COVER DESIGNER
Jim Dodson
Carter Publishing Studio

COPYEDITORS
Karen Doyle, Nancy Dickson

About the Author

WENDY LIPTON-DIBNER, MA is the President of Professional Impact, Inc., an International Training and Consulting firm that specializes in helping doctors and their staff to master the people factor. Her practical solutions have helped hundreds of medical and dental clients to provide a higher level of patient care, build a consistently productive and fulfilling workplace, develop strong relationships with colleagues, generate a steady stream of ongoing referrals, and achieve substantial increases in revenues despite ongoing changes in insurance reimbursement and the economy.

A social scientist with a firm belief in the power of research and an entrepreneur with a passion for unusual ideas that yield strong results, Wendy is making a significant impact throughout the healthcare community. Her entertaining and energetic style has received ovations from Akron to Australia, while her scientifically grounded strategies and proven formulas consistently yield measurable results for her clients.

Wendy received her Masters Degree in Sociology and Social Psychology from Duke University, has been in private practice, and has owned and managed five successful businesses. She was elected to the World Who's Who of Women and the International Who's Who Among Professional Women, and has been a respected consultant in corporate and healthcare environments for almost 30 years. An expert in organizational change, Wendy propels people to action by providing customized solutions and then identifying and breaking through the barriers that could sabotage their implementation.

Wendy is a member of the National Speakers Association and the Academy of Dental Management Consultants. She has published extensively in social science journals, is a frequent contributor to association newsletters and *The Journal of Medical Practice Management*, and hosts an ongoing forum and monthly column on PinkTooth.net. Her first book, *The ACTION Formula: The Shortest Distance Between What You Have and What You Want*, has helped countless readers to attain greater fulfillment and prosperity in their personal and professional lives.

In addition to conducting speaking engagements worldwide, Wendy works with her husband and partner, Dr. Hal Dibner, to provide consulting and in-house training workshops for healthcare practices and hospitals throughout the U.S. and Canada.

To learn more about Wendy and Professional Impact, Inc.:
Visit her website at www.Pro-Impact.com or
Contact Wendy directly at Wendy@Pro-Impact.com

Contents

Tables and Activities

TABLES

ACTIVITIES

Everyone's Mad for *M.A.D. Leadership for Healthcare*!

I was afraid of reading it too fast and missing important pearls! This book is AMAZING! A TOUR DE FORCE! A MUST READ FOR ANY HEALTHCARE PROVIDER WHO SEES PATIENTS AND FEELS PROUD TO PROVIDE LEADING EDGE CARE! I learned the science of medicine in medical training. I thought I had learned the art of medicine from my mentors as well. However, NOBODY can claim to be fully skilled in the art of medicine without knowing and using these powerful, yet simple tools that you outlined. This is the first book I have seen that systematically looks at how we can most effectively convince our patients to agree to the care that they need. Given the enormous implications that could have on public health, these original ideas will likely become a pillar for future investigation in this field.

Wendy, I knew you were special when you came out to consult for my practice. And I knew then that your ideas were very powerful. But still, this has really blown me away! I would be really surprised if this book is not excerpted for use in medical school curricula in the future. I feel an enormous sense of pride for you . . . this is such a home run!!!!

Daren Primack, MD, Managing Partner, Pacific Heart and Vascular Medical Group

I've spent a lifetime developing patient and practice management skills. I've read everything I could get my hands on, but nowhere have I ever read such a comprehensive, commonsense approach. It should be the bible of all healthcare practices, maybe for all businesses.

M.A.D. Leadership for Healthcare is not your ordinary "how to" book. This book unlocks the secrets of the human psyche — our own and that of the people we need to relate to on a daily basis in order to be effective and succeed.

Wise and witty, M.A.D. Leadership for Healthcare is easy to read, easy to teach and easily adaptable to the practice environment. If we all incorporate these techniques into our practices, we may actually have a reasonable answer to the health care crisis.

It's a masterpiece. I wish I'd had this years ago but it's never too late to get better. I can't wait to give out copies to my colleagues.

M. Constance B. Greeley, DDS, Private Practice, Orthodontics

If you don't think you need a book like this you are very wrong. If you are like me, and the vast majority of my colleagues are, you know nothing about managing people. You might think you know something but I bet you do not. We spend all our time learning and practicing the art of medicine and essentially no time learning business and management. It is these management skills, as I have come to realize, that are just as important as our medical knowledge, if you want a busy practice.

This book helps us understand how to better manage people. It teaches you how to understand what drives our employees, how to better relate to our employees, how to talk to our employees, and ultimately how to get them to do what you want them

to. When employees consistently do what you want them to do, your practice runs better and you make more money with less stress.

The lessons and explanations in the book are clear and easy to follow. Many of the ideas are new, and integration of them into your everyday life requires some thought. But if you take these concepts, practice them, and integrate them into your work life, you will have a much more productive and happy office. I can personally attest to that. I wish I had read this book before I started my practice 10 years ago as it would have saved me a lot of grief. I highly recommend this book to any and all physicians who have an interest in making their office run better and making more money at the same time.

Scott Wrye, MD, Private Practice, Plastic Surgery

This is a great book. It's an instructional "How To" guide to manage your practice life and your relations to your patients, your staff and colleagues, and to enlighten your personal life. Having had Wendy as the consultant of my orthodontic practice, I can testify how the book will guide a practice to evaluate all the interactions that are paramount in providing a service for people in a caring environment. After all, everything in the healthcare field is a service for people business. This book is a great, step-by-step description of how Wendy performs her magic in evaluating your practice and encourages your Team to give Five-Star patient care and in turn receive great financial rewards. I recommend this book to everyone in the health-care field. This book will definitely be required reading for the Orthodontic residents at the University of Illinois College of Dentistry.

I emphasize for first time readers the importance of thoroughly digesting and understanding Chapters 4 to 11 to realize the rewards of M.A.D.

Robert Manasse, DDS, Clinical Professor, University of Illinois at Chicago Department of Orthodontics, Private Practice, Orthodontics, Member of Board of Directors, Chicago Dental Society

Anyone truly committed to creating a work environment that is fun, productive, meaningful, and beyond the top of the Wow scale can embrace this book and make it happen. Filled to the edge of the page with Wendy's characteristic charm and humor, this manual is golden — chockfull with how-to's every step of the way, illustrations of the key elements, handy-dandy charts designed to make your practice life flow, and lots of success tips.

Having participated in the hands-on M.A.D. training and team building as only Wendy and Hal can do it, I can vouch for how well it works. We had a good, solid orthodontic practice, got M.A.D., rejuvenated ourselves and our team, and boosted our bottom-line into Unbelievable!

Now here you are, browsing in the Motivation and Practice Management section (could that be your deepest Desire calling?). You're scanning this book (the Resource you need) to actualize your Desire. Buy the book (Permission) and get going on the adventure of a lifetime . . . Action.

Johanna V. Manasse, Practice Manager (retired), Manasse Orthodontics, Ltd.

This is quite an effort — she has captured in detail the powerful techniques that she has perfected during her career as a business consultant. My staff and I worked hard with Wendy over many months to utilize these techniques. We have found them to be very useful in speaking to and understanding our patients as well as each other. Her techniques also allowed us to get out of our own way as we transitioned from an 80% insurance based practice to an 80% cosmetic, non-insurance-based practice. In helping us to get past our own barriers, we are now able to help our patients do the same.

The book is packed with not only descriptions of the techniques but various examples and scenarios encountered during Wendy's career. These real-world narratives are necessary to allow for group discussion and practice. The concepts in this book appear simple on the surface but they do represent a change that will require commitment from the doctors and their staff.

I recommend this book to anyone who is ready to step out of the drudge that modern medicine has become and into a world where the patient is the focus of attention.

Douglas M. Stevens, MD, Private Practice
Past President Lee County Medical Society,
Delegate to the Florida Medical Society

M.A.D. Leadership for Healthcare summarizes the successful techniques used by Ms. Lipton-Dibner in her very effective healthcare consulting business. This book is a blueprint for peace, prosperity, and understanding in medical and dental practices. Utilizing the techniques described in this book, our practice has enjoyed a better working environment, with happier office staff and higher conversion rates for our patients. Because of these techniques, the "difficult" patient has become a rarity. This book is a "Must Read" for struggling and thriving practices alike. Not just a great book on applied business psychology, this book can guide healthcare professionals to identify and achieve whatever they truly want!

Luke J. Curtsinger, MD, Private Practice, Coastal Empire Plastic Surgery

If you were to be able to magically change your practice into what you want, how would it look? Would each of your employees look forward to getting to work each day? Would they go out of their way to help your patients have a better experience with their visit? Would they treat each other with respect and humility, working hard to bring out the best in each other? Would they promote your practice as the greatest practice on planet Earth? This book can show you how to make this a reality. I have seen it happen in my own practice.

In this age of increasing medical practice complexity with growing costs and decreasing bottom line, finding and keeping good employees is mandatory for success. It is only by investing effort that you can hope to bring out the very best in each member of your staff. But how in our fast-paced lives do we get the training and the tools so that we are able to help our associates develop into the team we need? It is to this end that M.A.D. Leadership was written. This easy-to-read and understand text teaches the formulas that help get us to understand those human beings we have hired without being threatening or dominating. And, just as importantly, it shows us ways to help each employee to problem solve for him or herself, thus increasing potential and self worth.

For those of us who have been through a Dibner-lead motivational program, this text will be both a superb review as well as a handy reference guide. There is obviously far more in these pages than can have been taught in any two- to three-day session. Thus, reading and studying will lead to an even greater understanding and appreciation of the ACTION Formula and all that goes with it. Try reading a section each day before going to work. Your life and that of your employees will be better for it!

James W. Srour, MD, President and Managing Partner
Gastroenterology Associates of York

In dental school, they taught me how to fill a tooth, but not how to communicate with patients. In orthodontic school, I learned to straighten teeth, but not how to motivate my staff. Wendy Lipton-Dibner's book helps to fill this critical void.

She has written a "Must Read" for all professionals hoping to be extraordinary in the healthcare field. Gosh, I hope my competitors never get hold of this book!

Roger Haas, DDSMS, President, Haas Orthodontic Arts

As a "graduate" of a Wendy training session, I can say that this is "Wendy in a book." All of the information about the different languages, Action Types, and motivational words and phrases is there. It was a good review for me. In addition to this is the substance of her book "The ACTION Formula." In our practice, Wendy and Hal's coaching has been instrumental in helping us to bring patients in for appointments and get them to the operating room. Based on the principles in Wendy's book, we also have a PowerPoint presentation that we use to motivate patients, introduce our practice, and tell why we're distinct from other surgical practices.

If you can't get Wendy in person, buy the book. Your practice will grow, and you, your staff, and your patients will be happier and healthier for it.

Harold L. Kent, MD, FACS, Private Practice, Georgia Coast Surgical

M.A.D. Leadership for Healthcare is an enlightening and much needed text to help us understand why healthcare sometimes finds itself in a mess. As we look to serve, we perhaps forget (or never learned) why we are who we are, and how best to service the patients, our ultimate customer. Wendy brings insights into healthcare that have helped our large Heart and Vascular institute focus upon patiently and positively impacting patients' lives during their greatest times of fear and need. Really a super awesome job from an impressive lady.

Louis Cannon, MD, FACA, FCCP, FACC, FACP, Director,
The Heart and Vascular Institute of Northern Michigan, President,
the Cardiac and Vascular Research Center of Northern Michigan

I felt many emotions as I read this book. Wendy covers with wisdom and humor many of the topics that keep those of us in private practice awake at night. This is a Must-Read for anybody in any healthcare field. M.A.D. Leadership for Healthcare will be on my desk as a go-to reference book from now on.

Laura Dennison, PhD, Doctor of Audiology, Private Practice

Foreword

HEALTHCARE IS CHANGING, and doctors are taking note of it. These changes are causing doctors to experience increased stress as they work harder to see more patients in less time. There is also a significant problem with staff morale in many healthcare practices that in turn affects the patient experience. The time has arrived for a transformation of the methods that were used in the past to deliver healthcare to our patients. We need to infuse new techniques to take care of patients, to motivate our staff members to exceed patient expectations, and ultimately, to bring back the enjoyment that we once had in our practices.

While there are very few of us who can make changes in healthcare policy or improve the reimbursements for our services, all of us can make changes in our practice that will make the practice more effective and enjoyable for patients, staff, and doctors. This seems like a daunting task as most doctors are creatures of comfort and seldom venture out of their comfort zones. But there has never been a better time than now to initiate changes in your practice.

We need a solution and a remedy for the problems and issues that impact nearly every contemporary healthcare practice, and Wendy Lipton-Dibner's three-step M.A.D. Formula has brought it to us. Her formula will allow you to change your practice from the same ol'-same ol' to a new, vibrant, and effective practice that will attract new patients and ensure that they have a positive experience in the practice; provide an atmosphere that will energize your staff to take outstanding care of the patients; improve staff retention and partner effectiveness; and increase practice revenues.

Ms. Lipton-Dibner provides practical solutions to improve patient outcomes and satisfaction, increase your productivity, and ultimately allow doctors to enjoy their practices and leave at the end of the day feeling gratified that they have truly provided an outstanding service to their patients. Her M.A.D. formula — Motivate, Align, and Differentiate — applies to any practice from solo private practices to large multi-specialty and academic practices. Her techniques have been tested in hundreds of practices and have a proven track record of results yielding increased efficiency and productivity. The techniques can be easily accomplished with minimal added expense and with your existing staff.

So what have you got to lose? Put this book at the top of your reading list. Then don't just put it down and comment on how nice the ideas are, but put the ideas into action. Start by implementing a few of her techniques and watch the results for yourself. You won't be disappointed. Neither will your patients, your partners, or your staff. This book is a gold mine; so read it and pull out a few nuggets and weave them into your practice culture. Don't get angry, get M.A.D.!

Neil Baum, MD
Clinical Professor of Urology, Tulane Medical School
Author of *Marketing Your Clinical Practice —
Ethically, Effectively, and Economically*

Author's Note

THIS IS THE PART OF THE BOOK in which authors traditionally offer thanks for all of the help, support, and guidance they received from their parents, spouse, third cousin, best clients, closest friends, first grade teachers, and personal pet groomers. I too have many thanks to give, but I'm guessing you're not interested in reading about them. So instead, I'm going to use this space to tell you a quick story.

In the winter of 2000, my husband, Hal, and I took a seven-day cruise. At the time, Hal was in his 28th year as a private practice psychologist, and I was the president of a successful training and consulting firm. Occasionally, Hal and I worked together conducting programs for mutual clients. We were doing what we loved and making a good living.

Then, in the middle of the Caribbean Sea, we met Dr. Gary Saretsky. Determined to have a real vacation, we all agreed that we would refrain from discussing work. We had no idea about each other's credentials or "real" lives, and we didn't care. We laughed, we danced, we sang karaoke, and we became fast friends.

As the cruise was winding down, Gary finally broke the rule and asked, "So, what *do* you do?" In the interest of keeping to our original agreement, I simply said that I was a consultant, but Gary was curious and egged me on.

Never one to turn down an audience, I went into more detail. I told Gary about my somewhat eclectic background that led me from academics to business to private practice and ultimately to speaking, training, and consulting. I bragged a bit about my proprietary formulas and how I had helped Fortune 500 companies to increase their revenues by as much as 200%. Finally, I told him about the programs Hal and I did together with executive teams, resolving conflicts and building strategic action plans.

When I came up for air, Gary looked at me very seriously and simply said, *"My clients need you."* I asked him to explain, and he told me about his work in healthcare consulting and described some of his clients and the problems that kept them from increasing their success:

- A family practice that had team problems that kept them from running an efficient operation;
- A cosmetic dentistry practice that needed a new sales model to accompany their expansion plans;
- A cardiology group that needed to learn how to motivate their patients to follow treatment recommendations for lifestyle changes;
- A general dentistry practice that needed to help patients to say "yes" to the dentistry they needed, regardless of insurance coverage; and

- An orthopedic practice with 12 physicians who couldn't agree on much of anything except their desire to practice good medicine and build their success so as to pay for the $6 million building they'd just completed.

Gary invited me to speak at an event his company was sponsoring. I did a 45-minute presentation on leadership, and as I walked off the stage I was surrounded by a swarm of doctors who had questions, sought advice, and wanted contact information. Gary was right. They needed us.

Since then, Hal and I have worked with hundreds of healthcare professionals in medicine and dentistry. As our clients made changes, their success grew exponentially with reduced turnover, improved morale and productivity, satisfied patients, increased referrals and revenues, and a better quality of life. None of this would have happened if Gary hadn't matched his clients' needs to our solutions.

It was also Gary who introduced me to Nancy Collins of Greenbranch Publishing. Never one to turn away innovative approaches to practice management issues, Nancy is on the cutting edge of what healthcare practices need. She has provided me with a wealth of enthusiasm, counsel, and friendship as we worked together with her outstanding staff to bring you articles in *The Journal of Medical Practice Management*®, and now, this book.

If I were going to do the formal "thank you" thing (which I said I wouldn't), Nancy and Gary would be at the top of my list. They lit the path that allowed us to find the people who needed us most, and there is no way to know how many people they have indirectly helped along the way.

Truthfully, there's a really long list of people I'd thank if I were going to do the traditional "thank-you" thing. But I said I wouldn't. Besides . . . You've Got to Get M.A.D.! So, let's go . . .

Prologue

DR. GREAT AND DR. WONDERFUL went camping in the desert. After they got their tent all set up, both doctors fell soundly asleep.

Some hours later, Dr. Great woke Dr. Wonderful and said, *"Dr. Wonderful, look toward the sky, what do you see?"*

Dr. Wonderful replied, *"I see millions of stars."*

"What does that tell you?" asked Dr. Great.

Dr. Wonderful pondered for a minute, then said, *"Astronomically speaking, it tells me there are millions of galaxies. Time wise, it tells me that it is approximately a quarter past three in the morning. Theologically, it tells me the Lord is all powerful, and we are small and insignificant. Meteorologically, it seems we will have a beautiful day tomorrow. What does it tell you, Dr. Great?"*

Dr. Great looked up and said, *"Someone stole our tent."*

Sometimes we get lost in the details and lose track of what is right in front of our noses. We miss the obvious, the big "DUH" that, if only we'd seen it, might have enabled us to avoid a problem or build a greater success.

What is the great big DUH that is keeping you from being as successful as you could be?

After consulting with hundreds of doctors, working with their staff, meeting their patients, and comparing notes with other consultants who had worked in the practices before us, I can tell you without reservation,

The great big "DUH" in healthcare is the people factor.

Whenever people ask me what I do, I tell them, *"I help doctors and their staff to manage the people factor by learning how to communicate more effectively with each other and their patients."*

I remember the first time someone looked me straight in the eyes and said, *"Well it's a good thing someone is doing it."* He was a neurosurgeon.

Since then, I've heard a great many responses. In airports, restaurants, grocery stores, hair salons, pharmacies, book stores, and healthcare facilities, people everywhere want to talk about their experiences with doctors and their staff.

> *"I've got 18 different doctors, one for every two square inches of my body, and I can't get them to talk to each other."*

> *"Nobody cares any more. Just move 'em in and move 'em out."*

"I left my doctor. She was great, but her employees were impossible to deal with."

Patients aren't the only ones talking. Doctors have told me,

"Medicine isn't fun anymore."

"My malpractice insurance is higher than my mortgage payments."

"I've got so many people working for me, I don't know who is doing what."

"I can't make money anymore."

"I have to work two to three times as long just to make the same money I used to make."

"I've got more people handling insurance and billing than I do treating my patients!"

"I can't recommend a crown any more without some patient thinking I'm trying to take advantage of them and sell them something they don't really need."

"My biggest problem is finding good staff."

"My biggest problem is finding good partners."

"My partners and I only talk when we absolutely have to. Too much water has passed under the bridge."

"We're not bad people, just bad partners."

"I don't have time to be nice."

"Every vendor has something else they want me to sell. I'm not a salesman, I'm a doctor."

Practice administrators tell me,

"I dread our partner meetings. It's like herding cats to get them there, and if they do come, they fight worse than my teenagers."

"We can't keep staff. I'm constantly interviewing, hiring, and re-training."

"It's the gossip and the constant negativity that makes me nuts. Why can't they all just act like grown-ups?"

The answer is both simple and complex. The fact is that doctors and their teams have lost track of each other and their patients in response to a frenzied barrage of:

- Overbooked schedules;
- Transitions from old to new policies, procedures, and guidelines;
- The introduction of electronic record keeping;
- Risk management;
- Changing economic pressures;

- Legislative changes;
- Innovations in technology and sophisticated treatment options;
- Rapidly changing additions to pharmaceutical solutions;
- The introduction of new diagnostic equipment and testing options;
- Increased continuing education and certification opportunities for healthcare personnel;
- Media- and Internet-driven consumer education that increases patient demands for explanation and reassurance;
- Expert opinions that shift as quickly as new research comes in; and
- A consistent lack of resources that leads everyone to have to do more with less.

In point of fact, many of the innovative solutions of 21st century healthcare are causing people problems we never anticipated:

- Receptionists wear strained smiles as they try to communicate with patients who are complaining about time spent waiting, doctors who are complaining about holes in their schedules, and staff who are complaining about misplaced files and reports;
- While patients try to negotiate fees and co-pays, doctors try to explain about decreased revenues, changes in managed care, increased risk for litigation, and ever rising malpractice insurance costs;
- Referring doctors call for test results, while nurses work to hide their frustration and embarrassment as they discover that the tests were lost, misfiled, incorrectly ordered, or never processed;
- Dental hygienists complain about patients who don't want to hear the education they provide and who won't follow their recommendations for preventive care;
- Treatment coordinators complain about patients who don't show up for their consultations and about those who do show up, but say "no" to the procedures they want and/or need;
- In hospitals, nurses complain about doctors not answering their pages while doctors complain about pages they consider "unnecessary";
- Administrators describe Team problems at staff and partner levels regarding resistance to change, staff turnover, negativity, gossip, and low morale; and
- In board rooms from coast to coast, partners have difficulty reaching closure and consensus as they try to incorporate new and innovative solutions to increase their success.

As doctors and administrators search for answers to their problems, they look to practice management consultants for operational solutions to resolve patient flow, call scheduling, time management, charting and electronic records, billing and coding, risk management, and a myriad of other problems. In fact, millions of dollars are invested in consulting every year for the purpose of resolving operational details.

My own clients have confessed to spending massive amounts of time and money with competent consultants, only to fail to follow through on what they've learned.

I've seen the evidence. From solo practices to large hospitals, we find offices with unused manuals, cobwebbed workbooks, and unopened software piled under stacks of unused patient information brochures and marketing pamphlets.

Over the years, I've talked about this problem with dozens of my colleagues in medical and dental practice management who specialize in the operational side of healthcare. They all tell me the same thing:

The simple part of practice management is identifying the specific operational and clinical protocols, procedures, hardware, and software that will improve your outcomes. The hard part is getting people to use them immediately and consistently.

I have no knowledge regarding what is the most efficient way to organize patient flow in a 12-doctor practice or which documents need to be scanned or shredded. My expertise is the people factor: I know how to get people to do what you want them to do, and to do it with enthusiasm, positive attitudes, and consistent results. That's what this book is all about.

WHAT DOES IT TAKE TO GET PEOPLE TO DO WHAT YOU WANT THEM TO DO?

It takes knowing how to Motivate and Align all of the people associated with your practice and how to Differentiate your practice so that your uniqueness is understood and sought after by your community. Most important, it takes developing the desire, ability, and willingness to change.

The problem is that in healthcare today, most people don't know how to Motivate, Align, and Differentiate so as to create and sustain change. They know that they need to change, spend lots of money to create a change, dictate that the change should be made, expect that the change will be made, and then wonder why it isn't.

In the meantime, patients are mad, healthcare workers are mad, and most of all, doctors are mad. They are mad about their disconnection with their patients, their inability to bring in the revenues they want, their disrupted lifestyle, time lost with their families and friends, and not being able to give time to their patients. Mostly, they are mad about constantly finding themselves at the mercy of others who know nothing about what it takes to do what they do and losing track of the reasons that brought them into healthcare in the first place.

There is much to be changed in healthcare, but the first step is to stop the mad by addressing the "DUH."

It's time to master the people factor so that doctors, administrators, staff, and patients can come together to create a positive environment where everyone gets their needs met with grace and dignity.

When you master the people factor, the operational details are more manageable, the changes are embraced with enthusiasm, the tasks are better served, the results are stronger, and the revenues are higher.

With all of the changes that are happening in our economy and in national, state, and local legislatures, healthcare professionals have two choices: You can stand by and watch as doctors, staff, and patients get increasingly mad. Or you can take action, address the "DUH," and make a huge difference for people while increasing your revenues and building the practice you want. The fact that you're reading this book tells me that you've chosen to take action. The next step is

You've Got to Get M.A.D.!

Are you ready?

SECTION

Introduction

Chapter 1

In Search of a Good Night's Sleep

WHAT ARE THE QUESTIONS THAT WAKE YOU AT 2:00 A.M.? Are you thinking about your exciting plans for the future? Or are you bolting upright, heart racing, palms sweating, consumed by questions like:

> *How do I get my patients to change lifelong habits that are causing them harm? How do I get them to keep their appointments, be on time, and say "yes" to the procedures and treatments they need? How do I build strong and loyal relationships and reduce my risk for malpractice? How do I get my patients to go out-of-pocket for elective services and pay their bills in a timely manner? How do I get them to talk when I need information and stop talking when I'm ready to move on? How do I get them to trust me when I have only seven minutes to diagnose and treat? How do I get them to refer their friends and family members to my care?*

Or perhaps you are tossing and turning, wondering:

> *How do I get staff members to be self-motivated and proactive? How do I get them to behave professionally and sustain positive, be-of-service attitudes? How do I get them to work by my side as if they were virtual extensions of me? How do I get long-term employees to welcome and assist new hires? How do I get administrative and clinical personnel to understand and accommodate each others' needs? How do I create and maintain a well-oiled machine without threats and bribery? How do I get them to stop the back-biting and negativity and maintain a positive environment under stress?*

Or maybe you're pacing back and forth, contemplating:

> *How do I get my credentialed employees to follow my vision and coordinate their roles with those who are above and below their ranking? How do I get them to find the perfect balance between patient education and revenue-generating activities? How do I get them to learn and utilize effective leadership skills? How do I get them to take charge, but remember who's in charge?*

By now you've turned on the light, reflecting:

How do I get a group of independent doctors with differing objectives, perspectives, and processes to come together under a common umbrella and present a united front? How do I get people who were trained to work solo, to come together and work effectively and efficiently as a team? How do I get the rebels to play the political game? How do I get them to combine their clinical expertise with good communication skills? How do I get them to be willing to market, network, and grow the business? How do I get them to "play nice" with each other, colleagues, and referring doctors? How do I get those who love chatting with patients to speed up their productivity? On the other hand, how do I get those who are all about the technical aspects to stop and connect with their patients?

You pour some hot milk as you ask yourself:

How can we differentiate ourselves in the community as the go-to experts for our specialization? How do I get our staff and doctors to present a consistent, positive image internally and externally? How can I get the people in the community to understand that we're different and how we're different? How can we set ourselves apart from our competition so we can attract the kinds of patients, staff, and partners that we want?

Finally, you stumble back to bed grumbling your bottom-line challenge:

How do I get people to do what I want them to do?

If you are up nights asking yourself any of these questions, you're not alone. Your colleagues all over the country are up nights asking themselves similar questions and searching for practical solutions.

Here's a simple truth about healthcare in the 21st century:

Doctors, administrators, and staff are getting burned out. But it's not from doing the actual work. It's from not knowing how to deal effectively with people and get them to change.

I know a little about waking up at 2:00 a.m. I've spent a lifetime thinking in the middle of the night, going over in my mind all the patterns I'd seen, putting them all together in search of the formulas that would get people to do what I wanted them to do.

I remember the day I first discovered that I could get someone else to do what I wanted. My techniques were in the tadpole stages, but they were effective:

I stood up tall, put on my "cute" smile, cocked my head ever so slightly, and said, *"But if I go to sleep, who will keep you company?"* My mother burst out laughing, changed her mind, and let me stay up to watch a movie with her. I don't remember the movie, but I do remember that we had brownies . . . with ice cream.

Now I'm 51, and I still like it when people do what I want them to do. Of course, now I have certifications, publications, diplomas, and awards that say I'm an expert in the subject. I've also got solutions that work. After you read this book, you'll have them too.

Strange as it may seem, there are people who don't think about this stuff in the middle of the night. They genuinely don't worry about *how* things are done, *when* they are done, or even *if* they are done. That's not me, and it's probably not you, or you wouldn't be reading this book. I used to wish I could be more like those people who don't care. But now I think this is much more fun.

Be honest. Other than brownie sundaes, what's better than when you can get people to do what you want them to do? Especially when they do it without your having to ask them, plead with them, threaten them, bribe them, or hire someone else to make them.

On the chance that you are the kind of person who won't be able to sleep until you know where all of this is going, I'm going to give you the bottom line right now:

If you want everyone to do what you want them to do, all you have to do is establish rapid trust and rapport, and then apply targeted techniques that will allow you to motivate and align the people and differentiate your practice[1] in the community.

That's all there is to it. The rest of this book will show you how.

First, you'll read about proven, practical techniques to build rapport and develop trust in a quick and efficient manner through the **Four Languages of The M.A.D. Formula.** Then, you'll be ready to get **M.A.D.**:

Motivate people to action (your partners, your staff, your patients and their families, referring colleagues, vendors, students, the community at large, and yourself).

Align people to a common mission and action plan while encouraging individual strengths to create an environment that runs efficiently and enthusiastically, regardless of conflict and other stressful situations.

Differentiate your practice in your community by consistently projecting your uniqueness internally and externally.

---

[1] For ease of presentation, I use the word "practice" to represent all medical and dental facilities, from the smallest home-based solo practices to the largest hospitals and clinics.

"But I already do a lot of that stuff!"

Good!

If you're getting all the results you want, your practice is running smoothly, and you're living the life you want, then you're good to go. But if you want more, then read on.

I've worked with many clients who already had a good start on all three of the components of The M.A.D. Formula, but who needed some new strategies to enable them to take their results to a higher level. I've also worked with clients who had devoted their careers to clinical excellence and who had lost track of the people along the way. These clients needed to apply more of the techniques in this book in order to find a better balance and improve their results.

Whether you need only a few new strategies, or decide to apply them all, this book will give you what you need to master the people factor and enhance your success. Every technique and strategy in The M.A.D. Formula has been tested and proven throughout the United States and Canada, as well as internationally in Europe and Australia. It simply works.

I'm excited that you will soon be using The M.A.D. Formula because I've seen what it can do. My clients have found that they are able to help more people in less time and are enjoying the people more every day. Their practices are filled with happy, productive, energized people, and a consistent profit stream. They have rediscovered the passion that brought them into healthcare in the first place, and they sleep through the night, dreaming about the life they've come to enjoy.

This book isn't a panacea, and it certainly won't solve all of the problems in healthcare today. I believe it is a beginning, however, in that it will give you some strong solutions to manage the people factor. Who knows what you will accomplish from there.

If you have questions, please don't hesitate to contact me. I'm here to help.

Sweet dreams!

Wendy

Chapter 2

Overview

THIS BOOK IS DESIGNED to help you expand your perspectives and gain insights into how to work and live more effectively with people. How you choose to use the information will depend on your unique situation and position. Use this as a quick-reference book for specific goals, or read it cover to cover, immersing yourself in the theory and going one step at a time in the practical techniques until you have mastered The M.A.D. Formula.

You will find this book packed with information, explanations, and step-by-step formulas. Some of the techniques are quick and easy to apply, while others involve more complex processes and require you to make decisions about how to incorporate them for your unique organization.

There will be times when you will probably find yourself thinking "*I knew that*!" and kick yourself for failing to follow your own instincts. There will be moments when you may laugh out loud at the simplicity and common sense of these strategies, and other times when you discover the one piece of the puzzle that has been missing for you.

You will read true stories that cause you to raise your eyebrows and others that may bring a tear to your eye. Some case studies may lead you to worry whether their situation is happening in your organization while others may lead you to call an immediate meeting to get everyone to mimic their success. You will probably vacillate between skepticism, curiosity, and excitement as you find the formulas that fit for you as well as the ones that don't.

I will tell you what I tell my clients:

Whenever you find yourself doubting or questioning an idea, ask yourself one question: If I was guaranteed that I wouldn't fail, would I do it?

If the answer is "no," then that means it's not the right technique for your style or situation. If the answer is a tentative "yes," then that simply means you're not ready, so give yourself time to get comfortable using the technique in your practice. Consider rehearsing the techniques in safe environments with friends and family until you feel confident enough to bring them to work.

With a little bit of tweaking, every technique in this book will work at home with the same power as it does in your practice.

Once you've mastered a technique that once had you doubting yourself, remember how you felt in the beginning. It will help you to be a better teacher when you encourage others to use the techniques later on.

M.A.D Leadership for Healthcare is divided into six sections, with relevant information divided into separate chapters for easy reference:

SECTION ONE: INTRODUCTION

You're reading this section now. I think you've probably got this one figured out. Let's move on.

SECTION TWO: THE FOUR LANGUAGES OF THE M.A.D. FORMULA

This section will give you the critical background information you need to fully utilize the strategies and techniques in Sections Three, Four, and Five. Here you'll learn the science of building trust and rapport. You will also learn unique communication strategies that will allow you to expand and customize The M.A.D. Formula techniques to match your unique personality and the specific needs of the people with whom you are working. Specifically, Section Two will help you to:

- Understand the four sciences that form the foundation for using The M.A.D. Formula;
- Learn to rapidly build trust and rapport;
- Identify the communication needs of others within the first 30 seconds of contact;
- Understand how social background affects the decisions we make today;
- Identify and apply the five different States of Mind that are critical to communication;
- Discover how self-esteem plays a factor in what people do (and don't do);
- Develop a new understanding of people — how they think, what they feel, and why they do what they do;
- Find your personal comfort zones when working with people who are different than you; and
- Identify and conquer your blind spots.

Warning: The information in Section Two may permanently shift your entire perspective on people and yourself!

SECTION THREE: M IS FOR MOTIVATE

In this section, you will discover the missing link to Motivation and find the formulas that explain what drives people to say "yes" and "no." You'll receive powerful tools to help your team, your patients, your colleagues, and your family to get and stay Motivated, and develop skills that will enable you to:

- Distinguish and apply external and internal Motivation techniques;
- Conquer resistance to change among your team and patients;
- Strengthen and redefine your role as a leader;
- Learn about incentive programs and how they help and hurt your practice;
- Discover secrets for hiring the right people;
- Apply "praise" and "discipline" for maximum results;
- Apply The ACTION Formula to Motivate partners, staff, colleagues, and patients to do what you need them to do;
- Motivate yourself to action;
- Identify and break through your organizational success barriers;
- Build powerful scripts that will energize your incoming and outgoing calls;
- Significantly decrease no-shows and late arrivals;
- Incorporate a strategy to Motivate patients to follow treatment recommendations for lifestyle changes;
- Help patients to say "yes" to the elective procedures they want and/or need;
- Educate patients about your solutions without being "salesy" or pushy;
- Sharpen your case presentation skills;
- Handle and work through patient objections;
- Manage the financial presentation with style, grace, and effectiveness; and
- Dramatically increase your internal and external referrals.

SECTION FOUR: A IS FOR ALIGN

Section Four will help you to create and sustain powerful relationships between and among your doctors, leaders, staff, patients, and the community you serve. Here you'll find all new tools that will help you to:

- Identify your "Team of Sub-Teams," and get them all working together effectively;
- Create long-term relationships with patients and referring doctors;
- Build loyalty and commitment, internally and externally;
- Help others to build pride in themselves and their work;
- Establish a Success Agreement to limit threats and negativity on your Team;

- Resolve and avoid internal and external conflict;
- Discover the Language of Rules that guides the choices of every member of your Team;
- Manage uncomfortable emotions and difficult situations;
- Stop negativity and destructive gossip;
- Apply The Candor Formula to request behavioral changes;
- Use The Accountability Formula to avoid finger-pointing and blame;
- Use The Emotions Formula to de-escalate highly charged situations;
- Develop stress management techniques that will keep your practice positive and energized;
- Hold internal meetings that will encourage involvement and inspire follow-through;
- Create a provider-patient Alignment that will shorten your exam time, increase your impact, and reduce your likelihood of malpractice suits;
- Network with colleagues to maximize referrals;
- Create a mission statement that will inspire you and your Team; and
- Create a plan of action that will keep all of you moving forward enthusiastically and effectively.

SECTION FIVE: D IS FOR DIFFERENTIATE

Section Five is all about how to identify your uniqueness as a practice and build a reputation in your community that will allow you to attract the partners, employees, and patients that are the best fit for you. You will learn how to:

- Identify your specific uniqueness as a practice through practical and proven research methodology;
- Magnify your uniqueness internally and externally to help others to see the special differences you offer;
- Use subjective and objective research to determine what you can do that no one else is doing, and then do it;
- Engage your Team in Differentiation activities for maximum buy-in;
- Understand and apply the Attitude of Five-Star Service;
- Establish a strong market presence through community outreach seminars;
- Create and deliver powerful presentations that educate and motivate;
- Develop a strong reputation as the go-to experts in your area, without insulting your competitors; and
- Understand and apply strategies of image management both internally and externally.

SECTION SIX: NOW THAT YOU'RE M.A.D.

Section Six brings it all together with suggestions for next steps and an inspirational message. (No fair cheating! Save it for the end.) This section will help you to:

- Commit to change;
- Choose the techniques and formulas that are best for you;
- Go one step at a time to incorporate the strategies; and
- Stay confident while you transition to your M.A.D. practice.

This book is written in a conversational style and is designed to educate, inspire, and propel you to action. Learn, enjoy, and then pass it on to your Team. The more people who get M.A.D. around you, the more successful you'll be.

Chapter 3

How to Use This Book for Maximum Impact

ALL IN A ROW OR SKIP AROUND

Building a consecutive knowledge base will give you the most comprehensive understanding of the foundations and how-to techniques of The M.A.D. Formula, and make it much easier to hit the ground running. So, in the ideal world, you would read everything in this book in order. That said, each of the sections can stand alone, so if you need a quick solution to a current problem, go straight to the appropriate section and grab what you need. If you are a skip-around reader, I recommend that you read Section Two before you start skipping so that you are able to make sense of some of the techniques that follow. No matter what kind of reader you are, by the time you are done you will have a powerful set of techniques that will enable you to master the people factor.

THE WHY, THE WHAT, AND THE EXAMPLES

Some readers like to skim or speed-read their books. They don't have the time or patience to read everything. They just want to catch a few new ideas and move on. If this describes you, then go straight for the **Tables, Activities,** and **Bottom Line** summary paragraphs in each chapter. You'll get the "what"s without the "why"s or the "examples."

If you are a detail-oriented person, someone who likes to understand the "why" that explains the "what" of the techniques, as well as the "examples" that reveal techniques in action, then you will find everything you need right here. In fact, at times you may find more than you need.

I think live training is much more effective than conveying information in a book because of the interactive component. If you were in front of me, I could watch your face, your eyes, and your body language, and I would know when you "get it." At that moment, I would stop giving examples and move on to the next item you need to know. If we were together, I'd know if you need one more example or if you're ready to do an activity and try it yourself. Since we're not together, I have no way of knowing if you need me to explain a concept more completely or if you need to see it from a different angle. Because I'm not there with you and since I don't know your individual learning style, I have chosen to expand discussions whenever there is something I think may be a bit more complex. If you've got it, feel free to move on; and if you need more, just keep reading.

My hope is that whatever kind of reader you may be, you will find exactly what you need in precisely the manner that works for you.

PRACTICE SPOTLIGHTS

Throughout the book you will find Practice Spotlights, highlighted passages that will give you an opportunity to see how real practices used (and did not use) The M.A.D. Formula techniques. There are a few things I'd like you to know about these spotlights:

First, as I mentioned earlier, I will be using the word "practice" to represent all healthcare facilities, in medicine and dentistry, regardless of the size of the organization.

Second, all examples were obtained either through live observation during our site visits (visually or through video recordings) or by direct report from the clients.

Third, none of the names are correct. Throughout this book, I have used pseudonyms to protect my clients' confidentiality.

Admittedly, there's nothing better than having the opportunity to see these techniques being applied live and up close, but I hope these vignettes will help you to build a stronger understanding of the concepts and how to put them into action in your unique situation.

CRITICAL PASSAGES

All through Sections Two, Three, and Four you will find certain passages that are identified with a Success Icon[1] that looks like this:

---

[1] The Success Icon is my company logo. It symbolizes my firm belief that anyone can increase their success if they want what they will get as a result of the success, have all of the necessary steps to get them there and are willing to climb the steps all the way to the top.

These icons identify information and associated techniques that need to be used fluidly and naturally, without seeming like "techniques." The only way to make that happen is to make them familiar to you such that they become a part of your natural way of thinking. They need to be "second-nature." While these techniques work best when you follow the steps in order or use the provided language,

I do not recommend that you sit down and memorize any of this information!

Strict memorization of techniques and scripts will cause fake, sterile behaviors that will make you (and everyone else) uncomfortable and will ultimately fail. There are no cookie-cutter techniques in this book. They are all designed to be massaged to fit just right for you. The last thing I want is to create millions of little Wendy's running around the world doing everything the way I would do it.

My goal is to provide you with information that you can then translate into your own style — genuine and real.

Nevertheless, it's important that you absorb the information completely so you will be *able* to use it naturally. When you have to stop and think about how to use a communication technique, it forces you to lose track of the people. More importantly, at moments of stress when you need these techniques the most, you will not have time to run all over your office looking for your book!

Under stress, we regress.

When we regress, we return to the habits and behaviors that come most naturally to us without having to think about them. The only way to get the M.A.D. techniques to come out naturally during times of stress is to make them part of you so that they are as familiar as driving a car.

Mastering the techniques of The M.A.D. Formula requires muscle memory. They need to come out naturally and spontaneously, particularly in the moments when you haven't time to think.

So how can you get these techniques internalized with as little effort as possible?

After many years of searching, I've found the perfect formula for learning new material without losing a moment of precious time. The process is called "spaced repetition" and it works — quickly, efficiently, and flawlessly. Here's how it works:

People learn best when they are exposed to new material multiple times in spaced intervals. Elementary school teachers have long practiced this technique in repetitions of the alphabet and multiplication tables.

Think about how easily you learn the lyrics to your favorite songs. It's doubtful that you write to the artists, ask them to send their lyrics, and then sit down to memorize them. Chances are, you hear them playing in the background while you are busy doing something else. Then, over several weeks, you hear the songs again and again while listening to the radio or CD in your car or on your iPod while exercising. Each time you listen, more and more of the lyrics naturally seep into your brain, without your having to work at it. Next thing you know, you're singing along, making up your own words for the ones you never grabbed, harmonizing in full voice, and receiving standing ovations and raving cheers from the crowds of people who are drawn to your side (okay, well, maybe that's my fantasy and not yours). The point is, you learned the songs without even trying.

The same thing happens over the holidays when you're walking through a shopping mall. There you are, surrounded by noise, shoppers, twinkling lights, and ringing bells. You're focused on your goal: to buy the perfect gifts and get out in record time. As you leave the mall and walk to your car, you find yourself humming the tune that was playing over the loudspeakers in the mall. Now here's the thing: you never noticed that it was playing while you were in the mall. You didn't even know you *knew* that song, yet, here you are, humming away. The worst part is, you can't get the song out of your head for the rest of the day!

Do you wake up to a clock radio and then push the snooze button, only to find yourself in the shower singing a song that you never knew you'd heard? It stays with you all day long, popping up in moments of silence. How did that get in your head? More importantly, how do you get it out?!

Your brain is very powerful. It can learn when you're not even trying. In fact, it works best that way.

I invite you to take advantage of your brain's natural ability to learn by using the CD that is included at the back of your book.

I recorded it just for this purpose. It contains all of the key concepts and scripts with some extra commentary along the way.

Wherever there is a Success Icon, you will find a corresponding CD track. For the quickest route to learning, simply follow these directions:

1. Download the CD to your mobile device or place the CD in your car stereo or portable CD player.
2. Select the track(s) that you are most interested in learning. I suggest that you focus on learning no more than four tracks at a time.

3. Play the selected tracks (at least) two times a day for seven days in a row whenever you are doing activities where **your hands are busy but your mind is free to wander** (for example: shaving or putting on make-up, driving, exercising, doing dishes, walking the dog, or gardening).

4. Do not try to pay attention to the CD. Just let it play in the background as if it were the radio. Trust your brain. You will absorb key phrases and then translate those phrases in your mind to a language that fits your unique style and comfort zone.

5. After one week, play those same tracks two times a week for seven weeks, or until you've got it down.

Repeat these steps for every track you want to learn. Through the process of spaced audio repetition, you will become an expert in The M.A.D. Formula in no time.

Remember, the included CD is an adjunct to, not a replacement for, the book. It is designed to help you to quickly incorporate key concepts after you've read the associated chapters. Without the basis for understanding you'll get from the book, the CD will be largely meaningless to you.

ACTIVITIES

Throughout the book, you will find "Activities" to help you to think through key issues and experience the strategies that you will ultimately use with others. The more comfortable you become with the techniques, the more likely you'll be to actually use them in real time. Nothing succeeds like success! When you're ready, do the activities with your team. When you succeed, you can all jump up and down, applaud, and yell loudly. Or not.

NO SECRETS

There is absolutely nothing that you will read in this book that you have to hide from anyone else. In fact, I strongly urge you to tell everyone what you're learning and invite them to learn it too. I have clients who literally paste copies of their workbooks all over their exam rooms, operatories, labs, and break rooms. The best part is that patients notice these and ask about them! As staff and doctors discuss the different strategies and techniques of Motivation, Alignment, and Differentiation, patients are engaged and want to know more.

Take this book home, and share it with your family. Every single technique in this book will not only improve your business, it will help you at home. There are things you will learn here that our clients have called "life changing." If that is part of what you are looking for, then you'll find some of that here.

Imagine how your life would improve if everyone knew how to be accountable, self-motivated, and flexible in their communications so that they would speak your language. So,

Don't just use this ON people, use it WITH people.

Tell people you're in a learning process. Ask them to quiz you and practice with you. It will connect you to others in ways you never imagined, and maximize your efficiency far beyond where you are today.

BOTTOM LINE PARAGRAPHS

At the end of each chapter, you'll find a statement that will briefly summarize the chapter and highlight the take-away message from the discussion. This is largely there for the 50% of you who get frustrated by long explanations and want everyone to cut to the chase (you know who you are; the rest of you will learn about them in Chapter 5). In fact, if this describes you, then you will probably want to flip ahead in each chapter and read the Bottom Line paragraphs first. Feel free!

The rest of you, please don't worry about this. Your details will be there throughout the chapters, and the summaries will be at the end, precisely were you think they belong.

I hope you enjoy reading this book and that you will find it useful in your efforts to create change for your business, your Team, your patients, and your community. If you are at all like my clients, you will find that once you've mastered the people factor, you will be able to more fully enjoy your work and focus more on the passions that brought you to healthcare in the first place. And that's what it's all about.

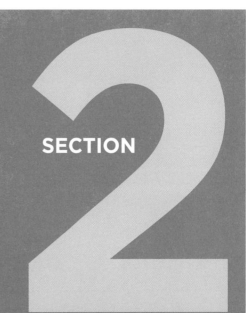

SECTION

2

The Four Languages of The M.A.D. Formula

Chapter 4

Building Trust and Rapport

IT'S SATURDAY NIGHT, and you're in the lobby of your favorite restaurant waiting for your table. It's really crowded, and you find a place to stand in the bar. You're sandwiched in between people, and you inadvertently step on someone's foot.

> *"Oh! I'm sorry,"* you yell over the room noise.

> *"Don't worry about it,"* he yells back, *"it's so crowded, who can move?"*

> *"Yes,"* you smile, *"You'd think they'd open up the patio, wouldn't you?"*

> *"You know, they usually do that. But then you have to deal with those mosquitoes . . ."*

And you're off and running, talking up a storm about the things the restaurant could and should do better to serve its patrons. In no time, you're moving on to discuss movies, books, the new library, where you went to school, who's running for mayor . . . The next thing you know, an hour has gone by, and as they call your table, you quickly exchange contact information and shake hands warmly.

How did that happen? You gave that person your phone number! You went on about things that you would never share with a stranger. For goodness sake, you told him about the time you flunked gym in elementary school! Somehow it all just seemed to be natural.

What makes two perfect strangers connect so quickly? How do two people who have never met suddenly feel like they've known each other forever?

It's a combination of factors, but the bottom line is this:

> **We build instant rapport when we form a quick opinion that the other person is "safe" and "speaks our language."**

How do we decide that a stranger is safe? A piece of that comes from a part of our brain that works out of our awareness, picking up on nonverbal signals from others and telling us whether we should approach or retreat.

We typically refer to that as "instinct." On the other hand, many of our decisions regarding the safety of strangers comes from our previous experiences. Our brain connects memories of people we have known or heard of that look, act, and sound similar, and if our stored memories are positive, the odds are that we will make a positive assessment of this stranger as safe.

Even if we don't have a good history with this "type," if the person speaks our unique language, we may let down our barriers enough to give him/her a chance.

So what is this "unique language" thing? Let's first define "language:"

Language is defined by the words and physical behaviors we use to express opinions, facts, and feelings.

From the moment of birth, everyone speaks their own unique language. We first develop our uniqueness as a function of our brain wiring, and the degree to which we are encouraged to bring out our natural talents and tendencies by others. Our unique language continues to get established as we experience the world and develop a unique vision of ourselves, other people, and the rules of living.

As we grow older, and have more experiences, our language continually changes, with new experiences blending in and layering over those that came before. The degree to which we allow our uniqueness to show to others is a function of our perceptions of what we have learned is safe and acceptable.

Here's the challenge:

No two people have precisely the same combination of biology and experiences, and, as a result, no two people speak precisely the same language.

Nevertheless, everyone has similarities, and the people with whom we feel safest are typically the people who come closest to speaking our unique language. In other words, we feel safest with those who seem to be **like** us. Even if someone is nothing like us, we can still feel safe with people who seem to **totally understand** us. We know this because they are able to speak our unique language. These are the people we trust. These are the people with whom we share our secrets and bare our souls. These are the people who we allow to see our vulnerability and our pain. These are the people we trust to help us, to advise us, and to take charge when we aren't able.

When you speak someone's language, that person will trust you. The faster you speak the person's language, the faster you will establish that trust. The M.A.D. Formula depends on this. Remember:

People need to trust you before they will allow you to Motivate them. People need to perceive that you are alike in the ways that are important to them before they will Align with you. Finally, people need to see all of this consistently before they will Differentiate you as the one to help them to achieve their goals.

So how do you speak people's languages when there are so many variations? I have found that there are four key languages that, when combined, allow us to build rapid rapport and trust. It is simply a matter of learning how to speak those languages and using them in your daily encounters with people.

DON'T PANIC! You don't have to use all four languages all the time. You can pick the one that is easiest for you, and master it. You will immediately see an improvement in your ability to build rapid rapport. Once you feel comfortable, add another language, and layer them together one at a time.

I use combinations of these four languages all the time, in every conversation; in every keynote address; in marketing, training, writing, and consulting with clients; and just socializing with friends. It's a skill like driving a car or typing on a keyboard.

You'll probably find it to be awkward and calculated at first. But in no time, you'll be speaking all four languages and wondering how you ever communicated with people before this!

So, let's start where it all begins, with The Language of Action Types in Chapter Five.

BOTTOM LINE

The ability to build rapid trust and rapport depends upon your skill at identifying the communication needs of others and then flexing your style to accommodate those needs. We can summarize those needs into four different "languages." While it is not necessary to speak all four languages, the more you can master, the more adept you will be at building trust and establishing rapport with everyone you meet.

Chapter 5

The Language of Action Types

NO DISCUSSION OF BUILDING TRUST AND RAPPORT would be complete without looking at the human brain and the way it influences our behaviors. Neuropsychologists have long been interested in studying the brain as it relates to our psychological processes and overt behaviors. Their work shows us that much of what makes us different from one another can be explained by looking at our brains. In fact, they have identified many key areas of the brain and found important connections between the brain and our patterns of behaviors, feeling, and thinking.

From Jung-Myers-Briggs[1] to the DISC system[2], different systems of identifying and categorizing people are utilized worldwide as respected methods of identifying the "personalities" of people. In fact, some of my clients have purchased licenses to utilize standardized tests that allow them to categorize candidates during job interviews, and many of my colleagues teach these systems in their programs. All of it works, but I was looking for a simpler, faster way that would allow anyone to identify on the spot another person's unique brain wiring.

The fact is that most of us don't have time to administer a Rorschach inkblot test[3]. We have to be able to look at people the moment they walk in the door and know how to build an immediate connection. We have to be able to pick up a telephone and, within 30 seconds, know how best to talk with the caller to establish rapid rapport and trust.

We don't have time to administer tests to everyone we meet; and when trust is at stake, we can't afford to be wrong.

After a careful review of the literature, I compiled a quick and easy system that will allow anyone to identify the unique brain wiring of another person. Rather than assessing personality, this system allows us to classify people into one of four "Action Types" simply by observing their overt behaviors.

---

[1] The Myers-Briggs Type Indicator is an assessment instrument based on typological theories originated by Carl Gustav Jung.

[2] DISC is a four-quadrant behavioral model based on the work of William Moulton Marston, Ph.D.

[3] The Rorschach inkblot test is a method of psychological evaluation used to examine personality characteristics.

Each Action Type has a set of behaviors that distinguishes the people in that group. All you have to do is learn these behaviors, identify them when you see them, and then flex your behaviors to incorporate behaviors from the other person's Action Type. If you share the same Action Type, there's nothing special to be done.

This process is ridiculously simple, and it simply works. In fact, you're probably doing some of this instinctively. Now we're going to take your natural instincts and make them work for you more effectively and consistently.

Let's start by describing the types of brains that are in the world.

INDIRECT AND DIRECT

We can divide the entire world of brains into two categories: some people's brain wiring leads them to display **Indirect** behaviors, while others are **Direct**. There are those who are out at the extremes, while others fall more into the gray areas. At the extremes, these two types are diametrically opposed. Let's talk about the extremes, and then we'll look at the shades of gray a bit later.

At the extreme end of the scale, Indirect people are shy and speak in very low volumes. They keep their arms close in to their bodies, and use subtle (if any) facial expressions. They are slow paced (physically and verbally) and take their time making decisions. They are quiet when they enter a room, and may stand at a distance patiently waiting to be noticed. They are methodical and have long attention spans.

On the other end of the scale we find the Direct people. At the extreme end, these people are loud and dramatic, and can be wildly expressive in their facial expressions and body language. They swing their arms away from their bodies and use their hands when they talk. They enter a room boldly and loudly, even slapping the counter, tables, chairs, themselves, and others to get attention. They are spontaneous and change subjects rapidly.

PEOPLE AND TASK

We can also divide the world of brains a different way: **People-Oriented** and **Task-Oriented**. Again, there are gray areas here, and some people's brains cross into both areas. For ease of discussion, let's look at the extremes.

People-Oriented brains focus on (I bet you didn't see this coming) people. They make eye contact immediately, touch when they talk, and may hug strangers when introduced. At a party or a professional function, they will get right up in your face, standing within three feet of your body, and shake your hand (the extremes will cover your hand with their free hand or touch you on your free arm while shaking your hand). If there were a fire in the building, they would first be concerned with the people, making sure everyone had gone to safety. No matter what they do, they always take people into account.

Task-Oriented brains are all about . . . well, you know where this is going. When they speak with you, they will focus their eyes on objects (files, instruments, computer screens, bottles, walls) rather than make eye contact. They prefer a rigid social distance of three feet or more, and, except at rare times with family and friends, they just don't do the huggy-touchy thing. In a fire, they will be the first to ring the alarm and grab the extinguishers. These are the people who you can count on to get the job done, particularly when they don't have to deal with people.

It's not that People-Oriented folks don't get tasks done, and it's not that Task-Oriented people don't care about people. But,

> **Under stress, we all go to our original brain-wired natural behaviors and focus on what we were born to see.**

PUTTING IT ALL TOGETHER

When we look at Indirect-Direct and People-Task, we discover that it is actually a grid that looks like this:

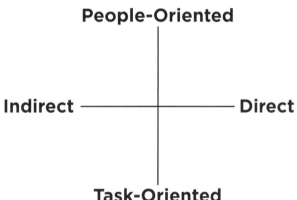

All of the categories come together to form four distinct types of behaviors that I call "Action Types," specifically Relater, Enthusiast, Thinker, and Commander.

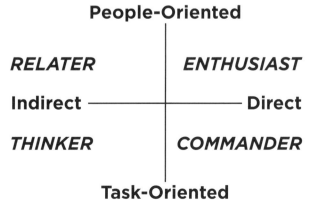

Relaters

People-Oriented and Indirect, Relaters are the people who will make sure that you get introduced to everyone sitting at your table. These are the people in your office who always have candy in their desk or locker, just in case someone needs a snack. They are the ones who will keep track of birthdays, get cards for others to sign, and make sure that everyone has what they need and want — often at their own expense. These are the "warm and fuzzy" people who remember everyone's names and avoid confrontation at all costs. They make your practice successful by focusing on the relationships among people.

Enthusiasts

Enthusiasts have many of the same qualities as Relaters in that they are all about the people. Contrary to Relaters, however, Enthusiasts are Direct, so their behaviors look entirely different. Enthusiasts are dramatic, upbeat entertainers who always have a story or joke to tell. They love to talk and talk (and talk). Enthusiasts are always creating a party atmosphere, decorating and rearranging furniture, putting smiley faces on daily sheets, and exclamation points in e-mails. Enthusiasts appreciate being recognized publicly with applause and awards. Their flair for drama and excitement will help make your practice positive and fun.

Thinkers

Task-Oriented and Indirect, Thinkers are the detail-oriented people who are focused on precision, accuracy, information, technology, data, and research. Meticulous, and purposefully slow, Thinkers will do whatever they can to avoid mistakes. They prefer order and predictability and may get testy if you surprise them with a change in their schedule. Thinkers keep your practice safe by focusing on the details and avoiding error.

Commanders

Task-Oriented and Direct, Commanders are bottom-line, no-nonsense, get-to-the-point people. Commanders are results oriented and goal-driven. They multi-task and never lose focus (although they often lose track of files and lose sight of people). Commanders will organize, strategize, and take control of any situation without being asked. These are the people that will keep your practice on target.

Table 5-1 summarizes the most common characteristics of each Action Type.

TABLE 5-1. Action Type Characteristics				
	Relaters	**Enthusiasts**	**Thinkers**	**Commanders**
Appearance tends to be	Casual Conforming	Fashionable Stylish	Formal Conservative	Businesslike Functional
Pace	Slow Easy	Fast Spontaneous	Slow Systematic	Fast Decisive
Workspace tends to be	Personal Relaxed Friendly Informal	Stimulating Personal Cluttered Friendly	Structured Organized Functional Formal	Busy Formal Efficient Structured
Social distance preference	Less than three feet	Less than three feet	More than three feet	More than three feet
Doesn't want	Confrontation	Loss of prestige	To be embarrassed	Loss of control
In an argument will usually	Submit Acquiesce	Attack Be Sarcastic	Withdraw Avoid	Dictate Assert
Enjoys	Appreciation	Recognition	Accuracy	Productivity
When making a purchase, needs to know	How it will affect their personal circumstances	How it enhances their status Who else uses it	How to justify the purchase logically How it works	What it does What it costs
Looks for	Close relationships	Flexibility	Preparation	Control
Values	Conformity Loyalty Compatibility with others	Playfulness Stimulating environment Acknowledg- ment Recognition	Correctness Thoroughness Precision Accuracy	Leadership Competition Results Measurable progress
Wants commun- ication to be	Pleasant	Stimulating	Precise	To the point
Wants to be	Connected	On stage	Correct	In charge
Gets frustrated by	Insensitivity Impatience	Boredom Routine	Surprises Unpredictability	Inefficiency Indecision
Decision-making	Careful	Spontaneous	Researched	Quick and definitive

THE VARIATIONS YOU'LL SEE

As I mentioned earlier, not everyone falls precisely into one quadrant. There are variations and gray areas. The ones who fall into the same quadrant all the time we call Singular-Action Types. Those who cross all four quadrants are called Multi-Action Types. And those who share either horizontal or vertical quadrants are called Dual-Action Types.

Singular-Action Types

Some people are in the center or outlying areas of their quadrant. Their Action Type is consistent whether they are relaxed with friends or under stress at work.

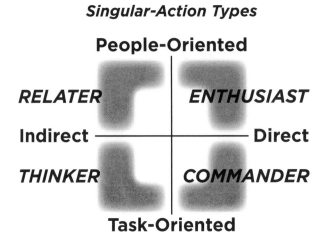

Singular-Action Types

Multi-Action Types

Some people fall right smack in the center where the vertical and horizontal lines meet. These people live comfortably in all four quadrants, portraying some of the characteristics of each Action Type, though never showing extremes in any one.

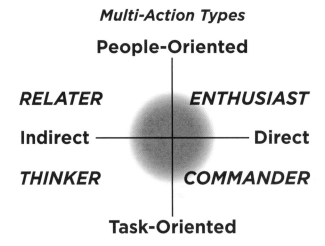

Multi-Action Types

Dual-Action Types

Many people find that they go between two Action Types. Regardless of which Dual-Type they may be, these people will always be on the horizontal or the vertical axis of the Action Type Grid.

Here are the combinations you will see:

True-Blue: Relater-Enthusiast

True-Blue Action Types

People-Oriented

RELATER   *ENTHUSIAST*

Indirect ———————— **Direct**

THINKER   *COMMANDER*

Task-Oriented

These people are always focused on people. They shift their pace, volume, and degree of expression, but never their focus.

Eye-on-the-Task: Thinker-Commander

Eye-on-the-Task Action Types

People-Oriented

RELATER   *ENTHUSIAST*

Indirect ———————— **Direct**

THINKER   *COMMANDER*

Task-Oriented

These people are always focused on tasks. They shift their pace, volume, and degree of detail-orientation, but never their focus.

Quietly Focused: Relater-Thinker

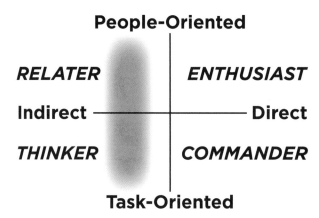

Quietly Focused Action Types

People-Oriented

RELATER   *ENTHUSIAST*

Indirect ———————— **Direct**

THINKER   *COMMANDER*

Task-Oriented

These people always display indirect behaviors, but shift their focus from task to people.

Go-Getters: Enthusiast-Commander

Go-Getters Action Types

People-Oriented

RELATER   *ENTHUSIAST*

Indirect ———————— **Direct**

THINKER   *COMMANDER*

Task-Oriented

These people always display direct behaviors, but shift their focus from task to people.

Diagonals: Enthusiast-Thinker, Relater-Commander (next page)

It is extremely rare to see people with brain wiring that crosses the diagonals of the grid. When you meet these people, you should know that they have extremely unusual brain wiring and can offer you a great deal in their flexibility as employees or partners. On the other hand, you may find them to be a little difficult to work with, since their behaviors are so inconsistent. You will often hear these types making self-reflective comments like, "I'm not sure who I am" and "I don't know if I'm doing what I was meant to do."

Diagonal Action Types

So what is *your* Action Type? Do you think you know for certain? Find out in Activity 5-1.

ACTIVITY 5-1. Identify Your Action Type
What is *your* Action Type? Are you a Singular, a Multi, or a Dual?
Make four copies of Table 1. On the first copy, place a check (✓) next to each characteristic that you think best describes you.
Give the second copy to your spouse, a close friend, or a family member. Ask that person to place a check (✓) next to each characteristic that he or she thinks best describes you.
Give the third copy to someone at work (preferably someone who works closely with you). Ask that person to place a check (✓) next to each characteristic that he or she thinks best describes you.
Look at all three charts. Count up the number of check marks next to each characteristic, and log that number on your fourth copy.
Time to assess your responses! • If one column has the majority of checks and there are scattered checks elsewhere, then that is your Singular-Action Type. • If you find that the majority of checks are split between two columns, or if your spouse, friend, or family member rated you in one column and your work associate rated you in an entirely different column, and your answers go half and half, then you are a Dual-Action Type. • If all four columns are equal, then you are a Multi-Action Type.
Note: If there is a big discrepancy between how you see yourself and how others see you, then this is important information since the image you are projecting is different than you realize. This may explain some of the responses you get from others that are confusing to you.

IDENTIFYING OTHER PEOPLE'S ACTION TYPES

First and foremost remember: these are *not* personality types. You don't need to know someone even slightly in order to figure out their Action Type. You just have to watch and listen.

**Action Types are strictly determined by behaviors,
and that's what makes this language so easy to use!**

To identify someone's Action Type, all you have to do is pay attention and follow two simple steps:

Step 1: Watch and Listen

In person or on the phone, simply watch or listen for one or more of the six behaviors shown in Table 5-2.

TABLE 5-2. Identifying Action Types: Indirect versus Direct	
Indirect	**Direct**
Closed and subtle	Open and dramatic
Softer-spoken	Louder-spoken
Slower-paced	Faster-paced

**The quickest way to distinguish an Indirect person from
one who is Direct is by the person's pace and volume of speech.
In personal encounters, you can add in the degree to which
their elbows move away from their bodies.**

Whichever of the six behaviors you identify, that narrows the field of choices. If you think a person is Indirect, then he or she can only be a Relater or a Thinker. If you choose Direct, then the only possibilities are Enthusiast or Commander. Now let's find out which, with Step 2.

Step 2: Zoom In

Now you're going to find out if the person is People-Oriented or Task-Oriented. In person, you can distinguish those who are People-Oriented from those who are Task-Oriented by choosing one or more of the six behaviors in Table 5-3.

TABLE 5-3. Identifying Action Types in Person: People-Oriented versus Task-Oriented	
People-Oriented	**Task-Oriented**
Eye contact	Focused on objects
Stands within three feet of you	Stands apart (three or more feet)
Touches you or others when speaking	No touch

Add the result from Table 5-2 to the result from Table 5-3, and, voila!

This is a little more complicated over the phone than in person, so, here's the secret: On the phone, listen for the *first statement* someone makes when you pick up the phone, then match that to the statement in Table 5-4 that comes closest to what the person said.

TABLE 5-4. Identifying Action Types by Phone: People-Oriented versus Task-Oriented	
People-Oriented	**Task-Oriented**
• "Good morning, I'm sorry to trouble you but is this Dr. A's office?" • "Will you please check your schedule, I'd like to make an appointment." • "I'm hoping you can help me, I need to refill my prescription." • "Hi (your name), my name is . . . and I was referred to you by . . ." • "How are *you* today?" • "Do you have any openings today?" • "Would you have a moment to give me directions?" • "I'm calling about your ad in today's classified section. The job sounds wonderful, are you still taking applications?"	• "Is this Dr. A's office?" • "I need to make an appointment." • "I need a refill." • "I was referred by . . ." • "I need to get in today." • "What is the charge for . . ." • "Where is the office located?" • "What are your hours?" • "Do you take insurance?" • "I saw your ad in the paper, and I'd like to apply. Is the job filled?"

The interesting thing is that there are eight examples on the People-Oriented side and 10 on the Task-Oriented side. Yet look at the difference in how much space each takes up in the table! What does that tell you?

OK, give up? I'll tell you the answer: People-Oriented types take more time on the phone than Task-Oriented types, and the more time you spend with them, the more trust you'll build.

People-Oriented callers will look to establish a relationship with you. Task-Oriented people will focus on what they need to accomplish.

Now that you've identified the Action Type, you're ready to speak their language!

In order to really master The Language of Action Types, all you have to do is listen to your CD or study Tables 5-1 to 5-4 and pay close attention to the specific communication and behavioral characteristics of each Action Type. Then, start watching people and practice. You'll be identifying Action Types in no time at all! Teach it to your staff, your partners, even your patients. You can have a lot of fun with this. Once you're confident in your ability to identify other people's Action Types, you're ready to speak their language (see Activity 5-2).

ACTIVITY 5-2. Identifying Others' Action Types			
Make a list of 10 people you know (family, friends, or co-workers).			
Next to each person, write down the Action Type that you believe that person to be.			
Show Table 5-1 to someone who knows this person, and ask for a second opinion.			
Finally, show Table 5-1 to the original person, and ask him or her to do a self-assessment. Have fun with this!			
Person	**Your Assessment**	**Second Opinion**	**Self-Assessment**
1			
2			
3			
4			
5			
6			
7			
8			
9			
10			

Speaking the Language of Brain Wiring

People often ask me, "*Why should I be the one to have to speak their language*?" Well, honestly, because you're the one who has the information. If you want someone else to do it, then teach it to them. In fact, the more people who learn this, the easier your life will be! Just remember one thing —

If you want people to learn from you, they need to trust you. The fastest way to make that happen is to speak their language.

In the ideal world, you will absorb all of the information in this chapter and use your CD to get the details into your brain. However, if you are a Commander or Enthusiast you are going to want something faster. So, Table 5-5 is a scaled-down cheat sheet to help you quickly learn The Language of Brain Wiring.

As you become more accustomed to thinking in terms of The Language of Action Types, you will begin to see where you may have been missing with some of your patients, staff, and partners. For example, there is nothing more disconcerting for an Indirect person than when a Direct person comes charging at them, arms swaying broadly, hand extended to connect in a firm handshake. On the other hand, if the two of you are both Direct, this behavior will help you to establish an instant level of trust and rapport.

People versus Task behaviors are particularly important with respect to the social distance, eye contact, and touching. Particularly in a healthcare

	Relater	Enthusiast	Thinker	Commander
Think to yourself	I have to connect person to person	I have to make this fun and be an appreciative audience	Facts, data, information	Bottom line
Begin with	• *It's important to both of us that . . .* • *We both agree that . . .* • *We both want . . .*	• *OK, let's look at the big picture.* • *The overall goal is to . . .* • *The general plan for today is . . .*	• *Let's go over the details.* • *I'd like to see the research.* • *This needs to be documented.* • *Tell me all of the steps you took to do this.*	• *Here's the point . . .* • *This is the bottom line . . .*
Use words like	• We • Us • Together • Relationship • Connect • Feel	• Very • Really • Fabulous • Wonderful • Excellent • Awesome	• Logically • For example • Specifically • Particularly • Detail • Precisely	• Result • Goal • Time • Point • Benchmark • Critical
Key behavior	Maintain eye contact	Emphasize facial and body expressiveness	Speak slowly and methodically	Speak quickly and clearly

TABLE 5-5. Speaking The Language of Action Types

environment, the assumption is that it is permissible for a doctor or assistant to get close and touch. This can be disastrous with a Singular Task-Oriented person.

This Practice Spotlight shows an example of what happens when you don't speak The Language of Action Types.

Practice Spotlight

Diane is a dental hygienist who has been practicing for over 10 years. She is a Singular Enthusiast, but doesn't know it because this is happening during pre-training observation.

Mr. New Patient is standing in the doorway quietly. Diane looks up, sees him, and bolts out of her chair, hand extended. He visibly retreats, but she doesn't notice.

She looks him straight in the eye (he looks down) and says, *"Hi! I'm Diane! Welcome! I'm SO excited you're HERE! This is awesome! Come on in, I'll get you started."*

With that, Diane puts her arm around Mr. New Patient's shoulder and guides him to the chair. He visibly cringes, but she misses that.

Mr. New Patient lies back on the chair looking uncomfortable. Diane reaches across him and puts on his bib, talking the whole while about all of the "cool" activities she'd done that weekend. She then sits on her stool and pulls up close to the back of his head.

"*So, let's see what you've got for me,*" she says as she leans over to look in his mouth, her mask only inches from his forehead.

Mr. New Patient squirms away, sits up, and says, "*I'm sorry, but I can't do this.*"

Diane gets up and walks around to touch his arm and look him in the eye, "*Please don't worry, I'm going to take very good care of you, and you really do need to do this.*"

Mr. New Patient allows Diane to go forward, but he never warms up to her, despite her Herculean efforts. At check out, he declines the offer to book his next appointment.

What happened here? Some might say there was no problem at all. After all, Diane delivered the service the patient needed. She was friendly, welcoming, and warm. So, did Diane do anything wrong?

If your goal is to build trust and rapport so that you can Motivate your patient to action, Align with your patient to build a loyalty that will lead to ongoing referrals and a long relationship, and Differentiate your practice as the one that is really exceptional, then the answer is "yes, there was something wrong."

Diane and her patient were on the diagonal. Diane should have scaled back her Enthusiast tendencies and adopted the behaviors of a Thinker. She has since learned the Language and now uses it with all of her patients. But how many people did she turn off in the meantime?

Practice Spotlight

Shayna is an Echo Technologist, working in a busy cardiology department of a major hospital. She loves her job and says that her favorite part is that she gets to talk to her patients all day long. Shayna is a Singular Enthusiast. She likes to bring fashion into her uniform, so, in addition to her neatly pressed scrubs, she always adds a little sparkle in her earrings, her shoes, or even her hair.

Shayna goes out to the reception area and locates her 3:00 o'clock appointment. She finds him sitting quietly in a far corner chair, head buried in a book. She's been warned by the front desk that *"he's a major Thinker."*

Shayna walks slowly toward him and stops about three feet away. Quietly she says, *"Mr. Patient?"* She waits for him to respond. He never looks up, but under his breath he says, *"Yes."*

"Will you follow me please, Mr. Patient?" She walks slowly, and he follows a short distance behind. She checks now and then, but refrains from her usual chit-chat.

"Please have a seat, Mr. Patient," Shayna says softly, looking down and staying on the opposite side of the small room. *"I need to get some additional details so that we can make sure everything is precise and accurate in your file. Would that be OK?"*

"That's fine," he says in a monotone.

Shayna goes through her questions, gives him a gown, and steps out without making any effort to be anything more than polite and efficient. When she returns, she moves her stool three feet from the exam table and sits down.

"Mr. Patient, I'm going to place these leads on your chest, would that be OK?"

"Yes," he replies. She gets up slowly, walks toward him, and says, *"Ready?"*

"Yes, go right ahead," he replies.

Shayna places the leads and then moves back. She pulls her stool over to the screen and sits down. As she does so, she talks with Mr. Patient, never making eye contact.

"I see that you are an accountant. I would imagine that the details of that can be stressful this time of year," she says slowly.

"Yes, that's correct," he says.

"Especially when people surprise you with last-minute changes," Shayna says.

Mr. Patient comes alive. He tells her about how most of his clients are "dependable" but there's always one who . . . She quiets him for the testing by saying, *"Hold that thought, Mr. Patient, I'll remind you where you left off, OK?"*

> *"OK,"* he says.
>
> *"I'm going to touch your chest with this wand, and you'll feel nothing but the wetness of the gel, OK?"* Shayna asks. When he nods, she conducts the testing.
>
> As soon as the test is complete, she takes a moment and says, *"So you were talking about the clients who surprise you at the last minute with extra documents."*
>
> He smiles and says, *"Luckily there aren't many."*
>
> When it's time to leave, Shayna stands up and says, *"Thank you for educating me, Mr. Patient. That was so interesting. I'll just take this out and give you a few minutes to get dressed."*
>
> As she walks out, he smiles and says, *"Thank you."*
>
> When Mr. Patient checks out, he says matter-of-factly, *"The technician did a good job."*
>
> Shayna considers that high praise.

Shayna had to work hard at that. This Thinker was her direct opposite, and she had to remind herself not to laugh too loudly or behave with too much expression. But her efforts were rewarded with a happy patient who trusts her.

The fact is that some people are natural "chameleons." They intuitively shift their style of behavior and always seem to know precisely what to do. Others need to study Tables 5-1 to 5-5 a bit before they get it. No matter which you may be, I promise you that your life will become much easier when you learn to speak the Language of Action Types. We'll talk more about how to use this when we start working through The M.A.D. Formula in Sections Three to Five. For now, all you have to do is:

> **Identify the other person's Action Type, then use the key words and behaviors of their type.**

It's just that simple. If you try to make it any more complicated than that, you're probably a Thinker.

PUTTING IT INTO ACTION

After you have listened to your CD and feel comfortable with the words and behaviors of the four Action Types, it's time to put it into your daily routine. Some people find that they "get it" immediately and have fun shifting from one Action Type to the next. Others feel more comfortable going in a stepwise fashion until they have mastered the process. Either way, the best way to incorporate the Language of Action Types is to start practicing it right now with Activity 5-3.

ACTIVITY 5-3. Practice Speaking the Language of Action Types
Make a copy of Table 5-5 and put it on your bathroom mirror so that you see it twice a day. Play your CD every day for a week. Then begin . . .
Week One: Use the Language of Action Types with family and friends. Flex your style with your friends and family to match their Action Types. Pay close attention to how their responses begin to change as you do this activity.
Week Two: Use the Language of Action Types with co-workers and colleagues. Consciously shift your style whenever possible, and start to notice how your stress level is reduced and your productivity increases.
Week Three: OK — you're ready. Trust yourself and start to use the Language of Action Types with patients (and everyone else in your life).

BOTTOM LINE

Our brains are wired to be one (or a combination) of four Action Types. Each Action Type displays a specific set of behaviors that is easily identified as Indirect or Direct, and People-Oriented or Task-Oriented. The key to speaking The Language of Action Types is to identify the individual's Action Type and flex your style to match more closely to theirs.

Chapter 6

The Language of Value Sets

BEFORE I TELL YOU what I'd like you to know in this chapter, I'll ask you to indulge me and do a quick activity. Doing this now will help you to achieve the most accurate response. Once you've read this chapter, your answer may be colored by your new-found knowledge. So, before you go any further, please do Activity 6-1.

ACTIVITY 6-1. Identify Your Value Set
Answer the following question by writing down the first thing that comes to your mind.
What made you choose the car you're currently driving?
Answer:

It's probably no surprise to hear that there is a distinct set of values that people use to make important decisions about whether to make a large purchase and, if so, specifically what to buy and from whom. These values also come into play when making decisions about career choices, education, and even how to raise a family. As I came to discover, these values also serve as one of the most important pieces in the puzzle of building trust and rapport.

Much of what we know about values comes from work that has been done by sociologists — specialists in the study of society and culture. These social scientists have given us great insight into people by studying the behaviors and opinions of different demographic groups. From those studies, they are able to tell us a great deal about the factors that cause us to do what we do. Of course, once we understand why we do what we do, we can then begin to figure out how to get others to do what we want them to do! That's when the fun begins.

Sociologists often look at people according to their **Socio-Economic Status (SES).** SES, also referred to as "social class," is a composite measure of income, education, occupation, and prestige. Through the years, there have been many studies that have used SES along with other factors such as race, ethnicity, age, and education to explain or predict patterns of behaviors ranging from which cereal we buy to whether our children are likely to engage in delinquency and, if so, what type of delinquency they'll choose.

I studied sociology and social psychology in college and graduate school and later went into social and organizational research. During the course of my work in this area, I conducted a study that uncovered something that I found to be intriguing. With respect to major buying decisions, the most common research results had historically shown that we could predict people's values and buying decisions by looking at their current level of SES. Contrary to these results, my studies showed that rather than current SES, a more accurate predictor of adult values and buying concerns was the demographic make-up of the significant others who influenced them as children. In other words, my studies showed that:

Regardless of current job, income, education, or prestige, people will make major decisions based (in large part) on the values they learned as children.[1]

What this means is that there are certain things about us that never change, no matter how successful we become! Further, it proves the old adage, "You can't always judge a book by its cover." Yet I have seen many doctors and staff members who refrained from offering an elective service to a patient solely on the basis of how the patient looked. The assumption was that because a patient was driving an old car or wearing discount clothing, he or she simply couldn't afford the treatment. This is not always the case, as you'll soon see; yet many patients walk away without ever knowing all of their choices.

VALUE SETS

By the time we are old enough to drive a car, each of us has developed a **Value Set (a combination of a values and concerns)** that we use when making important decisions. In my research, I found that there are two major Value Sets that people develop: one is about survival, and the other focuses on comfort. These values then lead to critical concerns in making major decisions and in choosing the people we trust to help us with those decisions.[2]

----

[1] We can gain deeper understanding (and complexity) by layering in factors such as age cohort (the time in history when children are raised) and differences in geographic areas where they were raised. For the purposes of this book, however, all you need to know is the general finding.

Value Set Type 1

People with Type 1 values and concerns were typically raised in communities in which people were focused on their family's safety and/or survival. This was typically the result of factors such as low income, work problems, war, illness in the family, or other life challenges that threatened financial security and/or life.

In many cases, an individual's family was not under any threat and may even have had significantly high income levels. However, if one or more of the adults in the child's life had strong memories of less fortunate times (such as those living through the Great Depression or Holocaust survivors) and spoke of these to the child, their Type 1 values would have been passed down.

Children learn Value Sets not only by their circumstances, but by what they are told.

Either way, Type 1 families typically raise their children with the set of values and concerns shown in Table 6-1.

TABLE 6-1. Type 1 Value Set	
Values	**Concerns When Making a Purchase**
• Financial security is when all bills are paid and you have everything you need to survive. • Education is a means to an end. For example, the reason people go to school is to get a good job. • Pride and self-esteem are derived from full ownership (the lower the debt, the higher the pride). • Respect is earned through hard work. Keep your head down, and your nose to the grindstone.	• Dependability • Reliability • Durability • Value for the money • Practicality • Usefulness

Value Set Type 2

Once a family has reached a certain level of financial status, and has been able to maintain that level for one or more generations, values begin to shift away from survival issues into the arena of comfort. Free from the fears of survival, Type 2 families are focused as shown in Table 6-2.

Now go back to Activity 6-1. Did your answers describe Type 1 Values such as dependability, practicality, durability, or value for the money? Did you

---

[2] Whenever I say that in workshops, someone usually objects. People just don't like the idea of being categorized into groups or told that they are so easily analyzed. But when these naysayers discover their Value Sets, they always laugh and say things like, *"Yep. That's me!"*

TABLE 6-2. Type 2 Value Set	
Values	**Concerns When Making a Purchase**
• Financial security is when you have everything you need and can get anything you want. • Education is an end in itself. Learning is its own reward. • Pride and self-esteem are derived from being accepted by those in higher positions than your own. • You earn respect from others by showing you don't have to work hard to accomplish something; ease of achievement is honored.	• Prestige • Status • Receiving and giving service • Ease of purchase • Ease of use • Comfort • Luxury

say things like, *"It got great gas mileage,"* or *"I could fit all of my kids in there,"* or *"It had a good safety record?"*

Perhaps your answers reflected Type 2 concerns such as luxury, comfort, or service, in which case you wrote things like, *"I just liked it," "It was ultra cool," "My neighbor got one," "It was just the right image for me,"* or *"I've always wanted a (brand)."*

Either way, your answer to the car question will reflect your Value Set.

When I found the Value Sets, I suddenly understood so many of the confusing aspects of people's behaviors that had never made sense. For example, it explained why Sam Walton (founder of WalMart) brought his lunch to work in a brown paper bag and why millionaires are seen driving 10-year-old vehicles. But it goes much further than that.

When we look at this in a healthcare environment, we can understand why:

• Some administrators will decline a change from a "perfectly good" filing system to an electronic medical records system.
• One patient will gladly use third-party financing to cover an elective healthcare procedure while another won't even use a personal credit card.
• Some patients will pay top dollar for a chemical peel at a medical spa, while others are completely satisfied with an over-the-counter scrub.
• Some patients are clamoring for teeth whitening while others aren't even aware of the brand of toothpaste they're using.
• Some staff will avidly watch continuing education videos while others will ask if they're being paid to do so.
• Some doctors will actively seek out continuing education long after they've met their annual requirements while others keep meticulous track of their continuing medical education credits.

Take some time and really think about the differences between Type 1 and Type 2 Value Sets and how they are playing out in your practice. You will find answers for many of the inconsistencies you couldn't explain previously.

Of course, there are exceptions to the rule. The greatest exceptions I found fell into two categories:

Exception #1

The first exception to the rule occurs when children are raised living with the behaviors of one Value Set, but are verbally told to pursue another. For example, a child raised in a Type 1 household might be told, *"When you grow up, I want you to have more than we did. Don't live your life like this. Get an education, become a success. Live the easy life."*

This could also happen in the reverse. A child raised in a Type 2 household has a coach he respects who constantly tells him things like, *"Don't get used to that easy life, kid. Nothing is worth anything if you don't work hard for it. It doesn't matter what other people think. It's what you think."*

In both scenarios, the child will carry both Type 1 and Type 2 Value Sets, and will be conflicted when making decisions about large purchases, schools, jobs and even whom he or she should marry.

Exception #2

The second greatest exception happens when a Type 1 person marries a Type 2 person and raises children. Here's what that might look like:

Let's imagine that she is Type 1 and he is Type 2. They fall in love, and everything is wonderful . . . until they start to plan their wedding. *"I want a small, intimate reception in my mother's living room. We'll cook the food ourselves and hand-write all of the invitations. We'll have to work hard for weeks to pull it off, but it's going to be a memory we'll cherish forever. Besides, I don't want to have to use credit and be paying off our wedding forever!"*

Our Type 2 groom has just received a new credit card, and he is ready to fill it up! *"Let's rent the ballroom at an upscale hotel downtown and get limousines to bring everyone down after the ceremony!"* he says. *"The invitations will be engraved, and the food will be catered by the best chef in the city; my father knows him, and he'll get us in. We'll get an announcement in the Sunday paper social column, and we'll be the talk of the town."*

Do we see a problem here? Well, yes, but love conquers all as they learn the art of compromise and go on to enjoy a long and happy marriage. As their son, Tom, grows up, he sees the different behaviors of his mom and dad and incorporates both sets of values.

Now let's fast-forward 22 years and watch as Tom is shopping for his first car. While drawn to a luxury sports car, he keeps thinking about the practical four-door sedan.

"I could carry all my products and files in the sedan, but I'd look like a jerk. That sports car is going to turn some heads. I can afford that sports car no problem, but what if it makes me look like I'm showing off? On the other hand, it might look good to pull up to the gym looking so successful. This one has better gas mileage, but that one is a real status mobile."

The fact is that Tom has both Type 1 and Type 2 Value Sets, and until he finds a car that is both practical and fits his image, he'll be riding the bus . . . in an Armani suit.

IDENTIFYING THE VALUE SETS OF OTHERS

When we communicate, we tend to use the language of our original Value Set. This is fine as long as we're communicating with someone who shares that Value Set. If not, we widen the gap between us, making it harder to gain trust and establish lasting rapport.

The solution is to learn to speak the language of both Type 1 and Type 2 Value Sets. Once you do, the next step is to identify people's Value Sets.

Method 1: The Car Question

The first and most direct route to discovering someone's Value Set is to ask the car question from Activity 6-1. Admittedly, it is an unusual question to be asking a stranger, particularly in a work setting, and some feel uncomfortable asking it. If you'd like to use it, you'll have a great time with it. It is a good ice-breaker, and everyone enjoys the conversations that come as a result. It is the fastest, most direct method to find someone's Value Set, and many of my clients have told me terrific stories about the fun they had doing it.

Here are the **Five Steps to Identifying Value Sets with the Car Question:**

Step 1: Ask Permission

Begin with something like this:

"I read a book that says we can tell a lot about how to communicate with people by asking them one simple question. It's important to me that you and I speak the same language, so I'd like to ask you this question to learn a little more about you. Afterwards, I'll tell you what I think your answer means, and you can tell me if I'm right. Would that be OK?"

Most people get curious and say *"sure,"* but once in a while, you'll meet someone who says *"no."* If that happens then let it go. That person has just given you important information regarding: (1) the degree to which that person typically trusts people: and/or (2) his or her Action Type (Commander). Just drop it. There are three other languages you can use that will help you to build trust with this person, so move on to one of those (see Chapters 5, 7, and 8).

Now, for the majority who respond positively, continue on to Step 2.

Step 2: Ask the Question

Ask the car question precisely as follows:

What made you choose the car you're currently driving?

Don't change it to "What do you like about your car?" or "What kind of car do you drive?" or any of the dozens of variations I heard when I was out doing follow-up coaching with clients. If you read it as written, it will demand that people access the kind of thinking that will tell us their precise Value Set.

Step 3: Listen

Listen closely to their answer. If the first thing they say falls immediately into the Value Sets as I've listed them in Tables 6-1 and 6-2, then you will hear words that define either Type 1 (value, dependability, durability, practicality, functionality) or Type 2 (image, status, ease of use, style, luxury).

If their answer is difficult to figure out, go to Step 4. If you think you've got it, go to Step 5.

Step 4: Probe

Sometimes you'll get a generic answer like, "*I needed a new car*" or "*I was looking for an inexpensive car.*" In this situation, probe by asking another question:

"*I'm sure there were several cars out there that would have been* (inexpensive, new . . . just fill in whatever they said). *So, I'm curious. What made you choose the one you chose?*" This will get them back on track.

In rare cases, you'll hear something like, "*I didn't choose it. My spouse/ parents/work picked it,*" or "*I don't drive. My son takes me,*" or "*I can't afford a car.*" No problem! Simply rephrase it and ask,

"*Well, if you were going to choose your own car, what would be the top reasons you'd pick one car over another?*"

Step 5: Feed It Back

Check your perception by feeding it back to them. For example, if you think your patient is a Type 1, you might test it by saying, *"It sounds like it's important to you that you get good value for your dollar and that the people who take care of you are people you can rely on. Is that right?"* If they say, "yes!" then you're right on target. Some will elaborate with something like *"a penny saved is a penny earned."* That's definitely a Type 1. If they respond with something like, *"No. I'll spend a little more if that means I'm getting good quality,"* you're with a Type 2. Simply respond with something like *"That makes perfect sense."*

Method 2: Listen to Their Language

Some people just aren't comfortable asking the car question, and others really don't have the time to work it in when seeing 100 patients a day. Whatever your reason, there is another way. While there is no other question that will give you the correct data as quickly or clearly as the car question (and I have spent a lot of time looking), there is another approach that is just as accurate.

Listen for key words in their speech that will come right at you like neon signs saying "Type 1," "Type 2." The words are listed in Tables 6-1 and 6-2. After a while, you will pick up patterns that will tell you their Value Set.

It takes a little practice to identify Value Sets, but as soon as you start you'll find that they pop out at you as clear as day. It's kind of like yellow Volkswagens. Years ago a friend told me that she was driving a yellow Volkswagen. I was amazed! I had no idea they produced yellow Volkswagens. That afternoon as I was driving home, I must have seen at least five yellow Volkswagens! The point is, we are surrounded by things we never notice, until someone points them out. You'll see what I mean when you do Activity 6-2.

ACTIVITY 6-2. Practice Identifying Value Sets
Listen to people in your work environment, and pay attention to the words they use.
Determine whether people are Type 1 or Type 2 by watching how they make key decisions.
When you have a few spare moments, go ahead and ask some people the car question by using Steps 1–5 above.

SPEAKING THE LANGUAGE OF VALUE SETS

Once you've identified a Value Set, you're ready to build trust and rapport by speaking The Language of Value Sets. Simply choose from the key words in Table 6-3, and plug them into your normal language.

For example, let's say you're with a Type 1 patient. Choosing Type 1 language, you might say,

*"You can **depend** on us to **work hard** to make sure you get what you **need**."*

Notice I've used all Type 1 language as shown in Table 6-3.

TABLE 6-3. Speaking the Language of Value Sets		
Value Set	**Key Words**	**Sample Phrases**
Type 1	• Need • Value • Dependable • Reliable • Practical • Hard work	• *You need to follow this plan.* • *It's a good value for the money.* • *You can rely on us.* • *This is a dependable drug.* • *The most practical solution is . . .* • *We're going to work hard to make this happen for you.*
Type 2	• Want • Success • Image • Priority • Ease of use • Comfort	• *You're going to want to follow this plan.* • *You'll have a successful outcome with this medication.* • *Your image will be safe since no one will be able to tell that you've had a procedure.* • *Your health is our first priority.* • *We're going to make this very easy for you.* • *Your comfort is important to us.*

For a Type 2 person, on the other hand, you might say:

*"It's a **priority** for us to make sure you get what you **want** and that it's an **easy** experience."*

> **If you're not sure about which Type someone may be, just pepper your language with a bit from both Value Sets.**

This way you're likely to say *something* the person can relate to and you will build a faster rapport. For example,

*"You can **depend** on us to make it a **priority** that you get everything you **want** and **need**."*

This seems so basic. Is it really that important?

Yes. Here's an example of what makes this language so valuable:

> **Practice Spotlight**
>
> Kelly is one of three receptionists in a very busy primary care practice. It's 3:30 in the afternoon, and Dr. W is running 45 minutes behind schedule. Kelly comes out to speak to Mrs. Patient.
>
> *"Mrs. Patient, I just want to let you know that Dr. W is running a little behind,"* Kelly says gently.
>
> *"What do you mean 'a little behind'?!"* Mrs. Patient replies, *"This is not*

> *OK. I have an important appointment across town, and I just can't be late. You people don't seem to care about your reputation in this community."*

OK, Kelly has just heard the magic words. Type 2 people talk about "reputation." Unfortunately, she doesn't know about Value Sets yet and continues with Type 1 language.

> *"Mrs. Patient, Dr. W is working very hard to get everyone in and . . ."* Kelly begins.
>
> Mrs. Patient collects her purse and gets up to leave. *"I've been a patient here for 20 years. I'd think I'd get a little more respect."*

Let's ignore the obvious issues regarding scheduling, patient flow, interdepartmental communications, and all of the other typical operational analyses. In the exact situation, if you were to change nothing about their operations, is there anything that Kelly could have said that would have made a difference? Very much so. I have found that using the Value Set language of others' clears the communication path and allows for problem resolution.

Here's an example in which a staff member applied the Language of Value Sets successfully in a similar scenario.

Practice Spotlight

Janice works as a combination office manager, receptionist, check in, check out, billing, filing, cleaning, ordering, and patient coordinator for a general dentist.

It's 7:30 a.m., and Mr. New Patient is sitting in the small reception area reading the newspaper. Dr. L calls Janice from her car. She's stuck in traffic and won't be there for another 30 minutes. Janice comes out from behind her desk and walks up to Mr. New Patient.

"Mr. New Patient, I just noticed your truck in the parking lot. It's a beauty. I'm curious. What made you choose that particular truck?"

"Yeah, I know, the guys always give me grief about it. But I always say 'what's wrong with a little flash?' Hey, if you want to be a success, you have to look like one, that's what my Dad always told us."

"That makes perfect sense," Janice smiles. *"Mr. New Patient, Dr. L just called in. She asked me to tell you that she got detained and won't be here for another 30 minutes. You're a top **priority** for her so she asked*

*me to see if you'd like to reschedule or whether you'd like to have some coffee and be **comfortable** for a bit. We want to **make this easy** for you, so which would you prefer?"*

Mr. New Patient rescheduled for the following week. In the meantime, he referred two friends, and I got an email from a very happy Janice. This is really simple once you've practiced. Begin with Activity 6-3.

ACTIVITY 6-3. Practice Speaking the Language of Value Sets
Once you have listened to the CD and have started to feel more comfortable with Type 1 and Type 2 phrasing, start practicing! Incorporate it into your everyday language, even if you're not sure you've identified someone's Value Set. The more comfortable you get using the language, the more smoothly you'll be able to apply it when the time comes that you need it to build trust, Motivate others, and get what you need.
HINT: Try it first with your family and friends!

BOTTOM LINE

Specific values and concerns learned as children form the basis of many of the decisions people make as adults. Simply put, you can take the kid out of the family, but you can't take the family out of the kid. There are two types of Value Sets: Type 1 (Survival) and Type 2 (Comfort). Each Value Set has its own language, and, when you use the words associated with it, you can more quickly and efficiently build trust and rapport.

Chapter 7

The Language of States of Mind

I'D LIKE YOU TO IMAGINE that it's 5:00 p.m. on a hot, humid Friday afternoon in summer. Everyone has left for the day to go home, to happy hour, to the lake, or to the mall, yet there you are, still working and all alone.

In the quiet of the afternoon, you hear the voices in your head[1] . . .

> *I'm so tired. I thought this day would never end.*
> *Where is everyone? Hey! They left!*
> *Why am I always the last to leave?*
> *Hey! She didn't finish that chart! How many times have I told her to complete the charting before she leaves?*
> *If you want it done right, do it yourself.*
> *I'm hungry. Did I eat today? Oooo, someone left donuts!*
> *Yeah, Pig, go ahead and eat the donuts.*
> *OK, OK, I'll be good.*
> *Oh, man those look really fresh. Maybe just a half.*
> *Pig.*
> *Wait a minute — I've been really good this week. Salads for lunch, worked out three times, besides, I deserve this donut. After the day I had, I'll go ahead and eat it.*
> *No, I'll just feel guilty if I eat it.*
> *OK, I'll stop on the way home for some frozen yogurt — 150 calories, leave out the bread tonight, and I'll be good to go.*

So, you get in your car and start to drive.

> *Who put this CD in there? Wow, that's really awful.*
> *OK, that's better.*
> *I really should call Bill. He's sent us a lot of patients, and I need to thank him.*
> *There — on the corner.*

---

[1] Don't even try to pretend you don't talk to yourself. Come on, it's just you and me here. Just be quiet and think about it for a minute . . ."*Hmmm, do I talk to myself? No . . . I definitely do not talk to myself.*"

Need I say more?

Good. A spot right in front.

You park your car and walk in to order your yogurt.

The clerk comes over and says, *"May I help you?"*

You smile and reply, *"Yes. I'll have a hot fudge sundae with butter pecan ice cream, whipped cream, and nuts . . . and two cherries."* So much for yogurt.

You take the sundae to your car (*I don't want anyone to walk in and see me eating this thing!*), and when it's all gone, you start the car to go home.

> *I shouldn't have done that!*
> *Oh but it was SO good! I could go for more.*
> *Pig.*

Sound familiar? Of course it does. Everyone has little back-and-forth conversations inside their heads (and out loud when they think no one can hear them). There are times when all of our voices are in agreement, and times when they get into all-out, drag-down fights!

So what are these voices, and what does this have to do with building trust and rapport so I can get people to do what I want them to do?

I'm so glad you asked. I am about to tell you about something that is so powerful, it will revolutionize the way you think about and work with people. When I learned about this, it literally changed my life. It helped me to make sense of my personal life, my professional life, and the unusual success of my previous business.[2] Let me explain . . .

UNDERSTANDING STATES OF MIND

Have you ever had a conversation with a friend in which he asks you what you want for dinner? You respond, *"Well, part of me wants pizza, and part of me is thinking Chinese."* Well, here's the truth — you really do have "parts" of you. In fact, you have five of them, and so does everyone else in the world.

For ease of learning, imagine that you actually have five teeny little people living inside of you.[3] These five people each have their own sounds, and each one makes you feel differently. If you let yourself, you might be able to see them in your mind's eye. These are your five States of Mind, and together they create a language all their own.[4]

---

[2] If you'd like to learn about my previous business and how it served as a laboratory for many of the techniques you're reading about here, please see Appendix I.

[3] I assure you, I've had a lot of therapy, and I'm really not crazy. I know you don't really have five teeny people inside you, it's just an example, so go with it, OK?

DEVELOPING STATES OF MIND

We develop our States of Mind from the moment we enter the world to approximately our third year of life. From that point on, we continue to expand our States of Mind, adding new information as we grow. Let's start at the beginning:

The First State of Mind: Natural Child

When babies are born, they are aware only of feelings and sensations like hunger, sadness, fear, joy, pain, and fatigue, as well as the visual and kinesthetic recognition of familiar people (such as parents). Uninfluenced by language or social rules, they sleep, eat, cry, play, and do whatever comes naturally without censoring their own thoughts or behaviors.

At the risk of sounding like a cereal commercial, this is what many refer to as "the child within." It is the part of us that feels, reacts without thinking, plays, connects to others, and intuitively knows whom to trust.

The Second State of Mind: Analyst

As babies begin to explore the world, they discover dangers and intrigues. Long before a baby has words to explain what she knows, she develops an encyclopedia of knowledge about the way the world works. *If I touch that it hurts . . . If I do this, it makes a loud noise, and Mom comes!*

As we grow older, and learn words, we are able to learn more about the world, how it works, and what to do. We use our Analyst as a computer to research, analyze, and make sense of everything around us.

The Third State of Mind: Critical Parent

We learn quickly that Mom and Dad don't think everything we do is cute. We crawl across the floor and stick a finger in the light socket. *"NO!"* someone screams. We have just witnessed our first Critical Parent response. Mom's Critical Parent State of Mind came to the surface, and leapt out to keep us safe. Of course, not everything that Mom fusses about has to do with safety. Sometimes she doesn't approve of something we do, while other times she just doesn't like it. The more things we do that are unacceptable to her (and all of the significant others around us), the more opportunities we will have to experience Critical Parent responses.

---

[4] It was Eric Berne who originally presented the idea for this concept in his teachings and writings about "Ego States" in the 1950s. Berne was the founder of Transactional Analysis (TA), and his contributions have long since been widely used in psychotherapy and in corporate consulting. I translated Berne's plan into my States of Mind system back in 1988 when I first started to use it to help sales professionals to increase their revenues. My clients found it to be simpler to understand and easier to apply. Nevertheless, the original credit goes to Berne (and to Dr. Hal Dibner who first introduced me to TA and helped me through my training and certification process).

As we grow older, we begin to treat ourselves the way we were treated. The Critical Parents we heard as children move right in and merge with our own Critical Parent inside of us. Eventually, all of the messages we heard get internalized, and we no longer require the external stimuli. We are perfectly capable of criticizing ourselves, telling ourselves all of the things we should and shouldn't do, should and shouldn't feel, and should and shouldn't be. In fact,

Most people "should" on themselves on a regular basis.

The Fourth State of Mind: Nurturing Parent

Luckily, there is another Parent that comes to our rescue, offering a balance to the Critical Parent. The Nurturing Parent provides the reassurance, loving safety, and coddling that all babies need. Where the Critical Parent provides the prohibitions, the Nurturing Parent gives us our permissions.

To the extent that we experienced Nurturing Parents from the adults in our environment, we will incorporate that into our own States of Mind and develop a part of ourselves that takes care of us and others according to our opinions of what others need.

The Fifth State of Mind: Socialized Child

The more a child learns and obeys the rules, the more he becomes an accepted member of the group. To the extent that we are social beings, we need that acceptance and learn to follow the rules of others. In order to accomplish this, we have to stop ourselves from doing what comes naturally. In other words, we have to contain our Natural Child and restrain ourselves from being who we really are. The Socialized Child takes over and behaves in socially proper ways.

It's easy to distinguish your Socialized Child from your Natural Child by thinking about the difference in the way you laugh in differing circumstances. Imagine this scenario:

You're out with friends, enjoying an evening of relaxation. Perhaps you've had a little wine, and someone starts to tell a funny story. You start to laugh. The more the story unfolds, the harder and louder you laugh until finally you're laughing so hard the tears are running down your face, and you can barely catch your breath.

You know that laugh, right? Now, compare that laugh to the laugh you emit when a patient tells you a funny story at work. You laugh, but perhaps it's a bit more contained. That is your Socialized Child kicking in, reminding you to follow the rules!

The Socialized Child also has another function. As we begin to experience the world around us, we take in lots of rules and begin to make our own rules that stay with us throughout our lives. We'll talk more about this in Chapter 20, but for now just remember this:

Your Socialized Child may be necessary in certain situations, but his or her job is to keep you from being real.

Each of The Five States of Mind has a distinct role in our thought processes and communications with others. Table 7-1 shows the specific responsibilities and roles of each State of Mind.

TABLE 7-1. The Five States of Mind		
State of Mind	**Responsible for**	**Role in Communication**
Critical Parent	• Protection and Prohibition • Opinions about ourselves and others that are negative • Stopping dangerous behaviors	• Criticism • Correction • Expression of negative opinions
Nurturing Parent	• Protection and Permission • Opinions about ourselves and others that are positive • Caring and nurturing	• Support • Encouragement • Expression of positive opinions
Analyst	• Fact gathering • Analytic processes	• Stating facts • Seeking facts
Socialized Child	• Following the rules	• Expression of socially acceptable behaviors • Play (within limits)
Natural Child	• Raw emotions and sensations • Natural play • Connecting with others • Intuition • Creativity	• Expression of genuine feelings and sensations • Play (no limits)

We can diagram The Five States of Mind like this:

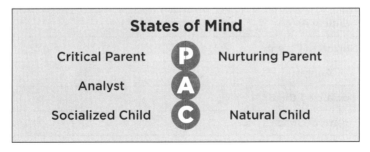

Although we talk about The Five States of Mind as separate parts,

At any given moment, all five States of Mind could be working simultaneously.

Right now as I write this chapter, my Analyst is churning away dictating the facts to be included in this chapter, telling my fingers which keys to press on the keyboard, watching the word processor tell me that I've spelled a word inaccurately, and then quickly looking it up to make sure I get it correct.

My Critical Parent pops in every now and then to keep me from getting carried away with stories and to scare me with criticisms like *"They're going to use this book for firewood."*

Luckily, my Nurturing Parent comes back to save me with reassuring reminders of the many clients who have found this information helpful.

My Socialized Child makes sure I follow social rules and keep this G-rated, while my Natural Child is popping in and out the whole time with humor, creativity, and ideas that make the process of writing this book fun for me, and hopefully for you as well (that was my Nurturing Parent again).

All day long, your five States of Mind are running around inside of you, helping you through tough situations and, perhaps, causing a few as well. Once you understand them, you can use them effectively. More importantly, if you want to build trust and rapport, it is supremely important to learn more about your own States of Mind, to identify States of Mind in others, and to master the process of maneuvering through it all. Let's start with Activity 7-1.

ACTIVITY 7-1. Identify Your States of Mind

Choose one day, and for the entire day, monitor your States of Mind. Notice the things you say to yourself and others. Pay attention to the tone of your voice along with the feelings and sensations inside your body as you engage in different activities throughout the day. At the end of the day, list the percent of time you spent in each State of Mind (ideally, it will add up to 100%).

State of Mind	Percent of Time
Critical Parent	
Nurturing Parent	
Analyst	
Socialized Child	
Natural Child	

HOW TO SPEAK THE LANGUAGE OF STATES OF MIND

Count up the number of people you typically see in a given day and then multiply that times the number five. That's how many people you *really* work with every day. If you've got five States of Mind, and each of the people you work with has five States of Mind, it's a wonder that anyone ever gets their message heard. Now do you understand why it's so hard to get people to do what you want them to do? Now do you understand why you needed that hot fudge sundae?

There are two simple steps to speaking The Language of States of Mind.

Step 1: Identify Their State of Mind

This is the easy part! Listen and watch for key indicators of States of Mind. I've listed them in Table 7-2.

TABLE 7-2. Identifying Others' States of Mind			
State of Mind	**Type of Communication**	**Sample Statements**	**Behaviors or Visual Cues**
Critical Parent	Opinion	• *You should or shouldn't . . .* • *You need to . . .* • *You are bad (or other belittling comments)*	• Pointed finger • Hands on hips • Frown • Harsh tone
Nurturing Parent	Opinion	• *You should or shouldn't . . .* • *You need to . . .* • *You are good (or other supportive statements)*	• Hand outstretched • Smile • Soothing tone
Analyst	Fact	• *This is true* • *That is false* • *It is 3:00 O'clock*	• Monotone
Socialized Child	Opinion or Feeling	• *I shouldn't . . .* • *I'm not good enough . . .*	• Fake • Sterile • Formal • Varied tone
Natural Child	Feeling	• *I like you* • *I love you* • *This is fun* • *Let's have lunch together* • *I'm so glad you're here*	• Emotional • Real • Varied tone

It can be confusing, because people often use multiple States of Mind at any given moment. The closer you pay attention, the more adept you'll become at identifying the key States of Mind that are at play in any situation. Start now by doing Activity 7-2.

ACTIVITY 7-2. Practice Identifying Others' States of Mind

Start paying attention to other people. Use your Analyst (to collect data) and your Natural Child (to engage your intuitive creativity), and observe the primary State of Mind being used by each person as the person speaks or acts. If you get stuck, refer back to Table 7-2.

HINT: Stay out of your Critical Parent. It isn't your job to draw opinions about whether someone is using the correct State of Mind for the situation. Just collect the data and determine which State of Mind the person is in.

Step 2: Parallel Their State of Mind

The next step is to begin to **pace** other people so that you move your State of Mind to fit with theirs. Unlike "mirroring" where the goal is to mimic the other person, pacing simply means paying attention to others and then keeping up with them rather than forcing them to keep up with you. Think of it as if you were walking with a friend. Your friend is a very fast walker, while you like to amble along. Pacing would require you to speed up your walk enough to keep up with your friend, but not necessarily enough to make you completely change what you like to do. Your effort to keep up will naturally invite your friend to slow down a bit so that you are pacing each other. With respect to States of Mind, pacing might look something like this:

Imagine that you are talking with someone who is in her Critical or Nurturing Parent. You might pace her by getting into your Parent like this:

Parallel Communications — Opinions

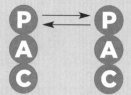

The food in this cafeteria is awful. They should do something about this.

I know what you mean. We should start a petition and get everyone to complain.

Or, speaking from the Analyst State of Mind:

Parallel Communications — Facts

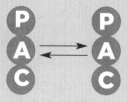

What's the special today?

The sign said "Yankee Bean Soup."

In the middle of lunch, you may hear her Natural Child State of Mind:

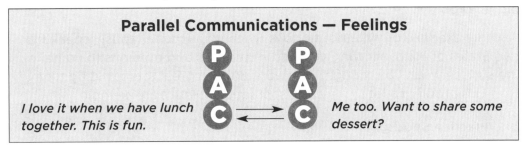

Parallel Communications — Feelings

I love it when we have lunch together. This is fun.

Me too. Want to share some dessert?

Sometimes, you will be approached from someone's Socialized or Natural Child State of Mind and hear it as a request for help. It might sound like this:

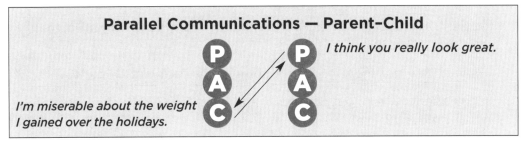

Parallel Communications — Parent–Child

I think you really look great.

I'm miserable about the weight I gained over the holidays.

Here's a tip: If someone says he thinks he gained weight, your responsibility is to deny that you've noticed. If you forget that, it's very hard to recover.

If you are with a patient, a Child to Parent parallel communication might sound like this:

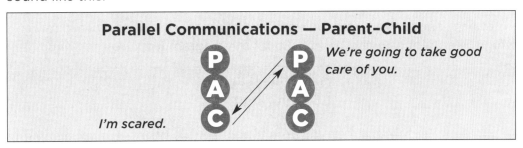

Parallel Communications — Parent–Child

We're going to take good care of you.

I'm scared.

WHAT NOT TO DO

As long as we parallel the others' States of Mind, we will have open communications and an opportunity to build trust. Rapport breaks down, however, as soon as we cross States of Mind. Here's an example:

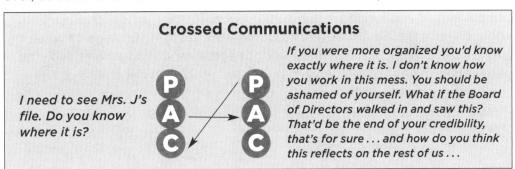

Crossed Communications

I need to see Mrs. J's file. Do you know where it is?

If you were more organized you'd know exactly where it is. I don't know how you work in this mess. You should be ashamed of yourself. What if the Board of Directors walked in and saw this? That'd be the end of your credibility, that's for sure . . . and how do you think this reflects on the rest of us . . .

Needless to say, the file never got retrieved. And now there is a much bigger problem.

Another example of what not to do is when you simultaneously speak from two States of Mind, allowing your "true" feelings and opinions to come to the surface when you thought you were doing a great job of hiding them. I see this problem a lot in my clients' practices. Here's an example:

> **Practice Spotlight**
>
> Rosie and Genita work together at the front desk of a dermatology clinic. They are engaged in a Parent-Parent conversation about a patient that just walked out the door.
>
> Rosie: *"Do you believe her? She thinks her stuff is the only stuff that matters, ya know?"*
>
> Genita: *"You got that right. Here comes Mrs. Patient. She's always late."*
>
> Mrs. Patient runs in, out of breath, and says, *"Hi Genita, am I late? What time is it?"*
>
> Genita puts on a smile, and in her most professional voice says, *"It's 2:30."*
>
> Mrs. Patient turns red in the face and says, *"Well, sorry! I did the best I could!"* and goes off in a huff to sit down.

What happened? Well, you can't see and hear what I saw and heard (and what the patient saw and heard). So let me diagram it for you:

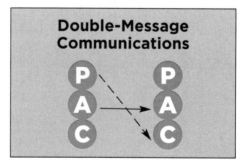

Double-Message Communications

Genita made an Analytical statement when she said, "It's 2:30." But her Critical Parent was lurking in the background, forming a negative opinion about the patient. So although her words were factual, her tone of voice was critical and accusatory, and her right eyebrow was slightly raised. The patient heard what Genita wasn't saying louder than what she said! The trust and rapport were broken.

**Unless you are an award-winning actor,
people always hear what you are trying *not* to say.**

If you're not sure what I'm describing, watch an episode of "Everyone Loves Raymond" and listen to the character named "Marie." She is a personification of a Crossed Communication, always pretending to be in her Nurturing Parent while her Critical Parent is throwing jabs at others with her tone of voice and facial expressions. Critical Parent thinking comes through no matter which State of Mind you use as your mask.

Here's an example of superb use of States of Mind. I'll note the States of Mind by using initials CP (Critical Parent), NP (Nurturing Parent), A (Analyst), SC (Socialized Child), and NC (Natural Child). Watch how Dr. D, a fertility specialist, consciously applies States of Mind to get through a potentially volatile situation:

Practice Spotlight

Dr. D is working in his office when Mr. Patient comes in for his appointment.

Dr. D (SC/A): *Good morning Mr. Patient, I'm glad to see you. Please come in, and tell me how I can help you today.*

Mr. Patient (CP): *I'll tell you how. You told my wife that you could help her get pregnant. You had no right to do that. Who the #&! do you think you are telling her that?*

Dr. D (NP to A): *You sound upset, do you want to tell me what the problem is here? Start at the beginning. What happened first?*

Mr. Patient (A): *OK. My wife came in yesterday, and you told her you could help her get pregnant.*

Dr. D (A): *And you are concerned about this because . . .*

Mr. Patient (NC/A): *Because I can't afford a kid! I'm working two jobs as it is! She's a teacher. She can't afford to take time off. And I don't know what it costs to do this, but it can't be cheap.*

Dr. D (NP to A): *Well I can see why you'd be upset. That makes perfect sense. Have you talked with your wife about this?*

Mr. Patient (A): *No.*

Dr. D (A): *What information do you need from me before you talk to her?*

> Mr. Patient (A to NC): *What's this gonna cost me? Will my insurance cover it? Will she be OK? And what if it's me that has the problem? I don't want to know if it's me that can't make a kid.*
>
> Dr. D (SC to NP to A): *I like both of you, and I wouldn't pretend to know what is best for your family. That decision has to be made by you and your wife. If you decide to pursue fertility treatment, then I will gladly tell you about all of the choices you have. But first, why don't you come with me and I'll introduce you to Ellen. She'll give you all the information you need so the two of you can talk about this clearly. If you have any questions, you can come back together and we'll talk some more, OK?*
>
> Mr. Patient (SC to NC): *Thank you, Dr. D . . . thanks a lot.*

The reason this went so well is because Dr. D paralleled the patient's States of Mind and then consciously moved the patient where he needed the patient to be by adjusting his *own* State of Mind first. I'm sure this seems complex, but it's really quite simple. Just listen to your CD and practice with Activity 7-3. It won't be long until you're speaking The Language of States of Mind as fluently as Dr. D.

ACTIVITY 7-3. Practice Speaking the Language of States of Mind
For the next three days, make a conscious effort to parallel communications with those around you. Avoid crossed communications at all costs!
When you're ready, start taking charge of conversations by changing your State of Mind, and notice how your partner changes his/her State of Mind in response. When it works, congratulate yourself! When it doesn't work, get into your Analyst, figure out where you missed, and then go right back out there. The more you use this language, the more you'll wonder how you ever communicated without it!

BOTTOM LINE

Everyone uses the five components of communication that we call States of Mind. For ease of learning, we think of these as five distinct parts within our mind: Critical Parent (negative opinions and prohibitions), Nurturing Parent (positive opinions and permissions), Analyst (facts and analysis), Socialized Child (learned opinions and feelings), and Natural Child (real feelings and sensations). By paying attention to others' States of Mind and consciously shifting our own, we are able to conduct more efficient communications that ensure greater productivity and a stronger level of trust and rapport with others.

Chapter 8

The Language of Chips

SOME PATIENTS ARE COMFORTABLE with themselves and others. They will tell you all about the things they take pride in, as well as the things they wish they'd never done. They'll confess to wishing their hair were a different texture, their bodies a different shape, or their personalities more wild or tame. They'll chat about their greatest accomplishments and their personal flaws with ease. They'll tell you that they are hurting, where they are hurting, and why they don't want to (or can't) follow your recommendations. While these people are willing to be honest and vulnerable with you, there is another group of patients who will do everything they can to protect themselves from anyone knowing that they might be less than perfect. These patients are self-conscious, uncomfortable, and even ashamed of how they look, what they do, and who they are. They believe that getting ill, growing older, or asking for help is a "weakness," so they are uncomfortable talking about it and giving you the data that you need to diagnose and treat. In fact, some patients are so ashamed, they never call you at all. They live in a bubble of low self-esteem and do everything they can to keep others from knowing about it.

We can find similar dichotomies when we look at partners and staff. Some are willing to try new things and to push the envelope of their capabilities. Their healthy levels of self-esteem allow them to consistently look for newer and better ways to accomplish practice goals. These people are in direct contrast to other members of your Team who are caught behind their veil of low self-esteem. Unwilling to cross into unfamiliar territory, these Team members hold onto the past and do all they can to maintain the status quo.

The fact is,

> **There is a huge disparity among people regarding the
> extent to which they like (or don't like) themselves,
> and this has a huge impact on your practice.**

Communicating with others means treading dangerously in the land of self-esteem, where all around you is a minefield waiting to explode. If you don't know how to manage that effectively, you're likely to step on a sensitive spot and experience an explosion that could potentially cause further harm to the person's (already low) self-esteem, damaging any opportunities you may have had to build trust and establish lasting rapport. Even the most rock-solid, longstanding relationships are at risk when you walk through the land mine of self-esteem.

RESEARCHING SELF-ESTEEM

I was overweight as a kid and received of a lot of teasing as a result. When I first learned about self-esteem in high school, I understood the reasons that all of that teasing had been so painful. I became fascinated in the area, and, in college, read all I could find about self-esteem. In graduate school, I received a grant to conduct research about self-esteem and how it might be connected to weight reduction in children. I developed and implemented a longitudinal study of 100 boys and girls who were attending an eight-week summer camp for overweight children. I interviewed the campers (and their families) before and after camp, then again at 6- and 12-months post-camp. I stayed at the camp all summer, ate with the kids, swam with the kids, and celebrated their incredible successes as they each went on shopping sprees to purchase new outfits to wear home. It was a wonderful experience for them and for me.

The results of my study proved what common sense would have predicted:

- Kids who had higher self-esteem going into camp were more likely to succeed (the higher the baseline levels of self-esteem, the greater the amount of weight loss and the longer period of time the loss was maintained).
- The greater the weight loss during camp, the greater the increase in self-esteem and the longer that increase was maintained (at eight weeks, six months, and one year).
- There was a direct relationship between self-esteem and total weight loss across demographics, medical history, and activity levels during camp.

This was no surprise. The big surprise came when I followed a hunch and filtered in one additional factor: the self-esteem of the cabin counselors. That analysis showed:

- The higher the self-esteem of a child's camp counselor, the more weight the child lost — *all other factors held equal.*

This piece of information set me off on an exciting quest to understand the power of self-esteem and leadership. I interviewed camp counselors after the summer and asked dozens of questions, searching for what made their self-esteem so integrally related to the success of the campers. I cross-checked their responses with a random sample of their campers, and here's what I found out:

- The higher the self-esteem of the counselor, the more likely he or she was to compliment children for every success, no matter how small.

The lesson was clear:

> **Nothing succeeds like believing you can do it**
> **and being recognized when you do.**

SELF-ESTEEM IN HEALTHCARE

During my onsite observation days, I've seen how a small compliment from a receptionist can send a patient almost skipping out of the office. I've seen the swell of activity that occurs when an administrator or doctor walks through and offers a pat on the back for a job well done. I've seen patients pump up their efforts in rehabilitation in response to the positive feedback of their therapists while other patients hang in through uncomfortable testing when their technicians praise their fortitude.

I've also seen the opposite. I've watched grown adults reduced to tears when they are ignored or, worse, belittled by their doctors. I have seen how a sideways glance or a snide comment can cut someone's productivity in half for the rest of the day. I've seen how one person's teasing becomes another's degradation. And I've watched patients sitting in reception areas, making eye contact and shaking their heads in response to the tension around them.

It's difficult to build trust in that environment. And without trust, you can't Motivate or Align, let alone Differentiate yourselves as a premier facility.

> **Self-esteem affects everything in your practice, from your**
> **effectiveness as a leader to the effectiveness of your care.**

It's critically important to understand self-esteem and to learn how to manage it effectively. If I have learned nothing else in my career, it's this:

> **Second to saving a life, there is nothing more powerful than**
> **the impact that one person can make on another's**
> **self-esteem — positively and negatively.**

DEFINING SELF-ESTEEM

Let's back up a moment and make sure we're on the same page about self-esteem.

Self-esteem is a measure of the extent to which we see ourselves as capable and lovable human beings.

Perhaps you've heard about studies that have been conducted with children to show the importance of self-esteem. One of the most famous was a study conducted many years ago at an elementary school. The children in the school were divided randomly in half. One half was told they were the "special and gifted" group. The other half was told nothing at all. The teachers were divided randomly as well. One group was told they were the "more talented" teachers, and so would be matched to the "special and gifted" children. The other group was told nothing but was simply assigned to the other group.

As the school year progressed, there were significant changes in the school. The children in the "special" group made amazing progress. Their grades went up, and their learning rate accelerated. Their teachers became more creative and found innovative ways to engage and educate their children.

The children in the non-labeled group heard that the other group had been labeled as "special" and made the logical conclusion that they, the non-labeled group, were the "dumb" kids. Their grades plummeted. Their teachers stopped trying because of their perception that they weren't good enough to teach the more talented children.

The research study was halted mid-term because it was considered unethical and harmful to the people in the school. But the initial findings were enough to wake up social scientists and teachers to the massive impact that self-esteem can have on a child's future.

Since then, we have seen a multitude of studies emerge showing the powerful role self-esteem plays in the human condition. This is because

Self-esteem is integrally related to the emotions of pride and shame.

In point of fact, shame is the most powerful emotion we can feel. There is no pill to cure it (although alcohol numbs it temporarily), and the longer a person carries it, the harder it is to dispel. If you question the power of shame, you need only look on the Internet and learn about the cultures in which people take their own lives in order to get away from their feelings of shame.

Pride, on the other hand, is an emotion that leads us to feel good about ourselves as people and to increase our productivity as workers. Pride gives us the belief in ourselves that allows us to accomplish more, to take more risks, and to build relationships with others.

So if pride is such a tremendous feeling, why don't more of us feel it? There are many answers to that question, but the bottom line is you can't feel pride when you have low self-esteem. In repetitive studies across the world, researchers have found that the vast majority of adults have low self-esteem. I heard it reported at a conference years ago that

> **Two out of every three adults worldwide have low to dangerously low levels of self-esteem.**

Two out of every three! When I heard that, my Critical Parent had all kinds of things to say about where we had gone wrong, and my Nurturing Parent was ready to rush out and save the world! The method I chose was to teach as many people as possible how to speak the Language of Chips. I'll show you what I mean:

LET'S GO TO MONTE CARLO!

I'd like you to imagine that I was to send you on an all-expense-paid trip to Monte Carlo. I'll pay for your first-class airfare, your suite at the finest hotel, and your ground travel through France in a chauffeured limousine. I'll take care of everything while you're gone: your patients, your family, and I'll even feed your cat and walk your dog.

To make it even better, as you get off the airplane, I'll hand you a special gift: a gold bag. When you look inside that bag, you will find *10,000 clay chips*. These special chips can be used at any casino in Monte Carlo, and the only catch is you have to use each chip at least once before you get on the plane to come home.

How does that sound? Will you go on the trip? (Please say "yes" because I can't hear you right now, so even if you say "no," I won't know it, and I will keep writing under the assumption that you said "yes" and, well, it will spoil the whole thing. OK? Thanks.).[1]

Now imagine the same scenario: I'll send you on an all-expense-paid trip to Monte Carlo. I'll still pay for everything, and I'll still give you a gold bag when you land. But when you look inside the bag, you'll find only *two chips*. Now everything else is still the same, so will you still go on the trip with me? (Come on, be a sport.)

OK, so now we have two identical trips where the only difference is the number of chips I give you. So, let's talk about the chips.

With 10,000 chips, I would imagine that your behavior in the casinos might be kind of exciting to watch. Perhaps you'd try some new games that you

---

[1] My publisher would want me to remind you that this is ONLY an example. No one at Greenbranch Publishing is going to send you to Monte Carlo. Sorry.

never tried before, take some risks that you'd never normally take because, what the heck? With 10,000 chips, what have you got to lose?

Now with only two Chips, I'm guessing your behaviors would be different. You'd probably be a lot more conservative and careful, watching every game, picking the one you might want to play, watching for hours until you were sure you understood, only to put the two chips back in your pocket and watch just a little longer.

The simple reality is this: the more chips you have, the more risks you take; the more risks you take, the more chances you have to succeed. It's just the way it is.

Now, here's the moral to the story:

Self-esteem is the same as a chip.

The more Chips (Self-Esteem) you have, the more risks you take in life, the more you put yourself out there, try new things, converse with new people, build relationships, and build your success.

The fewer your Chips, the more cautious and careful you are, and the less likely you are to take risks and try new things.

The more Chips you have, the more willing you are to network with colleagues, hire outstanding employees, and connect with goal-oriented partners.

The fewer your Chips, the more likely you are to keep a low profile and hire employees who do the same.

The more Chips you have, the more likely you'll be to listen to your M.A.D. CD, practice the techniques in this book; use them to build more trust and rapport with people; and then go on to Motivate them to action, Align with them individually and in teams, and Differentiate yourself as a practice that helps more patients to live longer, healthier, and happier lives.

The fewer your Chips, the more likely it is that you'll read this book and say, *"That was good, but well, we really don't have time for all of this."*

The more Chips you have, the more likely it is that you'll read this book and say, *"OK! Let's start with Chapter One and go one step at a time!"*

The more Chips you have, the more likely it is that you will be willing to change.

So, how many Chips have you got? Let's do a quick activity to find out.

ACTIVITY 8-1. Measure Your Chips

The following activity requires you to make two lists. It is most effective when you limit the time you take for each list *to only 45 seconds per list*. If possible, get a device that will count out 45 seconds and sound an alarm at the end (your cell phone may have this capability). Or grab someone and ask the person to time you! No matter what, *stop writing on each list after 45 seconds*.

When you're ready, begin.

List # 1 (Skill):

Set your timer for 45 Seconds. Now make a list of everything you can think of that you do *competently and capably*. Go!

		TOTAL ITEMS:

List # 2 (Heart):

Set your timer for 45 seconds. Now make a list of everything you can think of that makes you *likeable and lovable*. Go!

		TOTAL ITEMS:

Count up the number of items on both lists, and then I'll tell you about the test you just took.

This test is a derivative of a study that was conducted many years ago with six-year-old children. The children were given 45 seconds to say their answers out loud, while the interviewer wrote them down. The results of the study: The average six-year-old child was able to come up with a minimum of 20 items in each column.

So, how'd YOU do?

Please don't be surprised if you didn't fare quite as well as the children in the original study. I have done this activity with people all over the world, and without exception, in 29 years, I have never found an adult who is able to match the success of those six-year-olds. Here's what I think is going on:

When we are little, we get lots of Chips. People cuddle us and tells us how cute and special we are. We are filled with Chips and afraid of practically nothing. We run across the street, we climb up into trees, we run up to strangers and give them a big hug, and then we dive into leaves without knowing what's under them. We draw on walls, paper, and tables, proud of our masterpieces. We sing loudly, laugh loudly, eat everything that falls on the ground, and walk the planet as if it is ours for the taking.

Little by little, in their efforts to protect us, our parents teach us to be a little frightened, *"Don't cross the street without me."* Suddenly we're not so sure of ourselves.

Our teachers, in their efforts to educate us, teach us to draw between the lines, use the correct colors to properly represent the real world, and to beware of strangers outside the school walls.

Next, we meet the bullies. You know the type. These are the kids who tease and taunt the other kids. Perhaps we are a little shorter or taller or fatter or skinnier or lighter- or darker-skinned than the other kids. Perhaps we need glasses or our hair is too curly or not curly enough or we're too smart or not smart enough. Whatever our uniqueness, the bullies find ways to turn assets into liabilities; and little by little, our Chips are taken away as others catch on and continually comment on our differences.

Over time, the bullies get bigger, the homework gets harder, the games get more competitive, and the stakes get higher. We begin to experience our first failures. Perhaps we don't get chosen for the kickball team or get the part we want in the school play, or no one saves us a seat on the school bus.

Our parents wipe our tears and reassure us about how wonderful we are. They replace our stolen Chips and give a few extra (along with a cup of cocoa). But they can't keep up with the forces in the outside world. Sometimes they, too, contribute to the Chip taking, through unintended blows like, *"I wish you'd behave more like your sister,"* and *"I don't have time for you right now."* In some families, the blows are stronger as adults and older siblings take our Chips by saying things like, *"You'll never amount to anything"* and *"I wish you'd never been born."* If the blows are hard and frequent enough, we can develop a belief that we are "insignificant," "unworthy," or a "failure." We then carry that belief into the outside world.

Regardless of the Chips we receive or lose at home, we continue to grow, and the Chips come and go with each experience. Perhaps we don't get into our first choice of university but we get into a great sorority/fraternity, or we get a smile from someone sitting next to us in class but then we flunk our exam, or we do a great job in our classes but we don't get invited to the senior bash.

All along the way, our Chips are taken away, and new Chips take their place. the older we get, the more little failures we experience along the way, and the more we start to internalize those failures as a measure of our value as human beings.

Fast forward to the future, and we begin to find little lines appearing around our eyes and hairs turning gray. As our stomach starts to pooch, we look back on our successes and find them somehow overshadowed by the things we never tried, the things we tried but never mastered, and all of the people we lost along the way.

But we don't give up! We buy self-help books and go to motivational seminars, hang positive affirmations on our computer screens, and talk to ourselves in the rearview mirror. Pretty soon, we're reenergized and everything is great . . . until we come across a dreaded *"Difficult Person."*

You know who I'm talking about, right? Difficult People — the ones who brighten a room when they leave. These are the grown-up bullies. They one-up us, put us squarely in our places, and remind us about what we don't have and can't do. They gossip, they complain, they create chaos at every turn, lowering our productivity and inviting us to question our own competence and acceptability as human beings.

Do you want to know what makes Difficult People so difficult? It's that they don't have enough Chips. So what they do is try to steal ours!

So what can you do about all of this? Learn to speak The Language of Chips!

HOW TO SPEAK THE LANGUAGE OF CHIPS

Of the four languages, this one is the easiest to teach and, for many, the hardest to implement. There are three simple steps to speaking The Language of Chips:

Step 1: Discover Chip-Worthy Events

Many years ago, I had a mentor named Dr. Erving Polster who taught me something I never forgot:

> **Everyone you will ever meet will have at least**
> **one thing about them that you will find fascinating.**
> **Your job is to figure out what that is.**

There are many Chip-Worthy Events that happen all around you every day of the week. All you have to do is look for them. So what should you look for? There are two categories of Chip-Worthy Events:

Skill

Any time someone does something that is good, capable, practical, smart, accurate, effective, efficient, clever, accomplished, results-driven, impressive, admirable, interesting, knowledgeable, innovative, helpful, or just plain awesome, that is a Chip-Worthy Event.

Heart

Any time there is something about someone as a person that you find special, entertaining, likeable, lovable, endearing, personable, creative, sweet, funny, warm, welcoming, gentle, precious, nurturing, or just plain nice, that is a Chip-Worthy Event.

In other words,

> **Any time someone does what you want them to do —**
> **that is a Chip-Worthy Event!**

Now that you've identified the Chip-Worthy Events, you're ready for Step 2.

Step 2: Chip Them

This is simple to do for some people, and a little more difficult for others. What you're going to do is give a Chip. A Chip is more than a compliment, it's a recognition of something you like, followed by an explanation regarding what makes you like it. This combination is very powerful. Here's what to do:

> **Tell them what you have noticed that you like, and tell them**
> **what you like about it. If appropriate, add thanks at the end.**

There are two kinds of Chips: Chips for doing a Good Job (Skill Chips), and Chips for being a Special Person (Heart Chips).

The following Practice Spotlight is a series of examples of some of the many Chips I've heard my clients give out during the course of a workshop or a working day. It will give you a good picture of the breadth of possibilities when speaking The Language of Chips (Table 8-1).

TABLE 8-1. Practice Spotlight: Sample Chips	
Skill Chips	**Heart Chips**
You did a great job organizing your workstation, I like how you got all the clutter put away. Thank you.	*I appreciate how warmly you greet our patients. It shows your heart and helps us to stand out as a unit. Thank you.*
You are always on top of exactly what I need when I need it. I really like that because it makes me feel safe. Thank you.	*You always have a smile for me. That means a lot to me, and I just wanted to say thank you.*
Thank you for getting Mrs. Patient ready for me. It helped me to catch up, and now I'm back on schedule.	*You are the world's funniest person. You always have a joke ready at the times when I most need one. Thank you.*
No one ties a knot like you do. I bow to your skill.	*I feel safe with you because you are so accepting and nonjudgmental.*
You're a great teacher. You make everything so simple without making people feel stupid.	*You have a way of bringing joy to the worst days. I'm so appreciative of you for that. It's an art.*
Mr. Patient, you did a great job changing your diet. Look at your cholesterol numbers. Good for you!	*You're a really good listener. I feel like I can say anything, and you will just sit there and let me get it all out. And you never try and make me see things your way. Thank you.*
Ms. Patient, I can really tell you've been doing your exercises. Your range of movement is greatly improved.	*I love it when you come in. You brighten my day!*
I really appreciate how you include notes when you refer a patient to us. Your notes help me to understand your thinking and what you've done, and that helps me to team better with you. Thanks for doing that.	*I like being your partner because I know you have my back no matter what. I really trust you, and you know that's not easy for me.*

As you can see, there is really no limit to what you can Chip someone about. Simply find what you like, and let them know you like it. The more you Chip people, the more they will do what you want them to do.

Step 3: Don't Do a No-No

Some people get uncomfortable when they give out a Chip, especially a Heart Chip. This is particularly difficult for Thinkers and Commanders who get a little squeamish and label this "the touchy-feely stuff."

What typically happens when Chip-givers get uncomfortable is they try to lighten it up a little to take the seriousness out of the moment. How they do that is by adding a slug on the shoulder or a nervous laugh or even a sarcastic comment after they've given the Chip. The problem is that since so many people have low self-esteem, they have trouble believing that you would give them a Chip at all and actually have a hard time taking the Chip. When there is a little teasing along with the Chip, they pay more attention to the teasing, and less to the Chip.

So, the first No-No of Chip Giving is:

> **Never, never, never, never, never make a joke or tease someone when you give them a Chip. Keep it pure.**

The second No-No goes back to what you learned in Chapter 7 about Double-Message Communications. If there is any part of you that really doesn't mean what you're saying, the vulnerable little kid inside of them will hear it. So, the second No-No of Chip Giving is:

> **Never, never, never, never, never give a Chip unless every part of you agrees with it. It has to be real, and it has to be true.**

It is a vulnerable moment to give, as well as to receive, a Chip. If you can give it comfortably and from your heart, then it will go a long way toward building the trust and rapport that you need.

DO YOU HAVE ENOUGH CHIPS TO SPARE?

If your Chips are a little low (and whose aren't?), then you may find it a little difficult to give them away to others. The good news is that every time you give away a Chip, you get one in exchange because of the good feeling you'll get for having given a Chip to someone in need. In our culture, it is more common to take away Chips than it is to give them, so please understand when people are skeptical of your recognition, particularly if this is a big change in your behavior.

When you see someone's response, you'll be amazed by the power of your Chip. It can be a very humbling experience to give what you consider to be a "minor" Chip and watch someone's eyes tear in response. The person may even hug you. To my Task-Oriented readers, all I can say is, pull up your Chip-Giving panties and accept the hug. It may be the only way people know how to tell you what they're experiencing. Consider it an indicator of a job well-done.

No matter how much you may like the idea of doing this, the truth is that it's just plain hard to give Chips to others when your supply is on the low side. Here is an activity that will help you to build up your Chips quickly so you have plenty for yourself and plenty to share.

ACTIVITY 8-2. Building Your Chips
Every night for the next week, as you drive home from work or when you get into bed, take a moment and look back over your day. Think back on the things you did and said. As you relive the events of the day, ask yourself two questions:
Question # 1: What did I notice about the things I did today that proves I'm a capable person? Whatever answers you come up with, write them down on your list under the **Skill** category in Activity 8-1.
Question # 2: What did I notice about myself today that proves I'm a good person? Write down your answers under the **Heart** column in Activity 8-1.

If you do Activity 8-2 every night for one week, pretty soon you'll find that you have lots of Chips. Because if you are at all like most of the people I know, you are very Chip-Worthy. You just haven't taken the time to notice.

I think it's time. Don't you?

BALANCING YOUR CHIPS

When you were doing Activity 8-1, did you notice that it was easier to come up with Chips in one category versus the other? This is very common and can be directly associated with your brain wiring. People-Oriented folks are more likely to load up in the Heart area whereas Task-Oriented folks are all about Skill.

There is no right or wrong, but I do think it's important to recognize that unless you balance your Chips, you may find that you run into trouble in times of stress.

For example, let's say you have a bunch of Skill Chips. This is probably because you base your self-esteem on what you do. There's nothing wrong with that, until something happens and you can no longer do what you do. This is what happens when professionals retire or when patients get too ill to work. Many of these people find themselves getting depressed, in large part because they have no way of measuring their value. Task-oriented people need to pump up their Heart Chips so that when they are taken away from their jobs, they still know they are good and likeable people. In this way, they will have enough Chips to spur them on to go out and find new and appropriate activities from which they can build their supply of Skill Chips back to where they belong.

The same is true for Heart Chips. If your Heart list is full but your Skill list is lacking, this is probably because you measure your value by your relationships with other people. There's nothing wrong with that unless something happens to disrupt those relationships through retirement, "empty nest," separation or divorce, moving to another location, or the death of a loved one. When any of these events occur, People-Oriented individuals lose the stimuli that give them the Chips they need. The more isolated they become, the more Chip-starved they become, resulting in depression or illness. If you are People-Oriented, be sure to pump up your Skill Chips now to give you the strength you'll need should you ever have to get back out there and make new connections with people.

You might want to take a moment and go back to Activity 8-1 and add to your list so as to balance your Chips.

THE RIPPLE EFFECT

When you throw a pebble in the water it creates a series of ripples further and further away. Sometimes, if the pond is big enough, you can't even see the effect of your one little pebble.

This is how it is with Chips. When you give one Chip to someone, that person's Chips are exponentially increased in response. The more meaningful the Chip, the more powerful will be the outcome. This new-found pride leads that person, in turn, to spread Chips to others, and as each person builds up his or her Chips, the ripple carries it on and on, far beyond your vision. You can't imagine the impact you can make with one little Chip.

BOTTOM LINE

Self-esteem is critically important for human beings. Those with low self-esteem are less likely to be available to accept your efforts to build trust and rapport, and less likely to be willing to try new things or embrace change. The Language of Chips allows you to resolve this problem by providing others with units of self-esteem called "Chips." A Chip is a recognition of other people for something they do (Skill Chips) or for the goodness of them as people (Heart Chips). The more Chips you give, the more your own Chips will grow, and the ripple effect will have an impact throughout your practice, and beyond.

Chapter 9

Go Multi-Lingual!

I TOLD YOU EARLIER and I'd like to reiterate: it is not necessary that you speak all four languages of The M.A.D. Formula. The techniques you will learn in Sections Three, Four, and Five will still be effective. That said, each language that you add to your toolbox will give you that much more leverage, that much more flexibility, and that much more success.

The true skill (and art) comes when you begin to speak all four languages at once.

Breathe. You can do this.

First, remember that each language is simply another way of looking at, and talking with the same person. I'll show you what I mean.

Let's say you're attending a conference in St. Lucia (feel free to substitute any location you like). You're walking through the exhibition hall and stop to look at a new device that is supposed to give painless injections. As you lean in to hear more, you step on the toes of a woman. We'll call her Jill. Jill turns around slowly, and smiles. You apologize, and she offers her hand. "I'm Jill," she says as she shakes your hand lightly, "and this is my associate, Jack." Jill is clearly a Relater.

Jack goes back to looking at the display while you and Jill get into a conversation about the morning sessions. As you talk with her, you use Relater language, making eye contact, speaking slowly, and using words like "we" and "us."

Jill relaxes more, offering stories about what she's seen at the conference and the challenges of healthcare in the changing market. You parallel her States of Mind, sharing opinions, then offering facts, and laughing together at some of the suggestions you heard that morning.

During the conversation, she mentions the lunch at the other end of the hall. "*It's not fancy, but it's a good deal, and it'll do the job.*" Aha! She's a Type 1. Now, you continue doing the slow, connected Relater language and add in things about how much *hard work* goes into presenting at a conference and how *dependable* you've found this particular vendor.

As you sit down for lunch with Jill and a table of others, you offer her a few Chips, telling her how glad you are to have met her, how much you appreciate her thoughts on the new generation of sedation, and how much you've enjoyed her sense of humor after such a serious morning.

At the end of lunch, you exchange cards, and discover that she practices down the block from you! You tell her where you are located, and she replies that she's been looking for a specialist she could trust to refer her more difficult patients. She asks if you'd be willing to see some of her patients.

You smile (not too much), touch her lightly on the hand, and from your Natural Child you say, *"I'd really enjoy that."*

OK, time to leave St. Lucia and come back to reality.

What you just witnessed is the application of everything you've learned in Section Two. Just listen to your CD, and you will be doing this in no time at all.

In Table 9-1, you'll see the matrix of how all four languages fit together. Whenever you're talking with someone, simply start by determining the Action Type and then add each of the next three languages as soon as you're ready. If you can't figure out one language, just move on to the next.

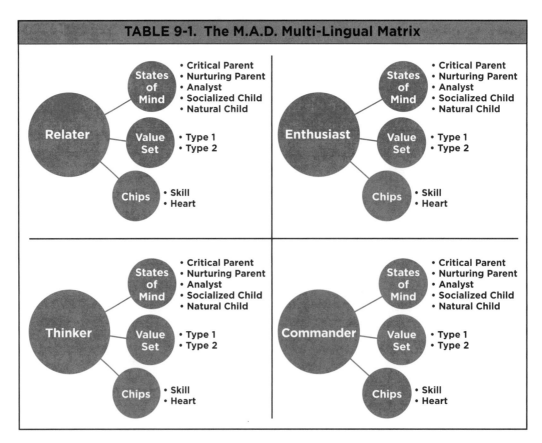

TABLE 9-1. The M.A.D. Multi-Lingual Matrix

If you're talking with more than one person, simply pepper words, phrases, and behaviors from each language that is represented.

If you're presenting to a large group, even if you don't know anything about the people in your audience, you can connect to all of them by continually speaking something from all four Languages and varying your style a little as you go.

Like learning any language, it takes time to master The Four Languages of the M.A.D. Formula. If you find that you just can't (or don't want to) do it, then teach it to someone who works closely by your side. As long as someone builds trust and establishes rapport, you'll be able to get done what you need to get done faster, more efficiently, and more consistently.

ONE LAST THING, THAT SHOULD REALLY GO FIRST

No matter how well you learn The Four Languages of The M.A.D. Formula, there is one more skill you need before you'll truly master it. The skill is **Listening.** There are many resources available to help you to enhance your listening skills. I'm going to narrow it all down to two simple steps. If you do both of these steps, you'll have it nailed.

Step 1: Commit

Make a commitment that you are going to listen. You really don't have to be interested, or even care about what the person is saying. You can try to talk yourself into being interested, but by the time you've convinced yourself, you'll have missed the important parts.

Commit to listen no matter what. If you find yourself being distracted, just remember your commitment by literally saying to yourself "Just listen."

Step 2: Turn Up the Volume

No matter what someone else has to say, you will lose focus when your States of Mind start to pop in and make personal comments in the background. Your Natural Child may be throwing wisecracks while your Critical Parent disapproves and tells you how disrespectful you are. Your Analyst is reminding you about picking up the dry cleaning, while your Nurturing Parent is badgering you that you should eat something before you get too lightheaded. Whoops, here comes your Natural Child again putting in a vote for pizza.

If you consciously try to quiet your own voices, you'll lose track completely of whatever the person in front of you is saying. Try it some time — you'll see what I mean.

Instead, imagine that there is a volume button on the person's forehead, right between the eyes, and push the up arrow to increase the volume.[1] As you imagine yourself increasing the volume of the person's voice, you will begin to focus automatically on his or her words. If you begin to lose track, simply push the button again.

Now you're ready to put it all together with Activity 9-1.

ACTIVITY 9-1. Practice Multi-Lingual Speaking at Work
Randomly select one patient from the schedule for the next day (ideally someone you don't know well). Make a commitment to yourself that when the patient comes in, you will go Multi-Lingual with the goal of establishing trust and rapport.
HINT: If you find yourself thinking, *"But I don't really have an opportunity to talk with patients,"* then maybe this would be a good time to change that. Go on out and say "hello" to the people you serve. Or if you're not set up for that, it's OK. Choose a colleague down the hall or a vendor that comes to call. If the person has a pulse, he or she is fair game.

MULTI-LINGUAL LIVING

Are you ready to branch out, and apply all of these skills outside of work? You'd be amazed at all the things you can do with The Four Languages of the M.A.D. Formula out in the real world!

Go Multi-Lingual at the gym, the grocery store, and the mall. Go Multi-Lingual with the PTA, your postal carrier, your auto repair mechanic, and the utility company customer service representatives (if you can find them). Most importantly, go Multi-Lingual with your spouse, your children, and especially your in-laws.

The more you use this, the more you'll find that everyone is responding differently to you, you're getting more of what you want, and people are starting to do more of what you want them to do.

Then, when you're ready to share the magic, teach others to do it too. Soon everyone around you will be building their Chips, taking more risks, gaining a better understanding of each other, and getting more accomplished along the way. When you go Multi-Lingual, everyone wins!

BOTTOM LINE

The Four Languages of The M.A.D. Formula can be used individually or as a set. Layer them in order, beginning with Action Types and going on from there. When you're ready, go Multi-Lingual with your partners, your staff, and your patients, and then expand it to all of the rest of your community, including everyone at home.

---

[1] No, not literally. Sheesh.

SECTION

3

M is for Motivate

Chapter 10

Motivation and Leadership

Motivate: To move to ACTION, to inspire or impel

IF YOU'RE LOOKING FOR A HIGH-ENERGY ENVIRONMENT, where people enjoy their jobs and give more than they are asked to give, where you have high referral rates, low turnover, and solid testimonials . . . then a Motivated Team is critical to your success. Even if you find the ideal team of people who bring their best every day, we know that people can lose momentum, and it is up to the leader to help them to stay on track.

A leader is a person who Motivates others to ACTION.

Motivation is critical to success, and the right leader is the most important piece of the puzzle. Ask any sports enthusiast, entrepreneur, or accomplished athlete, and you'll hear how the power of ongoing coaching and encouragement; continuous, positive expectations; unbending belief in themselves and their Team; and sheer determination can make the difference between a winning and losing Team.

Clients often ask me if they should bring in a "designated leader" who is responsible entirely for Motivation on a full-time basis. It's a great idea if you have a large Team and can afford it. This allows the leader to put all focus on Motivation and to ensure the implementation of the vision of the practice.

Most of my clients can't afford to hire a designated leader, and that may be the case with you. That said, perhaps you could find someone among your existing Team members who could be trained as a leader. If so, I would encourage you to consider training more than one. At the very least, every administrator, manager, doctor, physician assistant, nurse practitioner, dental hygienist, and patient coordinator needs to be an effective leader. In fact, if your goal is to substantially increase your revenues and elevate your reputation in the community, I'll tell you what I tell other clients who are in a similar position:

Any person in your practice who has contact with anyone you serve or employ needs to be an effective leader. In other words, he or she needs to know how to Motivate others to ACTION.

When I was five years old, I had two tiny turtles named Tipsy and Topsy. Every Sunday night, I would take them out of their terrarium to clean it. I'd place Tipsy and Topsy in a shoebox all the way at one end, and I'd put little pieces of lettuce at the other end of the box. I defy the Dallas Cowboys Cheerleaders to match the level of Motivational energy I sent out to those little guys as I'd root them to the finish line to get their rewards. Sometimes it took hours. Sometimes I had to give them a little push. Sometimes I had to wave the lettuce in front of their teeny little eyes. And sometimes I just had to be patient and let them know I was right there with them. But they always got there . . . eventually. Because I believed in them, I gave them enough incentive, and I never gave up on them.

Anyone can be a good Motivator. All it takes is enthusiasm and an undying belief in your Team. If you want to be an *outstanding* Motivator and a great leader, one who effectively moves people (and not just turtles), you need to know a little bit more.

CHARACTERISTICS OF A GREAT LEADER

In Table 10-1, you will see a list of characteristics of leaders that I created after reviewing countless books and articles that talked about successful leaders and then interviewing clients whom I felt displayed behaviors that encapsulated the essence of leadership. I summarized all of this into a 360-assessment instrument that I use whenever I work with a practice.

When you are ready to get your people on track to be leaders, give this instrument to them and invite them to assess themselves, and all others, according to each characteristic listed. You may be surprised when you see some of the results, but it will give you a good idea about where to get started in developing your leaders.

When you see the characteristics that are lacking, get everyone in a training program to develop those characteristics (all of the information for that can be found throughout this book). In the meantime, keep reading so you'll get a great score when they assess you!

UNDERSTANDING MOTIVATION

There are two types of Motivation, and both of them work. One allows you to Motivate people from the outside; the other gets people to Motivate themselves from the inside. One puts all of the responsibility on you and your business; the other is a partnership that takes most of the

TABLE 10-1. Characteristics of Effective Leaders: 360-Assessment Instrument				
Rate yourself and others on each characteristic listed below according to the following scale: 1) Never true, 2) Rarely true, 3) True about half the time, 4) Often true, 5) Always true				
Characteristic	**1 = Never true 2 = Rarely true 3 = 50-50 4 = Often true 5 = Always true**			
	Name A	Name B	Name C	Name D
Understands and believes in himself/herself and the practice mission				
Has written goals				
Has a precise ACTION plan for the attainment of his or her goals				
Is motivated to work the ACTION plan fully and persistently				
Is driven to succeed — both personally and professionally				
Is driven to help others to be successful				
Practices effective communication techniques				
Is willing to identify and work through the personal barriers that keep him/her from being totally effective				
Has a healthy level of self-esteem				
Has an assertive style (as opposed to passive or aggressive)				
Is skilled at productive confrontation and willing to confront				
Praises and disciplines effectively				
Effectively motivates others to take ACTION				
Maintains a positive atmosphere				
Holds effective meetings				
Nurtures others effectively				
Addresses and resolves all "unfinished business"				
Has the ability to see the big picture				
Has the ability to look to the future and visualize potential outcomes				
Has the ability to shift language and behaviors to match the listeners' needs				
Has the ability to handle emotions effectively (his/her own and others')				
Has the ability to build trust rapidly and establish long-lasting rapport				

responsibility off of you and puts it on to the people you want to Motivate. I think a good leader needs to know both so that he or she can factor in as many Motivating factors as possible.

EXTERNAL MOTIVATION

If you want a donkey to move forward, hold a carrot in front of his nose. He will move forward. Of course, then you have to give him a bite of the carrot. If you don't give him the carrot, after a while he'll figure it out, and he'll give you "the look" and turn his back on you. What happens next is not pretty. Trust me on this: it's just not good when a donkey turns his back on you. To avoid this problem, pay close attention and follow these six rules:

- **Rule #1: If you find the right incentive, and dangle it in front of them, they will take ACTION.** Hold out a carrot. When the donkey moves forward, give him a bite. Move it out further, and he will move forward in an effort to get another bite of the carrot.
- **Rule #2: Don't ever run out of carrots.** If you run out of carrots, the donkey will head to another farmer, and you will get stuck doing the donkey's work. The good news is you won't be cleaning up donkey mess. The bad news is you'll never get it all done alone.
- **Rule #3: The donkey has all the power.** Even if you have enough carrots and keep dangling them in front of the donkey, eventually the donkey will get full. Then, no matter how much you want the donkey to move, you're out of luck until he's hungry again.
- **Rule #4: Keep looking for new incentives.** If the donkey is full, you could try apples. Donkeys like apples. Even if the donkey is full, he'll move forward for a shiny red apple.
- **Rule #5: No matter what you come up with, they always want something better.** Of course, now that the donkey has the apples, you can forget about the carrots. He'll laugh at you if you offer him carrots. Have you ever heard a donkey laugh? It's pretty funny actually — unless you're busy worrying about what you're going to do with all of the leftover carrots in your warehouse and how you're going to pay for the apples. Also, you should know that eventually even apples will lose their appeal — especially when the donkey is full. When that happens, try sugar cubes. You'll have to go to the executive board to increase your budget. But hey — it's cheaper than trying to find and retrain another donkey.
- **Rule #6: If you like your donkey, just keep trying.** Search the Internet. Ask your colleagues. Check your cabinets at home. Get another loan at the bank. Bring in a consultant. Do whatever it takes to get that donkey to move. Of course, you may have to sell the farm to Motivate the donkey, but at least you'll still have the donkey.

I should also tell you that there are two Grand Rules that often override the previous six:

- **Grand Rule # 1: Don't hire a donkey.**
- **Grand Rule # 2: Always remember that employees behave just like donkeys.**

As you can see, we can learn a lot from donkeys. The most important lesson is:

External Motivation works, but it's temporary . . . and costly.

I spent many years consulting for major sales- and service-driven organizations before I came to healthcare. From utilities to trucking, from insurance to automobiles, and from real estate to investment banking, I watched leaders drive themselves to distraction trying to come up with external Motivation (incentive) programs that would keep their people striving for better and better results.

Healthcare organizations are battling the same challenges. If you give an annual bonus, then employees come to expect it, regardless of how well they do. In fact, they build their family budget planning for it. If you tie their bonus to an annual review, they get resentful when you tell them they didn't do what they should have done. You warn them that if they don't do better, they won't get a bonus next year either. We call that "Fear Motivation." Fear Motivation works in that it forces people to work "or else." The problem with Fear Motivation is that it creates havoc on Team morale and productivity. For the first quarter of the year, the employee is mad at you and doesn't perform well. In the second and third quarters, the employee does just enough to get by. Then, in the last quarter, the employee suddenly realizes he better get moving "or else," and you see a flurry of activity.

Since annual bonuses aren't as Motivating as we would like them to be, I have worked with clients to build incentive programs that are ever changing and directly connected to employee productivity. They pay cash bonuses to staff members for good customer service. They give cash and non-cash prizes to staff members who fill the schedule and keep it filled. This is effective, but it puts a tremendous pressure on the administrator to keep coming up with new contests and incentives.

I have clients in "elective" healthcare specializations who have installed highly creative incentive bonus programs that allow for weekly bonuses, giving staff an immediate and constant reinforcement for a job well-done. All incentives are directly tied into the practice as a whole, encouraging teamwork and group Motivation. Again, this is effective, but after a while, the hardest-working employee is the bookkeeper who has to keep track of it all.

Does external Motivation work? Yes. But any incentive you think of never brings the same spark of energy that it did the first time. Everyone loves to open an envelope and see a bonus check, receive a spontaneous $5, or get treated to a dinner out on the town courtesy of the doctor. But the problem is, once you start, you have to keep it up. And you have to keep making it better, bigger, and more exciting—not to mention equal among all the Team members.

My favorite story comes from a client in the south. After providing an extensive leadership and customer service program, I suggested that the client come up with some non-cash, recognition rewards for the employees to create a quick energy surge in the practice whenever it was needed. Here is an excerpt from an e-mail I received from their practice administrator two months post-training.

Practice Spotlight

. . . I want you to know that Dr. W took your suggestion about coming up with a little incentive program very seriously. Truthfully, I think he took it a little further than you meant.

A couple days after you left, he went and bought a brand-new silver Porsche, fully loaded with every bell and whistle you can imagine. He brought the keys in on Monday morning and hung them up in the break room with a sign that said "Employee of the week gets to drive this car on the weekend."

I'm telling you, Wendy, I never saw anything like it. Those girls were hopping! On Friday, Dr. W made the announcement that Lisa got the car for the weekend, and everyone hooted and hollered. She was one happy camper.

Of course, Monday morning everyone was buzzing around Lisa to hear about her weekend. I had to escort them back to work more than a few times. But by Tuesday, they were back to the business of trying to become the next lucky winner of the Porsche.

Last week, a couple of the girls asked me if we could have a meeting at lunch. When we got together, they told Dr. that they didn't want the car anymore. They had started talking about what would happen if they banged up the thing, and they said they didn't want that hanging over their heads. Even when Dr. assured them that he was covered by insurance, they agreed as a group that the more they thought about it, the more they didn't think it was so much fun any more.

Dr. W and I are going to meet next week to come up with something else. Do you have any suggestions?

When I said "non-cash" rewards, I was thinking more along the lines of movie tickets and pizza. In fact, there are many non-cash rewards you can use to insert a little energy boost into a flat group. I've listed them for you in Appendix II. But the fact remains:

External Motivation requires you to come up with new and ever increasing incentives to keep your people productive and happy.

And what about patients? Can you use external Motivation to get your patients to do what you want them to do (follow your treatment recommendations, keep their appointments, refer their friends and family, and pay their bills in full and on time)?

I have medical and dental clients with pediatric practices who give lollipops to their patients (sugar-free) along with stickers, toys, sweatshirts, and for the older children, cell phone minutes, music download gift cards, video rental gift certificates, and "mall bucks."

I know plastic surgeons who give free chemical peels with a breast augmentation, medical spas that offer complimentary facials with laser hair removal, and bariatric surgery practices that offer membership at a gym as an incentive for their surgical patients.

Does this work? Only insofar as patients have come to expect those kinds of rewards. So, if you don't offer them, they think you're behind the times. But does it really work to inspire and impel patients to say "yes" to better health? There are no statistics to prove or disprove the connection. I doubt that there is a direct connection there, but if your competitors are doing it, then until you master The M.A.D. Formula, you'll have to keep buying the mall bucks.

If you're genuinely interested in learning how to truly inspire people to ACTION by helping them to be self-Motivated, then I have a solution that works — permanently.

INTERNAL MOTIVATION

When Michael Phelps won his astonishing eight gold medals, it wasn't because someone was dangling cell phone minutes.

When a floor nurse stays long past her shift to sit with a patient whose family couldn't make it to visit, it's not because someone promised her a gold star on her locker.

When a hygienist spends unpaid weekend hours going for continuing education, it isn't because someone promised him a ride in a Porsche.

When people consistently give more than they're asked to give, it's not because someone offered more. It's because of an internal drive to achieve, to be proud of themselves, to do something for someone they respect, to prove something to someone somewhere, to be better than someone else, to break personal records, out of loyalty and respect to someone else, or any one (or combination) of thousands of other personal reasons. But here's the bottom line:

> **People are Motivated best by the voices inside their heads that tell them to keep on going, to strive for the best, and to achieve their dreams and goals.**

One of my favorite mentors was Paul J. Meyer, who many consider to be the father of Motivation. I learned a lot working with him, but my favorite memory was something he gave me on the back of a Christmas card back in 1988. To this day I have it etched in my mind:

> **Anything you vividly imagine, ardently desire, sincerely believe, and enthusiastically act upon must inevitably come to pass.**

The really powerful Motivational drive comes from inside of everyone. When you have that internal Motivation, then you can add in the necessary skills and resources to make it happen.

Internal Motivational drives can be summarized into two categories. Before I tell you what they are, let's do Activity 10-1.

ACTIVITY 10-1. Identifying Your Internal Motivational Drive	
Write down the very first answer that comes to your mind. Don't censor it. Here's the question:	
Why do you brush your teeth?	

If your answers were along the line of *"To keep them clean," "To have fresh breath," "So my spouse will kiss me,"* or *"To keep my gums healthy,"* then you are typically Motivated to **Gain a Benefit.**

If, on the other hand, your answers sounded like this: *"To keep them from falling out," "So I won't have bad breath," "So they won't be all slimy,"* or *"So I won't need dentures,"* then you are typically Motivated to **Avoid a Loss.**

When we know someone's Internal Motivational Drive, we can Motivate the person by shifting our language. We can Motivate someone who is driven to Gain a Benefit by saying things like *"Think about what you'll be able to do when this is done."* Conversely, we can Motivate the Avoid a Loss person with words like *"Think about what will happen if you don't get this done."*

These little communication tricks are effective, but not earth shattering. If you really want to use Internal Motivation to help people to get and stay Motivated, I've got a three-step formula that will help you to bring everyone in your life, at work and at home, to new heights of Motivation, drive, ambition, and follow-through. It's called **The ACTION Formula©,** and you'll learn all about it as soon as you turn the page.

BOTTOM LINE

Motivation is a key component to the success of your practice. Every practice needs to designate at least one leader whose responsibility it is to ensure that everyone gets and stays Motivated. The best leaders score highly across 22 characteristics of successful leaders. There are two types of Motivation: external and internal. Both work, but only internal Motivation is permanent and puts the responsibility where it belongs: on them.

Chapter 11

The ACTION Formula©

THE FORMULA YOU ARE ABOUT TO LEARN is a comprehensive, practical, and realistic leadership strategy that will allow you to Motivate yourself and others to ACTION through the process of internal Motivation. I'd like to give you some quick background information so you'll understand what makes it so powerful.

Back in the 1990s, I did some subcontracting work for an international seminar company that specializes in delivering one-day public seminars. It was a tremendous experience that gave me an opportunity to meet thousands of people while I traveled the world speaking in a different city every day, four days a week, three weeks a month for three years.

My seminars began at 9:00 a.m. and ended at 4:00 p.m., with a one-hour lunch break, a morning coffee break, and an afternoon snack break. All together, I had five hours to teach anywhere from 25 to 1000 attendees the skills they needed and to Motivate them to use those skills starting first thing Monday. At the same time, I was responsible for selling Motivational and educational books and tapes at the back of the room.

I received a pittance for conducting the seminar. The real money came from my back-of-the-room sales. The larger the city, the larger the audience and the higher my sales would be. We were assigned these "A" cities based on the track record we had shown for high sales and excellence in customer service evaluations. It was a tremendous challenge for me, and I loved it!

I poured my heart into every seminar, determined to inspire people to use the skills I was offering so that they could be more successful in their businesses and live richer lives. I saw my responsibility as twofold:

1. Educate with an entertaining and informative style; and
2. Motivate everyone to apply the skills they'd learned.

I received consistently flattering evaluations on my training and customer service, and large commission checks. In addition to getting the "A" cities, my success gave me credibility with the other seminar leaders, and I ended up serving as mentor to many of them. In addition, the company brought me in to train the hundreds of other seminar leaders so they could be more effective on the platform. I received awards from the company, and thank you notes and e-mails from participants all over the world. I was flying high. Until I received this note:

> *"Thanks for a fantastic day! My employees and I were so pumped when we left! The momentum lasted us through the next few weeks, but then it fizzled. Now we're back to where we began. What can we do to get back the motivation we felt when we were with you?"*

That started me on a furious campaign to figure out why the seminars weren't having the same lasting impact as my onsite programs. I determined that there were three differences between onsite programs and one-day seminars:

1. While seminars were a one-shot, five-hour exposure to the materials, onsite programs were longer, allowing participants to absorb the information more slowly and thoroughly through extended examples and opportunities to practice new techniques in a "safe" environment;
2. Whereas one-day programs were held in rooms filled with individuals from multiple corporations, onsite programs were exclusive to one company and always included the entire Team from the top down. This allowed me to add a component of Alignment into the seminar so that there was no chance of a rogue influence stopping the progression of change; and
3. Most importantly, onsite programs always included a distinct section designed to identify and eliminate any and all barriers to the success of the initiative. During that section, we would discuss personal and organizational challenges and find solutions to conquer all objections. Not one person ever left feeling anything but excited, comfortable, and looking forward to putting the new techniques they'd learned into motion. While I certainly told seminar attendees to find and break through their success barriers, they never had someone with them to walk them through the process and make sure everything was organized and everyone was on board.

I thought back on all the work I'd done working with people over the years, searching for the common thread that made some people take ACTION and others fail in the process. And then I found it. It was a combination of three factors that caused the permanent change, whether it was for one person or an entire Team:

In order for us to take ACTION to create a permanent change,

1. We have to want something (DESIRE). When I say "we have to want something," I mean there has to be a perceived benefit to making the change that is strong enough to light a fire within us so that we are willing to move mountains to make it happen. "Sort of" wanting may not be enough. **The degree of DESIRE has to equal the perceived difficulty of the ACTION to be taken.**

- **KEY #1**: Just because you may think the ACTION you want people to take is "no big deal," they may see it differently. It's their perception that counts here, since they are the ones who have to learn and implement new procedures (staff), make decisions to follow treatment recommendations (patients), or consistently refer patients to your care (colleagues).
- **KEY #2**: The benefit of taking ACTION (that is, the DESIRE) has to mean something to them personally. In other words, they have to be able to understand *specifically* how the benefit will enhance their life. The bigger the change, the more they have to be able to see what's in it for them. Remember, this is not EXTERNAL motivation, it's INTERNAL. So it isn't the carrot. It's what the carrot will do for them.[1]
- **KEY #3**: There is always more than one DESIRE:
  - **PRESENTING DESIRE**: The problem we want to solve or the solution we are looking to achieve;
  - **DESIRE 1**: The first logical benefit we see when we ask ourselves what an ACTION will get for us (typically comes from the Analyst State of Mind);
  - **DESIRES 2, 3, 4, etc.**: Additional benefits that we see in a step-wise sequence, in which DESIRE 1 leads to DESIRE 2, which subsequently leads to DESIRE 3, and so on. All States of Mind (Critical Parent, Nurturing Parent, Analyst, Socialized Child, and Natural Child) are engaged here, assessing all the possible benefits and how each will lead to the next thing or feeling we really want; and
  - **BURNING DESIRE**: This is the thing or feeling that we want most of all. It is the natural result of achieving all of the other DESIRES and typically comes straight from the Natural Child State of Mind.

2. **We have to be able to do the ACTION (RESOURCES).** I can't begin to tell you how many times an initiative has failed because someone didn't plan the details to ensure that everything that was needed in order to take the ACTION was accounted for. Every ACTION requires an understanding of the goal, the skills to make it happen, and often some sort of budget. In addition, there are personal resources such as health (people who are Motivated to take ACTION must be physically able to do what it takes to make it happen) and time (people have to consider their

---

[1] See the Donkey Rules, Chapter 10.

DESIRES as enough of a priority to allot the time to do whatever is necessary to take ACTION).

- **KEY #1:** Don't assume that people have what they need if they don't ask for it. Most people will put things on the back burner rather than face the prospect of having to ask for help or RESOURCES.
- **KEY #2:** When figuring out a RESOURCE plan, people need to work it backwards. For example, if you know that you will need $1000 in order to take ACTION, then the logical sequence of questions is: How will you get it? What will you have to reorganize in your schedule so you have time to do the ACTION that will get you the $1000? When will you have to start so that you'll have the $1000 in time to do everything you have to do to meet your deadline? The more detailed your questions are, the more likely you will be to have all of your RESOURCES in place.

3. **We have to be willing to take ACTION, and live with the consequences of that ACTION (PERMISSION).** The fact is that we have to be willing to change or we won't take ACTION to make it happen. In other words, we have to give ourselves PERMISSION to take ACTION. PERMISSION is best understood as the voices in our head that either encourage us to move forward or convince us to stop. Without PERMISSION, we sabotage initiatives (consciously or unconsciously), and the final ACTION inevitably fails.

Specifically, the goal here is to identify and break through any personal or organizational barriers that might lead us to feel anxious, self-conscious, or even mad about the change. Once that is accomplished, we can give ourselves PERMISSION and encouragement to take ACTION and enjoy the success the changes will bring.

- **KEY #1:** Many people lack PERMISSION without being aware that this is the problem. They may be missing the necessary Chips to take a risk and do something different, or they may have psychological or social rules that forbid them from doing certain things or behaving in certain ways. So the first step in PERMISSION is to help people to be aware when you think that they might be serving as their own success barriers.
- **KEY #2:** Very often a leader can help people to obtain PERMISSION by talking them through their personal barriers and providing support and encouragement.

There you have it, the three components of ACTION that are necessary to guarantee success. Together, they form a formula that is so powerful, I copyrighted it.[2]

The ACTION Formula:
Desire + Resources + Permission = ACTION!

Whether you want to help patients to make lifestyle changes or follow treatment recommendations for testing or procedures, whether you are looking to make a major change in your practice or simply trying to get resistant Team members to take ACTION, whether you are trying to get yourself back to the gym or off the couch to clean out the garage, it is critically important that you have all three components of the formula in place.

Think of it as a mathematical formula. The greater the ACTION, the greater must be your DESIRE for the benefits, RESOURCES to be able to make it happen, and PERMISSION to let yourself have it. The three components do not have to be equal in weight, but together they have to balance out their side of the formula. In other words,

- **You can really DESIRE something and be willing to give yourself PERMISSION to have it, but not have the RESOURCES to make it happen.** In this situation, you have to increase your DESIRE and/or PERMISSION so that you'll find a way to get the RESOURCES you need and not give up.
- **You can really DESIRE something, and have the RESOURCES to make it happen, but not be willing to give yourself PERMISSION to have it.** This requires you to identify the PERMISSION barrier and work through it, or else you'll have to pump up your DESIRE so that the thing you want means so much to you, you are able to ignore your fears or discomfort and go for it anyway.
- And finally, **you can have all the RESOURCES you need and be perfectly willing to give yourself PERMISSION, but find that it just isn't worth all the effort because you have no DESIRE for anything more than what you already have.** I see this situation a lot in complacent leaders, staff members who are nearing retirement, and among elderly patients. In this situation you have to explore the DESIRES in an effort to find a deeper, more meaningful benefit than what you/they have been able to see so far.

All three components must balance out or people won't take ACTION! Let's look at two examples:

> **Practice Spotlight**
>
> Mrs. Patient was past due for a colonoscopy. Eileen, a Physician Assistant, sat patiently and talked with Mrs. Patient, using The ACTION Formula and gently working through the DESIRE,

[2] ©2007 Professional Impact, Inc. *The ACTION Formula: The Shortest Distance Between What You Have and What You Want*; www.TheActionFormula.com. This is a fun little self-help book that teaches The ACTION Formula in a short, fast-moving parable about four office managers who become friends while working in a common building. My clients have found this to be a useful book for Team Alignment activities as well as gifts for patients who need help getting Motivated to make lifestyle changes.

RESOURCES, and PERMISSION components:

Eileen: *Mrs. Patient, it has been a long time since your last colonoscopy. We should really go ahead and get you scheduled for this, especially given your family history.*

Mrs. Patient: *I know. I'll call your office next week.*

Eileen: *Mrs. Patient, can I ask you a quick question?*

Mrs. Patient: *Sure.*

Eileen: *Is there any part of you that wants to put this off?*

Mrs. Patient: *Yes, I suppose so.*

Eileen: *Is there something we could be doing differently that would help you to feel better about having your test?*

Mrs. Patient: *No, it's not you. You've all been wonderful.*

Eileen: *Is it money, because I know that your insurance will cover you for this.*

Mrs. Patient: *No, I have good insurance. But I'd just like to get a refill on my medicine if you don't mind, and then I'll call y'all next week.*

Eileen: *It sounds like getting rid of your belly ache is important. What does the pain keep you from being able to do?*

Mrs. Patient: *Everything. When those cramps start, I can't get nothing done.*

Eileen: *When was the last time this happened?*

Mrs. Patient: *The other day. I was watching my grandkids while Jaimie was at the store.*

Eileen: *Jaimie is your daughter?*

Mrs. Patient: *Yes.*

Eileen: *How old are your grandchildren?*

Mrs. Patient: *3, 5, and 10.*

Eileen: *Wow! That's quite a family. You must love them very much.*

Mrs. Patient: *This is them last Christmas.*

She showed Eileen some pictures. While looking at the pictures,

Eileen kept talking.

Eileen: *Being in their life must mean a lot to you.*

Mrs. Patient just nodded.

Eileen: *Mrs. Patient, are you afraid that if you have the colonoscopy, you might find out that you have the same problem your mom had, and that you would have to miss seeing your grandkids grow up?*

Again, Mrs. Patient just nodded.

Eileen: *That makes sense, and I have no way of knowing what your test will show. I do know that the longer we put it off, the longer you'll have to walk around not knowing and the greater your risk would be if there is something going on in there. What is all this worrying doing to you?*

Mrs. Patient: *Probably making my stomach worse.*

Eileen: *Does that ever get in the way when your grandkids visit?*

Mrs. Patient: *Yes. I have to make them a different lunch because I can't eat what they eat or it will just set me off, if you know what I mean.*

Eileen: *Yes, ma'am I do. It sounds like we need to get this test done quickly so we can find the right medication for you so that you can stop worrying and be able to spend lots more enjoyable time with your grandchildren. What do you think?*

Mrs. Patient: *You got me there. OK, go ahead and set it up. I'll be there.*

ACTION!

Practice Spotlight

A solo dentist wanted to expand her practice to focus more on cosmetic dentistry. She hired us to help her, and the first thing I did was talk her through The ACTION Formula:

DESIRE: Desire 1: She was bored with general dentistry and wanted to focus on her artistic skills. Desire 2: She would feel more alive and proud to be working as a specialist. Desire 3: She could stop having to deal with insurance and could go to an all-cash practice. Desire 4: This would significantly lower her stress and allow her to have more fun. Desire 5: Lowered stress would reduce her migraine headaches. Burning Desire: With fewer headaches, she'd be more available to give attention and love to her special needs child at the end of the day.

RESOURCES: Her clinical skills were up to date. She had just purchased a new building in a high-end part of town. She had enough staff and equipment. What she was missing was the ability to do effective case presentations that would help her patients to understand what was actually involved in cosmetic dentistry and help them to make decisions without boring them to tears with too much technical information. Her staff needed to understand how to speak the Language of Value Sets, since they were all Type 1 people who would now be working in a Type 2 neighborhood, selling a Type 2 service.

PERMISSION: Everyone was excited about the changes, although they were a little nervous about whether they would be able to talk about something that they perceived to be "so expensive." The reality was that the fees they were going to be charging for a full-mouth restoration would be almost half of their annual salaries. The staff was having a hard time quieting the Critical Parent in their heads as they thought about the "frivolousness" of this "luxury" item. Once they were able to understand the connection between Chips and their service, they saw that they could help people to get rid of the appearance that was causing them to feel embarrassed and could help them to feel proud when they smiled. They decided that was worth any fee, and gave themselves PERMISSION to learn the techniques and help their patients to say "yes."

ACTION!

There are specific questions that you need to ask people in order to get a full understanding of where to intervene when applying The ACTION Formula. In the remainder of this section, we'll look at how to apply The ACTION Formula with specific types of people (staff, patients, partners, etc.). Each group requires a different application of The ACTION Formula, with changes to the wording of the questions and the timing of when and where to ask the questions. In Table 11-1, you will see the basic questioning strategy. I recommend that you hold off on using it, until you read through the following chapters to see the subtle, but critical differences in application.

When you think in terms of The ACTION Formula, you begin to identify and break through all of the barriers that keep people from moving ahead. It explains why patients say no, why training initiatives fail, and why executive teams go in circles. My clients have called it "the missing link" to Motivation, and I have no doubt that you'll find many ways to apply it as soon as you get comfortable with the approach. Let's move straight into the specific application chapters, and you'll be able to see for yourself how powerful this tool can be for you and your practice.

TABLE 11-1. The ACTION Formula Questioning Strategy
DESIRE
The goal is to find out what people truly want by giving them the opportunity to imagine how their life would be different if they received the benefits that would result from having done this ACTION. The strategy is to walk them through a process of identifying the benefits of taking ACTION and how each benefit would lead to the next. The questions you will ask will help them to envision their life AS IF they had already taken all of the necessary steps and already had what they have come to you to get. This "magical" thinking helps them to get away from their skepticism and doubt so they may dream about how life could be "if only" they would take the ACTION to have the health or appearance that they need and/or want. Keep asking questions until you help them to discover the benefit that is so personally rewarding, they are inspired to go ahead.
RESOURCES
Every situation is different, but in general there are key RESOURCES that come into play when taking ACTION: Skills or Knowledge, Money or Credit, Physical Health, Time, People to Help, Equipment and Tools, and Ability to Get From Point A to Point B (transportation for the elderly, physical space in the practice for expansion, etc.). The goal is to find out specifically what RESOURCES will be needed to accomplish the ACTION and to map them out in a step-by-step ACTION Plan that will ensure their attainment.
PERMISSION
The goal is to identify any reason that people might be unwilling to do what it takes to achieve the benefit or to live with it after the fact. Again, each situation is different (and we'll deal with those shortly), but the basic strategy is to ask questions that will help them to find the parts of the plan that will lead them to feel uncomfortable, and then to talk them through whatever needs to be done to resolve those issues for clear sailing.

BOTTOM LINE

People will be Motivated to take ACTION and make permanent changes only to the extent that they see the benefits, are able to do what it takes, and are willing to do what it takes and live with the consequences. The ACTION Formula takes all three components of success into account, allowing you to go step by step to achieve your goals.

Chapter 12

Motivate Your Staff

IN ALL OF MY YEARS AS A CONSULTANT, the most common question I've been asked is: *How can I get my staff to be Motivated?*

My response is typically: *Motivated to do what?*

Clients' answers vary with every practice, but the bottom line is always the same: *I want them to do what I want them to do without my having to remind them to do it.*

If you want to Motivate your staff without having to dangle costly carrots, simply follow these four steps:

Step 1: Hire the right people.

Step 2: Use The Language of Action Types, The Language of States of Mind, and The Language of Value Sets in all of your communications with your staff members.

Step 3: Use The Language of Chips to get them Motivated to consistently give you their best every single day.

Step 4: Use The ACTION Formula to increase Internal Motivation and help them to be excited, able, and willing to change.

Sounds easy enough, right? Let's go through the steps, one at a time.

STEP 1: HIRE THE RIGHT PEOPLE

You know all of the standard ways to find employees, so instead of insulting your intelligence by repeating them all here, I'm going to share my special secrets for finding the perfect people for your practice. Let me warn you, they're not traditional, so check the HR laws in your state. If these techniques are within your state laws, you will find the results are extraordinary.

Select the Right Action Type for the Position

I've gone into practices in which productivity was low and rearranged staff members according to their brain wiring. Not only was it valuable for cross training, but the energy, morale, and productivity soared when people began doing what they were born to do.

Think about the stress and subsequent loss of productivity that occurs when People-Oriented staff members have to spend their days stuck in cubicles staring at a computer screen. They need interaction and burn out quickly if they aren't given a position that allows them to use their natural talents. So what do they do? They leave their workstations to go chitchat with anyone who will listen, disrupting others' work, and sabotaging their own productivity. Get them out from their lonely cubicles, and place them in People-Oriented positions. You'll be amazed at how much happier and effective they'll be for you.

By the same token, stress levels soar when we ask Task-Oriented people to work in positions in which there is significant interaction with others. They complain about interruptions and distractions, and feel compelled to check and re-check their work for accuracy.

Don't make yourself crazy with this, but it is worth some time to stop and look at your people in terms of Action Types. Most particularly, I invite you to consider Action Types as a top priority when making hiring decisions. It will cost you a lot less time, money, and aggravation down the road.

Let's look at some specifics regarding Action Types and their best positions. On the People-Oriented side, Relaters do best in positions that are not likely to require strong confrontational skills (you don't want them in collections!). Use Relaters in positions in which they can connect to people and have an opportunity to build relationships. They are good with details and do particularly well at the Front Desk and in Medical and Dental Assistant positions. Remember, Relaters are the glue of your practice, so put them in positions where they will have the opportunity to bring people together. Enthusiasts are ideally suited as Receptionists, Patient Advocates, Treatment Coordinators, Practice Representatives, and any positions that require training or leadership responsibilities. Give them high visibility, and Enthusiasts will help you to shine.

On the Task-Oriented side, use your Thinkers in billing, transcription, clinical assisting (see Chapter 5 for best pairing recommendations), lab technicians, or any position where accuracy and meticulous attention to detail is the key. Avoid placing a Thinker in a position in which he or she has to relate with people all day long, particularly if the position involves fast thinking, constant surprises, and rapid delivery of information. I've seen Thinkers at the front desk and watched them spend their entire day with stress blotches on their face and neck.

Use your Commanders in Results-oriented, goal-driven areas in which they don't have to take orders from other people all day. Give them an opportunity to make things happen, and they will. Commanders are not the best Team players, but they are the best at organizing things and people.

They make great section or department heads (though they need to be able to flex to People-Orientation for leadership purposes), clinical assistants for Thinker doctors (they keep the doctors on task and moving along), and CFOs. If you can find a Commander-Enthusiast mix, hire this person for your Practice Administrator! This is not to say that Thinkers or Relaters can't succeed in the position, but they have to be able to flex to Direct behaviors on a regular basis.

Let's talk about doctors for a moment. I've worked with doctors from every Action Type, and each has assets and liabilities. Thinker doctors do best in quiet, slower practices in which they can take their time to solve problems and are given opportunities to conduct research. Commander doctors need to move quickly and get things done without having to manage the details of paperwork and building relationships. Enthusiast doctors will build you a tremendous reputation. These are the "schmoozers" who will be beloved by patients and colleagues. Keep an eye on them though — they'll throw off your schedule and lose track of overdue paperwork and "mundane" details like charting and dictation. Relater doctors tend to be nurturing and to want to spend time with their patients. This may be an asset or a liability, depending on your practice flow.

Remember, when it's time to pair assistants with doctors, pair Indirect with Indirect (Relators with Thinkers) and Direct with Direct (Enthusiasts with Commanders). Avoid pairing diagonals wherever possible.

Advertise the Position With Pizzazz!

There are many places to advertise your need for employees, such as Craigslist, newspapers, and community newsletters; hanging flyers in grocery stores, school libraries, health clubs, and local merchants; and sending direct mail to teachers in your community.[1] No matter where you choose to advertise, however, here are some suggestions that I always use with my clients that consistently yield a different and superior candidate pool.

1. **Target your ad to the correct Action Type by writing the ad in The Language of Action Types.** Go to Tables 5-1 and 5-5 and pull words that fit the Action Type you are hoping to attract.
2. **Write your ad, not about what *you* want, but rather about what *they* want.** It will make your ad stand out as different and will attract more confident candidates.
3. **Run your ad in atypical locations.** Most practices run their ads under "Healthcare," "Medical," "Dental," or "Office" headings. Sometimes your best candidate will be someone who wasn't considering a healthcare

---

[1] Consider high schools and universities as potential resources for non-credentialed employees.

environment. I've had clients run their ads under "Sales," "Reception," "Professional," and even "Telemarketing." Be creative and do some experimenting.

4. **Invest money.** The more money you spend, the higher caliber of candidate you are likely to attract. Go ahead and splurge a little. For higher paying positions, buy a display ad. Otherwise, buy the extra wide border. It's worth it!

Here are examples of ads that I wrote for clients with spectacular results:

ORTHODONTIC PRACTICE MANAGER

ARE WE RIGHT FOR EACH OTHER?

You have 10+ yrs Office Management experience. While you are extremely loyal, you would consider making a move to an environment where your true talents will be used and appreciated. People call you "a class act" and a "natural leader." You are task-oriented, goal directed, and you feel best when you're working with people. You have a great sense of humor. You are a planner, but you welcome spontaneity and change. If this sounds like you, then an outstanding opportunity awaits you in our unique practice. **FAX YOUR RESUME TO: XXX-XXX-XXXX.** We will contact you for an interview.

PATIENT CARE COORDINATOR

An unusual opportunity awaits you in our patient-focused optometry practice, as you welcome our patients and help them say "yes" to optimal vision. Generous compensation package, an outstanding team of fun, caring people, and continuing growth opportunities! **EXPERIENCE:** Sales or Reception **PERSONALITY:** People always tell you their secrets, you think fast on your feet and you are very curious. If this describes you,

FAX RESUME TO:
XXX-XXX-XXXX

PRACTICE LIAISON DIRECTOR

An outstanding opportunity awaits you in our patient-focused urology practice, as you help the medical community learn about the unique and comprehensive services we offer. **EXPERIENCE**: Sales (medical preferred). **PERSONALITY**: You enjoy talking with people, feel best when you're working, are called a "chameleon" by your friends and you always balance your checkbook!

IF THIS DESCRIBES YOU,
FAX RESUME TO:
XXX-XXX-XXXX

MEDICAL ASSISTANT

You are looking for a full-time position where you can help people of all ages while working towards your Certification. Your friends always tell you how good you are with people but your real talent is organization. Sometimes people tease you because you are so neat and careful. You like doing crossword puzzles and learning about history and science. You don't want just any job. You want to work with a group of people you like and respect. You have a High School diploma or equivalent plus a minimum of 2 years employment, and you're able to work evenings and weekends. If you want to work hard, make a good living and you can tell a good joke, then **FAX YOUR RESUME TO: XXX-XXX-XXXX**

You'll notice that these are not traditional ads. They reach out and speak to people. You can always check credentials and experience, but finding the right people takes a special edge. So,

Write your ads to attract the people, and the people you meet will be very attractive.

You'll also notice that all four ads require the candidate to fax their resume. I have found that this attracts a different kind of candidate, one who is patient and resourceful. Giving only your fax number will yield a candidate with a higher level of energy and more initiative than when you simply have them respond to the ad by sending in a cover letter or calling for an interview. It also allows you the opportunity to scan resumes before you are inundated by calls. If you are looking to keep your search quiet, use a fax number that will go directly to your computer or home.

Don't Wait Until You're Desperate

If you are desperate, you're going to make decisions that will haunt you later on. The Principle of Scarcity demands that you will make decisions based on fear rather than on a carefully calculated decision that takes into account the appropriateness of the candidate for the position and your Team. Waiting until you're desperate will lead you to hire by the Pulse Method (that's where you check to see if they have a pulse and if they do, they're in).

The best solution is to collect a pool of candidates and keep the pool updated every couple of months. Plan that once a month you'll run the ad and conduct a few interviews. You never know who you'll meet when you're not desperate. You may find someone that is so wonderful, you'll create another position just so you don't have to throw this person back into the pond where your competitors can swoop in and grab him or her! I know this seems like a lot of extra time and money, yet if you're willing to make this happen, it will pay off for you in the long run.

Share With Colleagues

Sometimes you meet a candidate who has great credentials and personality, but who just doesn't fit with your particular needs or Team. When that happens, ask the candidate's permission to share his or her resume with a colleague, and then call a couple of your colleagues and offer to pass on the candidate's resume. This act of good will can yield big points that you may cash in at a later time for coverage, referrals, and lots more. Down the line, you may even call them to let them know that you are looking for a certain type of candidate. They may have just turned down your perfect hire!

STEP 2: USE THE LANGUAGE OF ACTION TYPES, THE LANGUAGE OF STATES OF MIND, AND THE LANGUAGE OF VALUE SETS IN ALL OF YOUR COMMUNICATIONS WITH YOUR STAFF MEMBERS

The next piece of Motivating staff is being effective when you tell them what you want, particularly during training. Here are some tips to help you to get the best from your people by using The Language of States of Mind:

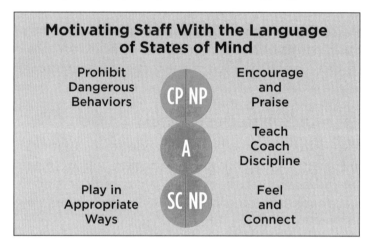

Make a conscious effort to use all Five States of Mind when you tell them what you want. Here's a great example.

Practice Spotlight

An administrator of a large practice was determined to make our training stick. She had worked hard to learn The Language of States of Mind since our Leadership Enhancement Workshop; and then, after the full practice had learned the language, she used it in communicating with them. Here's an excerpt from a follow-up e-mail she sent to me, describing an encounter with a member of her staff.

We were in the middle of cross training, and I had decided to tape the session. I'm so glad I did! Here's a transcription of my talking with one of the associates.

Me: *"Jodi, [Analyst] the number one goal here is to make sure there are no mistakes when you type this into the new system. If there's anything you can't read, don't hesitate to ask someone. [Critical Parent] I want you to listen, Jodi, this is my Critical Parent talking here — Don't make mistakes! OK. The truth is, [Nurturing Parent] I'm not worried about you — I know you'll do a great job because you are so careful with everything you do. That's why I picked you to handle this. [Socialized Child] I guess I'm just nervous because I know there is a lot at stake here, and I want to make sure we all get through the transition smoothly. So, [Analyst] let's just go through the steps one at a time.*

"First step, [Natural Child] take a couple of M&Ms and put them in your mouth. I'm serious! This system works best with chocolate. That's why I chose this one over the other three we looked at. OK, [Analyst] now look at the first chart, and find the patient number. OK, now find the place on the screen where. . . . Great! Go ahead and type it in while [Natural Child] I steal one of your M&Ms.

"I'm glad I had a chance to do this with you — it seems like I never get a chance to see you since you're all the way on the other side of the building. [Nurturing Parent] Oh that was good, now just [Analyst] move it over a little so it's aligned — perfect. [Natural Child] You know I think what they say is true — the blue ones really do taste different."

We got through the training in record time, laughing the whole time. I like getting in all the States of Mind when I coach, and it definitely helped that she'd had your training too so that I could come right out and say "Critical Parent" — it's a great communication shortcut because I could just say it instead of getting huffy but still trying to be nice. I don't try to be nice anymore. I just tell them what's happening. I think they like it better, and I can tell you I haven't had even a little headache in weeks.

What about the other Languages? As you learn about your staff members, begin to speak with them in the language that best relates to them. Discover their Value Sets and use Type 1 and Type 2 language to Motivate them to get the job done. Identify their Action Types and flex your words and behaviors accordingly. Make sure you're using all Five States of Mind at the appropriate times. Let's look at an example:

Let's say you have a clinical assistant who is a Type 1, Thinker. You have noticed that she responds best when you are in your Nurturing Parent. Your goal is to get her to keep your rooms stocked. You might say:

"You have been doing a really good job getting the patients roomed and ready for me in a timely manner. Thank you for doing that. One thing I'd like you to do in addition is to <u>work hard</u> to make sure that I always have a full supply of 4X4s in every room. I <u>need</u> to be able to <u>depend</u> on you for that so I don't have to run around looking for them. Can I <u>rely</u> on you for this?"

In the same situation, let's say you have a Type 2, Enthusiast who responds best to your Analyst with a little Natural Child thrown in. So, in this scenario you might say:

"You have been <u>SO</u> great about getting the patients roomed and ready. You've <u>really</u> aced that one, and I want you to know that <u>everyone has noticed</u> the <u>incredible job</u> you're doing on this. I want you to do one more <u>easy</u> thing that will help our <u>patients to see us</u> as more organized. I want you to set a <u>priority</u> to make sure that there is always a <u>ton</u> of 4X4s in every room. Don't make me run down the hall <u>like a maniac</u> looking for these things, because you know I don't <u>look good</u> doing the maniac thing, OK?"

But I don't want to have to do all that. I'm paying them good money to do their jobs and that's enough. You know, there are plenty of people out there who need jobs. If they can't do this, I'll find someone else. I don't have time for all this Motivation stuff.

OK. It's entirely your choice. Just consider one thing: It costs a lot of money to replace people. If you have an employee that is basically good at what she does, but who just needs to step it up a notch or three, then this is the perfect time to apply The Four Languages and watch the magic. It's much more fun to marvel at your magnificent application of these skills than to spend your time being mad at the employees who just "don't get it." There's a reason they don't get it, and it could be you! You can get mad, or you can get M.A.D.

STEP 3: USE THE LANGUAGE OF CHIPS TO GET THEM MOTIVATED TO CONSISTENTLY GIVE YOU THEIR BEST EVERY SINGLE DAY

Countless studies have shown that nothing Motivates employees more than being recognized for a job well done. Having worked as a consultant in both corporate and healthcare, I can honestly say that, while recognition is an important element of Motivation in all work environments, I have found it to be significantly more important in healthcare. I can't begin to tell you the number of practices in which I have found problems that came down to a lack of recognition.

Healthcare professionals work all day long pleasing others in an environment in which a mistake can mean a life. They have double the stress of much of the corporate world simply because of that double-edged sword. Nothing soothes that stress better than a Chip. You want to buy them a pizza, go right ahead. But a Skill Chip coupled with a Heart Chip will go a lot further. Serve pizza *while* you Chip them, and you've got a highly Motivated Team that will stay that way.

Practice Spotlight

We had reached the point in our workshop when we asked all 60 members of the team to talk about what they thought needed to be done to make their practice more effective. No one would say a word, although they were all shooting glances at one another when they thought we weren't watching.

I went to the hub of the practice, a medical assistant who had already shown that she was the one who everyone else in the practice came to with "the gossip." She was sitting on the floor, huddled up with three of her friends.

I asked her straight out, *"What do you think?"*

Stress blotches appeared on her face and neck. *"You really want to know?"* she asked.

"I think we all want to know. Honestly, I think your colleagues are counting on you to speak for them, so why don't you go ahead?" I said.

Her eyes welled up with tears.

"Are you afraid?" I asked. She nodded.

I asked the doctors and practice administrator to offer reassurance about job stability, and they eagerly assured her that she could be totally honest. So she took a deep breath and blurted out, *"It would be nice if we knew you appreciated us! We work so hard for you, and you never once give us even a thank you. We bring you great ideas, and you just ignore them or treat us like we're stupid. If you don't want to take our ideas then that's fine but at least once in a while could you please acknowledge that you value us as professionals or at least say 'thank you'?"*

As we looked around the room, all of the staff members were red-faced, and many were dabbing their eyes with tissues.

I asked them if she was talking for them and they all nodded, and a couple of them started to sob outright.

Dr. C stepped right up and started to say all of the things that he appreciated about each member of the staff, and tears came from his eyes as he apologized for the injuries he realized he had inflicted on his Team. Each doctor followed suit; and by the end of the hour, the Team was filled with an energy they hadn't experienced in many years. The next day I got an email from one of the physicians in which he asked, *"How did you get all those people to break through those emotional barriers?"* Admittedly, there was a strong foundation that had been laid to enable this event, but the real outcome came as a result of the willingness of the leadership to be accountable to their Team and to offer up a bunch of meaningful Chips at the right moment in time.

Don't wait for it to get to the point where you need a consultant's intervention. Starting right now, make a list of the staff members who report to you and make a commitment to

Give each member of your Team at least one Chip every day.

If you are a doctor, this could potentially mean that you will give dozens of Chips every day, to your partners, your front desk, your personal clinical assistants, your biller, your transcriptionist, your lab techs, your treatment coordinator, your financial coordinator, your PA, your Nurse Administrator, your Interns, and let's not forget your Administrator!

Is this a lot of work? In the beginning, it will seem like it. But if you put the time in, I promise you, the rewards you will receive will far surpass your efforts. People do meaningful things for you when they know they mean something to you. Besides, you will feel really good when you start getting Chips back! When the Chips are flying, the bottom line soars. It's just that simple.

Praise and Discipline

Whether you are Motivating a five-year-old or a 50-year-old, there comes a point when you have to stop behaviors you don't want and teach the behaviors you do want. In order to do that in a Motivational way that will inspire them to want to improve, I recommend that you use a formula that I learned many years ago called the **LB-NT Formula: LB =** Like Best**,** and **NT =** Next Time.

When people do something you don't like, find something about it that they did that you DO like, and tell them that. This is giving them a Chip and helps them to be better prepared for your correction. Next, tell them what you'd like them to do differently the next time they do it. Notice, you're not telling them that they did something *wrong,* only how you'd like it done *differently.* Here are a couple of examples:

Example 1:

Your employee completes all of the billing statements and gets them in the envelopes and mails them. She then punches out and goes home for the weekend. Two days later, your mail carrier brings back a basket filled with all of the envelopes. Your employee forgot to run the envelopes through the postage machine before she mailed them.

Non-Motivational Response: *I can't believe you did that! I thought you were more organized that that! Don't you realize we could have lost all of those statements? It's a good thing our mail carrier found them and brought them back. Try to be more careful next time.*

LB-NT: *I really like that you got all of the statements done on time, thank you! Next time, I'd appreciate it if you'd double check that everything is ready before you put them in the mail.*

Example 2:

For the past eight months, your partner has arrived over an hour late to the Executive Team meetings, disrupting proceedings and causing everyone to have to wait while your administrator catches him up on what was done before he got there.

Non-Motivational Response: *We are sick and tired of the disrespect you show us. I don't care what it takes, you have to either get to these meetings on time or we'll find another partner who will be more organized.*

LB-NT: *We all appreciate that you come to the meeting every month because you are an important part of our Team. Something we'd like you to do differently next month is to have your scheduler make sure that your 5:00 o'clock hour is blocked so that you can get here at the beginning of the meeting.*

KEY #1: The LB has to be about the same event as the NT or else it comes out all wrong: *I like how your scrubs are always neatly pressed. Next time you hand me an instrument, make sure it goes right into my hand instead of on the floor.*

KEY #2: Do not put the word "but" between your LB and your NT. "But" is a negating word in a communication, and takes away from the LB chip: *I like that you always answer the phone with a pleasant tone **but** next time I'd appreciate it if you would answer it before the second ring.*

KEY #3: Do not use the word "try" in combination with your "but" or you will get sent down the path of doom and gloom: *I like it that you take the patient history, but next time, try to get it right.*

The LB-NT Formula is a fantastic teaching and coaching tool in that it encourages students to know that they are making great progress and Motivates them to keep going: *I like the even spacing between your stitches, and next time I'd like to see you make them a little tighter.*

Praise and discipline doesn't have to be a scary or uncomfortable experience. It can be a Motivational opportunity to learn and grow as long as you use the LB-NT Formula.

STEP 4: USE THE ACTION FORMULA TO INCREASE INTERNAL MOTIVATION AND HELP THEM TO BE EXCITED, ABLE, AND WILLING TO CHANGE

One of the most dynamic ways to Motivate staff is to discover their INTERNAL Motivators and help them to reach their goals. You can do that by applying The ACTION Formula upon hiring and at each annual review. I teach this in all of my leadership training programs and have gotten nothing but rave reviews from the doctors and administrators who use it. Here's a transcription of a videotaped annual review session between Kathy (Practice Administrator) and Larry (Billing).

> **Practice Spotlight**
>
> Kathy: *OK Larry, we're going to do something a little different this year during the annual reviews, and I hope you find it interesting and helpful. I'd like to ask you some questions to understand more about your goals and dreams so that I can learn more about what I can do to help you to achieve them. Would that be OK?*
>
> Larry: *Sure, sounds like fun. But are we going to talk about my review today?*
>
> Kathy: *Definitely. If it's OK with you, I'd like to do this first so we can attach your review to your personal goals. I'm going to read some of the questions because this is new to me, and I want to make sure I do this right, OK?*
>
> Larry: *Fine with me.*
>
> Kathy: *OK, let's start with your personal Motivations. Larry, if you woke up tomorrow morning and magically found that this were the perfect job for you, what would it look like? Specifically how would things be on a day-to-day basis?*
>
> Larry: *Well, I think the job is pretty perfect already, Kathy.*
>
> Kathy: *That's nice to hear. There must be something that would make it more ideal for you. Go ahead and let your imagination go. I'm not going to hold anything you say against you. I'm genuinely interested in making sure you have everything you want and need. I'm going to be*

asking everyone these questions, so I'm not just picking on you. So, if you woke up tomorrow morning and magically found this were the perfect job for you, what would it look like?

Larry: *Well, to be honest, I wouldn't mind having a printer closer to my desk. I waste a lot of time every day waiting for the printer.*

Kathy: *Good, what else?*

Larry: *I don't know if you've noticed, but there's a lot of noise around me and that makes it very hard to talk on the phone. You know how much time I spend on the phone, and people are constantly talking all day long around me. I'm not saying they're doing anything wrong. It's all work stuff. But it's non-stop all day.*

Kathy: *Well, Larry, how would you suggest we might solve that problem?*

Larry: *I was thinking maybe I could switch desks with Corina. She walks away from her desk all day long to give her completed files to Barbara, and if they sat closer it would probably save her time too. Then I'd take Corina's desk and be in the corner where it's quieter. Also, Corina's right next to the printer so that would kill two birds with one stone.*

Kathy: *It sounds like you've thought about this.*

Larry: *Yeah, I guess I have.*

Kathy: *Good. Have you talked with Corina about this?*

Larry: *No. I didn't think I should say anything.*

Kathy: *OK, what else would make this job perfect for you?*

Larry: *That's it I guess.*

Kathy: *You guess?*

Larry: *Yeah, well . . .*

Kathy: *Go ahead. No judgments here, remember?*

Larry: *I'd like to learn to be an x-ray tech. I think I'd be very good at it, and I know how crazy it gets here sometimes and you could use another guy.*

Kathy: *Larry, that's awesome! So, let me ask you, if you woke up tomorrow morning and found that you were sitting in an area that was quieter, closer to a printer, and you were learning to be an x-ray tech, would that make things perfect for you?*

Larry: *Yeah!*

Kathy: *And what would all of that do for you on a day-to-day basis —
I mean, how would that change things for you?*

Larry: *Well, I'd be good, only more, you know, pumped.*

Kathy: *How so?*

Larry: *Well, don't get me wrong, I'm very happy with my job, but I've
always thought I could do more, you know? I think if I were working
towards the x-ray tech position it'd give me something to stand tall
about, ya know?*

Kathy: *Definitely. So Larry, is there anything you can think of that
would keep you from being able to do that?*

Larry: *Well, I can't afford to take off work to go to school.*

Kathy: *Have you thought about how you might work around that?*

Larry: *There are night classes at Community Tech.*

Kathy: *And . . .*

Larry: *I have to save for the tuition and books, but I could do that.*

Kathy: *OK, now here's another question. Is there anything you can
think of that would keep you from being willing to work during the day
and go to school at night so you could become an x-ray technician?*

Larry: *What do you mean?*

Kathy: *Well, when you think about doing it, how do you feel on the
inside?*

Larry: *Good!*

Kathy: *Only good? Anything else?*

Larry: *Well, it's a little weird, you know? At my age? What would
people think?*

Kathy: *How do you answer that question?*

Larry: *They'd think I'm too old.*

Kathy: *Would they be right?*

Larry: *Hell no.*

Kathy: *Then how can I help you to achieve your dream?*

Larry: *You would help me?*

> Kathy: *I'd like to talk about it with you, it depends on what you need, but I'd like to see what we can work out.*
>
> Larry: *Well, would you give me a recommendation for the school?*
>
> Kathy: *Absolutely.*
>
> Larry: *I know it's gonna be a while before I can graduate, but maybe when I start to learn I could maybe hang around and watch John a little bit?*
>
> Kathy: *If it's OK with John, and your other work is on schedule, I think that would be terrific.*
>
> Larry: *Awesome. So, am I doing OK with everything else? I mean, except for the noise and printer things, I really do like it here.*
>
> Kathy: *Let's talk about the progress you've made this year.*

Like many of my clients, Kathy grabbed onto The ACTION Formula and ran with it. But there are others who find it a little awkward at first, especially my clients who are perfectionists. Please understand, you don't have to be perfect on The ACTION Formula interview. Let the CD help you to get the general goals, and then let it come out in your natural style.

The people who have the most difficult time getting behind this approach are those who were taught that it is important to separate work from personal. If this describes you, I'd like you to take just a moment and consider this:

> **I have found that the more leaders try to keep the work environment emotionally sterile, the less likely they are to have energized staff and satisfied loyal patients.**

Don't get me wrong — I would never recommend that Leaders discuss their personal problems with staff, nor would I suggest that Leaders let down the boundaries that appropriately separate them from their employees or patients. However, the problem that I see everywhere is this:

In their efforts to keep clean boundaries and get personnel to focus on their jobs, many healthcare leaders have thrown the baby out with the bath water. They see this as a polarity, where they can either have well-behaved staff, or chaos. They tell their personnel to *"leave your personal lives at the door"* so as to avoid chatter about Saturday night dates, lost relationships, and difficult family problems. The problem is that they don't know how to help their employees to take all of that passion and channel it into passion for their patients and the jobs that need to get done. They view it as an all or nothing, and nothing wins.

When you help staff to identify their dreams and allow them to discuss their fears, embarrassments, and frustrations under a guided discussion, you develop loyal, passionate, and Motivated employees who will move mountains to protect your business, your doctors, and your patients.

If you are looking to build a highly Motivated staff, then the most efficient way to do that is to help them to build their personal internal Motivations. The problem is that people don't know how to find and build their personal Motivations on their own. If they did, they would probably have been exposed to this by someone who took the time and mentored them long before they met you and would have been doing it all along. In fact, with the right kind of support, upbringing, and education, they might even have ended up in *your* job. It's not too late! Help them grow with the ultimate goal of filling your shoes. This will leave your options open to grow even further.

Here's what you need to remember about your employees: They were all children once, and somewhere along the way, someone or something kept them from being able to grow to their full potential. Think of it this way: Every child begins as a dreamer. They are creative and whimsical, drawing blue buildings and pink skies and purple grass. If they have teachers who nurture that creativity and invite them to invent stories to match the richness of their dreams, they will grow to be creative employees who bring you innovative ideas. On the other hand, if the kids have teachers who stop creativity and dreaming, they will hear things like, "*Stop day dreaming and get back to work*" or "*Johnny, I want you to look outside the window. What color do you see there? Now draw me a picture that looks like that!*"

Many children in our country learn early to squash their creativity, to follow the rules, and to color inside the lines. The older they get, the more structured their environments become. Some would argue this is important for our society, and as a sociologist, I would never deny that. But I have to tell you that in healthcare this causes a problem. I see a lot of employees having their creative ideas shut down, their individuality diminished, and their passion quelled. Those are always the practices in which I find quiet rebellions, back stabbing, and gossip. It is in these practices that I hear the frustration of leaders as they describe employees who complain without presenting solutions of their own.

Leaders want innovation from their workers, but stop the possibility of that by insisting that the employees block the State of Mind that is responsible for creativity and innovation: The Natural Child.

You can't expect people to be creative unless you encourage passion and Chip them when they give it to you!

Admittedly, the non-dreaming kids grow up to be steady workers, and you need people like that. While the creative kids will likely be the thorns in your side, always looking for newer and better ways to do things, make a commitment to nurture that and you will find your practice consistently ahead of the competition.

Regardless of how your employees were raised, The ACTION Formula invites everyone on your Team to be creative by getting them to dream again. When you encourage them to dream, you'll be amazed at the possibilities. I'll show you how to do this as an Alignment activity in Section Four, and you'll see how powerful it can be when you use the synergy of your entire Team. In the meantime, start using it with your staff one at a time, and set proper boundaries so that the passion stays focused in the right direction.

Every so often, you may have an employee divulge something highly personal. It is critically important that you assure the employee that this conversation will never leave the office and that it will remain private and confidential. Ironically, it is these conversations that always end in dramatic turnarounds for staff. We have seen awe-inspiring changes come about in staff members who our clients had long ago reconciled to future dismissal. It is simply amazing what will happen when you give people some personal attention and help them to talk about their dreams.

My clients often ask me questions like, *"What if they dump a whole pile of problems on me?"* My answer to that is kind of rough, but here it is: if your employee has that many things going on, and offers no solutions, and no willingness to break through barriers, then you have a bigger problem on your hands than Motivation. You may have just discovered your fly in the ointment. At that point, it's time to start documenting very carefully what is happening with this staff member and start looking for a replacement.

The purpose of The ACTION Formula is to open up people's minds to the possibilities, let them know that you genuinely care about them as people, and that you'd like to help them to achieve their goals. It is not necessarily an invitation to complain. Often the interview will invite people to be more honest, and you will get valuable information about what is really going on in your practice. Don't punish them for that. Encourage them to partner with you in finding workable solutions, and don't make any promises that you can't keep.

When you are comfortable using The ACTION Formula, run with it. Follow-up with everyone, and use their DESIRES to help them to stay pumped during times of extreme stress. Get postcard-sized pictures of people's dreams and put the pictures on their workstations. Find little things that remind you of their goals and give them as spontaneous Motivational "thank you" gifts. If someone's dream is to build a home, give him two tickets to the Home Show that year. If someone wants a special car, find a

TABLE 12-1. The ACTION Formula Interview for Staff

I'd like to ask you some questions to understand more about your goals and dreams and so that I can learn more about what I can do to help you to achieve them. Would that be OK?

PRESENTING DESIRE:

If you woke up tomorrow morning and magically found that this was the perfect job for you, what would it look like?

DESIRE 1: Specifically how would your day-to-day life be different?

DESIRE 2: And if it (repeat exactly whatever they described in DESIRE 1), *how would that impact your day-to-day life?*

DESIRE 3: And what would that get for you?

DESIRE 4, etc: Keep probing, repeating *"What would that get for you?"* and *"What would that get for you?"* and *"What would that get for you?"* until you hear them say something that is particularly meaningful to them. You'll know they've said it because you will feel it, or you will see a slight flush of color on their faces or on their necks as they describe it to you. On rare occasions, you may even see a tear in their eye or they may burst out laughing! You have now discovered their **BURNING DESIRE.** When you hear their BURNING DESIRE, confirm its importance with something like *"And that's what you really want?"*

RESOURCES

Is there anything that would keep you from being ABLE to make that happen?

Tell me specifically what you'd need to make that happen.

HINT: If they tell you there are RESOURCES they need, then respond with:

Have you thought about how you would work around that?

What help would you like from me?

Remember it's not up to you to solve this problem, although you may discover there are actual tools, supplies, or skills that they need to better execute their jobs. Recruit them to partner with you in finding a solution, and make sure they have everything that they are entitled to as employees.

PERMISSION

Is there anything that would keep you from being willing to make that happen?

If yes:

And how do you think you might solve that?

CAUTION: If a staff member shares a personal secret regarding abuse, alcoholism, drugs, or other health issue, you are now into a Human Resources area and will need to follow your procedural manuals regarding referral to a competent professional.

toy version and leave it hanging from her locker. Little reminders that their dreams are important to you can go a long way toward helping them to stay Motivated.

Be sure to check in to make sure all RESOURCE needs are being met. I have seen employees lose Motivation when their managers fail to keep the closets stocked with necessary supplies. The little things become huge, and when that happens, the important things get neglected. Never underestimate the power of resentment. I have heard comments from employees like, *"Sure, he's driving a Mercedes, and we can't get any paper towels in the restroom."*

The ACTION Formula Interview shown in Table 12-1 is a powerful Motivational tool, but only if you are comfortable using it. I recommend to all my clients that you practice it first with family and friends (Activity 12-1).

ACTION Plans

When you use The ACTION Formula with a member of your staff, it is helpful if you write down the person's responses on an ACTION Plan as shown in Activity 12-2 (page 127). Consider having blanks printed up on duplicate forms with a place for both of your signatures. Give the staff member a copy, and keep one for your files.

One last piece of advice when Motivating staff:

**Don't just expect people to be grown-ups
and Motivate themselves.**

The only thing you'll get from that is a series of disappointments and frustrations. Dreams come true because we make them come true, not because we lie awake at 2:00 a.m. praying for the people in our lives to grow up. They're not going to grow up because people don't grow up. They just grow older and get bigger and learn to behave the way society dictates they should behave. They stop expressing their true thoughts, they stop dreaming, and they learn to settle for what they've got. I don't call that growing up. I call that giving up.

Don't expect others to grow up. Expect them to grow! And you are the role model for growth.

**If you want things to be different, you have to do something
different. When you change the stimulus,
you'll get a different response.
P.S. You are the stimulus.**

ACTIVITY 12-1. Practicing The ACTION Formula With Family and Friends

Before you use The ACTION Formula interview with staff, practice it at home with your family. Simply change the DESIRE question to one of these examples, or create one of your own! Then use the RESOURCES and PERMISSION questions as shown.

SAMPLE DESIRE QUESTIONS

Friends

If you woke up tomorrow morning and magically found you had everything you truly wanted, what would your life look like?
And if you had those things, how would your day-to-day life be different?
And what would that get for you?

Family

If you woke up tomorrow morning and magically found that your room was exactly the way you wanted it to be, what would it look like?
And if you had those things, how would your day-to-day life be different?
And what would that get for you?

If you woke up tomorrow morning and magically found that our life together was exactly the way you wanted it to be, what would it look like?
And if you had those things, how would your day-to-day life be different?
And what would that get for you?

If you woke up tomorrow morning and magically found that your school life was exactly the way you wanted it to be, what would it look like?
And if you had those things, how would your day-to-day life be different?
And what would that get for you?

If you woke up tomorrow morning and magically found that your relationships with your brothers and sisters were exactly the way you wanted them to be, what would they be like?
And if you had those things, how would your day-to-day life be different?
And what would that get for you?

NOTE: No matter which question you choose, follow it with:

And how would that affect your day-to-day life?
And what would that get for you?

RESOURCES

Is there anything that would keep you from being able to have that?

If Yes:

Have you thought about how you would work around that?
What help would you like from me?

PERMISSION

Is there anything that would keep you from being willing to make that happen?

If Yes:

How do you think you might solve that?

Don't rescue them. Simply help them talk it through to discover a solution by asking probing questions that enable them to come to their own conclusions.

ACTIVITY 12-2. Employee ACTION Plan

Employee:

MY DESIRES

MY RESOURCES

What I'll Need to Be Able to Take ACTION	How I'll Get It	Who I'll Get to Help Me	When I'll Start Pulling This Together	My Deadline for Attaining This Item

MY PERMISSION

What might keep me from being willing to take ACTION?

What will I do to change that?

What will I say to myself to remind myself that I want to do this?

BOTTOM LINE

Motivating staff involves four specific steps: (1) Hire the right people; (2) Tell them what you want; (3) Compliment them when they give it to you; and (4) Help them to get and stay Motivated so you get what you want. Use The Four Languages of The M.A.D. Formula, in combination with The ACTION Formula, and you'll have a consistently Motivated Team without having to dangle carrots.

Chapter 13

Motivate Your Executive Team

AN EXECUTIVE TEAM is a formal way of describing the group of people who own, and take profits from, your business. Your Executive Team may consist of one or more doctors (and potentially a vested Administrator), a doctor and spouse, or a board of directors that is composed of doctors and/or others who have business acumen but no clinical expertise whatsoever. The beauty (and the beast) of healthcare is the great diversity in how ownership is organized.

No matter who makes up your Executive Team, two things must be true if they are going to succeed in building a business that continually out-runs the competition:

1. **They must be Aligned with a common vision, mission, and ACTION plan; and**
2. **They must be sufficiently Motivated to change and grow.**

Sometimes we find that individual members of Executive Teams really are Motivated, but the Alignment problems on the Team are creating a dense fog that covers and suffocates their Motivation. In Section Four, I'll show you how to get and maintain Executive Team Alignment, but before you can Align your Team, the individuals have to be Motivated to change. So let's begin there.

I have worked with many Executive Teams who are Motivated and raring to go, and that is a very exciting experience. When I see an Executive Team who is determined to make whatever changes are necessary to bring their practice to a higher level of success, I know they are going to take the formulas and run with them and that we're going to see great things happen. It's fun to watch them launch their new protocols, stumble a bit as they find ways to fit the techniques to their uniqueness as individuals, and then soar when they have mastered the processes that allow them to use the techniques without even thinking about them. Their staff comes alive in response to the changes their doctors are making, and their patients make continual comments about the wonderful changes they see. Soon the news spreads to the community, and referrals begin to multiply. There is no limit to what you can accomplish when everyone is ready to change and grow.

I have also worked with many Executive Teams who are change-resistant. These Teams are exciting in a different way because they require us to use all of our tools as consultants to help them to get past their aversion to change. Let's look at these types of Teams.

In some Executive Teams, the members really do want their practice to grow and believe that this will happen if we get their staff to change (*That's why we hired you!*). While some of the Executive Team members are also willing to change, others think that they are fine as they are. The fact is that this situation limits success because of the simple reality that staff always take their lead from their doctors. Here's a perfect example:

Practice Spotlight

We conducted a full-practice training in "The Art of Motivating Patients To ACTION" for three plastic surgeons and their 30 staff members. The three doctors were in total agreement that the staff needed to learn and implement all of the techniques we provided, but only Dr. A was willing to participate with his staff in the three-month follow-up program. Dr. B and Dr. C went back to a "business-as-usual."

Dr. A encouraged his staff to learn and apply the new techniques, attended all of the Application Meetings, installed all of the new protocols, and instructed his scheduling coordinator to take charge of creating the new interview forms in the electronic medical record. He practiced role plays with his nurses and made sure that he personally used every technique from the workshop. He made it fun, and his Team had a great time with it.

One year later, we went back for our follow-up visit. Since our workshop, Dr. A's revenues had tripled, Dr. B's revenues had gone down 20%, and Dr. C's had stayed the same. We talked to the staff of all of the doctors. Dr. A's Team was pumped and couldn't say enough about how much fun they were having. Dr. B's Team was less enthusiastic. One of his nurses told me, *"No offense, but we thought that Dr. B didn't want us to use your stuff. So we just blew it off."* One of the front desk people told me, *"Dr. C said that she didn't have the time to do this stuff. So we figured if she doesn't think it's important, why should we bother, ya know?"*

Needless to say, we went back to the Executive Team and had a little chat.

There are many Executive Teams just like Dr. A's, where all of the doctors want their practice to change, and will invest time and money to get their staff to change, but where not all doctors are willing to *personally* incorporate new techniques into their daily routine.

The greatest challenge is found when most or all of the members of the Executive Team don't want their practice to change at all. This is a real challenge for the managing partner, CEO, or practice administrator who is charged with bringing a practice to a higher level of success. If you are one of those people, let me give you some ammunition as well as some practical tools:

A practice that fails to change, will fail.

It has often been said, "If you keep on doing what you've always done, you'll keep on getting what you always got." I have found that this just isn't true in business, and particularly not true in healthcare. Information and innovation change the face of healthcare every year, while markets become more saturated with competitors trying to eat into your piece of the pie.

Do you do something different and unique? Great! But watch your back because your competitors are learning from you. Once they figure it out, and begin offering something similar, you'll be sharing even more of the pie.

if you keep on doing what you've always done, you'll fall behind the pack.

Also, there is truth in the old adage that everything rolls downhill. High-energy Teams are led by Motivated, energized leaders, and if the Executive Team isn't willing to change, the employees will think it's acceptable for them to maintain the status quo as well. In fact, as long as we're doing clichés, let's talk about the one where dogs and owners tend to look alike. Do I need to spell that one out?

Motivating Executive Team members follows basically the same rules and guidelines as Motivating staff, with some exceptions.

Step 1: Hire the right people.

Step 2: Use The Four Languages of The M.A.D. Formula to tell each other what you want.

Step 3: Use The ACTION Formula to get them Motivated to consistently give you their best every single day.

Let's go through each step to see how to apply it with your Executive Team.

STEP 1: HIRE THE RIGHT PEOPLE (AKA BRING IN THE RIGHT PARTNERS)

Too often, we see doctors and practice administrators who are brought in because of their credentials, experience, or even willingness to relocate to a remote area, without consideration of how they will actually fit with the rest of the Team. Everyone goes out to dinner, has a chance to chat with the candidate, and even the spouse and children. The administrator says, "*I like her*"; the partners say, "*She's nice,*" or "*She will fill the gap in our capabilities,*" or "*There's no one else,*" or "*It's a competent body that will lower our call time,*" and you're done.

Is this a good way to pick a partner? Maybe. Is it the *best* way to pick a partner? Well, let me put it this way — would you choose a marriage partner after one or two dates and a look at the person's curriculum vitae?

When candidates show their pleasant and articulate selves in an interview setting, they are doing the same thing that dating singles do in the beginning of their relationship. In the beginning, you shave before dinner, never talk with your mouth full or use profanity, apologize politely if you have to take a cell call, and, of course, take great pains to match your socks. There are flowers and specialty meals served with candles and music, and there is never a discussion about who gets the remote.

The real test comes the first time one of you gets stressed over work, gets sick or injured, or encounters any other situation that creates the opportunity for one of you to be in a vulnerable situation. How you handle that moment will tell you more than you ever learned while sharing a bucket of popcorn at a movie (which, now that you mention it, you never really wanted to see but you went ahead because you knew the other person wanted to see it).

Some people make it through that stage; and when they feel safe enough to show their true selves, discover that they were saving the best for last. These are the special marriages that provide a lifetime of closeness, safety, dependability, friendship, and passion. You're perfect together.

But you don't have that kind of time when selecting a business partner. You don't know how this person is going to behave when under stress, sick, tired, angry, pressured, and surrounded by potentially litigious patients and over-worked staff. That's when you find out if your partner is made of the stuff that will lead you to feel proud that his or her name is on your letterhead.

The fact is, a business partnership is a marriage. You must go into it with full knowledge of your partner to be. You need to know that in the trenches and in the community, this person will speak with the same voice as the rest of your partners. This is one area in which outside help is worth the investment. Find an outside consultant who will evaluate the entire Team and the candidate for psycho-social fit and neuro-psychological propensity to leadership, and don't make an offer until you've received validation from someone who isn't caught in the forest.

STEP 2: USE THE FOUR LANGUAGES OF THE M.A.D. FORMULA TO TELL EACH OTHER WHAT YOU WANT

The Executive Team has to learn and speak The Four Languages of The M.A.D. Formula for reasons that are obvious and not-so-obvious:

1. It will help you to communicate more effectively as a Team so that you can get the job done more effectively. When the Executive Team speaks The Four Languages, people do what you tell them to do. It's just that simple. When you use it with each other, there are significantly fewer miscommunications, and the Team presents a united and consistent approach to staff, patients, and the community. When you give each other Chips and use the LB-NT Formulas with each other, you learn that you are valued as partners and respected as doctors. This is critically important and helps you to stay Motivated and positive in the face of day-to-day pressures.
2. The Executive Team serves as the model for all who follow. If all of you don't speak The Four Languages, you are sending a clear message that you don't think it's important. At the risk of beating a dead horse, if you don't change, neither will anyone else . . . including your patients.
3. Speaking The Four Languages will allow you to feel comfortable with the idea of recruiting another doctor who is a different Value Set or Action Type than the rest of you. This can be a tremendous asset to your Team, but will be a nightmare if you're not prepared to speak the person's language. I always advise clients to bring in different Action Types and Value Sets to round off the Team and to allow for a broader offering for patients. But I recommend this only after they have shown proficiency and comfort speaking the languages and flexing their styles. The more you speak The Four Languages, the broader your world will become.

STEP 3: USE THE ACTION FORMULA TO GET THEM MOTIVATED TO CONSISTENTLY GIVE YOU THEIR BEST EVERY SINGLE DAY

Whenever we do an Executive Team Retreat, we always start with The ACTION Formula. It is a powerful tool that will allow each member of your Team to address his or her personal Motivations and to make sure that the practice is designed to get each and every one of you precisely what you want. When each of you is assured that the model of your practice has been designed with your personal dreams and goals in mind, then you will find ever increasing energy and drive to do those things everyone hates to do.

I've seen doctors who were lax in dictation consistently finishing early when they see the connection between that accomplishment and spending more time with their kids, or fishing, or reading, or biking, or whatever their particular DESIRES may be. I've watched doctors who were completely unwilling to go out and network to build referral bases suddenly hitting the pavement when they are made aware of the connection between that activity and their new home or boat or car or Ivy League tuition for their kids.

Use The ACTION Formula with your entire Team, connecting everyone's personal DESIRES to the organizational goals, creating a list of RESOURCES and an ACTION Plan for their attainment, and addressing any PERMISSION barriers that may be present, and you will create a Team of Motivated and energetic doctors who will lead the rest of your practice to achieve consistent growth and improvement.

Be sure to revisit your ACTION Plan whenever you bring in a new partner. This will help that individual to incorporate his or her wants and needs and will allow the new partner to get on board with your vision a lot sooner. We'll revisit this issue when we talk about Aligning your Team.

The best way to get an Executive Team to use The ACTION Formula is to do it yourself so that you can honestly rave about its power. I invite you to take some time over the next week or so and begin to write out your ACTION Formula (Activity 13-1). Then, go to Activity 13-2, and write out your ACTION Plan. Walk the talk. It will come back to you in many ways — all of them good.

You spend every day helping others to get what they want. It's only fair that you do the same for yourself. Dare to identify and then capture your dreams. It will make you a better leader, a better healer, a better friend, a better parent, and a happier person. At some point, it has to be your turn.

BOTTOM LINE

In order for the Executive Team to function effectively, each member of the Team must be given the opportunity to get and stay Motivated. This involves the same steps as discussed for staff, with some additional strategies reserved for those who shoulder the bottom line responsibilities of owning the business.

ACTIVITY 13-1. Your ACTION Formula
Write out your own ACTION Formula here:

DESIRE

If you woke up tomorrow morning and magically found that this were the perfect practice, department, or hospital for you, what would it look like? Get very specific here.

If your practice, department, or hospital became as you've described it, how would your day-to-day life be different? Again, get very specific.

And if your day-to-day life changed as you've described it above, how would that impact the rest of your life (health, joy, fulfillment, relationships, family life, social life, etc.)?

And what would all of that get for you?

And what would that get for you?

Keep asking yourself *"what would that get for you?"* until you've found your BURNING DESIRE. You'll know you've reached it because you will have a physical response to the picture you've created.

RESOURCES

Is there anything that would keep you from being ABLE to make that happen?

What, specifically, would you do to work around that?

PERMISSION

Is there anything that would keep you from being willing to make all of this happen?

And how will you resolve that?

ACTIVITY 13-2. My ACTION Plan

MY DESIRES

| |
| |
| |
| |
| |
| |
| |
| |

MY RESOURCES

What I'll Need to Be Able to Take ACTION	How I'll Get It	Who I'll Get to Help Me	When I'll Start Pulling This Together	My Deadline for Attaining This Item

MY PERMISSION

What might keep me from being willing to take ACTION?

What will I do to change that?

What will I say to myself to remind myself that I want to do this?

Chapter 14

The Truth About Motivating Patients

WHAT DOES THE TITLE of this chapter say to you? Does it pique your curiosity or heighten your skepticism? Whenever we go in to present a program on how to Motivate patients, the title of the program elicits a range of responses. I always send a flyer for practice-wide distribution, announcing the program, the contents, what participants can expect to experience, and what it will allow them to do. But regardless of what I write, staff and doctors always develop their own perceptions of what the title *really* means.

The administrator usually sends out an e-mail with the flyer attached and writes his or her own comment. That comment sets up the program, and the subsequent responses from the team.

> **ATTENTION:**
>
> **"Professional Impact is coming to help us to communicate more effectively with our patients."**

"Good, we need that," they say, referring to everyone in the practice other than themselves.

That sounds like a good idea to some, while others predict it will be *"another waste of time."*

> **ATTENTION:**
>
> **"Professional Impact is coming in to do some motivational training."**

> **ATTENTION:**
>
> **"Professional Impact is coming in to get us to motivate our patients to action!"**

Ooops. Up come the walls of resistance.

Doctors and staff alike go into Critical Parent, spewing opinions about their roles as professionals and expressing concern in pre-training questionnaires with comments such as, *"I'm a doctor, not a salesman."* Some go into Analyst, with statements like, *"How are we going to find the time to do that?"* Many respond from Socialized Child with comments like, *"I don't want to be 'pushy'"* or *"I would never want to sound 'salesy'."*

What happened? After many years of watching this and asking for feedback, I learned the answer. When people hear the word "Motivate" attached to the word "Patients," they interpret that they are being told they should "Sell." This brings up a host of associations with uncomfortable shopping experiences during which they felt pressured to buy something they didn't intend to buy.

During pre-training assessments, I watch and listen as these professionals, ironically, portray precisely the behaviors they most fear. Here are some examples of statements I've heard during our pre-training, onsite assessments:

> **Practice Spotlight**
>
> *"You have to lay off the cigarettes. End of discussion."*
>
> *"Doctor's schedule is filling up, so you better book now."*
>
> *"You have to exercise and eat a healthy diet. I say that to you every year, and this time you have to listen to me."*
>
> *"You should know better than to skip your meds. You have to take them twice a day."*
>
> *"This is the best supplement we've ever sold! We just got it yesterday, and we're running out. You should buy two."*
>
> *"You're crazy if you don't do this. You know you want to."*
>
> *"The doctor said you should get this. You want one or two?"*
>
> *"Our doctor is the best in town. Don't bother looking anywhere else."*
>
> *"You should buy a second pair of glasses."*
>
> *"We've got a special going this week: if you book a breast augmentation before September, we throw in a free facial."*

But wait . . . there's more . . . if you buy today, we'll include a Ginsu knife set, matching serving spoons, and a real, plastic display case! Order now while supplies last!!

Honestly, I have been amazed by the pushy and salesy nature of some communications in healthcare. People complain about that kind of behavior from car dealerships and department stores, so what makes you think they're not complaining about you as well?

I have watched patients' body language as they retreat from the people they have come to for help. I have seen patients crumple a prescription and throw it in the trash as they walk out the door. I have seen healthcare professionals who use their positions of authority to pressure patients to do what they want them to do, and those who fail to encourage patients at all. Is there a middle ground? Absolutely, but first let's get something clear about "selling."

SELLING OR MOTIVATING

What is "selling," really? According to a variety of online dictionaries, selling is defined as:

1. To exchange or deliver for money or its equivalent
2. To promote
3. To be popular on the market
4. To attract prospective buyers
5. To be approved of
6. To gain acceptance
7. To persuade another to recognize the worth or desirability of something

Whenever I show this to my clients, they tell me that all seven statements represent things they think their practice should be doing. The gray area is in the last sentence, "To persuade another to recognize the worth or desirability of something." What is the "something" you are trying to sell?

**Are you selling what your patients want,
or what you want to sell?**

Are you persuading, pressuring, or guiding? Are you communicating information and helping people to make choices, or are you telling them what you think they should do and expecting that they will just do what you tell them because you're wearing the lab coat? Are you pressuring patients with fear or encouraging them with possibilities?

Motivating patients to ACTION is the process of helping patients to understand the choices that will enable them to get what they truly want, and to break through the barriers that might stand in their way.

Most can understand this in terms of helping patients to make decisions about cosmetic enhancements, but how does Motivating patients to finish all of their prescribed antibiotics help them to get what they truly want in life? That depends on the patient, but one thing is certain: when patients are ill, they aren't able to accomplish all they want to do, nor can they be fully present in their personal and professional relationships.

Your interventions allow people to live their lives more fully.

Don't underestimate the ripple effect of the smallest intervention or the impact you have in people's lives.

THE SEVEN TRUTHS OF MOTIVATING PATIENTS

There are seven truths you absolutely must understand before you can master the art of Motivating patients.

Truth #1: Nobody wants what you do.

It's true, and I'm really sorry to be the one to tell you this, but it's simply a fact. Except for a very rare group of people who enjoy medical and dental procedures for the attention they get, the fact is that most patients do not want what you do.

Patients don't want you to stick instruments or fingers (gloved though they may be) into orifices; they don't want you to cut, burn, slice, or freeze anything that is attached to them; they are not at all interested in having bodily fluids drawn, pulled, or sucked; they do not want any part of themselves removed, and if they do want something removed they certainly don't want to go through the process of *getting* it removed; and they definitely do not want you to cut their skin anywhere for any reason whatsoever at any time, even if you are going to sew it back together again.

Nobody wants what you do.

But don't quit yet . . . there is good news in Truth #2.

Truth #2: Everybody wants what they will get because of what you do.

Everybody wants something in their lives that they can't get unless they have clear sinuses; a regular heart beat; blood flowing smoothly through clear veins and arteries; joints and muscles that move with ease; eyes that see; ears that hear; teeth that chew; stomachs that can handle whatever got chewed; babies with 10 toes; children who laugh, play, and don't miss school days; longevity; sleep; energy; stamina; dignity; self-sufficiency; and a youthful appearance without distortion. You can help them to have these things so that they can go on to live their lives freely and with zest. There is, however, another problem . . .

Truth #3: Patients need help making the connection between what they want and what you do.

The simple truth is that most of your patients have no idea what you really do and, quite frankly, many don't really want to know. Even with all of the increasingly educated patients (thanks to Internet and media), no one will ever really understand what you do.

When people are ill or in pain, they aren't always thinking clearly about the big picture and how their lives will improve or what will happen in the future if they will go ahead and have the test you want them to have or fill the expensive prescription for the medicine you want them to take or make the lifestyle changes you recommend or have the surgery you think they need. When patients are in pain (physically or emotionally), they are not thinking about the future when birds will sing and all will be right with their world. They are focused on the present, the immediate loss they will experience if they do what you want them to do (taking time off from work for testing or surgeries, giving up cherished vices, experiencing recuperative pain, or paying out-of-pocket for elective procedures and services). They need your help to make the connection between what you want them to do now and what your treatment will allow them to do in the future. But,

**It can't be the future as you envision it.
It has to be their dreams and goals.**

When you help them to attach your treatment to their dreams and goals, they will be more Motivated to do what you want them to do. Well, except for Truths 4 and 5:

Truth #4: Patients have to be ABLE to do what you recommend.

What may seem like a simple treatment plan from your perspective, may in fact be a genuine hardship for your patient. When we've asked patients whether they think they will be able to do what their doctors have recommended, we hear comments like:

Practice Spotlight

"I can't afford it."

"I can never remember to take pills."

"I just can't get to physical therapy with my schedule."

"I live on the road. I can't always predict how much salt is in the foods I eat."

> *"To be honest, I've never been much good at swallowing pills."*
>
> *"I can't have surgery now — who'll take care of my kids?"*
>
> *"My husband will never agree to this"*
>
> *"I'm not really sure I understood what she wants me to do."*

In the hit TV series "House," Dr. House tells us his fundamental rule: *"Patients always lie."* While that may or may not be true, I have consistently found that many patients won't tell you about their ability to follow your recommendations unless you ask them. Even then, if the problem is such that it leads them to feel embarrassed, you won't get the whole truth unless you've developed a strong foundation of trust and rapport. They have to know you speak their language and will not judge or criticize them in any way.

Truth #5: Patients often stop themselves from letting themselves have what they really want.

When you're seeing 100 patients a day, you probably aren't taking the time to find out whether or not a patient is completely Motivated to take ACTION on your treatment recommendations. Even if your patients tell you they have every intention of following through, things change when they leave the safety of your office and begin to think about real-world concerns. They question you and themselves, and start thinking about all of the ramifications of your treatment recommendations. They experience varying levels of fear and anxiety, or may feel angry about having to experience the side effects or disruptions to their lives.

The more they think about it, the more patients experience varying levels of what we commonly refer to as **Buyer's Remorse.** If they find even the smallest down-side to your treatment plan or the changes they'll experience as a result, they will sabotage their own success (consciously or unconsciously).

Buyer's Remorse in healthcare is most easily understood by looking at weight reduction. Having counseled hundreds of men and women in weight reduction programs, I have seen how Motivation and program adherence decline as patients get closer to goal. When we talk about this, they tell me about the ways in which their life is changing and the challenges they have to face. Their new, attractive bodies elicit a different kind of attention then they have been accustomed to, and they don't know how to handle it. Whereas buying new clothes had been something they'd looked forward to, it turns out they really can't afford a new wardrobe. Spouses are beginning to behave differently toward them, with jealousy or new types of attention. Old friends are moving away, and people who never talked to them previously are suddenly inviting them to lunch. The stress of these changes makes them long for the familiarity and safety of being overweight, leading them to sabotage their own success. Of course they don't see it that way. They just suddenly begin to start giving into their "cravings."

Buyer's Remorse is a common problem throughout healthcare, and you can help patients through it, but you have to know to look for it. You have no way of knowing what patients will think about after they leave your office and reenter their "normal" lives.

For example, you recommend a certain test, and your clinical assistant offers to make the call to book it. Your patient interrupts and says, *"I'll have to call you after I check my calendar at work."* While driving back to work, other issues prevail, and your patient talks himself right out of taking ACTION.

The good news is that there is a way to identify possible road blocks and help your patients to clear the path. That leads to Truth #6.

Truth #6: Your impact is far-reaching.

When you help your patients take ACTION on your treatment recommendations, you heal more than their immediate pain, you give them the ability to live their lives. The relationships you build and the help you provide allow your patients to go out and do what they need to do and what they want to do. These successes enable them to increase their Chips and make a stronger impact on family, friends, and co-workers. You will probably never know how far your impact extends into a patient's life, not only from your clinical interventions, but from the personal connections you've made along the way. Keep that in mind when you wonder why you should spend an extra minute with a patient. If making a difference is important to you, know that the difference you make goes well beyond the walls of your practice.

Truth #7: Most practices have no idea if they are Motivating their patients to ACTION.

Even if they think that Motivating patients to ACTION is a great idea, most practices do not keep track of their successes and failures. Most practices keep great records and statistics regarding (for example) financials, credentialing, patient histories, reimbursements, and employee sick days. Some have newer computer programs that allow them to keep even better statistics regarding how many patients call in, book and keep appointments, etc. But ask a doctor or administrator the percent of patients who actually followed their treatment recommendations last year, and you're likely to hear something unspecific like, *"All of our patients do what we tell them to do,"* or *"If they don't come back, we figure they're OK."*

In pre-training assessments I always ask doctors and staff to estimate their percentages, and the differences vary by large amounts. In fact, at a recent meeting with my colleagues in the Academy of Dental Management Consultants, we all noted the discrepancies we see in practices regarding staff and doctors' perceptions of their own case acceptance percentages.

I recently conducted an informal survey of several of my clients in a variety of specializations (Cardiology, Gastroenterology, Bariatric Surgery, Family Medicine, Orthopedics, Plastic Surgery, Facial Plastic Surgery, ENT, Ophthalmology, Optometry, Orthodontics, Cosmetic Dentistry, and General Dentistry) and asked them the following question:

Have you got the most recent statistics from your professional association about the number of patients who walk away and don't have the procedures they consulted about, the number of patients who don't fill prescriptions, and the percent who don't follow through on test orders?

Without exception, all responded by saying that they were unable to find statistics published by their associations that addressed these questions. Many kept statistics on their own since we had begun working together, and some gave me other information, such as:

- "The percentage of morbidly obese adults in this country is about 6%, but only 200,000 to 300,000 bariatric operations are done every year in this country."
- "The current level of appropriate colon cancer screening is supposedly just under 50%."
- "I don't know what those stats are; except at a meeting I attended two years ago, a consultant stated goals (not necessarily true) of 80% of patients who contact the practice come in for a consultation, and overall 50% of those patients who contact the practice went on to have something done."

But the most common responses were like these:

- "I couldn't find anything. I looked . . ."
- "It is more likely monitored by the cash practices because it affects their bottom line more dramatically. In cardiology, people are afraid not to take the docs' advice, and it is less expensive to do so because insurance defrays part of the cost. However, it would still be valuable information to know and invaluable to have strategies to impact it."

Are your patients following *your* recommendations? Let's do some research and find out. Activities 14-1, 14-2, and 14-3 will help you to track some key numbers in your practice. HINT: Use the strategies in Chapter 12 to Motivate your staff to collect your data accurately and with enthusiasm!

ACTIVITY 14-1. Are We Motivating Our Patients to ACTION? (Front Desk)							
Make copies of this chart, or recreate it in an Excel file. Keep track of all incoming calls for four consecutive weeks by indicating the time of call and then placing a check (✓) in all columns that fit.							
Time of Call	New Patient	Repeat Patient	Called for Information	Booked Appointment	Canceled Appointment	Changed Appointment	Other (please describe)

If you offer elective services, make copies of Activity 14-2, and find out how you're doing. If you offer a wide variety of elective services and/or products, extend the chart. The more detailed your statistics, the more effective you will be at analyzing your current status and developing a plan for increasing your revenues.

For non-elective services, complete Activity 14-3. In order to get a complete picture, you will need to conduct follow-up calls to patients. I recommend that you pull a random sample of 10% of your patients. This will give you a good baseline from which to view your practice and the degree to which you are successfully Motivating your patients.

At the end of your four weeks, look at your statistics to determine where you are doing well and where you could improve. Set your goals, and use the techniques in the next chapter to help you to achieve them.

THIS IS TOO MUCH WORK — WHAT'S THE BIG DEAL?

Trust and credibility only open the door to future conversations. They don't guarantee that people will do what you tell them to do. People need to be Motivated to change or else your recommendations may fall on deaf ears. In many practices, if patients don't follow your recommendations to the letter, they could become sicker or even die. For this reason alone,

Part of your risk management procedures must include patient Motivation strategies.

ACTIVITY 14-2. Are We Motivating Our Patients to ACTION? (Clinical — Elective)					
For the next four weeks, keep track of each of the following statistics					
Statistics to Be Kept	Week 1	Week 2	Week 3	Week 4	Average
Total # of new patient visits					
# of new patients who said "yes" to your treatment recommendations					
# of new patients who responded to your treatment recommendations with, *"I want to think it over/talk to someone else"*					
Total $ amount of new patient conversions					
Total # of returning patient visits					
# of returning patients who said "yes" to your treatment recommendations					
# of returning patients who responded to your treatment recommendations with, *"I want to think it over/talk to someone else"*					
Total $ amount of returning patient conversions					

Regardless of where you are in the healthcare system, you need to know how to Motivate patients. In mainstream, traditional models of healthcare, you just don't have time to sit and Motivate people on every test, procedure, or change they need to make. You need a shortcut, and I've got one for you: clear strategies you can apply to Motivate your patients in short spurts of time.

As we see more and more doctors opting out of managed care, we see an ever-increasing need for specialized communication strategies in helping patients to say "yes" to what they want and need. Patients need your support and guidance in making decisions that involve cash outlays for preventive health, ongoing maintenance, and care of existing health concerns, as well as education regarding options for enhanced health choices. While your status provides you the luxury of being able to spend more time with these patients than in the traditional model, you too, need a communication shortcut to Motivate them to ACTION.

ACTIVITY 14-3. Are We Motivating Our Patients to ACTION? (Clinical — Non-elective)					
For the next four weeks, keep track of each of the following statistics					
Statistics to Be Kept	**Week 1**	**Week 2**	**Week 3**	**Week 4**	**Average**
Total # of new patient visits					
# of prescriptions written					
# of prescriptions filled					
# of tests ordered or prescribed					
# of tests completed					
# of patients who were given recommendations for lifestyle changes (alcohol, drugs, cigarettes, food, exercise, etc.)					
# of patients who report that lifestyle changes were made successfully					
# of those patients for whom we were able to validate their self-report					
Total # of returning patient visits					
# of prescriptions written					
# of prescriptions filled					
# of tests ordered or prescribed					
# of tests completed					
# of patients who were given recommendations for lifestyle changes (alcohol, drugs, cigarettes, food, exercise, etc.)					
# of patients who report that lifestyle changes were made successfully					
# of those patients for whom we were able to validate their self-report					

On the elective side, patients need a lot of help in Motivating themselves to ACTION. The more choices there are in medicine and dentistry, the more patients are actively sifting through the media and internet, talking with friends, and taking anecdotal accounts of what is safe and not safe, what can be done and what should never be done, how to know if a procedure is right for them and if a given doctor is the best fit for their needs. It's true what they say, "A little information can be dangerous," and by the time they come to you, they are genuinely interested, though often misinformed. They need to understand what is possible and not possible for their unique health and financial situations.

If your patients are physically fit for the procedures you recommend, if they can financially manage it, and if they really want the differences your intervention will make in their lives, who better to help them than you? If you don't help them to understand their choices, think through their barriers, and figure out their questions, they will leave your practice without saying "yes." Then if they meet someone else who helps them think it through more completely, they may go ahead and put their healthcare in the other person's hands.

You know your practice best. Are you sure you want to let a patient go and be treated by someone else just because someone in your practice didn't take a couple of extra minutes with the patient? Are you sure that the next practice will give the patient the same level of care you might have given?

And what about your protection? If a patient leaves without fully understanding all of her choices and having all of her questions addressed, what does that do for your risk management?

If you don't help your elective patients to say "yes" to the treatments that are in their best interest, you may have done them a disservice and may be setting your practice up for a loss.

When you take the time to Motivate your patients to ACTION, it requires more of your time in the beginning and significantly decreases the amount of time you have to spend down the line. In the long run, it's the best thing you can do, for your patient and your practice.

BOTTOM LINE

Motivating patients to ACTION means helping them to understand their choices and clearing the path so they are able and willing to do whatever will help them to get what they really want and need. There are truths you need to understand in order to effectively Motivate your patients, but the most important is simply this: if you don't understand how to help your patients to think through their choices and make competent decisions, you may not be doing all you can to help them **and** to protect your practice.

Chapter 15

The Five Rules of Motivating Patients to ACTION

SHOULD YOU MOTIVATE your patients to ACTION? Obviously I think so or I wouldn't have included this chapter. But it's a fair question, so I'd like to take a moment to explain my opinion about what makes this so important.

I used to walk through department stores with my eyes down. If anyone wearing a badge tried to make eye contact with me, I'd quickly look away. If they offered to help me, I'd automatically say, *"I'm just looking."*

Then I had a shopping epiphany. Go ahead and laugh but this was huge! I suddenly realized that no one can MAKE me buy anything. No matter what they say, no matter how much they may push or how much they stand to benefit from my purchase, the fact remains that I'm the one who decides what I want and don't want.

The job of the sales professional is to educate me and help me to understand my choices so I can make informed decisions. If I don't want what they are offering, I can say "no." But if I don't allow them to educate me, if I don't tell them my concerns and let them offer missing data, then I will draw conclusions about the value of their offering that are based on erroneous assumptions. In the end, I will lose out on what could have enhanced my life.

I began to wonder how many things there were in life that I never knew existed, how many services were right there within my reach, and how much I'd missed because of my arrogant assumptions that I knew it all or because of objections I may have had to the style of the people who were trying to educate me about my choices.

I started asking questions about items I was considering for purchase, asking for opinions and talking through my mixed thinking about whether to go ahead. I began doing the same thing with my doctors. I had to educate them about how to educate me, but once I did, they blossomed.

This new way of communicating led them to talk with me about a different level of care, preventive services, more sensitive testing, and a wide range of options for health and wellness that they'd never offered because the services weren't covered by insurance, and so they assumed I wouldn't be interested.

I opted to go out of pocket for many healthcare services because the more I learned about the possibilities, the more I wanted to take ACTION and improve my chances for a longer, healthier life. Instead of nodding my head and privately thinking *"OK, well I'm never going to do that,"* I said it out loud, and allowed them to tell me things I didn't know that helped me to make better decisions for my health.

> **What if all healthcare professionals were able to help their patients to get educated and Motivated to make the changes they need to make?**

> **What if all patients understood their choices and made active decisions to enable them to live longer, healthier lives?**

> **What if in all healthcare experiences, there were people who patients really trusted, people who would educate them about their health choices, show them the possibilities, and encourage them to permit themselves to have the best health and appearance possible?**

There are many things patients need in order to live long and healthy lives. From breaking addictions to incorporating lifestyle changes, from annual examinations to sophisticated testing, from taking vitamins to managing insulin injections, but no matter what,

> **Patients need your help so they can get Motivated to take ACTION and sustain lifestyle changes.**

I have a cardiologist client and friend who once sent me an e-mail that said, *"Our patients listen to what we say because our recommendations save their lives."* I have no doubt that his patients listen to him or that your patients listen to you. But unless you can say with certainty that every one of your patients is taking prescribed medications as they are prescribed, flossing their teeth, having regular colonoscopies, showing up for all required testing and procedures, following your treatment recommendations for healthy lifestyle changes, and feeling and looking as well as they could possibly feel and look given their unique health and financial situations and personal goals, then I invite you to ask yourself

> **"Have we mastered the art of Motivating patients to ACTION?"**

There are five rules to follow in the process of Motivating patients. Once you have these mastered, you will be able to consistently:

- Build strong trust and rapport with your patients in a shorter amount of time;
- Help your patients to get Motivated to make decisions and follow through with ACTIONs that will be in their best interest for improved health and/or appearance; and
- Set the stage so your patients will get what they really want and need.

When you've mastered The Five Rules of Motivating Patients to ACTION, then you can vary your approach to fit the unique style of your practice and your own comfort.

RULE #1: KEEP A RECORD OF PATIENT M.A.D. CHARACTERISTICS.

There is no reason for everyone in your practice to have to assess each patient on their own. Work as a team. As one of you recognizes a characteristic, simply log it in the chart or patient record.

It is necessary to have the M.A.D. characteristics easily accessible so that you can look quickly and know what to do to speak the patients' language. This will permit you to build a deeper level of trust, leading them to give you the information you need to Motivate them effectively.

The first thing to do is to create a place in the patient file or record where you can keep track of M.A.D. information for your patients. If you are using paper files, insert a small table at the front of the chart that looks like Table 15-1. Right now the chart may look complicated, but soon you'll recognize the abbreviations quickly and easily and know that

> **Value Sets** are abbreviated as **T1** (Type 1) and **T2** (Type 2)

> **Action Types** are abbreviated as **R** (Relater), **E** (Enthusiast), **T** (Thinker), and **C** (Commander)

> **States of Mind** are abbreviated as **CP** (Critical Parent), **NP** (Nurturing Parent), **A** (Analyst), **SC** (Socialized Child), and **NC** (Natural Child)

The ACTION Formula abbreviations are

> **PD** (Presenting DESIRE); **D1**, **D2**, **D3**, **D4**, **D5**, and **D6** (subsequent DESIRES); and **BD** (Burning DESIRE)

> **R** (RESOURCE Barriers)

> **P** (PERMISSION Barriers)

TABLE 15-1. M.A.D. Charting											
T1	T2	R	E	T	C	CP	NP	A	SC	NC	Chips
PD						D1					*List Date of Chip*
D2						D3					
D4						D5					
D6						BD					
R											
P											

I promise you, these abbreviations will become as familiar to you as "MD" (medical doctor), "DDS" (doctor of dental surgery), "DMD" (doctor of dental medicine), and "TMI" (too much information).

When you identify the M.A.D. characteristics of your patient, simply circle the appropriate boxes for The Four Languages of The M.A.D. Formula and record dates to note when you give a patient a Chip.

Once you have established rapport, you'll be able to use The ACTION Formula with your patient (I'll explain how in a minute). Write in the details for The ACTION Formula (PRESENTING DESIRE, other DESIRES, BURNING DESIRE, RESOURCE Barriers, PERMISSION Barriers) in the spaces provided on the patient's M.A.D. chart.

Imagine that you conduct The ACTION Formula Interview with a patient. As you talk with him, you discover that he is a Type 1 Enthusiast who responds best when you communicate from your Nurturing Parent. You would log that in the M.A.D. Chart by circling T1 (Type 1), E (Enthusiast), and NP (Nurturing Parent). The patient tells you the initial symptoms that brought him in to see you, describing persistent headaches and unrelenting fatigue. You log that under Presenting Desire (PD). Using the specific questions of The ACTION Formula, you continue and ask the patient about the benefits of relief from his symptoms. The patient tells you that he would get more energy, be able to get more done at work, would have more energy to spend with his family, would have a happier family, would have more fun at home, stress would go down, and he would be able to get a great night's sleep. You log all of that in the M.A.D. Chart by noting each benefit in its own DESIRE box (D1, D2, etc.). You continue with the interview, and ask the patient if there's anything that would keep him from being able to do what it takes to get well. He tells you that he travels extensively for work and isn't able to commit to anything that requires a regular schedule. You log that information in the RESOURCE box (R).

Finally, you ask the patient whether there is anything that would keep him from being willing to follow treatment recommendations and log his answer under PERMISSIONS (P). You tell him that you are deeply impressed by how well he has articulated his situation and thank him for the trust he gave you. Then you log your Chip by noting the date. Table 15-2 is an example of how the completed M.A.D. chart might look.

TABLE 15-2. Sample M.A.D. Chart											
(T1)	T2	R	(E)	T	C	CP	(NP)	A	SC	NC	Chips
PD Headaches and fatigue						D1 Increased energy					*List Date of Chip* 1/4/08 5/3/08
D2 More accomplished at work						D3 More energy to spend with family					
D4 Happier wife and kids						D5 More fun at home					
D6 Less Stress						BD Get a good night's sleep					
R Extensive travel schedule requires flexibility in Tx plan											
P Skittish about needles											

Keep this information taped or stapled to the front, inside cover. I have clients who have chosen to have custom file folders preprinted so that the M.A.D. Languages are on the outside and The ACTION Formula information (DESIRES, RESOURCES, PERMISSION) is on the inside where it is private. You can also use pre-printed, self-stick labels and then paste the label on the inside cover of your file.

Most electronic health records have the ability to insert fields where you can subsequently select the appropriate responses for each category.[1] No matter what your system of data keeping, the goal is that anyone who works with that patient will always look first at the patient's M.A.D. Formula information so that they will know immediately how best to communicate with this patient to establish rapid trust and rapport and to Motivate the patient to ACTION.

RULE #2: SPEAK THE FOUR LANGUAGES OF THE M.A.D. FORMULA.

I can't stress enough the importance of choosing patient-specific communication strategies. The more members of your practice who speak the patient's language, the better able you will be to Motivate him or her to ACTION.[2] Here's a quick review with specific application to Motivating patients:

[1] Many electronic health records systems also allow you to create patient questionnaires. Ask your EMR representative for help in this area.

[2] This is another opportunity to practice Motivating your doctors and staff regarding the importance of accurate record-keeping and follow-through with the strategies of The M.A.D. Formula. This will become even more important as we get into Sections 4 and 5.

The Language of Action Types (See Chapter 5)

The easiest time to make an assessment of your patient's Action Type is when the patient first walks in the door. Because of this, your receptionist is ideally suited to take charge of this area of the patient assessment. If the receptionist doesn't see or talk to the patient, then the first person to see your patient (patient coordinator, clinical assistant, clinical provider, or doctor) needs to assess the patient and then log the information into the patient's chart or record.

The Language of Value Sets (See Chapter 6)

Listen to your patient to determine whether he or she is using Type 1 or Type 2 language. If you have time and it is appropriate, ask the car question. If you aren't sure of your patient's Value Set, no problem. Pepper your communication with language from each.

The Language of States of Mind (See Chapter 7)

As you get to know your patient, you will begin to notice that he or she responds best to you when you are in a particular State of Mind: Parent (Critical or Nurturing), Analyst, or Child (Socialized or Natural). Make a note of that observation for future reference.

Many research studies have been conducted to determine how people make purchasing decisions, indicating that people use both logic and emotion. The order of which comes first is the key:

> **People buy on emotion and justify their purchase with logic.**

I love it! And it's tax deductible.

Do people make decisions that involve healthcare with the same process? Yes. In fact, your patients decide whether or not to follow your treatment recommendations based on three specific issues:

1. **Opinions:** Do they find your practice, your people, you and your credentials worthy of trust?
2. **Facts:** Do they understand the facts of their condition and the plan you have recommended?
3. **Feelings:** Are they experiencing emotions and physical sensations that are strong enough to make them want to change?

If you diagram the patient decision-making process with States of Mind, here's what you get:

States of Mind		
Parent	P	20%
Analyst	A	20%
Child	C	60%

Sixty percent of the decision is made from the Child State of Mind!

This fact has surprised many doctors when they look at their case presentations and realize that they have been balancing their presentations all wrong! The same is true for the patient education that is offered by clinical professionals such as hygienists, physician assistants, nurses, nurse practitioners, physical therapists, and medical and dental assistants. These professionals are so busy focusing on the facts that they want to deliver, that they fail to balance that with other key factors.

When you present or educate, you have to do more than present the facts. You have to IMPRESS THE PARENT and SELL THE CHILD![3] Here's what you need to remember:

Patients don't change unless they are experiencing some kind of pain that is more painful than the process of making the change or the fear of what the consequences of that change might be.

In preventive education, the key is to help your patients to experience the excitement and relief of what life could be like IF they were pain-free and/or looked as they wanted to look. When you are trying to help patients to change addictive behaviors or to undergo treatment that may be painful or uncomfortable in and of itself, you really need to access their emotions to bring it home.

Sometimes the best way to make that happen is to talk about your own emotions with respect to their situation. Here is a Practice Spotlight that serves as an excellent example of incorporating the 20-20-60 rule.

Practice Spotlight

Analyst	*"I have your test results, Jim. If you look at these numbers you will see how much your disease has progressed since your last visit. These numbers here show the amount of oxygen you are able to get into your lungs without an oxygen tank. It's supposed to be 100. Do you see where you are?"*
Natural Child	*"I've been your doctor for over 20 years; and, to be honest with you, Jim, I am really scared about what could happen to you if you don't quit smoking now."*

---

[3] This is particularly difficult for clinicians who are uncomfortable around expressions of emotions. We'll talk about this more in Section Four.

Nurturing Parent & Analyst	*"I know you enjoy smoking, and the last thing I want to do is see you have to give up something that brings you so much joy. On the other hand, I've seen what can happen to people who are experiencing the kind of symptoms you've got. They get worse so that they can't breathe without help. They lose the ability to run around and play with their grandkids. I know how much you enjoy your weekends with John and Katie, and you might not be able to run in the park with them if you keep on smoking.*
Natural Child	*"But it's not just that, Jim, I am afraid that if this gets worse, you'll start to feel what it's like to not be able to breathe. It won't be long after that until we start to see some other things happening to you that are too scary to think about right now.*
Natural Child & Nurturing Parent	*"But the thing that scares me more than anything is that if you keep on smoking, you will lose your free-dom. You've been with me a long time, Jim, and I know that your freedom means a lot to you. Smoking is going to make your disease worse, and you'll lose your freedom. You may need to be hospi-talized, you may need constant care, and your kids may not be able to keep you at home.*
Critical Parent & Natural Child	*"I know we've always managed to pull you through, but if you keep smoking, I won't be able to make you better. I'm sorry to sound so threatening, but you're in a bad situation, and I need you to see your choices.* *"From my clinical opinion, you have two choices: Keep smoking, and cheat yourself and your family out of the time you could have spent together; or quit smoking now, and then we can talk about ways to help you to live healthy and free."*

By the time this doctor got halfway through, both he and his patient had tears in their eyes. The doctor's willingness to be vulnerable with his patient allowed him to get to his patient right where it counted—in his heart. You may not need the 20-20-60 rule for every patient on every visit. But I suggest you get in the habit of presenting that way and use it on a regular basis. Your patient may not need the Motivation today, but who knows what will happen tomorrow, or 10 years from now.

Your impact will stay with them long after you have forgotten the things you said.

ACTIVITY 15-1. Check Your Percentages

The next time you give a presentation to a patient (case presentation or patient education), pay close attention to the details of which States of Mind are being included. Note the number of facts you offer, the degree to which your behaviors and appearance invoke a trust response, and the extent to which you are eliciting emotions that will lead the patient to take ACTION. If possible, record your case presentation, and literally *count* each category. If you are giving too many facts and ignoring the other two States of Mind, it's time to make some adjustments!

The Language of Chips (See Chapter 8)

When a patient is ill, frightened, or in the throes of making decisions, one of the best things you can do is offer the patient a heartfelt Chip. People need a self-esteem boost when they are making difficult decisions. As you'll see in Section Five, the more Chips you give, the more patients will perceive you as caring and giving good customer service.

It's easy to forget about giving Chips on every visit, but if you keep track of your Chips you'll get in the habit quickly. To keep yourself honest, create a place in the patient record to keep track of how many Chips you have given to the patient. Using the "Chip Log" will keep everyone accountable and serve as a valuable reminder for future visits.

Keep giving out the Chips. It will make a big difference for your practice, and you'll find your day to be a lot more joyful.

RULE #3: APPLY THE ACTION FORMULA.

My clients have found that The ACTION Formula is the most powerful tool they have to Motivate their patients. When you use The ACTION Formula with your patients, it will allow you to find out what they really want from you, their perceptions regarding how your intervention will impact the rest of their lives, the barriers that would keep them from being able and willing to take ACTION, and the ways in which they need your help to break through those barriers.

Using The ACTION Formula on the Telephone

The ACTION Formula is useful in every area of your practice and begins from the very first phone call. Table 15-3 provides an example of a script you might use at your front desk or call center. The script is strategically designed to allow you to build a connection with patients by phone while you obtain demographic and insurance information, and it allows you to apply The ACTION Formula to Motivate patients to make and keep their appointments, and to arrive on time.[4]

TABLE 15-3. The ACTION Formula for Incoming Calls
Initial Response
Thank you for calling (practice), my name is (you), how may I help you today?
Response
I'll be happy to help you with that! Again, my name is (you), and you are . . . ?
Response
PRESENTING DESIRE and Initial Information
Tell me, (patient name), what is the problem you'd like us to help you with?
Response
(Patient name), I'm really glad you called! We'll do everything we can to help you. Would you spell your name for me so I can make sure I get it right? And I need a day and evening phone number so we can reach you, please.
Response
Thank you. Is it OK to identify our practice when we call these numbers? Do you have a cell phone you'd like us to have in case you're not at either of the other numbers?
Response
Insurance (optional)
(Patient name), were you planning on using insurance to cover your (treatment, services, testing) with us?
If "Yes":
I'd like to get some information about your insurance to save you time when you come in; would that be OK?
Get insurance information.
Schedule Appointment
OK, let's find you an appointment. Do you prefer mornings or afternoons?
Response
We can see you on (day) at (time) or on (day) at (time). Which would be better for you?
Response

(Table continues next page)

---

[4] You may want to review Chapter 3 regarding strategies for learning scripts without memorization so you and your staff can apply each strategy in the script without sounding fake. If you sound scripted, you will defeat the point of the script, that is, to build trust and rapport and make a connection with your patient by phone.

TABLE 15-3. The ACTION Formula for Incoming Calls *(continued)*

New Patients Only

(Patient name), do you have access to the Internet?[1]

If "No:"

No problem, (Patient name). I'm going to mail you a small packet of information so you'll know as much as possible about us before you get here. I'm also going to send you some information forms to fill out to save you time when you come in. Where can I mail your package so you'll be certain to get it?

If "Yes:"

Great, (Patient name). I'd like to invite you to visit our Web site so that you can learn more about us before you get here and so that you can download and complete some informational forms. This will save you time filling out paperwork when you come in and allow us to help make sure all of your information is in our records. Do you have a pen so I can give you the Web address? *Give Internet information.* While you're on the site, you're welcome to sign up for our patient newsletter. We will send you monthly tips to help you to (*stay healthy, keep looking your best, etc.*). Our patients have really enjoyed that.

RESOURCES

OK, (Patient name), now is there anything that might get in the way of you being able to keep your appointment on (day)?[2]

If "Yes":

Find another day/time when there would be no conflict.

PERMISSION

(Patient name), as much as we'd like to think otherwise, we know that not everyone looks forward to coming in to see us for the first time. So I always ask our new patients this question: If you were going to talk yourself out of coming for your appointment on (day), what would you say to yourself?

If they indicate that they would talk themselves out of it:

Then what would you say to yourself to talk yourself back INTO it?

Response[3]

OK, (Patient name), would you like me to help you with directions, or do you know how to find us?

Response

If they need directions, refer to your Web site for interactive directions, offer to include directions with the packet being mailed, or talk them through directions right then.

Tracking[4]

(Patient name), whom may we thank for referring you to our care?

Response

Log the information

(Table continues next page)

> ## TABLE 15-3. The ACTION Formula for Incoming Calls *(continued)*
>
> **Final Comments**
>
> It's very important to us that all of our patients get the best possible care we can provide, so please let us know if you think of anything you need or want.
>
> (Patient name), I look forward to seeing you on (repeat appointment day and time). We are very proud of the fact that, unless there is an unusual emergency, our patients are seen right at their scheduled appointment times, so I would appreciate it if you would make every effort to be on time. Also, please remember to bring in your completed forms, and if you have any questions before or after you get here, please don't hesitate to let me know. Again, my name is (you). See you on (appointment day)!
>
> ---
>
> [1] This section assumes that you have a Web site with information about your services, your personnel and downloadable forms. If you don't have this, I'd urge you to consider it. There are many competent people out there who can help you make this happen for a relatively low investment. In today's competitive environment, it definitely helps to have a good Web site.
>
> [2] This line is really important. We see an increasing number of patients who call for appointments from their cell phones while driving or when they are away from access to their work and home calendars. They grab the first appointment that you offer, without remembering that they have alternate plans. When you give them a second chance to think about the day of the appointment it often jogs their memories, and you will hear comments like *"OH! Now that you mention it, I've got to xyz that day. We better plan a different day."* This will save you repeat calls for rescheduling as well as reduce your no-shows.
>
> [3] Most people will tell you something they'd say to themselves, and often this will be a humorous response. On the rare occasions when they indicate that they don't know what they'd say, your response is: *Well, if you need someone to talk you back into it, just give me a call, OK?*
>
> [4] This is to help you to track your marketing efforts and to thank referring doctors and patients.

Admittedly, adding some ACTION Formula questions to your phone interview will increase the amount of time for your incoming calls. In reviewing the statistics of clients who actively use this approach, however, I have found the benefits far outweigh the extra time spent on the phone. We have seen significant decreases in reschedules, no-shows, and late arrivals, as well as increases in the number of patients who complete paperwork in advance of arrival.[5] When you Motivate your patients by phone, they do what you want them to do!

Using The ACTION Formula Face-to-Face

As you get to know your patients, you will have opportunities to gather information about their DESIRES, RESOURCES, and PERMISSIONS regarding their health (and appearance if you offer medical or dental, surgical or nonsurgical cosmetic enhancements). Depending on your particular type of practice, you may want to gather information in stages or you may prefer to perform a full interview. Let's look at both models.

[5] For high-volume practices, consider hiring a part-time employee to fill in at hectic phone times during your week and/or creating a separate call center. The benefits will more than pay for themselves.

The Interview

The ACTION Formula Patient Interview takes 4 to 10 minutes (average 6), and can be conducted by anyone in your practice who is willing to learn it, available to do it, and comfortable talking with patients. It is ideally suited for the medical or dental practice that offers elective services as well as for cash-pay, boutique practices, but it is entirely workable for any practice with sufficient space and personnel.

The interview can take place in a consultation room before the patient is walked back for clinical services, or it can take place in the exam room or operatory. Let's look at it in ACTION, and then I'll walk you through it:

Practice Spotlight

The following is a transcription of a conversation between a medical assistant and her patient that was recorded during an in-house coaching session. It shows an excellent example of The ACTION Formula interview and how the medical assistant used the information she attained to help Motivate the patient to take ACTION on the doctor's treatment recommendation.

Medical Assistant: Mr. Patient, I'd like to learn a little bit about you and your health goals so that I can make sure that we understand the kind of help you need from us. Would that be OK?

Patient: Sure.

Medical Assistant: Do you prefer Mr. Patient or Carl?

Patient: You can call me Carl. Mr. Patient is my father.

Medical Assistant: (Laugh) I totally understand. Call me Tricia.

Patient: OK.

Medical Assistant: So tell me a little bit about you, what do you do for work?

Patient: I'm at the south plant; I'm a day shift supervisor.

Medical Assistant: I can't tell from your tone of voice. Is that a good thing or a bad thing?

Patient: (Laugh) It's a good thing. It's just been a long week. We had to lay off some people, and it was rough.

Medical Assistant: Oh, I'm sorry to hear that.

Patient: Yeah, it'll be OK, but things are a little tense on the line right now.

Medical Assistant: I'll bet. So let's talk about you for a minute. I'd like to find out more about how we can help you, so let's get to your goals. If you woke up tomorrow morning and found that you felt exactly the way you wanted to feel, what would you feel like?

Patient: I'd get rid of this pain in my leg.

Medical Assistant: OK, I'm writing this down for the doctor, it's your right leg?

Patient: Yeah.

Medical Assistant: Would you describe it as sharp or dull?

Patient: Both. It wakes me at night, it gets me at work, and sometimes I have to pull over when I'm driving. It kind of shoots down from here to my foot. It's driving me nuts.

Medical Assistant: OK, I know Doctor will have some more questions for you when he comes in. I don't know what he'll find or if he can definitely help you, but he's an excellent doctor and I know he'll do everything he can for you.

I'm curious, Carl, if you woke up tomorrow morning and found that your pain was gone, how would that affect your day-to-day life?

Patient: I'd get more done at work, that's for sure. I'm up for a promotion, but I can't get my s*** together and get all the documentation I need. I'm just too beat from being up all night with this damn leg.

Medical Assistant: Sounds rough. So, now you've really got me curious. If you got rid of your pain and got a promotion, how would that change things for you?

Patient: It would get me off the line and move me upstairs. More meetings but a lot less noise and some good perks.

Medical Assistant: Would the perks be enough to change other things in your life?

Patient: (Laugh) Yeah, you could say that. There's this house my wife and I have our eye on. I'd be able to get that.

Medical Assistant: That sounds interesting. What kind of house?

Patient: It's an A-Frame on a lake. I've always wanted a house with my own dock. And of course, a boat!

Medical Assistant: Awesome! So, Carl, is there anything that would keep you from being ABLE to let us help you?

Patient: Well, I have good insurance through the plant, so that's no problem. But if I need anything like surgery, that could be a problem because I have to be careful about time off from work, especially right now.

Medical Assistant: OK, so we have to be careful to schedule whatever you might need around your work schedule, right?

Patient: Definitely.

Medical Assistant: I'll be sure to introduce you to Jenny after you talk with Doctor. She'll help you figure out whatever you need to know about scheduling tests or whatever Doctor says you need.

Patient: Great, thanks.

Medical Assistant: I see a lot of people with pain like you've got, and I feel so bad for them. Sometimes no matter how much they want their pain to go away, there is something that holds them back from going ahead with doing what Doctor recommends. Maybe they think about how their life would change, or sometimes it's the actual treatment itself that worries, them—it's different for everyone.

Carl, is there anything that you can think of that might keep you from being willing to get tests or have treatment for your pain?

Patient: Hell no. I want this gone.

Medical Assistant: Great, then let me go get Doctor for you.

The doctor recommended that the patient get an MRI of his lower back, but the patient left without scheduling the test. The Medical Assistant called him at work later that afternoon and asked him if he wanted her help scheduling the test. He declined. She pursued it.

Medical Assistant: Carl, we had a good talk earlier, so I'm gonna stick my nose where it doesn't belong, OK?

(Patient talking—unable to record)

Medical Assistant: Something must have happened between before you saw the doctor and when you left because you seemed pretty charged to do whatever you could to get rid of your pain when we were talking. So what happened?

(Patient talking—unable to record)

Medical Assistant: That makes sense. Ya know, Carl, it sounds like maybe you're doing what we talked about—stopping yourself because you're worried about what the test will be like. Is that what's going on?

(Patient talking; unable to record)

Medical Assistant: Did you fill the prescription the doctor gave you?

(Patient talking; unable to record)

Medical Assistant: It's a pill that will relax you for the test.
(Patient talking; unable to record)

Medical Assistant: I don't think so. I think Doctor gave it to you because a lot of patients feel the same way you do, and so he probably wanted to make sure you'd have it if you needed it. There's only one pill in your prescription.

(Patient talking; unable to record)

Medical Assistant: Right. You'll be totally relaxed, and you'll probably sleep right through it and dream about your new house with your boat docked right there!

(Patient talking; unable to record)

Medical Assistant: (Laugh) Perfect! Just make sure you have someone drive you to your appointment because you'll be groggy for a while and shouldn't drive home.

(Patient talking; unable to record)

Medical Assistant: I don't know for sure, but it would probably be best to schedule your test at the end of your work day so you can just go home afterwards.

(Patient talking; unable to record)

Medical Assistant: (Laugh) Do you want me to connect you to Jenny so you can schedule your test?

(Patient talking; unable to record)

Medical Assistant: OK, good, hold on one second, please.

This patient had done what so many patients do. He had talked himself out of following the doctor's treatment recommendation because he was embarrassed to tell the doctor that he was claustrophobic. Because the Medical Assistant had built a relationship of trust, she was able to discover his PERMISSION barrier and help him to make a positive decision to take ACTION.

OK, now let's break it down. Table 15-4 provides the script for the interview, which you will adjust to fit for you. I am giving you several examples here, to cover different medical and dental services. The possible variations are endless, so use your imagination to create the best fit with your particular menu of services and products.

Table 15-4. The ACTION Formula Interview for Patients: Elective and Non-Elective Services	
I'd like to learn a little bit about you and your goals so that I can make sure that I understand the kind of help you want or need from us. Would that be OK?	
If "yes," continue.	If "no," reply with: *OK, no problem. Let's get to the reasons that brought you here* and move on to **PRESENTING DESIRE**.

Identify Patient Characteristics

Tell me a bit about yourself, are you from here originally? What do you do for fun? What do you do for work? (Ask only one question, whichever you choose, that will allow the patient to talk for about one minute. While the patient is talking, observe his or her behaviors and language and assess his or her Action Type, Value Set, and favorite State of Mind. As soon as you've got those figured out, move on.)

Transition

Next I'm going to ask you a few quick questions that will help us to understand exactly the kind of help you want/need (pick one based on Value Sets) *from us, OK?*

NOTE: Approximately 1 in 25 patients say "no." If that happens, forget The ACTION Formula Interview for now, and switch to a fact-based question like: *"What brings you in to see us today?"*

PRESENTING DESIRE (health — medical)

(Patient name), if you could wake up tomorrow morning and find that you felt exactly as you wanted to feel, what would you feel like?

Follow-up question: *How is your ideal health different from how you're feeling now?*

PRESENTING DESIRE (appearance — body)

(Patient name), if you woke up tomorrow morning and magically found that your body looked exactly as you wanted it to, specifically, what would it look like?

Follow-up question: *Look in the mirror here, and tell me, what do you see that you like, and what would you change if you could?*

(Table continues next page)

Table 15-4. The ACTION Formula Interview for Patients:
Elective and Non-Elective Services *(continued)*

PRESENTING DESIRE (appearance — face)

(Patient name), if you woke up tomorrow morning and magically found that your face looked exactly as you wanted it to, specifically, what would it look like?

Follow-up question: *Look in the mirror here, and tell me, what do you see that you like, and what would you change if you could?*

PRESENTING DESIRE (health and appearance — dental)

(Patient name), if you woke up tomorrow morning and magically found that your smile looked and felt exactly as you wanted it to, specifically, what would it be like?
Follow-up question: *Run your tongue around your teeth, and tell me what you feel that you like and if there's anything you feel that you don't like.*

Follow-up question: *Now, please look in the mirror here, and tell me, what do you see that you like, and what would you change if you could?*

DESIRE (These questions are the same for all specialties. Simply select "feel" or "look" where appropriate.)

I'm curious . . . if you felt/looked that way, how would your day-to-day life be different?

Probe further by choosing any of the following questions (the goal is to help your patients to actively picture what life would be like if they achieved their DESIRES):

• *What would you do that you can't do now?*

• *Where would you go?*

• *Who might you spend more time with?*

• *How would this affect you at work?*

• *How would this affect you at home? Socially?*

• *What clothes would you wear that you don't let yourself wear now?*

• *What special events would you be looking forward to that otherwise you might have dreaded?*

Chart each answer as **D1, D2, D3,** etc.

D4

And if (repeat exactly whatever the patient described), *how would that impact you personally?*

D5

And what would that get for you?

D4, etc.[1] and BURNING DESIRE

Keep probing, repeating "*How else would that affect you?*" and "*What would that get for you?*" until you hear the patient say something that is particularly meaningful to him or her. Watch for a flush of color or listen for a spike of emotion and then ask, "*And that's what you really want, isn't it?*" If yes, move on. If no, continue probing.

(Table continues next page)

Table 15-4. The ACTION Formula Interview for Patients: Elective and Non-Elective Services *(continued)*

RESOURCES

Is there anything that you're aware of that would keep you from being ABLE to let us help you to (fill in the patient's goal)*?*

Tell me specifically what you'd need to make that happen.

HINT: If the patient tells you there are RESOURCES he or she needs, then respond with:

Have you thought about how you would work around that?

Will you let me know if we can help in any way?

Remember it's not up to you to solve the problem, and it's more empowering for patients if you don't rescue them with suggestions or opinions. Recruit them to partner with you in finding a solution and offer facts when appropriate.

PERMISSION

You know, sometimes no matter how badly our patients want to (look/feel) better, there is something that holds them back from going ahead with doing what it takes to make that happen. Sometimes they think about how their life might change, sometimes it's the actual treatment itself that worries them—it's different for everyone. Is there anything that you can think of that might keep you from being willing to (fill in the patient's PRESENTING DESIRE)*?*

If "yes,"

And how do you think you might solve that?

Continue to ask leading questions to help patients discover a solution on their own.

CAUTION: If a patient shares a personal problem regarding domestic violence, abuse, rape, or other personal threat, refer to your practice guidelines for how to manage confidential information that may put your patient at risk. Be prepared to offer referrals to competent professionals in your community.

---

[1] There is no rule about how many DESIRES the patient will list. I offer the D1 to D6 as a guideline to help you to keep track of the different DESIRES the patient states. The later in the discussion, the more personal the DESIRE will be, so D1 will be more "surface" while D6 will be more private and "deep." BURNING DESIRE could appear from the onset with an emotional statement about why the patient wants your help. If that happens, don't worry about D1 to D6. You found what you needed.

Again, all of the information you gather in The ACTION Formula interview will be written on the M.A.D. Chart (Table 15-1) and made a part of the patient's permanent record.

Collecting The ACTION Formula Information Over Time

When patients come in for treatment, there is usually someone who collects and updates information before the doctor comes in. This is a perfect time to throw in a couple of questions from The ACTION Formula interview and to find out more about your patients. On one visit, ask about the DESIRES. The next time the patient comes in, bring it back up and ask the RESOURCE question. If you have time, go for PERMISSION, or else wait until the next time. It could take one to two years before you get all of the information, but if you are diligent and make it a commitment that all patients will have completed records, you'll get it done.

The key to long-term collection of information is to give your staff the freedom and time to be able to spend with your patients so that they can get this done. From a customer service perspective, it can buy doctors a little extra time to catch up and keep your patients happy while your assistants are getting the information you need to Motivate them to ACTION. It's a win for everyone.

RULE #4: GO MULTI-LINGUAL!

When you and your staff know how to use The ACTION Formula interview and the information it provides, and combine that with your ability to speak The Four Languages of the M.A.D. Formula, you'll find countless ways to use the information to motivate your patients. Here's a great example:

> **Practice Spotlight**
>
> A patient who had been in the practice for over 10 years, came in for an appointment with her hygienist. The practice had just completed our training, and the hygienist was excited to try the new interview. She used her notes, asked all of the questions, and the information went into the patient's record.
>
> About four months later, we had returned for our follow-up coaching session with the practice. By coincidence, the same patient called for an emergency appointment. The doctor on site that day wasn't the patient's regular doctor, but he had access to the electronic health record that had the M.A.D. information carefully logged and ready to use.
>
> It was fun to watch what happened next.

Patient Record xxxxxxxxxxxxxxxxxx Professional Ballet and Jazz Dancer, eats lots of raw fruits and vegetables, no gum or candy, no floss but 'keeps meaning to' **Mother (deceased) perio problems by age 40.**

T1	(T2)	(R)	E	T	C	CP	NP	A	SC	NC	Chips
PD Healthy gums						D1 Reduce likelihood of problems					*List Date of Chip* 9/4/07
D2 Keep own teeth						D3 Look good when smiling					
D4 Catch better parts						D5 Dance in NYC Ballet Co.					
D6 Prima Ballerina						BD Make grandfather proud					
R None											
P Pain Phobic and slow to trust doctors.											

The doctor was a Type 1 Commander who spent most of his time in his Analyst, but the patient was a Type 2 Relater who was usually in her Natural or Socialized Child (totally different). The doctor did a good job of speaking the patient's language and used her ACTION Formula information to break through the strangeness of being the on-call doctor.

> Putting his hand on the patient's arm he said:
>
> Doctor: *I know you're concerned about pain, and I think we can fix this without you having to feel anything at all. It's a minor crack, and it will be easy to reinforce it and make it look good for you at the same time.*
>
> Patient: *Oh, good. Thank you.*
>
> Doctor: *I see you're a dancer. Do you have any performances coming up?*
>
> Patient: *This weekend.*
>
> Doctor: *OK then, we will make it a priority to be sure your tooth looks great when you get back on stage with your colleagues. I'm going to use a bonding material that will reinforce the strength of your tooth while matching the color of the rest of your smile. This will allow you to bite into fruit without worrying, and you'll be able to smile into the spotlights when you're on stage. Is there anything else you want me to look at while I'm here?*
>
> Patient: *To be honest, I don't really like the color of my teeth. As long as we're doing this, can we pick a lighter color of the bonding stuff and then make all of the rest of them match?*
>
> The doctor had time in his schedule and was able to provide the patient with everything she wanted and needed.

Notice how well the doctor incorporated the M.A.D. language in his presentation. This was a key in his success since the patient had a history of difficulty building trust with strangers.

He also did a very good job of explaining facts and benefits.

> **A presentation needs to include the facts of what you will do and the benefits the patient will derive as a result.**

When telling a patient about your treatment recommendations, services, or products, the closer you can tie it to his or her personal situation, the faster the patient will be Motivated to take ACTION. This is accomplished by incorporating The Language of Action Types and The Language of Value Sets into your presentation, and then partnering that with the personal information you have from the patient's ACTION Formula. This multi-lingual presentation formula is very powerful. Here's how to make it work for you.

Let's say you are talking to a patient about a total hip replacement. You choose the key facts you want the patient to know. Ever mindful of the 20-20-60 rule, you will talk about benefits of the hip replacement by *making a connection between what you are going to do and what the patient is going to get*. Then, during your presentation, you will speak the patient's unique language.

Table 15-5 is an example of different statements you might make about a hip replacement for different types of patients in your practice:

TABLE 15-5. Multi-Lingual Motivation	
Service: Total Hip Replacement	**Sample Facts**
	The damaged hip is removed.
	A prosthetic device is inserted into the leg and attached at the top for stability during the healing process.
	Bone grows into the stem, creating a strong and tight fit.
Benefits	
Relater: Your body will grow bone into the device creating a strong and tight connection. The relationship of the prosthetic with your natural bone will allow you to walk smoothly and without pain.	
Enthusiast: This particular device is used by the top orthopedic surgeons all over the world.	
Thinker: The device is specifically measured so as to most accurately fit for your height. Current research shows that it has the best results for patients of your age and fitness. It weighs one pound and is made of titanium and porcelain.	
Commander: It will allow you to do what you need to do.	
Now consider how you would talk about this with each of the two Value Sets	
Type 1: This device is durable and has been shown to be very dependable in all of the studies.	
Type 2: You'll have some discomfort from the surgery, but we will do everything we can to make this an easy experience for you.	

Now, just select one statement from each category, and you have your presentation:

- **Relater, Type 1:** *We'll remove your damaged hip and insert a prosthetic device into your leg and attach it here for stability during the healing* process. *As you heal, your own bone will grow into the stem of the device creating a strong and tight connection. The relationship of the prosthetic with your natural bone will allow you to walk smoothly and without pain. This device is durable and has been shown to be very dependable in all of the studies.*

- **Relater, Type 2:** *We'll remove your damaged hip and insert a prosthetic device into your leg and attach it here for stability during the healing process. As you heal, your own bone will grow into the stem of the device creating a strong and tight connection. The relationship of the prosthetic with your natural bone will allow you to walk smoothly and without pain. You'll have some discomfort from the surgery, but we will do everything we can to make this an easy experience for you.*

- **Enthusiast, Type 1:** *We'll remove your damaged hip and insert a prosthetic device into your leg and attach it here for stability during the healing process. As you heal, your own bone will grow into the stem of the device creating a strong and tight fit. This particular device is used by the top orthopedic surgeons all over the world! It's durable and has been shown to be very dependable in all of the studies.*

- **Enthusiast, Type 2:** *We'll remove your damaged hip and insert a prosthetic device into your leg and attach it here for stability during the healing process. As you heal, your own bone will grow into the stem of the device creating a strong and tight fit. This particular device is used by the top orthopedic surgeons all over the world! You'll have some discomfort from the surgery, but we will do everything we can to make this an easy experience for you.*

- **Thinker, Type 1:** *I will remove your damaged hip and insert a prosthetic device into your leg and attach it here for stability during the healing process. As you heal, your own bone will grow into the stem of the device creating a strong and tight fit. The device is specifically measured so as to most accurately fit for your height. Current research shows that it has the best results for patients of your age and fitness. It weighs one pound and is made of titanium and porcelain. This device is durable and has been shown to be very dependable in all of the studies.*

- **Thinker, Type 2:** *I will remove your damaged hip and insert a prosthetic device into your leg and attach it here for stability during the healing process. As you heal, your own bone will grow into the stem of the device creating a strong and tight fit. The device is specifically measured so as to most accurately fit for your height. Current research shows that it has the best results for patients of your age and fitness. It weighs one pound and is made of titanium and porcelain. You'll have some discomfort from the surgery, but we will do everything we can to make this an easy experience for you.*

- **Commander, Type 1:** *I will remove your damaged hip and insert a prosthetic device into your leg and attach it here for stability during the healing process. As you heal, your own bone will grow into the stem of the device creating a strong and tight fit. This device is durable and has been shown to be very dependable in all of the studies and the bottom line is that it will allow you to do what you need to do.*
- **Commander, Type 2:** *I will remove your damaged hip and insert a prosthetic device into your leg and attach it here for stability during the healing process. As you heal, your own bone will grow into the stem of the device creating a strong and tight fit. You'll have some discomfort from the surgery, but we will do everything we can to make this an easy experience for you, and the bottom line is that it will allow you to do what you need to do.*

Remember, the formula is 20-20-60. So, the more facts you give, the more benefits you need to throw in to balance it out.

Now it's your turn. Use Activity 15-2 to get an idea of how you would talk about different services, treatments, surgeries, or products in your area of specialization.

When you use multi-lingual Motivation strategies, patients believe they can trust you, and they tell you what they really want. The more they open up to you, the more you will learn the secrets that will help you not only in Motivational conversations, but often in designing their treatment plan.

RULE #5: BE AWARE OF SCARY WORDS.

There are certain words that can be scary to patients because of the associations patients make when they hear the words. Table 15-6 contains a list of words that can be scary, along with recommendations for replacement words. Please notice the comments next to each so that you can make sense of my recommendations. I would never want you to do something without understanding the reasoning behind it.

Whenever I teach this in a workshop, I challenge the group to avoid scary words for the remainder of our time together by telling them that I am going to charge them 25 cents for each slip, and I promise that at the end of the program I'll give the money to the administrator to buy pizza for the Team. You wouldn't think it would add up to much, but you would be amazed at how often these words get used! The worst offenders are always the patient coordinators, receptionists, check-out staff, and ALL of the doctors. In fact, I've had many occasions when a doctor will throw a $20 bill into the cup yelling *"OK, I'm covered for the rest of the workshop*!" People throw in checks, IOUs, dollar bills, and once we got a lottery ticket! They cover each other's debts, run to the lobby for more change, and stack their quarters in front of them, hoping they won't be the next to slip. The best

Activity 15-2. Practicing Multi-Lingual Motivation
Choose a service that you offer in your practice. Write out three facts about that service that a patient would need to know.

Service	Facts
	....
	....
	....

Now write out how this service might benefit each of the Action Types (if you need help choosing words, go back to Chapter 5).

Relater

Enthusiast

Thinker

Commander

Now write out how this service might benefit each of the Value Sets (if you need help choosing words, go back to Chapter 6).

Type 1

Type 2

Now put it all together!

was when someone threw in her Snickers bar! I figured that was my tip. There's a lot of laughter, and people learn the rules quickly.

Don't fool yourself — this is harder than it looks. We had a client several years ago who had a terrible time with this. In hopes of helping him catch on, his Team had created enormous, colorful posters, and hung them all over his private office. When we went back to do his follow-up coaching, I walked into his office and laughed so hard I couldn't breathe. The one that really got me was hanging directly above his desk:

"THE COST OF PRICE IS $20!"

TABLE 15-6. Word Choices		
Scary	**Preferred**	**Reasoning**
Contract	Agreement	When people hear the word "contract," they perceive that they are trapped. If they have had bad experiences, they will picture lawyers and court battles. "Agreement" is just as binding, it's just friendlier.
Price	Fee Investment	"Price" is what you see at the discount store *"Good morning shoppers, in aisle 3 we have a blue light special on root canals and angioplasty."* Don't cheapen yourself or your services.
Cost	Fee Investment	"Cost" is heard as a loss of security: *"What's this gonna cost me?"* There is a time when you might use the word purposefully to Motivate your patient to ACTION, as in *"What will it cost you if you don't have the surgery now?"* Otherwise avoid it.
Pay	Handle	*"How do you want to pay for this?"* Again, this cheapens your image. Consider instead, *"How would you like to handle your bill?"*
Any word that would not be understood by a six-year-old child.	Simple words that don't require the listener to wonder what you're saying. This doesn't mean that you *treat* them like they are six years old. Only that your WORDS are so simple, a child of six would easily understand you.	Most people will not tell you when they don't understand something you've said. It's a Chips thing—most people would rather pretend they know something than admit they don't. Remember, patients need Chips if they are going to take ACTION, so don't put them in a position in which they feel one-down because they don't understand what you are saying. This is particularly important for patient Motivation, patient education, and risk management.
Oops, Whoops, Yikes	NOTHING!	Do I really need to explain this one?
Waiting Room	Reception area	Again, this is obvious. No one wants to wait, but everyone wants to be welcomed!

Eliminating scary words isn't difficult, but it takes practice to break old habits. Get started now with Activity 15-3.

ACTIVITY 15-3. Find and Replace Scary Words
The next time you have a Team meeting, have a brainstorm session and make a list of scary and preferred words. Start off by suggesting words like "Needle," "Cut," "Blood," and see what the Team comes up with. Have fun with this, but let the Team know this is serious and that you all need to agree to avoid these scary words whenever possible.

When you follow The Five Rules of Motivating Patients to ACTION, you will build a strong relationship of trust with your patient, and open the door for your patient to tell you everything you need to know to provide better diagnostics and treatment. When you offer your treatment recommendations, your patient will understand more completely your plan and will be able to connect your treatment with his or her unique situation. It's a powerful tool that will help you and your patient get what you truly want.

BOTTOM LINE

The Five Rules of Motivating Patients to ACTION allow you to communicate with your patients in a customized process that permits you to determine precisely what they want, the barriers that would keep them from being able and willing to let you help them, and the solutions that would help them to break through their barriers. When you follow these five rules, patients are significantly more likely to accept and follow through on your treatment recommendations. The process can be used in any type of practice, by phone and in person, and will yield higher levels of patient commitment in place of unreliable patient compliance.

Chapter 16

Invite Your Patients to Take ACTION!

THIS IS THE PART of Motivating patients that makes most clinicians wince. It's one thing to diagnose and prescribe, but it's quite another thing to ask your patient to make a commitment to proceed. This is particularly true if you are recommending a treatment that is not covered by insurance. Let's look first at the issue of money, and then we'll look at ways to invite your patients to ACTION in elective and non-elective, self-pay and covered treatments.

THE MONEY BARRIER

In the old days, there was one authority: the doctor. The doctor told patients what they needed, and the patients understood that they had to provide the fee for the doctor's services (with cash, pies, chickens, or pigs). In today's healthcare environment, we have several authorities: the doctor, the media, and the patient's insurance company. The patient looks to these authorities to determine what is (and is not) "necessary" treatment. Of course, only "necessary" treatments are reimbursable to the patient, and now that patients have learned that they are entitled to get reimbursed for healthcare services, they want to have only those services that are covered. Think of this for a moment, not as a "good" or "bad" thing, but only as a fact.

> **The fact is that in today's healthcare environment, patients believe they are entitled to have their services "covered" by insurance.**

This phenomenon has put doctors (and other healthcare personnel) in the position of doing more than diagnosing and treating. Now you have to deal with the money aspect of your services; bargaining, bartering, and negotiating while, at the same time, assuring patients that a given treatment is necessary regardless of whether their insurance company deems it so.

I always tell my doctor clients that there is no need for them to have to be involved in this aspect of Motivating patients. In fact, I think it's better if doctors separate themselves from the process, assuming they can afford to hire personnel to handle it for them. Talking about financials and insurance coverage can be embarrassing for patients, and it's better to allow them to keep their relationship with their clinicians free of any discussions regarding their financial situation. It also helps to stop the inevitable tendency of doctors to lower their fees in response to their patients' requests for "discounts." Not all doctors suffer from this problem but many have a strong propensity to give away their services to patients who can easily afford them, simply because the patients ask them to barter or bargain.

Your clinical training is for cutting skin, not fees.

Many practices have designated employees whose entire responsibility it is to help patients to sign all of the necessary forms and credit applications, choose dates for procedures and services, and understand additional options that might be available.

This is a great thing except for one little glitch:

The patient knows he or she is about to leave the safe cocoon of the doctor's domain and is now going to talk to "the money person" (cue organ music). In fact, I have heard many doctors refer to these staff people by saying, *"Come with me, and I'll introduce you to the money lady."* Can you say "salesy?"

Anyone who has purchased a car knows what comes next! After you choose your car, the car salesperson goes off alone to some unknown place where he or she will serve as your advocate and liaison to the mysterious "general manager" (who no one has ever actually seen). Once the "deal is made," the friendly car salesperson walks you across the entire showroom in front of the knowing, sympathetic eyes of all the other friendly car salespeople and their equally confused customers.

At the end of the long walk, you enter "The Financing Office" where you will feel exactly as you did as a child in the principal's office. Now you hear about still more ways to part with your money through extras like satellite radio and roadside assistance packages. You begin to sit a little straighter and unconsciously lay both hands over your checkbook.

The "principal" taps on his computer and suddenly informs you that your credit isn't as good as you thought it was (that stupid free offer that wasn't free forever and expired *only* if you canceled it, which, it seems, you never did). Next you learn that your teenager wrote too many checks on your account, and you haven't got the cash for the down payment. You hand the "principal" your credit card only to discover that it is maxed out because your partner mistakenly ordered the new copier on your personal card. You put your guard up and lock it in.

No, "The Financing Office" is not a happy place.

This is precisely what patients are expecting as they walk your hallway to the office of your (cue organ music) Financial Coordinator.

Let's see if we can correct that image. First, it's great to have a Financial Coordinator, but consider a different title such as "Treatment Coordinator," "Scheduling Specialist," or "Cosmetic Coordinator." In the ideal world, this person will also conduct the initial ACTION Formula interview, creating a smooth transition for the patient who now returns to the "Patient Consultation Room" to talk about planning options with someone he or she already likes and trusts. If you are on a computer network, your Coordinator will already have your recommendations on his or her screen and will be able to generate paperwork by the time the patient has been escorted back to the consultation room by your assistant.

When it's time to invite your patient to take ACTION, there is a specific process that I have found to be quite effective. It allows your Treatment Coordinator to bring together everything you've learned about the patient and allows your patient to carefully think through the options before taking ACTION.

THE NINE STEPS TO INVITING YOUR PATIENTS TO TAKE ACTION

Whether you are recommending a "covered" treatment plan or an out-of-pocket service, there are nine steps to Inviting Your Patients to Take ACTION, and I recommend that you follow all of them in order. These steps will allow you or your representative to walk your patient through the decision-making process, taking all things into consideration, and giving your patient an opportunity to think things through with someone who really understands the details of the case. Using the steps will reduce the number of times you hear phrases like, "*I need to talk it over with my spouse*" and "*I need to think it over*"; will enable you to significantly increase the number of times you hear "yes"; and will help you to limit your canceled procedures (due to Buyer's Remorse) and noncompliance. There are specific questions and statements associated with each step that come together to form powerful scripts. Let's look at the individual steps first, and then I'll show you the scripts.

Step 1: Find the Final Straw

Most patients do not come in to see a doctor on a whim. Unless they are having an emergency, the odds are that by the time they call you, they have been thinking about calling for quite some time. Patients will cut out an article or an ad and put it on their refrigerator, only to dig it back up a year later when an event occurs that serves as the catalyst that propels them to take ACTION. They will get your name from a friend or referring doctor, and then put off calling until something comes up that they just can't ignore.

It is important that you find out what was the original catalyst, or "Final Straw," that led your patient to make the call because, unless you can see these patients on the same day that they call, most will forget the experience of physical and/or emotional pain that they felt in that Final Straw moment. Days, often weeks go by, and by the time they see you, they are more focused on the pain they will have to endure in the future (financially and/or physically) then on the pain that led them to seek your help in the first place. So you need to bring them back to the Final Straw moment so that they can have all the data to determine whether the benefit of taking ACTION outweighs the downside.

Make mention of the PRESENTING DESIRE (the actual problem they want resolved) and then ask them to tell you about the moment that they finally decided they'd had enough and picked up the phone to call. In the telling of their story, they will rekindle the fires that brought them to your door.

Step 2: Review Treatment Plan

Most patients have no real understanding of what their doctor has proposed for treatment. Their head is spinning with dozens of thoughts while the doctor is, first examining, and then making his or her recommendation. If the service is cosmetic or if patients are seeking help for problems that resulted from the patients' lifestyle (such as weight- or smoking-related illnesses), they are often embarrassed that they need the help in the first place. This embarrassment leads patients to lose track of much of what the doctor says when he or she is describing treatment recommendations.

It's important for the patient (and your risk management) that your Coordinator review the treatment plan with the patient in simple, nontechnical terms, as well as repeat the technical terms that the patient heard from you. If you skip this step, you may find your patients balking during preop, yelling that they never agreed to this or that. This is worse than Buyer's Remorse, and dribbles over into Angry Buyer. That's not a pretty place to go, so be sure to cover this step cleanly and clearly, but don't overdo it. I've seen people who purposefully try to frighten patients out of taking ACTION. Offer only the pertinent facts, make certain the facts are understood, and know that you've done what you need to do for everyone's protection.

Step 3: Risks of Waiting

This is my favorite step because this is when you are going to sit back and let the patients sell themselves on taking ACTION. You will accomplish this by inviting your patients to tell you about the downside of putting off the treatment plan. The language is very specific here, so it's important that you follow the script for this step. But the general plan is this:

If the treatment is **non-elective**, you will mention two to three health risks of putting off the treatment and then ask your patients to tell you what other risks they envision. If the treatment is **elective**, then you will let your patients know that this treatment is not a life or death concern and that it is perfectly OK for them to postpone it. You will note that there will be some slight risks, and lightly discuss how they will have to wait a little longer to get one or two of the DESIRES they told you about earlier. Next, you invite your patients to tell you what the risks are as they see them.

At this point, your patients will work very hard to sell you on the fact that they should absolutely not postpone the treatment.

Note, this is not in any way unethical. If the patients don't think there are any risks in postponement and are not ready to go ahead, they will see your effort as kind and helpful and express gratitude for your willingness to let them "off the hook."

Step 4: Empower the Patient

One of the most difficult things for patients is the sense of powerlessness they feel when they get involved in the healthcare system. In healthcare, there is a long history of placing patients in situations in which their choices are taken away, and others make decisions on their behalf. From the moment you tell them to remove their clothes, they are at your mercy, stripped of the trappings that they depend on to help them to feel powerful in the outside world. This is no different in dentistry where, although permitted to stay fully clothed, they are locked in position and social distance rules are destroyed as one or more people hover over them. Unable to talk and afraid to move for fear of getting hurt, patients experience powerlessness and loss of control.

Now, here they are, free again, in your consultation room. They are about to be presented with your fee, and they know they will have to decide if they are going to take ACTION.

No one can make a firm decision and feel confident about that decision unless they feel grounded and confident.

So you will help them to feel strong again by reminding them that they are completely in control of the situation, and that they alone hold the key to deciding whether they move forward and get the DESIRES they mentioned. Then you will help them to Motivate themselves further by inviting them to think about other ways they will benefit from the treatment plan.

Step 5: Introduce the Investment (Elective or Out-of-Network)

If your treatment recommendations require your patients to go out-of-pocket, this is the time to tell them your fees. The biggest challenge I see in my coaching is that Coordinators put way too much emphasis on the dollar amount when the emphasis should really be on what the patient will get as a result of taking ACTION and receiving the treatment or surgery.

Just state the fee and move on.

Do not linger, do not say the number and then pause while the echo of your voice calling out that number wafts through the air ringing over and over and over again through the dense silence of the room. I'm not kidding. Look at Activity 16-1, and try it yourself!

ACTIVITY 16-1. The Communication Echo
Grab a friend and have him or her say something to you and then fall silent. Notice how the echo of his or her last word rings through your mind.
Now have the friend say this out loud and be quiet afterwards: ***Five Thousand Dollars***
Do you ear the echo? ***Dollars . . . dollars . . . dollars . . . dollars . . .*** Is this what you want your patient to remember most from your meeting?

Here's what I recommend: Right before you mention the investment amount, take a breath that will last you through the next two sentences. You'll describe what the fee includes, announce the fee amount (the number, but leave off the word "dollars"), and then tie it all to the patient's BURNING DESIRE.

Step 6: Give a Choice

At this point, patients think, "*Should I do this or not*?" When that is the decision they are looking to make, they get caught up in comparing "yes" and "no." We can make this easier for them by offering a different set of choices that will lead them to consider the details of what would happen if they decided to go ahead. Assume the answer is "yes," and then offer choices about the WHEN, WHERE, and HOW of taking ACTION. Believe me, if the answer is "no," they'll tell you! We'll talk about how to handle that in Step 7.

In the meantime, please know that there is nothing more empowering than being given a choice. The choices you offer can be anything from scheduling dates to methods of payment. The important thing is this:

After you offer the choice, be silent and wait for a response.

Under no circumstances are you to talk until your patient responds, no matter how long that takes. There's an old rule in selling, tried and true through the ages:

In a large purchase, the last person to talk is the one who loses the money.

Just sit quietly, and everyone will win.

In Table 16-1, you will see an example of a script that incorporates the first six Steps to Inviting Your Patients to Take ACTION. Listen to the script on your CD so that you get the general idea in your head. The only step that needs to be precise is Step 3 (Risks of Waiting), otherwise feel free to use language that fits your unique style.

Inevitably, many patients will object when they hear the details of the plan or the fees. So now you need to know how to handle their objections effectively.

Step 7: Handle Objections

One of the biggest sources of problems I see in Motivating patients to ACTION is that healthcare professionals do not know how to properly handle their patients' objections. This is due to two factors:

1. They hear the patient's objections as rejection or criticism; and/or
2. They honestly don't know what to say in response.

Let's look at each separately.

They hear the patient's objections as rejection or criticism.

Many people think a patient's objection is a rejection of them personally or a criticism of their treatment plan. The truth is, the majority of objections are nothing more or less than a patient's request for help. Let me explain what I mean.

Imagine that we really did go on that trip to Monte Carlo, and in the middle of a day excursion into a remote area of France, you take ill. Imagine further that you don't speak any French at all, and the people in the clinic speak no English whatsoever. If you are a doctor or clinical professional, imagine for a moment that you are just a regular person with no credentials or clinical training whatsoever.

TABLE 16-1. Inviting Your Patient to Take ACTION (Steps 1–6)
Step 1: Final Straw
(Patient name), you told me that what brought you in today is that you are looking to (Insert PRESENTING DESIRE). *I'm curious, this didn't just happen overnight. You've probably been thinking about this for some time. So what was the final straw that made you decide to pick up the phone and call us?*
Step 2: Review Treatment Plan
OK, so the doctor has told me that the best road to get you to (PRESENTING DESIRE) *is* (TREATMENT PLAN). *Do you have any questions that the doctor didn't address about the treatment/surgery, recovery, or anything else?*
Step 3: Risks of Waiting
You know, the truth is, you could put this off for a little while — it's not like it's a life or death procedure that has to happen tomorrow. It's really important to us that you do this when you're ready, and not a minute before. Now granted, there would be a few risks in putting it off, like you'd have to wait a little longer to be able to (insert one or two DESIRES). *I'm curious— what risks do you see in putting this off?*
Step 4: Empower the Patient
Let's be clear about something; this is your body and you can do anything you want to do — you have all the power here. Is this something you'd like to postpone, or are you anxious to get (insert DESIRES 1 and 2). *I know you said you want to* (insert DESIRE 3), *and* (insert DESIRE 4), *right? How else do you imagine your life will be different once your* (health/body/face/smile) *is where you want it to be?*
Step 5: Introduce the Investment
Great, so, let's get that for you! [breathe] *Now, the fees for your treatment include* (state everything that is included) *and come to a total of* (amount). [do not breathe] *So the only question you have left to answer is how quickly we're going to begin the process of getting you on the road to* (insert BURNING DESIRE)! [breathe]
Step 6: Give a Choice
Would you prefer to have your surgery on a Tuesday or a Wednesday?   *Do you want to start with your upper teeth or do your full mouth?*   *Do you want to schedule your preoperative appointment in the morning or afternoon?*

Through sign language, you manage to tell the people in the clinic where you are hurting, and you write down the phone number of your family back home. They are very nice to you in the clinic, but you really don't understand a word they are saying. All you know is you're sick and scared and alone.

Several people examine you, and then someone who you think is a nurse comes over to you with a pill and a glass of water. You stare at the pill. You don't know these people, and you have a history of allergic reactions to medications. You're afraid to take this pill without knowing what it is, but if you don't take it, you could get worse.

What do you do?

I have presented this scenario to people all over the world, and I get three different responses.

Group A: *"I'd just swallow it, and take my chances."*

Group B: *"I'd just get up and leave, and try to find a hospital that spoke my language."*

Group C: *"I'd keep complaining until I could find someone to explain to me what the pill is."*

The people in Group A are just like your easy patients. They do everything you say without question. We know the people in Group B have no intention of following the doctor's treatment recommendation, so they are gone.

Now here's the really interesting question: Would the patients in Group C bother to complain or ask questions at all if they had no intention of taking the pill? I propose that the answer is "no." In my experience,

> **Patients only object because they want to go ahead and they need more information before they can comfortably take ACTION.**

There are Four Categories of Objections:

- **No way, no how:** These people criticize your plan or your fees but they don't actually leave your office. You will typically get this response from Commanders.
- **I can't afford it — it's too expensive:** Some patients genuinely can't afford your help because they have no cash, no credit, and no Great Aunt. Apart from this relatively small percentage of people,

> **The vast majority of patients say "I can't afford it" because it is a socially acceptable way of saying "no."**

The "I can't afford it" objection is akin to "I'm just looking." It gets you to leave them alone. What I've found through many years of experience in managing objections is that most people who say they "can't afford" something are actually afraid of something but are too embarrassed to say so. When you give them an opportunity to talk about it, they always share their concerns. While sometimes their fear far outweighs their desire to take ACTION, more often than not their fear is due to a miscommunication or misunderstanding about what the treatment will involve, or a concern about how others will be affected by their decision. When their fears are put to rest, patients spring to ACTION.

- **I need to think it over:** These people aren't saying yes or no, they simply need time to sort through all of their States of Mind (opinions, facts, and feelings) before they will be ready to decide. You will hear this most often from Thinkers and Relaters. The problem is that if you let them go off on their own to think it over, they will be bombarded by opinions from relatives and friends who know more than the doctors because they saw a talk show that explained everything in detail. They would be much better off having the opportunity to think it over with you first so you can be sure to correct any miscommunications and answer any clinical questions they might think of during the process of thinking it through.
- **I need to talk it over with . . . :** These people aren't saying yes or no, they are either in a relationship that requires them to discuss major decisions, or they genuinely need to talk with someone else before they will feel comfortable saying yes or no. You will typically get this response from Relaters and Enthusiasts, and occasionally from Thinkers.

The important thing to remember is that if the patient has stayed, it is not a rejection of you. The patient just needs your help to sort it all out and/or some time to make a decision.

They honestly don't know what to say in response.

The patient objects, and you are stymied. You know you should say something, but you just can't think of what you should say. So you simply smile and say, *"No problem. Just let us know if you change your mind."* Now I just want you to stop and think about this for a minute. If patients go to all the trouble to come to your office, fill out paperwork, and submit themselves to tests, prodding, and questions, does it make sense to you to just let them walk away without at least helping them to think it all through and make sure all of their questions are answered? Honestly, if you let them go, the odds are they will take their questions to someone else who knows how to help them figure out what to do. Who will that "someone else" be? Your competition? I honestly believe that part of customer service in healthcare is to make sure that every patient is given the opportunity to think through major decisions with a member of their healthcare team. Who is better equipped to help with that than you or your representative? So let's look at how to do that.

Just as there are Four Categories of Objections, there are specific methods for handling each. In Table 16-2, you will find scripting for handling each objection category. Again, I remind you to listen to your CD so that you can get the ideas in your head and allow the concepts to come out freely in your own style.

TABLE 16-2. Handling Objections		
"No Way, No How"		
No problem (patient name). May I ask you a quick question?		
If "yes," go on to next question.	If "No, I have to go:" *That's perfectly OK. I'll leave this information with you, and if you have any questions at all, please call or e-mail and I'll get right back to you. I'm glad you came in today, let me show you out.*	
What's scarier, doing this or not doing this? (No matter which they choose, you continue.)	If the response is *"I'm not scared of anything,"* you respond with, *"What's your concern?"* You will typically hear the questions that the patient never asked the doctor. After all questions are addressed, return to Step 6 of Inviting Your Patients to Take ACTION, and repeat the patient's choices.	
OK, what's scary about doing this? (No matter what they say, go on to the next question.)		
OK, what's scary about NOT doing this? (At this point, patients will start talking themselves back into taking ACTION. Just be quiet and see where it goes. If the patient indicates he or she is ready, return to Step 6 of Inviting Your Patients to Take ACTION and repeat the choices. Otherwise, if the patient still hesitates, continue.)		
So the real decision that has to be made is how long you're willing to wait before you can (fill in the patient's answer to what's scary about NOT doing this). *So, (patient name) . . . how long <u>are</u> you willing to wait?* If the patient says he or she really needs to postpone, then say: *That's perfectly OK. I'll leave this information with you, and if you have any questions at all, please call or e-mail and I'll get right back to you. I'm glad you came in today, let me show you out.* If the patient is ready to move forward, reiterate the choices from Step 6 of Inviting Your Patients to Take ACTION and schedule the procedure/treatment/etc.		
"I Can't Afford It — It's Too Expensive"		
Yes, it is a lot of money. Would you like me to talk with you about credit or financing options?		
If "Yes," talk through financing and then Return to Step 6 of Inviting Your Patients to Take ACTION.	If "No" *I'll just leave this information with you . . . (Patient name), I'm curious about something — if you could afford to do this, would you do it?*	
	If "Yes" *Well, when you're ready, we'll be here for you. I'm glad you came in today, let me show you out.*	If "No" *What is it that concerns you?* Talk through the patient's questions and if appropriate, go to Step 6 of Inviting Your Patients to Take ACTION. If not, end with: *If you ever change your mind, we'll be here for you. I'm glad you came in today, let me show you out.*

(Table continues next page)

TABLE 16-2. Handling Objections *(continued)*	
"I Need to Think It Over"	

I understand perfectly, (patient name), and I want you to take as much time as you need to think this through. [pause] *Can I ask you a quick question?*

If "Yes," go on to next question.	If "No, I have to go:"
	That's perfectly OK. I'll leave this information with you, and if you have any questions at all, please call or e-mail and I'll get right back to you. I'm glad you came in today, let me show you out.

What is it you want to think about, is it the fact that you'll (insert DESIRE 1)?[1]

Probable Response: *"No, that's not it."*

Could it be the fact that you'll (insert DESIRE 2)**?**

Probable Response: *"No, that's not it."*

Honestly (patient name), could it be the money? [nod your head]

Possible Answer #1: Yes, It's the Money

I hate it when I really want something and I can't afford it. Frankly, even if you could afford it, you're probably like some of our other patients — they put everyone else's needs before their own — saving their money for something their kids might want or need before they'd spend it on themselves. Is that how you feel?

(No matter what the response, you go on.)

Well, I want you to take as much time as you need to think about this. One thing I might invite you to add to your thinking is a very important question: Is getting (insert DESIRE 3, DESIRE 4, BURNING DESIRE) *worth $____? Only you know the answer to that.*

Sit still and smile. The patient will either take ACTION or move to leave.

If the patient takes ACTION, repeat Step 6 of Inviting Your Patient to Take ACTION. If the patient indicates that he or she is ready to leave, continue.

I really want to thank you for giving me the chance to talk with you today. I'd like to call you in a few days to see how you're doing on your thinking, would that be all right?

If "Yes," continue.	If "No":
	Then please feel free to call me any time you'd like to talk.

When is the best time to reach you, morning or afternoon?

Make a date to talk on the phone.

Possible Answer #2: No, it's not the money...it's...

Address the patient's concerns with information or apply the responses under "No Way-No How."

(Table continues next page)

TABLE 16-2. Handling Objections *(continued)*
I Need to Talk It Over With. . . .
I understand perfectly. I want you to take as much time as you need to talk about this. I'm curious — how are you going to sell him [or her] *on this?*
Help them talk it through with you. You might even role play it!
When can I call you to find out what happened?
They'll give you some day, or they'll say they will call you. Either way . . .
(Patient name), don't let him or her talk you out of this. This is about taking care of you so you can (insert DESIRE 1, DESIRE 2, DESIRE 3, DESIRE 4, BURNING DESIRE).
Sit still and smile. The patient will either take ACTION or move to leave.
If the patient takes ACTION, repeat Step 6 of Inviting Your Patients to Take ACTION. If the patient goes to leave:
I really want to thank you for giving me the chance to talk with you today. I'll talk with you on (DAY).
[1] What you're doing here is reminding the patient of some of the benefits that the patient said he or she wanted. The goal is to get to the point that you can ask about money challenges without embarrassing the patient.

Let me reassure you about these scripts. If your words come from your heart, your patients will genuinely appreciate your efforts to help them to think through their problems and decisions. Here's an example:

Practice Spotlight

Patient: I appreciate your time, but I'm going to need some time to think this over.

Treatment Coordinator: I understand perfectly, Kellie. This is an important decision, and I want to encourage you to think about it all you want. May I ask you a quick question?

Patient: Of course.

Treatment Coordinator: What is it you want to think about? Is it that you'll get back the stomach you had before the baby?

Patient: No, that's the whole idea!

Treatment Coordinator: Is it that you'll be able to wear a bathing suit this summer?

Patient: I've been thinking about that all winter. I was worried about the scar but Dr. H showed me where it will be so I think I'm going to be fine.

Treatment Coordinator: Kellie, could it be the money?

Patient: Yeah. I really didn't think it was going to be so much. I don't know where I got the idea it was $2000! Anyway, I just can't rationalize spending this kind of money when I've got a new baby and I'm not working. It's just not fair to my husband.

Treatment Coordinator: That makes total sense, and I want you to take as much time as you need to think this through. One thing you might add to your thinking is this: Is $5000 worth being able to get into your old clothes, lose your self-consciousness with your husband, and get your confidence back when you're out with friends? Only you can decide that.

Patient: (Laugh) Well, when you put it that way, I could spend a lot more than that on a new wardrobe and a divorce attorney (laugh).

Silence

Patient: This is stupid, I really want to do this thing. When can you get me in?

Treatment Coordinator: Are you sure?

Patient: Totally. Like you said, it's my body, and I can do what I want. This is what I promised myself when I got pregnant. I'm not going to have any more kids, so why should I waste one minute when I could be living in the body I want?

Treatment Coordinator: Good question.

Patient: Yeah well, I'm done with the questions. Sign me up.

Treatment Coordinator: OK!

ACTIVITY 16-2. Role Plays

In Appendix III, you will find instructions for how to run Team role play activities that will enable everyone involved to achieve confidence using these techniques. In Appendices IV through X, you will find sample M.A.D. Charts derived from transcripts of videotaped patient interviews in medicine and dentistry that you can use in your role plays.

Follow the instructions in Appendix III, and remember to make sure that everyone experiences success! The goal is to help everyone to become familiar with The ACTION Formula Interview and the first seven Steps of Inviting Patients to Take ACTION, while at the same time enabling everyone to develop facility when using the M.A.D. charts.

Start with conducting The ACTION Formula interview and then move to Inviting Patients to ACTION Steps 1 through 6. Once everyone is comfortable, start throwing in some objections and practice Step 7. If you make this a fun experience, then everyone will be excited about incorporating these techniques into their daily routines.

HINT: I suggest that you *allow people to hold scripts in hand and help each other along.* The goal is not perfection. The goal is comfort and familiarity with the process. Expect laughter galore as they work their way through the different examples. I hope you'll join in the fun!

Now that you know the first seven Steps of Inviting Your Patients to Take ACTION, you're ready to practice with your Team with Activity 16-2. Have fun with it!

Step 8: Send a Thank You Note

Remember when your grandmother told you to send a handwritten thank you note to your Aunt Edna for the flannel pajamas that didn't fit you and made you itch? Well, at the risk of sounding like your grandmother, I'd like to suggest that you bring back that long-lost tradition.

In a world of electronic signatures and cryptic responses, there is nothing

> **Thank you for visiting** *(Practice Name)* **on** *(DAY)*. I enjoyed meeting and talking with you, and I am particularly grateful for the trust you showed me in telling me about your goals and concerns.
>
> I am looking forward to working with you further so that we can begin the process of helping you to *(DESIRE 3)*.
>
> Respectfully yours,

For patients who say "yes" to taking ACTION

> **Thank you for visiting** *(Practice Name)* **on** *(DAY)*. I enjoyed meeting and talking with you, and I am particularly grateful for the trust you showed me in telling me about your goals and concerns.
>
> I am looking forward to talking with you on *(DAY, TIME)* so that I can answer any other questions you might have.
>
> Respectfully yours,

For patients who say they want to think it over or talk it over with someone

Thank you for visiting *(Practice Name)* on *(DAY)*. I enjoyed meeting and talking with you, and I am particularly grateful for the trust you showed me in telling me about your goals and concerns.

I am looking forward to meeting you again at some time in the future. In the meantime, I wish you the best of success and good health.

Respectfully yours,

For patients who say "no"

more dramatic than a handwritten thank you note from someone in your practice. In the ideal world, it would be signed by either the Treatment Coordinator or the Doctor. The content of the thank you note can be anything you choose. Here are sample thank you notes that I created for my elective clients:

I know, I know . . . you don't have time to hand write thank you notes. I have three words for you: *high school students*. I have many clients who hire high school seniors to come into their practice part-time at minimum wage to do some odd tasks like filing, etc. If they have good handwriting, set them up at a desk, and let them go for it!

I have a client who takes his thank you notes home and pays his teenage daughter $0.25 per note.

True Confession:

OK, I'll be straight with you . . . This is an idea that everyone loves but few pursue consistently. One of my favorite clients recently confessed to me that they had switched over to word processed thank you letters on letterhead because they just couldn't afford to allow an employee to take the time to hand write them. I'll tell you what I told them:

Do what is best for you and your practice, but if you can find a way to put this into ACTION, it will pay off for your business and your reputation.

Step 9: Follow Up

No matter what, it's important that someone in your practice follow up with patients after they have booked their procedures/treatments/surgeries.

Patients appreciate a quick call to make sure that they are still ready to go and haven't thought of any extra questions. Apart from being great customer service, this helps patients stay on course and avoid Buyer's Remorse.

If they do say they've started to think twice about it, suggest that they make a list of all of their concerns and you'll call them back in a few days. If the doctor is available, have him or her follow up with the patient. Otherwise, have a clinical assistant, physician assistant, or nurse follow up. This is important, not only to Motivate your patient to ACTION, but it will also serve you well in the risk management department.

PULLING IT ALL TOGETHER

None of us has a crystal ball. We don't know how our patients will use the gift of health and good appearance to create fulfilling lives for themselves and their families. We can't possibly know how one intervention might create a snowball reaction that will lead our patients to win the lottery or the Nobel Prize. One thing is certain, however. If you allow patients to leave without making every effort to Motivate them to ACTION, you haven't given them all you have to offer.

BOTTOM LINE

Inviting your patients to take ACTION is a combination of steps that helps patients to make positive decisions to follow through on your treatment recommendations. It involves applying The Four Languages of the M.A.D. Formula, The ACTION Formula, and specific scripts for discussing fees, handling objections, and following up with patients. While it takes a concerted effort on behalf of everyone involved, it will pay off in dividends by improving your practice revenues, your reputation, and your patients' lives.

Chapter 17

Who Else Can You Motivate?

NOW THAT YOU KNOW HOW to Motivate yourself, your partners, your staff, and your patients, who else shall we add to your list? How about referring colleagues, community leaders, and staff members of other healthcare providers with whom you interact? How about all of the potential patients out there whom you have yet to meet? What about family members and friends?

The truth is, you can use the strategies throughout Section Three to Motivate everyone you meet, and everyone you hope to meet. Rather than reiterate all of what you've already read, let me offer you some quick ideas to apply what you now know about Motivation in other areas of your business and your life.

Incorporate The Four Languages of The M.A.D. Formula into everything you write and say.

In Section Five, we'll discuss some specific strategies and techniques for marketing and Differentiating your practice. For the purposes of this discussion, just remember that every communication you make must target your audience and speak their language. The good news is, you now know all four languages! Make it a part of your everyday life. The more you use it, the more you will build trust and speak directly to the hearts and minds of the people you want to reach.

Remember: Be sure to spread lots of Chips wherever you go! People like to be around others who help them to feel good about themselves!

USE THE ACTION FORMULA EVERYWHERE YOU GO

Do you send thank you gifts to your referring colleagues and patients? Now do a little bit more:

Do some investigating, and find out more about their personal ACTION Formulas and then target your gifts to help them to reach their DESIRES or to break through RESOURCE or PERMISSION barriers. For example, let's say one of your best referring colleagues mentioned to you that she always wanted to learn to cook, but never had the time to do anything about it. You might hire a well-known chef to come to your colleague's home and prepare a meal, teaching as he cooks.

Assign someone in your practice to do some investigating by calling staff members from your referring practices. Tell them to be honest and explain that you are looking to give a special gift to their doctor and that you'd like to get a little personal information about the doctor.

Take some time when you're doing rounds to sit and talk with a hospitalist or floor nurse. Tell the person about The ACTION Formula and give a sample by asking a DESIRE question. Pay attention to the person's answers. Not only will you learn more about what kind of thank you gifts the person might appreciate, you'll also develop a different kind of connection that will go a long way toward the person being Motivated to do what you want him or her to do.

Your gifts don't need to be expensive, but the more personal they are, the more they will mean.

Remember, The ACTION Formula is a valuable tool to help you to analyze what is *blocking* Motivation. When people aren't doing what you want them to do, you can let it frustrate you to the point of distraction, or you can sit down with a legal pad and analyze the barriers to success by looking at each element of the formula. For example, let's say that you are the director of a research project in your hospital. You have 10 doctors involved in your research; and at first glance, they all look like competent people who should be able to get the job done. Yet, week after week, your numbers are falling short of where they could be. So you look at each doctor, one at a time, across the three components of The ACTION Formula, asking yourself these questions:

1. (DESIRE) Have I checked with each doctor to make sure the doctor understands what's in it for him or her to be involved in this project? Consider personal lives and how they would be affected positively.
2. (RESOURCES) What, precisely, does each doctor need in order to be able to fully participate in this study, and does each doctor have what he or she needs? Consider time, space, staffing, and supplies.
3. (PERMISSION) Are there any emotional barriers that would make any or all of the doctors unwilling to participate? Consider internal resentments, fear of failure, and even fear of success and the consequences that would come as a result.

Once you have determined what each doctor is missing, fix the problem yourself or partner together for complete success. Remember,

> **More often than not, Motivating people to ACTION means identifying and breaking through barriers so they are excited, able, and willing to do what you want them to do.**

WALK THE TALK

You can only influence people to the extent that your ACTIONS match your words. People trust you when you do what you say you're going to do, when you keep your promises, and when you practice what you preach. Now that you've finished this section, I invite you to go back to Chapter 13 and review Activity 13-1. The more you work your personal ACTION Formula, the more powerful you will feel, and the more Motivated you will be to help everyone else to get what they truly want and need.

BOTTOM LINE

All of the information in Section Three can be applied to help you to Motivate people inside and outside of your practice. The more you use these techniques, the more you will master them and the more success you'll build for your patients, your Team, and yourself.

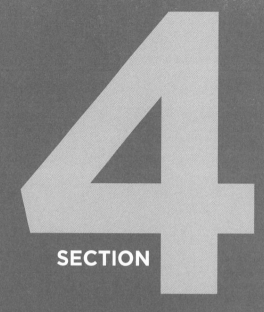

A is for Align

Chapter 18

The Power of Alignment

Align: To bring into cooperation or agreement; to adjust two or more elements to improve the relationship or function; to adhere to a prescribed course of action

HAVE YOU EVER SEEN a musical show or heard a symphony orchestra? Perhaps you sat in an auditorium proudly watching your child star in a school performance or took your family to see an elaborate show on Broadway. Maybe *you* had a role in a play, sang with a chorus, or played an instrument in a band. If you've had any of these experiences, you know that it takes a lot to put on a great show.

Imagine for a moment that your Team members were serving as the cast, crew, and orchestra in a musical show. What would their performance be like? Would the scenes run smoothly? Would all of the individuals behind the scenes, in the orchestra pit, and on the stage combine their talents to create a masterful piece of art? Would the chorus sing beautifully in synchronized harmony, or would one or more singers stick out sounding shrill or out of rhythm? Would each member of the orchestra come together to create a solid sound, or would the first violinist put down her bow because someone else got a better place in the spotlight? What would members of the audience say during intermission? Would they return to their seats for Act Two? Would they tell their friends about the performance, and if so, what would they say? Thumbs up? Thumbs down?

When we attend a performance, our experience as a member of the audience is based on a combination of factors, but the greatest impact will come from the skill of the director. It is the director's job to choose key personnel and work with them to create a product that sells tickets. The director must Motivate and guide all performers to give their best. And while each individual brings varying degrees of skill and talent, the director must help everyone to Align and perform as one unified ensemble. Our enjoyment of the show, and the reviews we give, will depend entirely on the ensemble's success at the hands of their director. Of course, all of that is made possible by the financial backing and support of the producers, who must be Aligned in their plan for the business so as to generate significant revenues and develop a solid reputation for excellence.

Let's run with this metaphor and look at three examples of how different levels of Alignment can affect the final product of a musical show. Then we'll look at how this fits for you and your practice.

Show #1

The producers can't agree on anything but saving money so they settle for an inexperienced director who is willing to take a low salary. They refuse to waste time with planning meetings or to spend money on advertising. They give him a minimal budget, instruct him to do his best, and head off to their favorite vacation spots for the winter.

The director takes the first 10 people who show up for auditions, holds a few rehearsals, tells everyone to learn their parts, belittles them when they make mistakes, and threateningly reminds them to "*Work hard and keep your personal problems to yourself.*"

On opening night, the house is one-third full—mostly friends and relatives of the performers. The orchestra begins, the stage crew forgets to open the curtain, and it goes straight downhill from there. The actors miss cues and skip entire pages of the script so that the storyline is soon lost. The chorus is out of synch with the orchestra. One of the dancers trips over another, causing a vaudeville-like moment during an otherwise serious scene. Soon everyone is off, singing notes that aren't particularly on key, trying desperately to make up for others' mistakes, and making it increasingly worse as they go. The ensemble's discomfort translates to the audience, and everyone finds the show painful to watch.

At the end of Act One, you bend down pretending to search for something while others put their hands together in obligatory applause. When the houselights go up for intermission, you walk out to the lobby and keep on going. You tell your friends to avoid the show, and they repeat the warning to their friends. The bad news spreads quickly throughout the community, and the show soon closes.

Show #2

The producers are smart enough to know what they don't know so they hire an experienced director and give him a fair salary with an incentive bonus for delivering a hit. They explain that despite the ailing economy, this show has to succeed. They give him a reasonable but inflexible budget, agree to do a bit of advertising on local radio, and promise to do more if the director proves that he can deliver.

The director recruits an experienced group of performers and brings them all together for a meeting. He hands out the scripts and tells them that he expects them to work hard as a team, be professionals, and build a good show. They rehearse nights and weekends; and while there is often someone missing or late, the director keeps on going, reminding them that they are professionals, that they are a team, and that they need to keep working hard to build a good show. He brings in a vocal instructor, an acting coach, a set design consultant, and a choreographer, and they all put their marks on the troupe. Their skills increase with each rehearsal, but they are too busy working hard to stop and notice.

A week before opening, the director hands a stack of flyers to the actors to put up throughout the community. The actors voice their objections saying this isn't part of their jobs, but he reminds them that they are a team and that they have to be professionals and work hard to build a good show.

Back in their dressing rooms, the actors complain about the cheap flyers, about not being appreciated, and about their inadequate exposure in the media; the musicians bicker about whether they are supposed to accelerate on measure 24 and wonder what's wrong with them that *they* weren't selected to hang flyers; and across the hall, the stage crew gossips about the prima-donnas who won't hang up the stupid flyers and about the self-centered musicians who leave empty cups and water bottles in the pit. All the while, the director sits alone in the theatre reviewing the budget, proud of the team he has built.

On opening night nearly all of the seats are filled. The orchestra begins, the curtain goes up, and the actors enter. The scenery is appropriately designed, and the dances are clean and well executed. The singers are accurate in their notes and rhythm, and the orchestra follows the conductor with precision. Everything is perfect . . . yet something is missing.

When you look closely, you realize that each individual is working hard and consciously thinking about his or her performance. Singers move their lips with flawless technique. Dancers take two steps stage left then turn on a dime and return precisely two steps back. The conductor raises his baton up on beat one, and down on beat three. The performers' smiles are pasted on and never falter as they sing and move on cue. It is a technically perfect performance, yet it is cold and distant. There is no passion in their music and no connection between the performers on stage or the people they seek to entertain. They earn your respect for their obvious skill, but they never get your heart. You applaud politely, and leave your program on the seat. The next morning at breakfast, you tell your colleagues that the show was OK, but not really worth the money.

Show #3

The producers have unflappable respect for each other's opinions, and chat amiably as they ride together to meet the director-candidate at their favorite restaurant. During dinner they explain their vision to produce a show that will go down in history as a profoundly important contribution to the arts. They ask for her input and are impressed with her ideas and her easy style. She seems to understand them completely, and the more they talk, the more it seems that they have known her forever. The producers look at each other and nod with a silent code of consensus, then tell the candidate that they are impressed with her credentials and vision. They trust her completely and give her the job with full freedom to follow her instincts and do what she thinks is best for the show. They give her a generous budget but offer her an incentive to bring in the show under budget. They promise to market the show using a variety of media, to be there if she needs them, and to stay out of her way so she can build their dream.

The director advertises for the specific types of people that she wants in her show; and when she has everyone selected, she brings them on a weekend retreat. She opens the retreat by explaining the producer's vision, adds her own, and then asks for input from her troupe about how they see each scene. She invites the orchestra members to brainstorm with the singers about how they can come together to build the musical plan, and facilitates their discussions so that everyone moves forward with positive energy and productivity. She works with the actors and helps them to see how their roles will merge with others to create a realistic story. She encourages everyone to identify and bring out their uniqueness, teaches them how to rehearse for maximum productivity, reminds them that every person is critical to the end product, and makes sure that everyone understands that while they have a huge responsibility to work hard, they should never get so serious that they forget to make it fun. They make a commitment to each other that they will give nothing less than their best and leave knowing that they are a part of something unusual.

In the weeks that follow, the director continues to mold the group into a solid product. They work hard at every rehearsal, but she always remembers to give Chips to all members of the cast, orchestra, and crew. She recruits the people who show natural leadership to Motivate the others and their enthusiastic efforts make it that everyone arrives each night on time and ready to go. She holds weekly meetings to celebrate their progress as a team and to give everyone notes on how they can improve for even greater success.

The night before the premier, the director invites the producers to watch the dress rehearsal. The producers arrive on time and sit quietly in the back. When the show ends they applaud with gusto and compliment the ensemble for all of the hard work and commitment they brought to the show.

On opening night, it is standing room only, and the orchestra is warming up. Media representatives have come to review the show and are whispering excitedly in anticipation.

The lights go down, the conductor raises his baton, and the performers take the stage as if they own it. The actors have amazing presence and deliver their lines with potent intention. The singers have mastered their craft so completely that they transcend technique and send out resonant sounds that seem to float on the music of the orchestra. Dozens of dancers swirl and move around the singers and actors. And as the orchestra builds to a huge crescendo, it seems as if they are all performing only for you. Their passion projects beyond the footlights and straight to your soul. You are mesmerized, completely unaware of the patrons sitting around you; and the effect leaves you breathless. When the performance ends, you jump to your feet, applaud wildly, and purchase the CD on your way out. You talk about it for weeks, telling everyone you know about the amazing ensemble, how wonderful they were, and about the impact they had on you personally.

So . . . How's *your* show doing?

THE PERFECT PRACTICE

Have you ever visited a practice that was completely Aligned? The doctors and staff were so synchronized you were completely unaware of phones ringing or other patients and were only aware that they were there to help you. From your initial inquiry call to the moment you picked up your prescription, it was a flawless experience. The doctors and staff seemed to enjoy their work and each other, and smiled easily when they spoke with their patients. All the while you were there you had a sense that they knew what they were doing, yet they didn't seem to be working as much as they were just moving together and talking with people. You felt safe enough to be vulnerable and comfortable enough to laugh. There was never a moment of doubt that each member of the practice was a part of a well-oiled machine, yet they were human and real and it felt good to be around them.

"That's what I want!"

Of course you do. Who wouldn't want to work in a practice that is filled with people you can count on to represent your vision and carry forward your mission and plan?

A well-Aligned Team finds innovative and creative solutions to keep your business growing, your patients well cared-for, and your environment positive and energized.

A well-Aligned Team helps each other to help their patients. They encourage each other to capitalize on their uniqueness as individuals, yet are so in synch that you can't tell where one begins and the other ends. A well-Aligned Team enjoys working together and is loyal to the practice.

A misaligned Team, on the other hand, can create problems. These problems can be as inconsequential as everyone in the office thinking it is someone else's turn to make the coffee or as dangerous as everyone thinking that someone else already gave the patients their medications. A misaligned Team can cause serious problems that could impact your patients, their families, and your practice.

A misaligned Team can cause damage to the reputation and revenues of the practice, as well as to the safety of patients and the Team itself.

If you do nothing else this year, I recommend that you make Team Alignment your number one priority.

The process of Alignment is much easier than you might think, regardless of whether you are starting from scratch with a new Team or realigning a long-standing Team. The first thing you need to know is

Team Alignment is different than Team building.

Team building is a powerful intervention that teaches people to put their individuality aside and assume like behaviors in the pursuit of a common goal. Team building is great for a temporary swell of activity when you have a special project like a large mailing or community event, but

The problem with the Team building approach is that it is temporary.

By design, the purpose of Team building is to ignore the individual's needs in the interest of the Team. Everyone walks together around a common idea, and the goal is to get everyone to walk in the same direction in the same way all the time.

In the real world, this is virtually impossible to sustain long term unless everyone on the Team is experiencing a common stressor, such as war, competitive sports, or a short-term event like an end-of-year push for increased sales.

The "all for one and one for all" mentality just doesn't hold up against the day-in, day-out reality of working in healthcare. Individual needs keep cropping up and inevitably become more important than the needs of the Team. The more individuals you have on your Team, the more often things crop up.

Where Team building yields a simple melody, Team Alignment creates a wealth of different notes and instruments, soft and loud, sharp and flat, brass and strings, all playing together in a perfectly synchronized symphony of sound.

Every instrument is strong enough to stand on its own, and while it may be spotlighted from time to time with a brief solo, it is at its best when harmonizing with all of the other instruments. Together they create a brilliance of artistry that no one can resist. That is Team Alignment.

> **Team Alignment enables all members of the Team to maximize their individuality and to fit their unique assets with every other individual in an intricately woven tapestry of strength that allows everyone to attain their individual goals while in pursuit of a common mission.**

Yeah, ok, that sounds great. But who has time for this?! First I have to Motivate them and now I have to Align them too? This is NOT what I signed on for. Besides, it sounds a little too touchy-feely for my tastes.

Think of it this way — employees are like teeth. They only will function effectively to the extent that they: (1) grow in the same direction; (2) fit together side-by-side; and (3) have an owner who pays attention to them individually and as a Team by getting in close every day to clean off any and all bacteria that has collected over time.

Team Alignment isn't about hugging and singing Kumbaya. It's about

- Using specific communication formulas that enable you to create a positive, productive and safe work environment;
- Building working relationships with staff, colleagues, and patients that are strong, durable, and rewarding;
- Having a workable plan to get you through normal day-to-day ups and downs and the inevitable bumps in the road;
- Knowing how to manage the "personal" in a field that strives for "professional";
- Identifying the barriers to your Alignment and knowing how to break through them;
- Capitalizing on your Aligned Teams to maximize your profitability;
- Minimizing stress and maximizing joy, and;
- Focusing on making a difference, instead of fighting to work out the differences.

Is it possible to have an Aligned Team? Absolutely, and I'm going to show you how. First, I'd like to highlight some truths you need to know about Teams so that you'll have a clear understanding of why it is such a critical piece of The M.A.D. Formula. Then, in the rest of Section Four we'll look at the specific formulas to make it happen. Once you apply these formulas, you and your Team will be able to consistently manage the inevitable challenge of working in tight quarters with other people while undergoing a constant barrage of ongoing demands from each other and the people you serve.

THE 10 TRUTHS ABOUT TEAMS

There are 10 general truths about healthcare Teams that you need to know before you can effectively Align your Team.

Truth #1: Misalignment can be very costly.

Permit me tell you a story that will explain why it may be in your best interest to Align your people.

Practice Spotlight

A large urology practice brought us in to facilitate an Executive Team meeting for their CEO, CFO, and 10 physician partners. During the course of our time there, we discovered that there were many unmet goals that had been set by the team in years past. As we explored the situation, we soon learned that disagreements among the partners had led to a history of long meetings where issues were continually put aside *"for further discussion."*

The CEO and CFO were aware of the problems, but they were being well-compensated and confessed that they were afraid to step on toes or rock the boat. So, in an effort to avoid a confrontation with the physicians, the CEO asked us to gather data regarding other avenues to increase their revenues.

As we worked our way through the practice, we began to see a trend. The staff members were huddled together in camps, angry at those who were outside their departments and particularly at the physicians for what they called *"mistreatment."* As we investigated further, we found the first of several problems:

Stuffed in the back of a cabinet were hundreds of unfiled Explanation of Benefit (EOB) forms dating back over the course of a decade. When we counted up the lost revenues, it represented hundreds of thousands of dollars.

When we asked the three employees what made them decide to cheat the doctors this way, one spoke for all of them, *"We were trying to make a point, but nobody ever said anything. After a while, it got to be a game — you know 'us against them.' Hey — they don't care what we do down here, so why should we care about them?"*

If this had been a one-time phenomenon, it would be bad enough. But this is only one example of the many ways we've seen doctors, employees, and patients respond when they aren't Aligned. It can be very costly.

Truth #2: The practice looks different depending on where you sit.

Any sports fan will tell you, the game looks different depending on where you sit in the stands. The further up you go, the broader your perspective, but the less you are able to make out the details without a powerful set of binoculars. Permit me to serve as your personal "binoculars," so that you can have a closer look at some of the trends I've seen while working with practices around the world.

In most practices, everyone works unaware of the realities of what others are experiencing.

Doctors are unaware that after completing an exam with a kind and respectful patient, the same patient turns around and treats the staff with rude and belittling behaviors. They don't realize that what they consider to be an analytical correction is often heard by their staff members as a harsh criticism. They don't notice that their failure to respond to a colleague's call can send a message that gets misinterpreted as disrespect.

Staff members are often surprised to hear that their doctors are overwhelmed by the sheer quantity of critical decisions that define their day-to-day existence. They hear their doctor's tone and assume anger when, more often than not, it's fear. They see a patient's cranky behavior as a reflection of their doctor's tardiness without ever considering that it may be a symptom of the patient's problem. Caught up in the stress of managing the nonstop demands of their own jobs, staff can lose sight of the problems of others or the impact they have on their patients and Teammates.

One of the best examples of perspective can be seen in this Practice Spotlight:

Practice Spotlight

We had returned for our onsite coaching for a facial plastics and aesthetics practice. With patient permission, we were video-taping initial consultations so that we could review the videos later for coaching.

The first patient went into the patient consultation room with the treatment coordinator and they completed her ACTION Formula interview. The treatment coordinator then came out of the room to inform Dr. A about the M.A.D. Characteristics of the patient so that he could go in prepared to flex his style to build rapid trust and rapport. Since this was relatively new to the Team, it took them eight minutes to talk this through. In the meantime, the patient was waiting in the room, and the camera was running the whole time. When Dr. A was up to speed, he and his nurse went in the room for the consultation.

At the end of the day, we reviewed the tapes. The Team had done a fabulous job of using the techniques, and we gave them lots of Chips. Then we showed them the first video, and the Team had a rare and valuable opportunity to see a piece of their practice through their patient's eyes.

We all sat quietly and watched the patient interview. Everyone applauded at the great job their treatment coordinator had done. We watched her exit the room, and then we watched the patient wait . . . and wait . . . and wait . . . They suddenly realized what had happened and wanted me to fast forward the tape, but I asked them to sit it out.

We all sat there staring at this patient for the entire eight minutes. Do you have any idea how long it really takes for eight minutes to pass? We watched her begin with a magazine, shift in her seat, check her watch, go back to the magazine, check her make-up, clean out her purse, check her watch, switch to a different chair, walk around, check her watch again, and on and on until everyone on the Team was squirming uncomfortably. Needless to say, Dr. A and his staff didn't like this view of their practice. They made a firm commitment that this would never happen again and talked together about how they would ensure this change would stick.

It's amazing what you can see when you have an opportunity to sit in a different part of the stadium.

Ironically, the people who have the best view of your practice are your patients. They hear you on the phone, sit in the reception area, walk your halls, and wait in non-soundproofed rooms; hearing, feeling, and seeing your practice from one of the highest points in the stadium. They don't catch all the details, but their vantage point gives them a wide perspective of your practice. They form an opinion of what they see and then, like the game of telephone, they spread what they've seen from friend to friend, each in turn embellishing and changing the story as they pass it on.

What are they saying about you? Are they talking about your impressive Alignment?

I am a strong believer in sitting in all areas of the stadium when we work with a practice. Through pre-training questionnaires, surveys of patients and referring colleagues, telephone interviews, and onsite observations, we can get a widely differing view. What fascinates me is that the patterns are always the same when a practice is misaligned.

The pattern goes like this: The first pre-training questionnaires to arrive are always "perky" and positive, with cute little smiley faces and easy-to-read handwriting. Typically from doctors and staff who have been with their practice for less than six months, these eager-beaver newbies are still working hard to learn their jobs and the people around them. They write comments like *"I'm looking forward to working with you," "I love my job,"* and *"I think everyone here is very nice."* It soon becomes clear, however, that they are still in the locker room and haven't made it out to where the action is.

As the veterans begin to fax their responses, we get a clear view from the field. Job descriptions are included, with passages circled with bold exclamation points and question marks written in. They add extra pages, providing details of the problems they see in their organization. They write statements like *"You said I should be honest, so here you go . . . ,"* or *"I don't know why you're coming — this place will never change,"* or *"We're good people, but we're understaffed, and we just haven't got the time to be nice."*

Just recently I received a response that said, *"We've had so many consultants over the years and nothing has ever changed. I'm afraid to get excited if I'm only going to be disappointed again."*

Administrative staff members write about clinical personnel and how they "mess up" schedules, fail to complete records, and get all of the doctors' attention. Clinical personnel write about their front desk and how they overbook patients, fail to call no-shows, eat in front of patients, talk about their boyfriends, and go out for too many smoking breaks. Employees in the front and the back describe moody doctors who come in late, miss meetings with partners, snap at patients and staff, and score poorly on key characteristics of leaders.

Of course, we ask doctors to complete questionnaires as well. While not all comply, those who do often use the opportunity to vent about partners and employees, and talk about how much they are looking forward to our coming so we can change everyone else.

Patient accounts and referring doctor surveys reflect wide ranges of perspectives depending on the frequency of contact with the practice, but if there is the least bit of misalignment it is always noted by these two groups.

At the top of it all is the administrator. He or she usually has the clearest perspective, able to see all areas of the practice. That said, from their box seats, administrators are still too close to the field to get the aerial view and are typically surprised when they see the aggregate results of their surveys.

The long and short of it all is simply this: in a misaligned practice, everyone is living in their own world, unaware of how they fit with or impact the others, or what they personally can do differently to meet the needs of their colleagues and patients.

Practice Spotlight

A group of five family practitioners hired us to conduct a Motivating Patients to ACTION program for their 55 staff members. The staff questionnaires reflected typical comments, while the doctors and practice administrator questionnaires were nondescript.

We asked the doctors and administrator to say a few words to launch the meeting. The administrator spoke of her excitement about the new system they were going to learn. Three of the doctors echoed her comments, the fourth said he thought it was good timing since he'd just joined the practice, and the eldest doctor said, *"Y'all better learn a lot 'cuz this is costing us a s*** load of money."* No one laughed.

As the morning began, the majority of staff members sat, arms folded, with pastries on top of their unopened workbooks. They wrote notes back and forth, rolled their eyes, and ran to the restrooms during interactive activities. At break, they went outside to smoke and were late to return. This was unusual, because we typically have Teams engaged and interacting from the very start of our programs.

At lunch, we told the doctors that we had some concerns about what was going on. Without exception, they told us they thought their staff members were thoroughly enjoying the program and that we were doing a great job.

After several attempts to engage the staff with no success, we decided to separate doctors from staff. When I had the staff alone, I asked them point blank what was going on. They unloaded a litany of complaints ranging from mild issues of miscommunication to serious allegations of harassment, negligence, and abusive behaviors. They spoke of one male doctor who would routinely walk into the ladies restroom and pull assistants out because they were needed to find charts or draw blood. They talked about having their purses searched because another doctor thought they had been stealing.

When I asked what made them stay in the face of all of this, they told me that the doctors had warned that they would be "blackballed" if they ever tried to leave. While there were significant differences in the problems cited by administrative and clinical personnel, they all agreed that the problems they were describing were too severe to ignore. While they varied in the degree to which they were willing to express their concerns, they unanimously reported that they would not change or learn any new systems until the doctors apologized for how they had behaved and agreed to change.

Meanwhile, on the other side of the building, Hal[1] was talking with the doctors and practice administrator, who were comfortably reiterating how pleased they were with our program. They reassured him that the staff worked well together and had no problems. One implied that the only problem they had was "a female thing" and went on to ask Hal about what made women who work together end up menstruating together. The female doctor was looking visibly uncomfortable as I walked in the room. I asked how things were going, and Hal filled me in.

I took a deep breath and gave them the news that their 55 staff members were launching a virtual mutiny and that they refused to budge

---

[1] Hal Dibner, PhD, my husband and business partner.

until the doctors heard them out. The doctors and administrator were visibly shocked to hear that their staff members were so "unhappy."

Needless to say, we dumped the Motivating Patients program and went to a Team Alignment program. There was a lot to discuss, and some significant changes had to be made. Of course, there were several different perspectives that had to be sorted through regarding the events that the staff members had described and somewhere in the middle of it all we found the truth. Once their perspectives were Aligned, they were able to put together a plan so that everyone's needs could get met. They left in a much better position for having found the courage to be honest.

Ironically, we never did the Motivating Patients program, but the Alignment of the Team was enough to double their gross revenues by the next year.

Sometimes the hardest part of my job is watching people, who have good intentions, learn the truth about how their intentions were missed through the smog of their behaviors. It never ceases to amaze me how so many people, who do so much good for so many people, could be so completely blind to their own impact.

Truth #3: There are Teams within Teams, and all Teams must be aligned.

In sociology, a group is defined as two or more people. I think of a Team in the same way. A Team can be a doctor and a patient, a doctor and working spouse, or all of the people in a multicampus hospital. When you Align your Team, it's important to look at your total Team as well as all of the combinations of Sub-Teams.

Practice Spotlight

After working together for more than ten years, the eight cardiologists were losing ground. Their revenues were dropping substantially, and when they looked at their reimbursements, it turned out that wasn't the problem. They had heard of some work we'd done with some of their colleagues, and they brought us in.

During my initial call with the practice administrator, I discovered that the practice was losing referrals to a competitor group. As the story unraveled, it turned out that there was a long history of toe-stepping and backstabbing that had led to an extremely high rate of turnover among staff and some very unhappy doctors.

When I asked the administrator to tell me about her perception of the doctors, she outlined a series of camps within the Executive Team. Dr. A, Dr. B, and Dr. C served together on the managing committee but Dr. C and Dr. A had some bad blood between them. Dr. D and Dr. E were best friends until Dr. E did something that Dr. D found morally unforgivable. Nowadays they barely spoke except to give reports after they had been on call. Dr. X had a problem with Dr. Y, and while he seemed to be OK with Dr. B, he would not allow Dr. Z to see any of his patients. The stories went on for two hours.

As she ran through the complex maze of politics describing a history of broken and reformed alliances, I typed furiously. When I read back to her everything she'd told me she burst out laughing and said *"it sounds like a soap opera!"*

She quickly backpedaled, and assured me that her doctors and staff were hard-working, dedicated professionals who did a great job caring for their patients and that there were only a few little problems that needed to get fixed. I reassured her that the only difference between her practice and the hundreds of others we'd seen was that her people were in a different building.

At the Executive Alignment Retreat, the doctors exchanged pleasantries and took their seats like errant children. Board-certified, accomplished professionals, they were understandably embarrassed that they had to call in consultants to help them unravel the mess they'd made.

Their situation was the result of three extremely common challenges:

1. Since it was an extremely busy practice with outreach to five different towns, there was never enough time to get together as a group and find solutions to problems as they occurred. This led to an accumulation and snowballing of issues that made everything seem overwhelming and insurmountable. They just needed a chance to talk it out, explain misperceptions, and apologize for all the unintended pain they'd caused.

2. They were all uncomfortable with confrontation and needed some basic skills that would allow them to get through it quickly while preserving each other's dignity.

3. They had a common tendency to point the finger at each other and to avoid personal accountability, and they needed a process that would allow for all parties to recognize how they'd contributed to any given situation so that it could get finished.

The partners were a solid Team when they left their retreat, and during our follow-up calls they reported great results. But that wasn't enough to increase their referrals. The problems among the partners had had a ripple effect that was far reaching.

There were problems among the employees, who battled with each other daily as they tried to please their doctors, each of whom had different requirements regarding how they wanted their rooms, their schedules, etc. The misalignment of the staff led to a perception by the patients and referring doctors that the practice wasn't "friendly" or "organized" and led to a steady stream of resignations among staff members.

The hospital complained about the practice's "customer service" as hospital-employed Physician Assistants and Hospitalists waited end-lessly for pages to be returned and patients to be seen in the ER. This misalignment led the hospital to start paging "the other guys" instead.

While each doctor individually had built strong Alignments with his or her individual patients, the doctors did not speak well of each other to their patients, so patients were adamant about wanting to see their "own doctor." This misalignment put a tremendous strain on each partner to work long hours, left many patients having to wait unneces-sarily to get the care they needed, and led a few patients to litigation because they believed they were being maltreated when a different doctor changed their medication or treatment plan and their primary doctor told them it had been a bad decision.

All of this combined to create a situation where every day the practice lost more and more market share to a group that was far less experi-enced or equipped to handle the cases that these doctors could do.

Every Team was misaligned, and the only way to get the practice to grow was to work one Team at a time and then put them all back to-gether again. We got it done, but the amount of money it cost the practice in lost referrals, lost employees, and increases in malpractice premiums would take years to recoup.

Truth #4: Just because your Team "works well together," does not mean they are Aligned.

In an Aligned practice, all members share an identical vision, complimentary perspectives, and coordinated processes for communication. They openly discuss any challenges that keep them from comfortably and efficiently performing their jobs and follow agreed upon formulas to avoid or resolve any conflicts that may arise. They work without threats and know how to manage stress and difficult situations. If a new person comes onto the Team, everyone works to make sure he or she is brought into the fold and understands not only the job, but the mission and the process of the Team.

> ### A Team who works well together but isn't Aligned may be just as productive as an Aligned Team, until there is some disruption or change to the status quo.

All it takes to rattle an unaligned Team is a change to the status quo, such as a move to another office, the introduction of electronic medical records, a shift in focus or addition of new services or specialties, switching from insurance-based to cash-pay, the exit of a beloved teammate, a new practice administrator, or the incorporation of one or more new employees or doctors. Without Alignment skills, the people who "work well together" flap around like fish out of water.

Practice Spotlight

Three dentists and their Team of 17 employees had worked well together for 20 years when the eldest decided it was time to retire. The exit of the eldest was very sad for the Team, as he had been a mentor to the other two doctors and a beloved leader to the employees.

The elder's departure was soon eclipsed by the recruitment of the young, handsome, energetic Dr. A who had been practicing in a nearby city. Everyone was friendly to Dr. A, but left him on his own to get settled while they focused on the task of alerting patients about the retired partner, finding an assistant for Dr. A, and running the day-to-day operations of a busy practice.

Approximately two years later, the practice contacted us regarding a Motivating Patients to ACTION program. As I spoke with the treatment coordinator, I heard something in her voice that led me to ask whether the members of her practice were open to change. She admitted that they were "*pretty stubborn about change*" and that they were having "*a few problems.*" I told her that I thought it would be a waste of their time and money to force people to learn and install a new system of working with patients before they got all of their own people in Alignment. She agreed and we made plans for a Team Alignment program.

The Team arrived to their retreat and everyone was in high spirits. They walked in the room laughing and kidding around with each other with the comfort and familiarity of a group that had been working together for more than two decades. And then there was Dr. A and his assistant. While they joked with everyone else on the Team, they sat at the edge of the U-shaped table, slightly apart from the others. At lunch they did the same thing, choosing seats that kept them apart from the rest of the group.

When the trend continued into the second day, we brought it up to the Team. The chatter stopped and everyone froze. The practice administrator flushed red, and one of the other doctors tilted his chair back far from the table. No one spoke. One of the assistants got a tissue out and started to blot her eyes while others shot side glances across the room.

As the stories unfolded, we learned of a series of minor miscommunications that had led the older members of the Team to make false assumptions about Dr. A and his assistant. This in turn led Dr. A to perceive that he was being rejected and that no one wanted him there. He subsequently created a wall between himself, his partners, and the staff. The only one who he felt safe with was his assistant, a Commander who was glad to keep it all business. The problem was that he was an Enthusiast who needed the interaction of friends and laughter.

In addition to the problem with Dr. A, there were Team members who were still sad for the loss of the elder doctor. They were holding on to the "old ways" that the doctor had used when he ran the practice and were resisting the new senior partner's attempts to make improvements in the business.

Another of the staff members was spearheading a massive campaign to help the practice to become 100% Occupational Safety and Health Administration (OSHA) compliant. She was very proud of what she was doing there, but felt that the other members of the Team were ridiculing her and were slow to comply with new procedures and protocols.

Another staff member had experienced some problems at home and had never told any of her Team members. They knew she was acting strangely, but figured she was mad at them for something.

Another staff member came up to us during a break and asked us to talk to her coworker because she was afraid that there was something really wrong but didn't know how to approach her. As it happened, there was a serious physical problem that had been developing that was causing her to behave differently, but everyone had ignored it because they didn't want to embarrass her by mentioning anything.

The vicious circle of false assumptions, inaccurate conclusions, and lack of effective communication had created a complicated web that was seriously interfering with the Team's ability to move forward.

How does it happen that so many small (and not-so-small) events could cascade into such a crippling situation?

This leads us to Truth #5.

Truth #5: A tiny splinter can handicap the strongest person and destroy a Team.

You're sitting on your deck, enjoying a beautiful spring day. You pop off your shoes and lean back to rest when the phone rings. As you jump up to grab the phone you pick up a little splinter in your foot. It pinches for a second but you forget about it as you get involved with the details of your call. By the time you get back inside, you can't see the splinter. You know it's in there, but you can't find it. *Oh well,* you think to yourself, *it'll work its way out,* and you go on about your day.

A few days go by, and the cells around the splinter begin to rebel against the presence of this strange entity. Little by little, infection sets in, and you begin to notice a strange little pain on the bottom of your foot. You've long forgotten about the splinter, and you can't imagine why your foot hurts. You inspect it, but it just looks a little red. *Well, if it keeps up I'll have someone look at it.*

A few more days go by, and now you find that putting weight on your foot causes it to hurt even more. You begin to favor the foot with a limp. By the end of the day, you have a backache from forcing your body to walk out of its normal alignment. You resolve to see someone about this tomorrow.

When you call for an appointment, you discover that the first chance you can get in will be on Monday . . . three more days. *OK, it'll be fine.*

Over the weekend, you continue to favor your sore foot as the muscles in your back spasm even more. Now you have a terrible headache, and your vision is slightly blurred from the tension. You can't stand it any more. You find a tranquilizer that you had left over from whatever-that-was, and you take it. The muscles relax. But so do you, and you're down for the count. You sleep all afternoon, and on into the night, missing the banquet where you were supposed to present the Chairman of the Board of your hospital with her Lifetime Achievement Award. Fast asleep, you never hear the phone ring.

The next morning when you awaken, your foot still hurts, and you hobble over to your computer to check your email. There in your inbox is an email where the subject line reads "Don't Bother." When you open it up, the message says "to come in on Monday."

All of this because of a tiny splinter.

At any moment, someone, somewhere in your practice could pick up a tiny splinter. The type of splinter and the degree to which that splinter grows into a full-fledged infection will depend on a number of factors, all of which we'll go over in Chapters 19–21. For now just know that the solution is to provide a simple process for reporting and removing splinters before they cause permanent damage, and make sure everyone knows how to use it now, before they need it.

Practice Spotlight

He had written several text books, mentored hundreds of students, and saved countless lives in the OR. This brilliant vascular surgeon was widely revered for his hands and his attention to detail. His patients loved him, but his partners? Not so much.

There was no question that he was a good doctor and a good man. But he had developed what his senior partner called *"an attitude problem."* Dr. J did not play well with the other children. We filed that for future reference and flew in to conduct the Executive Team meeting, the purpose of which was to facilitate the process of setting goals and a plan of ACTION for a practice-wide customer service program.

As we sat talking with the group of surgeons, we watched Dr. J carefully. He had a quick mind and a big heart, yet something wasn't quite right. When I was presenting, he was engaged and offered outstanding ideas in response to my questions.

I gave the partners an activity to begin outlining the plan and the partners launched into it. As they were strategizing and brainstorming, however, Dr. J sat quietly and stared into space. His face was beet red and his hands were locked so tightly that his fingers were starting to turn white. We let this go for a bit to see where it would go. The doctors finished the activity and had come up with a plan, except Dr. J had never offered an opinion and had never been invited to do so by the others.

We asked for Dr. J's opinion on the plan, and he went from 0 to 90. His explosion was large and loud, filled with accusations and anger. The chain reaction was immediate, as the entire group lashed back with everything they'd never said but had clearly been thinking for some time. The next few hours were like a scene on a football field where 22 men are crumpled up on top of each other and the referees are methodically unraveling the heap of men to find the little pigskin at the bottom.

In this case, the pigskin was a broken promise. The doctor had been promised that he would be the head of a lab, but soon after he took that on, the job was taken away and given to someone else. Regardless of whether the decision was a good one for him and for the overall practice, the bottom line was that he was disappointed by the decision and angered by what he perceived to be a broken promise.

The initial splinter festered and led him to develop the "attitude" that subsequently led to a set of behaviors that were destructive to his image and that of the group. Dr. J was a member of the group, but he had nothing to do with the group. He did his own thing and presented frequent demands for changes to policy and procedures to accommodate his personal needs. No one ever doubted his dedication to his patients or his incredible expertise as a surgeon. But he wasn't Aligned with the rest of his partners, and they began to resent his rogue style. The employees of the practice and referring colleagues began to complain about his behaviors, although his medical assistant defended him as the *"best doctor they had."* Several times they thought about breaking up the partnership because of the damage that had been done to the trust, and Dr J discussed it regularly with his wife. He didn't want to stay where he wasn't wanted, but they really didn't want to pack up and start all over again.

They got it worked out, and the practice was able to continue to benefit from his lifesaving hands. But the scar tissue from that initial splinter still aches every now and then and requires brief interventions.

Please remember, splinters are typically nothing more than a nuisance, but can be deadly if left untreated for extended periods of time.

Truth #6: Beneath the credentials, titles, job descriptions, lab coats, blazers, and scrubs are real people who have real needs and real feelings.

Everywhere we go, we hear doctors and administrators preaching variations of the healthcare mantra: *"Personal and professional don't mix. Leave your personal feelings at the door."* At the risk of opening a can of worms, where exactly do you draw the line between personal and professional?

You are entitled to run your practice in whatever way you see fit. I would only invite you to stop a moment, think about a few facts, and then draw a clear line wherever you think it belongs. Here are some things to think about:

- I've seen plastic surgeons who in an effort to block their own feelings, lost the ability to recognize the emotional pain of their prospective patients. This led them to dismiss and discount problems that their patients perceived to be serious enough for intervention. They simply didn't see the effect these "minor" blemishes had on the patients' self-esteem.

- I've seen dental hygienists who were so busy trying to be "perky and pleasant," they were oblivious to their patients' anxieties and discomfort, causing them to miss opportunities to make hygiene an easier and welcomed experience for their patients.
- I've seen pediatric oncologists who blinded themselves to their patients' pain because they themselves couldn't handle it, leaving their patients' feeling alone, scared, and misunderstood.
- Feelings are your brain's natural way of alerting you to *danger*. If you force yourself to ignore your feelings, you will also lose your ability to rapidly distinguish when something is wrong.
- Feelings are also your brain's natural way of alerting you to *pleasure*. If you force yourself to ignore your feelings, you will also lose your ability to rapidly distinguish when something is good for you, your Team, or your patient.
- If people are encouraged to "keep their personal things to themselves," you may never learn when things need to be addressed in your practice.
- If you choose "not to feel" or to "turn off your emotions," then you will literally have to block off the part of your brain that experiences emotion. While many have been able to accomplish this, they didn't anticipate the side effect: **When you shut off your feelings, you stop feeling *everything***. That leads to an inability to appreciate success or care about problems. You can become clinically depressed and make no efforts to change or enjoy your practice or your life.

Healthcare is filled with passionate, caring people who have been trained not to get involved with each other or their patients but rather to remain "friendly but distant." There are some real problems that come with this:

- Patients don't like distance. They want to know that their healthcare providers feel sorrow in the face of their pain and joy in their recovery. They want to know a little bit about the people they depend on. They want their healthcare staff and providers to know them as more than a patient ID number. In addition to care, they want relationships.
- Employees don't like distance. Longevity and loyalty come in response to a deep connection with fellow employees and doctors. This can only happen when they develop friendships and connections with each other. When employees are taught not to feel, they are taught not to care.
- Doctors *act* like they like distance. But from the thousands with whom we've spoken, it turns out they would really like to be able to find the gray area so they can enjoy their partners, patients, and employees more fully and still have something left to bring home to their families at the end of the day.

In your efforts to clean your workplace of the "personal," have you thrown out the baby with the bathwater? Could you build better loyalty, longevity, and commitment among your Teams if you were just a little less formal and a little more "real?" Could your build better Alignment with your patients if you were a little freer to feel and properly express emotion? What would happen to your reputation if all who crossed your path felt comfortable being "themselves" in your presence?

Practice Spotlight

After an Executive Team Alignment with five gastroenterologists; a Leadership Team Alignment with the practice administrator, doctors, and department heads; and a third session with all of the physician assistants, it was time to get the entire practice together for their customer service training.

It was a combination pep rally and training session and the energy in the room was sizzling as each of the Leadership Teams got up in front of the room and talked about what they'd learned in their sessions. Everyone was involved, taking notes and enthusiastically participating in the activities. We were heroes. And then came lunch.

Somewhere between the salad and the brownies, I got pulled away by a group of staff members who wanted to tell me "the truth" about their practice. There was nothing I hadn't heard, but I was surprised that they felt reticent to bring these challenges to their doctors. When I asked them, one responded, *"He'd never understand. He's got it made. It's not like he's got problems like we've got."*

I shifted gears and moved everyone into a huge circle of 100+ people. For the next two hours, we went around the room and asked each and every member of the practice to finish this sentence: *"Between the time I wake up and the time I get to work, I . . ."*

Some of the stories were funny, others were serious, but everyone told their story honestly. No one hogged the floor. In fact, most people were a little skittish about having the spotlight on them. But each took his or her turn, gaining courage from those who had gone before, and the time flew by.

Without exception, every employee described a full-time job at home as well as at work. Some had young children, others had aging parents, but everyone had someone who depended on them. No one told stories of *being* taken care of, but only of caring for others. Single mothers talked about holding down second jobs or going to school at night, several spoke about how their spouses worked different shifts and how they never saw each other but for brief moments as they passed the baton for their children's care. Some were battling chronic pain, two were battling breast cancer, and others had debilitating disorders. Not one person in that room reported that they got more than five hours of sleep per night during the week.

When it came to be Dr. A's turn to speak, he told his Team that he felt guilty that his life was so much easier than everyone else's. His ultra-Enthusiast medical assistant turned quickly and said *"Are you KIDDING?! I wouldn't trade my life for yours! You have everything on your shoulders: the patients, us, the business, the hospital, not to mention your wife and kids. We've got it SO much better than you."*

Everyone applauded and Dr. A sat down, profoundly moved.

At the end of the day, when we did our debriefing session with the doctors, they all agreed that those two hours were the best they'd ever spent as a Team.

If you want your Team to enthusiastically embrace their jobs and Align with others to create a powerful force that can handle anything that comes its way, you have to encourage them to be real. You can teach them where to draw the line, but I strongly recommend that you avoid black and white statements or you will lose the richness of the rainbow that is available to you from and with your people.

Truth #7: A mission of many is more powerful than a vision of one.

If you browse the Internet and look at the Web sites of different healthcare practices, you will find a wide variety of mission statements. Some talk about being "patient-centered" while others commit to "state-of-the-art" treatment. Some mission statements read like bumper stickers, while others look like carefully crafted reflections of someone's vision. Some were written by doctors, others by administrators, and others by outsiders, hired to do the job on behalf of the Team. The more closely you look at these things, the more you can tell which are real and which are manufactured, which describe what the practice actually does, and which speak about the practice's ideal.

Do you have a mission statement? And, if so, who wrote it and what do you suppose your Teams think of it?

What do your patients think of it? How about your colleagues and referral sources? Do any of them comment on how "it spoke to them" in some way?

What do *you* think of your mission statement? Does it propel you out of bed, exciting and enticing you to bolt enthusiastically out your door into torrential rain at 5:00 o'clock in the morning?

When I wrote the mission statement for my business, I wrote it for myself. It was designed to help me to stay positive in the face of long travel days, and hotel beds that went *klumph* when I sat down. Then one night, as I stretched across three chairs in an airport terminal watching the snow fall and praying that my little bag of trail mix would last until they reopened the airport, I knew I needed something to remind me that I was doing this for more than the money. So, I took out a pen and, on the back of my itinerary, I wrote the following:

> **Our mission is to make an impact on every life we touch by moving people to ACTION. We accomplish this mission by providing the necessary knowledge, skills, and insights that enable people to take control of their lives. It is our hope that by helping others to grow, they will in turn make a positive impact on every life they touch.**

It got me through that night and every night since for the past 20 years.

I have had many moments throughout my career when I have thought *"I can't believe they actually give me money to do this! This is so much fun!"* But, like every professional, I've also had moments when I thought, *"they're just not paying me enough to do this."* My mission statement always gets me through those moments. Does yours?

Ask your staff to tell you the mission of your practice, and watch the deer-in-headlights expression on their faces. If it weren't so sad it would be kind of comical.

Once I asked the practice administrator of an inpatient rehabilitation center if she thought they were enacting their mission statement. Her precise words were, *"Oh yeah, I've been meaning to look at that thing. Is it still hanging in the lobby?"*

Part of the process of Team Alignment is to get everyone behind your mission. Sometimes that's a simple matter of sitting down and talking it through to make sure that every individual interprets the message such that they: (1) understand it; (2) are Motivated by it; and (3) are able to enact it every day.

Every one of your employed Sub-Teams need a mission statement, in addition to that of the full Team.

I always urge my clients to come together to create a Team mission statement that may, or may not, serve as the practice mission statement as well. When that happens, the result is electric.

Practice Spotlight

Here are some mission statements that were written by Teams after their Alignment workshops. The cool thing about them is that every single member of the Team participated in the creation of their mission statement.

1. General Dentistry: One Doctor, Spouse Practice Administrator, and Full Team

   Our mission is to help people to improve their lives by enhancing their smiles.

   We accomplish our mission by carefully, kindly, and conscientiously providing excellence in dentistry while we connect to our patients, ask questions, respect their time, share thoughts and opinions, and help our patients to enjoy the personal changes that come as a result of achieving good dental health.

   It is our hope that by using a Team approach to helping others, we will provide artistic and creative solutions that allow each of us, and every single patient, to feel the freedom that comes from getting what we all truly want.

2. Cardiology: Three Doctors and Full Team Mission Statement

   Our mission is to deliver the highest quality medical care to the community in an environment that is safe, calming, nurturing, and supportive both to our patients and ourselves. We do this by listening, learning, showing respect, smiling, and enjoying what we do. By doing this we make a positive difference in people's lives and we show our appreciation for our patients, ourselves, and our community.

3. Orthodontics: Three Doctors and Full Team

   Our mission is to make a difference by creating customized smiles that our patients can be proud of for the rest of their lives.

   We accomplish our mission by applying 400 years of combined experience in world-renowned techniques of orthodontics, by taking pride in discovering and developing the uniqueness of each and every patient, by believing in the skill and dependability of our Team, and by never taking shortcuts.

It is our hope that by staying loyal to each other and our patients, we will continue to know the pride and excitement, the laughter and security, and the self-satisfaction that comes from spending every day amazed by the joy that we bring to every life we touch.

4. Gastroenterology: Five Doctors and Leadership Team Mission Statement

Our mission is to inspire every associate of our practice to feel an ever-increasing excitement as a successful part of our Team and to walk beside them as we build our self-worth together.

We accomplish our mission by consistently modeling the actions we request of others, encouraging them to adopt these behaviors in all they do, and offering recognition for their efforts and achievements.

It is our hope that by providing the best possible care to our associates, we will feel the pride and joy that comes from knowing we've created a unique environment in which we can all feel special.

Truth #8: Transference is alive and well and living in your practice.

In psychoanalytic theory, transference is defined as "an unconscious redirection of feelings or thoughts about one person to another." Theory proposes that, when we see someone in our present who does something that in some way reminds us of someone or something from our past, we respond in the present *as if* we were with the person from our past.

As it turns out, this theoretical construct is more real than you might think and refers not only to people who sat on the psychoanalytic couch of Dr. Freud, but to people who are sitting right there in your reception area, your exam rooms, your operatories, your call centers, your board meetings, and your morning huddles. Transference is real, and you need to know how to recognize it before it shoots your Team out of Alignment.

Here's an example:

One of your most dependable staff members is sitting at her station scanning pages into electronic patient records. You come up and ask from your Analyst State of Mind, *"Do you have any idea when you'll be done here? I need you to do something for me."* She turns in her seat and lashes out at you *"I'm going as fast as I can!"* Clearly, something isn't right here, so you invite her into your office.

You offer her a seat and you lean against your desk right in front of her. She looks up at you and tears well up in her eyes as she yells, *"I work so hard and you never notice. Nothing I do is good enough for you!"*

You are surprised at the response. It seems totally out of proportion to the situation and you can't imagine where it came from. You respond with the statement you learned at a seminar you went to years ago, *"OK, Mary, maybe we need to take a few deep breaths and then we'll talk about this."* It doesn't take long before you discover that this particular technique wasn't all it was cracked up to be. She gets up and runs from the room.

What happened? You have just been the recipient of transference. For whatever reason, you remind Mary of someone from her past (who may or may not still be in her life). This person may have been difficult to please, someone who withheld praise, or a thousand other possibilities. Twenty years later, Mary finds herself in a stressful job and puts the face of the other person onto you. She does everything she can to win your approval and recognition, unconsciously trying to get you to make up for what she never got from the other person — acknowledgement and pride.

Of course, there's no way you can ever make up to her for what she wanted from someone else. But your "failure" catches up to you, and she lashes out at you with the words she never got to say to the original person.

STOP! This is MUCH too weird. Are you telling me all of my people are whackos?!?!

No. I'm telling you all of your people are normal. Oh . . . and you probably do it too.

> ### Practice Spotlight
>
> Tom received a promotion and took over as the new department head for the hospital blood bank. He had worked hard for this and was proud of his achievement. Tom was the most experienced person in the department, and it made perfect sense to everyone that he would get the job. So it was confusing to him when Sue gave him the cold shoulder every time he asked her to do anything.
>
> The tension between Tom and Sue started to affect the others in the department, and even people who dropped in knew something wasn't right. Pretty soon, the gossip mill took over, and the administrator decided it was time for an intervention.

During the course of our discussions with the Team, we asked everyone for input regarding the source of the problems. They all pointed at Sue, but she denied any problem at all.

On a hunch, I asked her to tell us who Tom reminded her of from her past. At first she couldn't think of anyone, and then suddenly she started laughing and laughing. Sue had a contagious kind of laughter and pretty soon everyone was laughing, even though no one knew why they were laughing. As she wiped her eyes and caught her breath, she told the group what was going on.

I have a twin brother. I was always the good kid, doing all my homework, making my bed, and getting good grades. I never gave my parents any trouble. But my brother, he was a terror. He copied my homework and got detention at school when he got caught. He was always causing my parents problems, and they always laughed it off saying he was just being a boy.

When we turned 16, my parents bought us a car to share. They kept the keys and we had to come to them for permission to drive it. The thing is, they always gave the car to him. It didn't matter how good I was or how hard I worked at school or helped around the house, he ALWAYS got the keys. They said a boy needed a car more than a girl because he had to pick up his date and I could go with my friends. It seems like the only time I ever got to drive the stupid car was when my mom needed something at the store. "You're a much better shopper than your brother!" OH that made me SO mad.

No one spoke. She just looked all around the room at her Teammates and finally locked eyes with Tom.

OK, here's the thing. I really wanted that job. And when you got it, maybe I was a little jealous but I really am happy for you, and I do think you deserve it. I guess it was just the car all over again.

I'm not suggesting that you walk around asking everyone to share all of their potty training foibles with you. I do think it's important to be aware of this, however, since it will go a long way to help you to make sense of a lot of what happens in your practice.

Remember: it isn't your job to make up to people for all of the experiences they had before you ever met. I do think it's the job of every leader to be sensitive to the fact that everyone has someone who did them wrong at some point in their life, and that they bring that baggage with them when you let them into your practice.

Truth #9: The most productive Teams have common objectives but not necessarily common methods for their attainment.

One of the biggest complaints we hear from doctors and their staff concerns the differences in work styles that they see among their Team. Staff members complain that the doctors have different requirements for everything from room setup to which vitals they want. Doctors complain because staff members work at different speeds, have a different touch when handing over instruments, and a different way of dealing with their unique "quirks."

Team Alignment does not require that everyone do everything precisely the same way.

In fact, depending on the job, sometimes requiring all employees to do things the same way is not the best plan because it forces everyone to go outside the boundaries of where they would naturally be most effective. I recommend that you map out the work styles of all Team members and then match those who have similar work styles so that they can work closely together in Sub-Teams in a fashion similar to "PODs[2]." Depending on the size of your practice, you might have any number of Sub-Teams in both administrative and clinical areas.

Another solution for Team Alignment of work styles is to create a list of doctors' style requirements so that staff members can easily access it as a reference and post the list in plain vision in administrative and clinical areas. For the details of how to make all of this work, I refer my clients to my colleagues who specialize in the operational side of practice management. My role is to make sure you understand the truth of what happens when you try to fit a square peg into a round hole and make them work together. You end up consuming massive amounts of chocolate, alcohol, or whatever your particular vice may be. Which leads us to our final truth:

Truth #10: Everyone has a glass; and no matter how big or small it is, it takes only one drop of water to make it overflow.

Just as a chain is only as strong as its weakest link, a Team is only as strong as its most stressed-out member. By definition, healthcare is a stressful profession, and while the people who are attracted to work in the field tend to be stronger and more resilient than the average run-of-the-mill, umm, consultant, the fact is that everyone has a limit. Do Activity 18-1, and you'll get a precise understanding of what is going on in your practice.

[2] A POD is typically defined as a Team of clinical (and often administrative) personnel who are assigned to work exclusively with one doctor for a given shift or on a full-time basis, but PODs can be clinical/administrative, all clinical or all administrative.

ACTIVITY 18-1. Understand the Stress of Healthcare

Take a glass of water and fill it to the brim. Carefully put it on the counter and then, using a water dropper, place one drop of water at a time into the glass. Every time you think it is going to over flow, you'll find there is room for just one more little drop.

After a few rounds of this, you might start to get a little cocky, putting the drops in faster, virtually daring the glass to overflow.

Then suddenly, with no warning at all, you'll put in another drop, looking no different than any drop that came before, but this time the glass will overflow all over your counter, your floor, and your brand new designer shoes.

That is the stress of healthcare.

Being aware of stress, and knowing how to relieve it before it impacts your practice, is the responsibility of every member of your Team. Generating a Team plan for how to avoid, manage, and resolve stress is one piece of getting your Team Aligned.

WHAT DO YOU DO WITH ALL THESE TRUTHS?

It's a strange phenomenon, but often I find that when leaders understand these 10 truths, they have a paradigm shift and their practice immediately starts to change in response. Nevertheless, you have to make a concerted effort to Align a Team, and there are dozens of strategies and formulas to make that happen. It may seem a bit overwhelming at first glance, but it's really only a matter of making a commitment to address the key elements of Alignment.

While you may not be ready to address every element today, the more elements you integrate into your practice, the closer you'll be to attaining a practice that will give you precisely what you want. How can I know that? Because the practice will be directed by you! As the director, you get to choose which elements to focus on in any given quarter, which Team members need more coaching, and who are your stars. As the director of Alignment, here are the elements you'll need to work into your plan:

THE SIX ELEMENTS OF TEAM ALIGNMENT

Element #1: Clear Communication

All members of the Team communicate in a manner that ensures they understand and are understood by every other member of the Team.

Element #2: Team Trust

There are strong levels of trust between and among Sub-Teams.

Element #3: Common Mission

Every member of the Team (and potentially each Sub-Team) works together to build their own mission statement and has a plan for the enactment of their mission over time.

Element #4: Coordinated Individuality

There is a process for getting the most out of every person on the Team by identifying and coordinating differences in individual work styles so that you are able to maximize the assets of your individuals and create Sub-Teams who enjoy each other and achieve maximum productivity.

Element #5: Conflict Circumvention

There is a concrete plan in place to encourage Team members to manage and resolve internal and external conflicts.

Element #6: Sustained Energy

A clear commitment is made to apply strategies to manage stress and sustain a positive and energized environment for all Sub-Teams and the Team as a whole.

Chapter 19 gives you the strategies and formulas to address Elements 1 through 4, Chapter 20 will show you how to manage conflict and difficult emotions, and Chapter 21 provides a plan to keep your practice moving forward in the face of constant change. Once you have the basic elements in place, you'll be ready to focus on your Sub-Teams, so Chapter 22 provides key tactics to help you to Align with patients, and Chapter 23 focuses on the other Sub-Teams of your practice so you can direct them all in a symphony of Alignment and strength. When you have addressed each element throughout your Team, you will know the joy of synchronicity and synergy, and the word will spread about the magnificent ensemble that you direct. Imagine the thrill of your audiences (patients and colleagues), the pride of your performers (doctors and staff), and the delight of your producers (Executive Team)! Lights . . . camera . . . ACTION . . . it's show time!

BOTTOM LINE

Every healthcare practice is composed of a combination of Teams within Teams, all of which need to be aligned. Unlike Team building, which discourages individuality in pursuit of a common goal, Team Alignment is a process in which individuals are encouraged to maximize their unique assets while in pursuit of a common goal. Team Alignment requires the application of formulas that streamline communications and maximize productivity while creating a professional environment that honors the human condition. This, in turn, creates an ongoing atmosphere of trust and loyalty that provides a consistent stream of referrals and satisfied patients.

Chapter 19

Orchestrate Your Alignment

BEFORE YOU CAN FULLY Align your Team, you need to make it clear who is *on* your Team!

Begin by asking yourself one question:

Who is affected by, and has an affect on, our practice?

Once you have that figured out, diagram it. Here is an example of a typical healthcare Team diagram:

In this example, there are 10 Sub-Teams, which together form Team 1, aka The Practice. While each Sub-Team stands alone, it may interact or overlap with any or all of the others. The more interaction there is between and among Sub-Teams, the more important it is to define the dynamics of your

Team and address the Alignment elements. What does *your* Team look like? Do Activity 19-1 and define your Team.

ACTIVITY 19-1 Define Your Team		
Create a diagram of your Team. Begin with Team 1 (The Practice), and then add in all the Sub-Teams that define your practice.		
Next to each Sub-Team, write in the benefits of getting them fully Aligned internally and with the other Sub-Teams. I'll start you off with some ideas.		
SUB-TEAM	**BENEFITS OF ALIGNMENT**	
Executive Team	Common vision for practice More productive meetings Shorter meetings! Reduced conflict Improved image Increased likelihood of attracting potential partners	Increased likelihood of shared responsibility for practice and patient management Increased trust Improved patient care Increased referrals Increased revenues
Administrative Team	Improved work flow Improved morale Improved impact on patients Increased productivity Increased creativity	Reduced stress Reduced mistakes Reduced turnover Fewer sick days Reduced resistance to change
Clinical Team		

Now that you've diagramed your Team, make sure all of your Sub-Teams get a chance to see it. Consider hanging a copy in your reception area to show your patients that you consider them a part of your Team, and then start working the Elements of Alignment.

Let's start with Element #1.

ELEMENT #1: CLEAR COMMUNICATION

You will never be able to form Alignments unless everyone is able to deliver a message and know that it will be received precisely as it was intended.

Here are some tips to help you to ensure that your communications flow smoothly on a consistent basis.

Step 1: Eliminate Assumptions

I'm sure that at some point in your professional career, some consultant or mentor wrote the word "ASSUME" on the board and drew two vertical lines to explain why you should never assume anything in a communication. The problem is that usually the people teaching this assume you get what they mean! So, let me spell it out for you.

There is absolutely no way to be certain that another person's words mean the same thing to him or her as they mean to you. This is why you ask your patients for clarification when they say *"it hurts."* When a patient tells you she is in pain, you don't jump to treat until you find out the what, when, where, and how of the pain. You start asking questions like, *"Where does it hurt? What makes it worse? When is it worse? Is it sharp or dull? Is it constant or intermittent? On a scale of 1 – 10 . . ."*

If a colleague says, *"I'm hurt that you didn't invite me to lunch with you,"* do you begin to ask questions to clarify what he meant or do you assume you understand? The word "hurt" could mean something entirely different to your colleague than it means to you. In fact, over the years we have asked thousands of people to explain what the word "hurt" means to them, and have received a wide variety of responses:

> Hurt = *disappointed, sad, embarrassed, mad, humiliated, frustrated, sad and mad, sad and embarrassed, mad and embarrassed, mad and scared, sad and scared, disgusted, and/or the sensation of actual physical pain in the stomach, head, and/or "heart"*

Of course, "hurt" is only one word. The Second Edition of the *Oxford English Dictionary* lists 171,476 words, and an additional 47,156 words that are considered obsolete. It also lists 9,500 words that it considers to be derived from other words. And that's just English. Many of our healthcare Teams are filled with people for whom English is a second language. Add in the total number of words in their dictionaries, and we have a lot of room for misinterpretation.

**When it comes to words, the simplest thing to do
is to keep it simple.**

As I mentioned in Chapter 14, always use words that a six-year-old child would understand. This will narrow down the likelihood of miscommunications and keep everything crystal clear.

Communications that involve feelings and emotions can be extremely dangerous when you are looking to form an Alignment. While this varies across gender, age, and culture, speaking clearly about emotions is not always comfortable for adults. In their efforts to preserve their dignity, they grab onto formal, "grown-up" words that don't tell you clearly what they are really experiencing. So, you fill in your assumption of what their word means.

So what?! I know what they mean. Pretty much. What difference does it really make?

I'm so glad you asked!

Imagine that you are talking with a colleague who says, *"I'm so frustrated about the new rules for reimbursement!"*

You respond with, *"There's no point in getting mad about it, there's not a thing we can do to stop it."*

He says, *"Who said anything about being mad? I'm terrified! I'm losing money right and left. I might have to close my doors if this keeps up. I thought you might have some ideas, but I can see you are clueless."*

So much for Alignment, but what actually happened?

This is a classic example of assuming. When your colleague used the word "frustrated" he didn't mean what you thought he meant. This is because for you, "frustrated" represents some level of "mad." It could be just a mild mad or it could be a great big mad. But it always means "mad."

For your colleague, "frustrated" means "scared." This is an entirely different emotion. Your response led him to believe that you didn't understand him. This is a common miscommunication and is a major problem in Alignment.

Table 19-1 lists the most common words that cause miscommunications, with simple words to explain what they typically mean.

One of the greatest challenges of Alignment is to remember that

Your ability to create or sustain Alignment is contingent upon your ability to understand and to be understood.

It's critically important that the words you choose always express what you really mean, and that you ask questions of others when you're not absolutely sure what they are trying to tell you.

To make it even more daunting, research has shown that words only account for a small part of communication. Specifically,

7% of the impact of a communication comes from the WORDS you use, 38% comes from your TONE, and 55% is VISUAL.

Table 19-1. Communicating Your Emotions With Simple Words	
Complex	**Simple**
Frustrated	Mad, scared, mad and scared
Disappointed	Sad, mad, or combination
Hurt	Sad, embarrassed, mad, humiliated, disgusted, disappointed, etc., see page 235
Anxious	Scared
Depressed	Sad, mad, or combination[1]
Agitated	Scared, mad, or combination
Irritated	Mad, scared, or combination
Hopeless	Sad, scared, or combination
Confused	Scared, mad, or combination
Helpless	Mad, scared, sad, or combination
Guilty	Sad, mad, scared, or combination
Betrayed	Mad, embarrassed
Jealous	Mad, scared, or combination
Hate	Mad, disgust, ashamed, or combination
Trust	Not scared, comfortable
Safe	Not scared, comfortable, cozy
Overwhelmed	Scared or a combination of many feelings
Resent	Mad, sad, or combination

[1] If someone says he or she is "depressed," do not rule out the possibility of clinical depression. You may need to refer to a professional for proper assessment. When in doubt, ask some clarifying questions like, "What are you experiencing exactly?"

Consider this for just a moment.

From posture to facial expressions, we send a message everywhere we go that may help or stop our efforts to Align with others. This can be a challenge, particularly when we interpret someone's body language to mean something that is inaccurate. The classic example is folded arms. If people fold their arms in front of them, it could mean that they are angry or unavailable for change, but it could also mean they are standing comfortably, protecting an aching back, trying to get warm, or protecting an ailing stomach. If you don't really know what it means, but assume that you do, your response could cause a miscommunication and threaten your chances for Alignment.

If your listener can't see you, the visual aspect of your communication process is eliminated, which means that

When you're on the telephone, or if you're standing behind or out of sight of someone, 93% of your message comes from the tone of your voice!

Is it any wonder that it's hard to form Alignments? There are so many chances for misinterpretations. The simple formula is this:

If there is any chance that there may be a discrepancy between what someone says and what you understand, ask a question.

There are many questions you can ask someone to clarify a communication. Table 19-2 lists some examples:

TABLE 19-2. Clarifying Questions
• You have a funny look on your face, what are you thinking?
• I know what frustrated means to me, what does it mean to you?
• Something seems wrong, what's going on?
• I can't tell from your tone if you're mad or something else, what's up?
• What is it like for you, will you describe it to me?

Another common miscommunication revolves around the word "feel." Many times you will hear people use the word "feel" when they are describing something that isn't actually a feeling. The way you can tell is that they will begin their sentences with *"I feel like," "I feel that," "I feel as if,"* or *"I feel as though."* If the words that follow the word "feel" are not actual emotions or physical sensations, then what you are hearing is not actually a feeling, it's a perception. Compare *"I feel scared that you aren't going to be able to do this procedure"* to *"I feel like you just don't get it!"* The first sentence comes from a combination of Natural Child and Analyst. It tells us clearly what is going on with you and helps us to understand that you are being impacted by what we are (or aren't) doing. That information helps us to Align with you so that we are more compelled to change. The second statement comes from your Critical Parent. It tells us your opinion of us and forces us into the Child State of Mind where we are likely to feel ashamed, scared, or mad. Stuck in our response to your statement, we are likely to start thinking about the way you spoke to us and lose track of what you were trying to tell us. And what if you're wrong about us? What if we *do* "get it" but are paralyzed with fear of failure because we don't think we have the skills to do what you want us to do? You've missed a valuable training opportunity where you could have shown us how to work through our fear and trust our instincts, or reminded us that it is always OK to ask for help. Here's the problem:

When you state your perceptions instead of your feelings, you run the risk of alienating your listener and defeat your efforts to Align.

Similarly, when others give you their perceptions rather than their feelings, it's important to stop and find out precisely what they mean so that you don't make false assumptions and risk misalignment.

Table 19-3 gives some examples of how to respond to perception-based statements.

TABLE 19-3. Managing Perception-Based Statements	
Statement	**Clarifying Response**
I feel like I'm going to explode!	*What's going on? What are you going to explode about?*
I feel that you never listen to me!	*What am I doing or not doing that leads you to think that?*
I feel as though we're never going to get this project done.	*What specifically is making it hard to finish the project?*
I feel as if nothing I do is enough.	*How would you know if you had done enough?* *What will be your benchmark for success?*
I feel like today is going to be a long day.	*What's going on that you feel that way?*

Some people look at this chart and think *"Wow! This is great!" while* others think *"That is WAY too much trouble."* Here's what I think:

Pick and choose the tools and formulas that fit for you.

Anything you do to get more clarity into your communications will help you to Align with the people on your Team. The more you do, the faster you will get Aligned and the longer you will stay that way.

And why is that important again?

Because when you are Aligned with people they are more likely to do what you want them to do.

Oh yeah — got it.

Step 2: Use The Four Languages of the M.A.D. Formula

In the ideal Alignment scenario, every single person in every Sub-Team would understand and use The Language of Action Types (Chapter 5), The Language of Value Sets (Chapter 6), The Language of States of Mind (Chapter 7), and The Language of Chips (Chapter 8). Begin by building your own facility with the languages, then encourage your Executive and Leadership Teams to follow suit. Soon the ripple effect will take it all the way down the line and spread out to your patients and colleagues. Remember,

> There are no secrets! Share your knowledge with patients, colleagues, vendors, and everyone you meet. Why should you have to do all the work to establish the Alignment?

Step 3: Make a Communications Map

As you discover the different languages of individuals on your Team, create a communication map so that everyone knows how to travel the territory of your Team and avoid all the potholes. If you have a Team of 50 or fewer doctors and staff where your Sub-Teams interact frequently, create one huge map and hang it in your break or locker room. Larger Teams may choose to make maps of their Sub-Teams and then distribute them to all other Sub-Teams. No matter which way you choose, a communication map is very simple and will look like the example in Table 19-4.

TABLE 19-4. Sample Communication Map				
Team Member	Action Type	Value Set	Favorite State of Mind	My DESIRE
John	T	1	A	To write a text book
Mary	R	1	NP	For all of my children to go to college
Karen	C	1	A-NC	To get my certification
Judy	R	2	SC	To lose 20 pounds
Teresa	T	2	A	To get a research grant
Doug	E	2	A-SC	To own a boat
Luke	E	1	NC	To be the top providers in our county
Meghan	R	1	A	To spend more time with my kids
Jeremy	C	1	A-CP	To go to Africa
Sarah	T	1	A	To pass my board exams

When your communication map is clearly in sight, it makes it easier for everyone to remember to shift their styles with their Teammates. One thing I would suggest, however: move it around every now and then so it isn't hanging in the same place. Don't let it become like the choking poster that's been hanging in your break room for years — you know the one — it's right on the wall under the announcement about last year's holiday party and your assistant's recipe for brownies.

You will notice that there is a column for "DESIRE." While this column is optional, I have found it brings Teams together when they know each other's DESIRES, support each other's ACTION Plans and celebrate successes along the way. While this appears to have nothing to do with your practice, the positive energy and loyalty that it creates is well worth the effort. Remember, you helped them to make the connection between work and personal when you asked the question *"If you woke up tomorrow morning and found that this was the perfect job for you . . ."*[1] Their DESIRES are what will give them the Internal Motivation to do what you want them to do. That's a good thing.

Step 4: Beware of Technology

The larger your Team, the more likely it is that individuals will go long periods of time without communicating face-to-face and discussing how they can meet each other's needs more effectively. Particularly with the onset of electronic communications, there is less call for face-to-face interaction. Email can be a great tool to help people to stay in touch and establish tight Alignment, but while this innovation is a great time saver, it often causes miscommunications that can ultimately break down your Alignment.

First, remember that while words are only 7% of a communication, in email that's all you've got. That means the words are 100% of your communication! Even if you make wide use of "Emoticons," italics, bold fonts and underlining and are very careful about when you use FULL CAPS, it is difficult to relay your intended tone in email. As a result, a lot of assumptions and miscommunications are made in email. Consider the following example:

John looks at Mary's response and thinks, *"Wait — can't do <u>what</u>? Can't meet? Can't talk? Can't do EMR? Is there a system problem? I thought we solved that. Wait — is she mad at me? Oh, man, I couldn't make it to her stupid birthday party last month, and I bet she still hasn't*

---

[1] See Chapters 10–12.

forgiven me. Well, I couldn't help it that I had to work late. I bet I was the only one who never got there, and she's never going to let me off the hook for that. Well, two can play this game."

FROM: John   TO: Mary
SUBJECT: Re: Re: Meet

Fine.

Mary receives John's email and thinks, *Oh good. He probably can do it without me anyway.*

John stays mad. He's mad because he thinks Mary is mad. Of course, Mary was never mad. But she will be, probably in about a week when she finds out that John just dropped the project.

This happens a lot, and we can expect it to happen with more frequency as practices become even more technologically sophisticated.

Another problem with building Alignments in email is due to the Multigenerational Gap of the 21st century. Innovations in healthcare have meant that people are living longer and staying more active for longer periods of time. This means that there is a strong likelihood that you could have an age difference of up to 70 years between members of your Team!

In addition to the obvious differences in work styles, perceptions, and cultural influences, the wider apart the generations, the less they have in common regarding the degree to which they prefer email to face-to-face communications. Some older Team members may blatantly refuse to purchase a computer or cell phone, some Baby Boomers are just now beginning to bite the bullet with respect to web-based technology, the majority of Generation X are completely caught up and won't go anywhere without their cell phones, and the Generation Y group is texting so much that they will likely create a new source of revenues for orthopedic physicians who specialize in carpal tunnel syndrome.

The younger the Team members, the less adept they will be with face-to-face interactions, and the more impatient they will be with those who want that, particularly since they know they can interact any time with a quick flip of their cell phone and a few rapid strokes of the teeny tiny keys that the rest of us need glasses to read. *Sigh.*

Be aware of the differences and preferences in communication, and make sure that everyone understands the best ways to communicate with everyone else on their Team.

ELEMENT #2: TEAM TRUST

The strategies and techniques listed in Element #1 will go a long way toward your ability to achieve Element #2. That said, there are two additional steps I recommend to build strong and lasting trust on your Team:

Step 1: Seek to Define "Trust" on Your Team

"Trust" is one of those tricky words that can mean different things for different people. For many, it means they know they can count on you to do what you say you're going to do. For others, trust is about honesty and integrity, commitment and promises. The safest and most effective way to define "trust" is to ask a question:

> *What specifically will you need to see, hear, or experience before you'll be able to completely trust me (us)?*

Ironically, simply the fact that you are asking that question will launch the process of Alignment. When you take the time to ask, people realize that you care about what they need. Of course, there are people who will be surprised by your question. These people will look at you like you're an alien and say, *"I have no idea!"* No problem, simply walk them through it with clarifying questions like:

- *Would it be helpful to you to know a bit about my background or experience?*
- *Would you like to know the thinking that goes behind the choices I make?*
- *Would you like to watch me do things first so you are sure I am competent?*
- *How often would you want to get together before you'll know you can count on me?*

The more clarifying questions you ask, the more they will see your sincerity, and that will go a long way toward building trust, no matter what it means to them.

Step 2: Walk Through Fire Together

There is nothing that will build trust faster than when two or more people go through an emotionally charged experience together. There are all different levels of these experiences that occur in every practice on a regular basis, but most people fail to acknowledge that anything has happened and therefore miss the opportunity to solidify their trust for each other.

When people don't acknowledge a difficult experience it is typically because they believe professionals should always be cool, calm, and collected. This leads them away from acknowledging that anything happened. They dismiss the situation by putting on a smile and never bringing it up again. While this may help them to sustain a sense of bravado, it does nothing to Align the Team or build trust.

It is significantly more effective to acknowledge an experience than it is to pretend it never happened.

Whether you simply make a quick comment or go through a full debriefing will depend on the severity of the experience. Table 19-5 lists some examples of how you might respond with a quick acknowledgement to build Alignment and trust.

TABLE 19-5. Walking Through Fire	
Experience	**Sample Response**
Six incoming lines ring simultaneously and, at the same time, three patients arrive for their appointments. Two Team members handle it all smoothly.	• High five, low five • Wink • Smile • Fist-to-fist • *"And that's the way it's done!"*
End of month payroll is due and the computers freeze. Your IT Team (your spouse and teenager) is away looking at colleges. Everyone chips in, and you get it all figured out.	• *"Now that's what I call a close call!"* • *"Did you plan this?"* • *"Maybe we should all take a course or something?"* • *"That deserves a pizza — I'm buying!"*
The fire alarm goes off with patients present, all are evacuated safely, and it turns out to have been a small fire on another floor.	• *"Well* that *was fun."*[1] • *"It's a good thing we cleared those boxes from the emergency exit!"* • *"I thought for sure it was us!"* • *"Glad it wasn't!"*
Patient is afraid of needles, and the two of you get through it successfully.	• *"You are a real trooper!"* • *"We make a good Team."*
Code Blue, patient survives.	• *"That was a little too close for comfort."* • *"Good work everyone."* • *"It went like clockwork."*
Code Blue, patient doesn't survive.	• *"That was rough."* • *"Are you OK?"* • *"We'll get through this eventually."* • *"Does anyone want to talk about it?"*
[1] A little playful sarcasm can go a long way to lighten a difficult situation.	

One of the fastest and most effective ways to experience an emotionally charged event that is extremely *positive* is to come together for the purpose of creating a Team mission statement, which brings us to Element #3.

ELEMENT #3: COMMON MISSION

I can't stress enough the importance of developing a unique Team mission that is generated by all of the members of your Team. This simple activity will bring you a tighter Alignment than you can possibly imagine. When people are given the opportunity to talk in a group about what brings them all together every day, the Team rises to a new level of awareness of how much they share in common. The experience is uplifting and the end product is one that will help to sustain the Alignment for years to come. Simply follow these four steps:

Step 1: Schedule Your Mission Statement Creation Day

Scheduling a day for an entire Team to come together is the most difficult step of this process. While you want everyone to be present, that isn't always feasible. Obviously, the larger your Team, the more difficult it is to get everyone in one room at the same time, not only because of schedules but because of coverage. In the ideal world, everyone would be there at the same time. If there is no possible way to make that happen, then divide each Sub-Team into halves or thirds and run your activity in shifts. The important thing is that you have representatives from each Sub-Team in every session so you can get a well-rounded perspective from each group.

There is no way to predict how long it will take to create your Mission Statement because it depends entirely on the detail orientation and size of your group. The more Thinkers you have, the longer it will take because all of the details will have to be covered. While the details will be minimized with a practice full of Enthusiasts, every idea will be accompanied by dramatic examples and stories that will be entertaining but could also be lengthy. Commanders will give you quick one-liners (leaving you in the position of having to draw out their thoughts) and your Relaters will make sure that everyone else has a chance to be heard, forgetting to join in themselves. From start to finish, you can plan that you will have your Team Mission Statement in approximately two to three hours.[2]

Once your Mission Statement is completed, create an ACTION Plan that flows directly from that. The development of your ACTION Plan can take anywhere from one to five hours, depending on how creative your Team is and the degree to which your organizational ducks are already swimming in a row throughout your practice. You don't have to do your Mission Statement and your ACTION Plan in the same day, although that is ideal because the momentum and emotional charge is at its peak from having just created the Mission Statement. Nevertheless, all of this can be accomplished in stages if that is your preference.

[2] When we work with a Team to create a Mission Statement, it typically takes much less time, but that is because we are in the middle of a program that is already in progress and so a lot of the ground work has already been established to get everyone on the same page. Pulling a Team together for the sole purpose of creating a mission statement and ACTION Plan requires you to do some teaching first. I'll explain that in Step 2.

Step 2: Create Your Mission Statement

There are probably as many perspectives on how to create a Mission Statement as there are practice management consultants. I will give you my approach, but it is not necessarily any better than anyone else's, it's simply different than the others.

For a group of 50 or less, get a flip chart pad and easel (with colored pens). For larger groups, use a combination laptop with LCD projector. You may even be able to find an overhead projector in the back of a closet somewhere. That is the best choice of all for any size group.

Introduce your plan by explaining what you're going to do and why. For example, you might say something like this:

> *Each of you brings a unique talent to our practice with a unique perspective on our job and our patients. When we put all of that together into one building, it results in the unique combination of services we provide to our patients and their families every day. I'd like for us to find a way to describe that by creating a Team Mission Statement.*
>
> *We have a practice mission statement that we put together years ago, but that doesn't reflect all of who and what we are today. So today we are going to work together to create a new Mission Statement. I'm asking all of us to work together on this because I believe the more we come together to define our practice, the better our practice will be.*
>
> *Here's how this is going to work. I'm going to ask you to give input to a set of questions by calling your answers out loud while I write them up here on the flip chart. After we get all of your responses up here, I will put them together into sentences and ask you to read them. If you think they represent us effectively, we're done. Otherwise, we'll keep going until every single one of you says "that's us!"*
>
> *It's very important that each of you contributes to this for one important reason: this Mission Statement is for us. It isn't meant as a marketing tool for our patients. If you decide you want to share it with them at some point, that's up to you, but the main point of this is to provide all of us a strong tool that we can use on the worst days, when we don't want to get out of bed in the morning or when we can't wait to leave at the end of the day, to remind us that we do this because we want to,*

> *because we believe in doing something that means something, and because we believe in each other. Our Mission Statement will help us to remember all of that, and keep us going when we need an extra boost. I'll talk you through the details in a minute, but first, does anybody have any general questions?*

Next, write the word "WHAT" on the top of your flip chart and ask:

What, specifically, do we do in our practice? Just call it out. Tell me everything you can think of that we do here every day.

Write down phrases as they speak. By the time you are done, you may have several pages for the WHAT of your practice that look something like this:

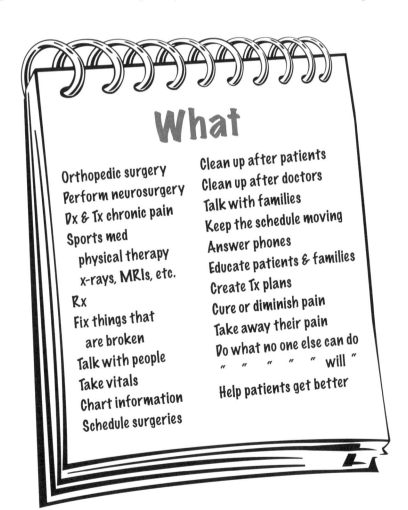

When you think that you have drawn out all of the WHATs, move on to the HOWs and ask:

OK, how do we do all of these things? How do we make them happen?

As before, write everything they say on the flip chart. Urge them to be creative, and applaud spontaneity and humor.

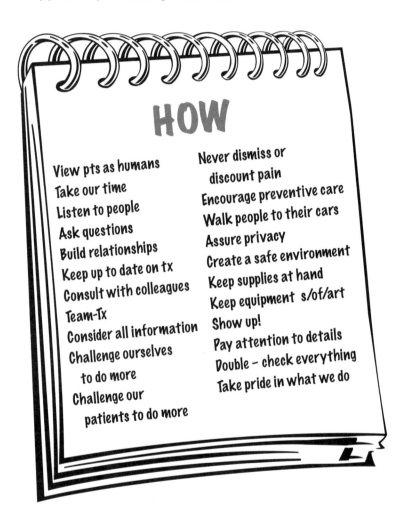

HOW

View pts as humans
Take our time
Listen to people
Ask questions
Build relationships
Keep up to date on tx
Consult with colleagues
Team-Tx
Consider all information
Challenge ourselves
    to do more
Challenge our
    patients to do more

Never dismiss or
    discount pain
Encourage preventive care
Walk people to their cars
Assure privacy
Create a safe environment
Keep supplies at hand
Keep equipment s/of/art
Show up!
Pay attention to details
Double – check everything
Take pride in what we do

Now, the final piece, it's time to figure out what drives the engine of your practice. So, you're going to ask your Team about their personal Motivations for doing the things you do:

Why do we do this? What are the reasons each of you works so hard? What makes you feel proud about what you do? The truth is that we could all work somewhere else, or do something else. So why do each and every one of us choose to do what we do? And why do we choose to do it here with this particular group of people?

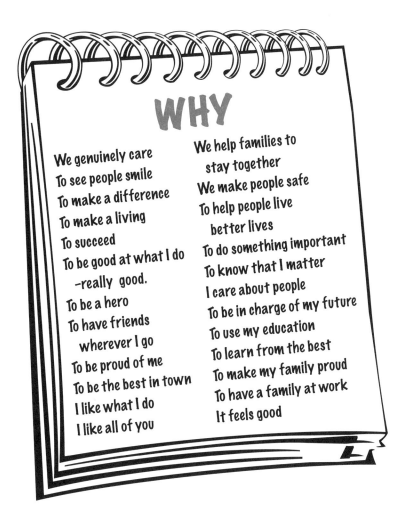

OK! You have all of the pieces to the puzzle. Now send everyone off on a 30-minute break while you build the statement. It's not hard. Just lay all three flip charts in front of you on the floor and stare at them for a few minutes. As you stare at all of these words, you'll begin to see patterns. Using different colors of markers, circle the statements that go together.

**There is no right or wrong to how you do this.
Because you were there to listen during this process,
you will know how the Team intended this to be.**

Begin your Mission Statement with:

Our mission is to . . .

And then create a summary of all of the "WHATs." You may need to create a run-on sentence or two. I promise you, your third-grade teacher will not hit you with a ruler. Remember, it doesn't have to be perfect. It only has to be reflective of your Team's intent. Save one or two for the final paragraph.

Next, add your "HOWs" by finishing this statement:

We accomplish our mission by . . .

Again, simply pull together everything your Team said and create summary statements. It's OK to use words that they didn't say, as long your words mean the same thing. The most powerful Mission Statements use many of the Teams' own words and phrases, so go ahead and throw those in! Don't worry about using every one. There's one more chance in the next paragraph.

At last, the final step. This is going to be a two-phase paragraph. In the first, you are going to grab a few more of the WHATs and HOWs and complete this sentence:

It is our hope that by . . .

OK, time to get down to the depth of your soul and bring it home. You see, the real secret of the mission statement is the emotion it evokes. When you read it, the words should give you goose bumps, bring a tear to your eye, or make you want to throw your arms up to the ceiling and yell, *"YES!"* So, let your creativity and heart come out here, and summarize the "WHYs" they gave you by beginning with:

We will . . .

Now read what you've written out loud and pay attention to how it sounds and feels as you read it.

Our mission is to cure or diminish our patients' pain by providing treatment, surgery, and rehabilitation through our knowledge and experience in orthopedics, neurology, sports medicine, physical medicine, and physical therapy.

We accomplish our mission by staying up to date on all aspects of treatment, viewing our patients as human beings, educating them about their choices, taking a Team approach to treatment, using state-of-the-art equipment, paying attention to every detail, building strong relationships, and never dismissing or discounting our patients' pain.

It is our hope that by continually learning from each other and our patients, challenging ourselves and our patients to strive for the best, and never giving up, we will feel pride in our accomplishments and the friends we make, and continue working as a caring family who helps other families to live better lives.

When your Team comes back in the room, announce that you have finished their Mission Statement and that you would like them to read it out loud to see how they like it. Remind them if there is anything they want to change, you will do that together after they've read the entire statement.

Have them stand close together, away from their desks,[3] and then get ready to go. Pump them up a little bit by saying things like, *"Are you ready?" "You did a great job putting this together!" "OK, here we go, 1 . . . 2. . . . 3."*

Project the first line on the screen, and then scroll down as they read each line.[4] Read it with them. Remember, you're a member of this Team too!

When you're all done, turn off the projection and ask

> *What do you think?*

The discussion that follows will tell you whether you need to tweak it, or if you're all set.

HINT: Keep your ego out of this. You're not going for a Pulitzer Prize. You are simply pulling together all of the thoughts of your Team. This is a Team effort all the way.

Don't be surprised if someone suggests that you should make your Mission Statement public. I have clients who have hung theirs in their reception area, posted it on their Web site, and sent a press release to area newspapers. The one that really touched me was a client who had their Mission Statement inscribed on an enormous wooden and brass plaque and had everyone sign their name underneath it. They surrounded this with 8 x 10 color photos of everyone in the practice. It took up an entire wall and was the first thing you saw when you walked in the practice door. It was simply awe inspiring.

Don't feel that you have to use this as a marketing tool. The important thing is that it is an Alignment tool, so make sure it is hung prominently somewhere in your practice so that all of your Team can see it. It doesn't have to be for public viewing at all.

Step 3: Create Your ACTION Plan

Your Team ACTION Plan comes directly from your Mission Statement and is similar to the one I showed you in Chapter 12 except designed for your entire Team. Ask each person to write down the answer to the following question:

If we were to actively work our Mission Statement every day, what would that get for you personally?

---

[3] OK, I have to confess, this is the part of the program when I have them all hold hands. It's sappy, I know, but it just always feels right. Do what feels right to you.

[4] I use PowerPoint for this and insert an animation for the entire Mission Statement called "Color Typewriter." When you use this animation, it scrolls out your statement one word at a time at the perfect speed for reading aloud. It's very dramatic and makes it a little easier to keep everyone reading at the same speed.

When everyone has finished, go around the room and ask them about their desire.

HINT: Ask clarifying questions if their DESIRE is too general. For example, let's say someone responds with *"I'd be more Motivated to go to work."* You might probe by asking *"And if you were more Motivated, how would things be different for you?"* Write down the answer and move to the next person. Table 19-6 gives you an example of how your ACTION Plan would look at this point in the process.

TABLE 19-6. Team ACTION Plan — DESIRES	
OUR DESIRES	
Team Member	**DESIRE**
Sally	I would laugh more during the day which would make me enjoy my work more and make everything more fun. That would reduce my stress, and my headaches would probably stop.
Kurt	It would be easier do deal with the cranky patients and that would let me make a bigger difference for everyone, which would ultimately make me feel better about myself.

When you have everyone's DESIRES listed, go to RESOURCES.

Break everyone into smaller groups (if possible, make sure each group has a representative of each Sub-Team), give them one to two hours, and tell them to answer all of the following questions as completely as possible:

- *What, specifically, will we need so that we will be able to enact everything in our Mission Statement?* (tools, skills, education, people, supplies, time, equipment, space)
- *How will we get each of these items (one at a time)?*
- *Who will take the lead to make sure each of these items is secured?*
- *Who will help on each item?*
- *When will we start?*
- *What is our deadline for completion?*

Before you send them off to work on their ACTION Plans, announce to your Team that every single idea will be reviewed by the Executive Team and give them a date when they will receive a response from the Team for each of their suggestions. Ask them to keep that date in mind when choosing start and deadline dates. Tell them to be creative and to think as if money were no object, but remind them that money *is* an object and that not every idea will be taken.

I suggest you give each group a chart as shown in Table 19-7 so that they can keep their discussion organized, and then send them off where they can talk without distraction from the other groups.

TABLE 19-7. Team ACTION Plan — RESOURCES					
OUR RESOURCES					
What We'll Need	**How We'll Get It**	**Who Will Lead**	**Who Will Help**	**When We'll Start**	**When We'll Finish**
New MRI technician	Call the school, run an ad in the newspaper?	Kellie	Jane	2/17	3/17
Coordinate physical therapy and surgery for pre- and post op!	Educate patients about the importance of doing both (especially for cash-pay patients) Revamp coding Educate front desk Educate all clinical associates	Jim	Nan	2/18	3/18

When everyone returns, debrief the activity by asking how they did. You'll hear various responses ranging from *"great"* to *"it was tough."* Listen carefully to what they say and you'll learn things about your Team and your practice that you may not have known such as how to help them to elevate their results through targeted training, where you are missing valuable RESOURCES and who excels at organization and strategic planning.

The next piece of the Team ACTION Plan is the PERMISSION section. In this particular activity, we don't do individual PERMISSION barriers. The goal is to discover practice-wide challenges that would block the enactment of your Mission Statement.

Ask this as a question and encourage a Team discussion:

What might keep us from being willing to take ACTION on our Mission Statement?

Any of the following three things will happen:

1. Everyone will answer positively with statements like, *"Nothing! We're doing this!"* or *"Just hand us the credit card, and we're ready to go!"*

If this happens, give lots of Chips for their great attitudes, remind them of your Executive Team meeting to determine budgets, and move to the next step.

2. You will hear mixed responses, some positive, and some skeptical like, *"Well, it all makes sense sitting here, but what happens when we get back and we've got 80 patients a day? Who has time to think about all of this then?"*

Send that back to the Team and ask them to respond. They will talk about it and together they will Align (one way or the other) to build a solution.

3. They will respond negatively, balking about all the work they have and how they're not being paid enough (yada-yada-yada).

Now you've discovered that there is a serious problem that needs your attention, because where there is negativity, there are usually splinters that have festered (in other words, unresolved conflicts have built up on the Team). We'll address this more completely in Chapter 20. In the meantime, if this happens during your ACTION Planning, assure your Team that you will work through this and find a solution, and redirect them to making sure that their DESIRES are strong and their RESOURCES are accurately outlined.

The exciting part of all of this is the energy you will feel in the room as everyone works together to find solutions. They will want to do all of this for one reason:

It's their Mission Statement, and their ACTION Plan. They created it and now they want to see it through.

Try very hard not to wink at your partners or to put out your hand for the cash that you are owed when you bet each other regarding whether or not this would work. Save all of that for later. Now is the time to pass out the Chips and celebrate your success!

Step 4: Review Your Mission Statement With Patients, Colleagues, and Vendors

Since Team Alignment includes all of your Sub-Teams, the more people you can include in the adoption of your mission, the more Aligned will be your Team. Assuming you have received permission from your partners and employees to share your Mission Statement with those you serve, then the next step is to make that happen.

The simplest way to share your Mission Statement is to hang it in plain view, put it on your brochures, include it in your newsletters, and make sure it's clearly displayed on your Web site. But if you *really* want to use your Mission Statement to strengthen your Alignment with people, then talk with them about it. There are many creative ways you can do this. Here is one:

Give new patients a copy of your Mission Statement at the front desk after they complete relevant paper work. As you hand them the card, say something like:

> *"Mr. Patient, we are very glad you've chosen to come to us. This is our Mission Statement. I'd appreciate it if you'd take a quick minute and read it while you're waiting for Dr. Y. It will help you to get a better sense of who we are and what we strive to do."*

Then, when the patient goes back, your assistant will continue the discussion. *"Mr. Patient, did you happen to look at our Mission Statement?"*

If the patient says "no," then say *"OK, no problem, I just want to make sure we're the right practice for you. Please let me know if you have any questions."* Then go on with your regular procedures.

If the patient indicates "yes," then say *"Does it sound like we're the right practice for you?"*

This will create a good beginning to Aligning your new patient with your practice and will also help you to project an image that your practice is just a little different than average.[5]

If you want to see the power of Mission Statements, do Activity 19-2. After you've done it, take it home and do one with your family!

ELEMENT #4: COORDINATED INDIVIDUALITY

One of the greatest challenges of any organization is to bring together a Team of unique individuals and get them to coordinate their efforts. You can take the typical route, and enforce a code of behaviors that forces

---

[5] We'll talk more about that in Section Five.

ACTIVITY 19-2. Write Your Personal Mission Statement

The next time you are sitting on a train, on a plane, or in a cozy chair on a rainy day, write out your own What, How, and Why responses and create your own Mission Statement. Hang it at home or in your office, use it as wallpaper on your computer, or keep it in your wallet. The day may never come when you need it to give you strength, but in case you do, it will be there for you.

---

everyone to lose their individuality and melt into the sameness of their Team. The alternative, and the one I recommend, is to identify the uniqueness of each individual and then maximize the degree to which you can capitalize on their assets by grouping them with other individuals who will work well together. Remember:

> **When people are encouraged to be who they really are, the energy soars, the creativity is maximized, and they work even harder to be the best Team members they can be.**

The more you know about your Team members, the more you can create work Teams, set up work stations, etc. This is easily accomplished through a simple survey of your Team and then a coordination of all responses by one person. The survey is shown in Table 19-8.

Before you distribute the survey, do Activity 19-3!

ACTIVITY 19-3. What Is Your Work Style?

Be the first on your Team to take the Work Style survey! Remember, the more honest you are, the more you'll get an accurate picture of how to Align your own Sub-Team within the practice.

Once you've got all of the surveys done, organize them by Sub-Team and do your best to put people together with similar styles. It may take a little time, but it will take a lot less time than having to sort through squabbles over the "little things."

Now that you have worked through the first four elements of Alignment, you have a Team who is more Aligned and who will probably stay that way . . . unless something goes wrong. The final two elements of Alignment will help you to manage the more difficult areas of working with people in a healthcare environment so you can assure that your Team stays Aligned no matter what.

BOTTOM LINE

The first step in Team Alignment is to apply key strategies to assure clean communication and the development of trust. Once this is accomplished,

TABLE 19-8. Work Style Survey					
The following brief questionnaire is designed to help us to create as comfortable a work environment as possible for everyone on our Team. Please answer each of the following questions honestly. There is no right or wrong answer! When all surveys are in, we'll put all the results together and talk about how we can use the information to create the ideal work environment for everyone.					
Please read each of the following statements and then choose one of the following numbers to indicate the degree to which the statement describes your work style preference for each by placing a check (✓) in the column to indicate: 1) Never true 2) Rarely true 3) True about half the time 4) Often true 5) Always true					
Statement of Work Style	**1**	**2**	**3**	**4**	**5**
I work slowly and methodically.					
I jump right in and deal with the details as I go.					
I have to clean off my desk before I can work.					
I keep piles and know where everything is.					
I get caught up in what I'm doing and lose track of time.					
I write notes on sticky pads.					
I talk to myself out loud.					
I like to have music playing when I work.					
Noise bothers me when I'm working.					
I don't like to be interrupted.					
I enjoy stopping to talk with people.					
I forward my phone to voice mail.					
I need to know who's calling right away.					
I think best when I talk through the problem with someone.					
I think best when I'm alone.					
I prefer to sit rather than stand.					
I eat while I work.					
I like to save everything up and do it all together.					
I like to do things as they come up.					
I get sarcastic when I get stressed.					
I get irritable when I get stressed.					
I get punch-drunk (laughing) when I get stressed.					
In a crunch, the best way to help me is to leave me alone.					
In a crunch, the best way to help me is to make me laugh.					
In a crunch, the best way to help me is to chip in and work.					
I have a unique talent or skill that I think would help our practice. I know how to _____.					

help your Team to create a common Mission Statement and an associated ACTION Plan. Finally use a survey to assess the individual work style preferences and unique assets of your Team members and then coordinate them to create ideal work Teams that will bring out the best in every member of your Team.

Chapter 20

Conquer Conflict!

FROM THE OUTSIDE, it looks like you are doing everything you should be doing. You've read the practice management books and articles, you've attended practice management sessions at your association meetings, you've reviewed your operations with your favorite consultant, and it seems that you're doing everything right.

So why haven't your revenues soared like all of the theories say they should? Here's what I've found,

> **When you've done everything you're supposed to do and you're not as successful as you should be, something is going on with the people factor of your business.**

We know from Chapter 11 that there are only three components of ACTION: DESIRE, RESOURCES and PERMISSION. Let's assume that the people on your Team know what they want, and they are able to get it, but you're still not where you should be. Partners aren't networking for referrals or seeking additional education or credentials, employees are doing only the minimum and rarely offering to do more, there is negativity throughout your Team, patients are saying "no" to your elective services, and you're hearing complaints about your customer service. What is causing all of this? I have one word for you:

Conflict

Element #5: Conflict Circumvention

There are two types of conflict, both of which can impact your success: **External Conflict** and **Internal Conflict.** Let's look at both.

External Conflict occurs when two or more people become misaligned. This can be the result of any number of factors, from miscommunications to broken trusts. When External Conflict occurs, the involved Team members need a safe method for working through and resolving the conflict. This is a big topic that doesn't always have simple solutions. To the degree that the conflicts are manageable, there are some strong communication formulas you can use to work through them.

The challenge is that even the most dynamic formulas are useless unless we are willing to apply them. So, before we go through the External Conflict formulas, let's look at Internal Conflict.

Internal Conflict occurs when one or more of your States of Mind disagree.

The classic example of Internal Conflict is when you're standing in front of the refrigerator, holding the door open and talking to yourself as you look inside:

I want something but I don't know what I want.
Hey that's cold, close the door!
I have no idea what that is, but I'm not eating it.
Carrot sticks—I should eat those.
Yuck.
Oh! Cake!
Don't do cake, you'll be up all night.
Just a little piece.
One piece leads to two.
I should have the carrot sticks.
Oh! Is that beer?

Sound familiar?

As we saw in Chapter 7, these little conflicts are perfectly normal. But some Internal Conflicts can serve as barriers to our own success. Those are the ones we need to talk about here.

THE LANGUAGE OF RULES

Every individual has a unique set of personal success barriers that I call **The Language of Rules.** This language develops from the time we are old enough to understand the "DO"s and "DON'T"s of life. The first time you reach for something and someone says "no," you begin to learn that just because you want something, it doesn't mean you're going to get it. You also learn that if you behave a certain way you will be more likely to get what you want (and avoid what you don't want) from the people who control that (usually the "grown-ups"). Your Language of Rules expands as you learn all the rules of what to be, and not be, do and not do, think and not think, feel and not feel, and have and not have.

We develop our Language of Rules first through our exposure to others. We learn rules from people verbally and nonverbally as they tell us rules, such as *"be a success,"* but we are also *shown* the rules by virtue of how our significant others behave. When we see our parents get up early, go to work, come home late, and stay up doing paperwork or cleaning the house, we learn that this is what grown-ups do, and these behaviors become part of our rules about how we are supposed to behave so that we can follow the rule and "be a success."

We watch the behaviors of those around us, and then interpret them as how girls behave, how boys behave, what professionals do, etc. Sometimes we incorporate these rules into our internal Language of Rules, and other times we make new rules in which we rebel against what we see and vow never to behave as we see others do. Either way, our Language of Rules expands with each rule we incorporate.

We also inherit rules that are passed down to us from our parents, siblings, grandparents, aunts, uncles, cousins, teachers, neighbors, clergy, and peers. For example, let's say little Johnny is visiting his grandparents for the weekend. As he sits on his grandfather's knee, he hears, *"Johnny, always remember, the Jones family is a hard-working, loyal family of men who always do what they say they're going to do. Jones men support their wives and children and work hard their entire lives to keep their families safe. Carry the Jones name proudly, and remember that no matter where you go or what you do, you will always be a 'Jones'."* Johnny has just inherited a bunch of rules and will spend the rest of his life making decisions that allow him to live up to his Language of Rules. Even during the times when part of him knows that he really needs to slow down or take a vacation, he will make himself rise to the occasion, because he is a "Jones."

In addition to the rules we learn from others, we also give rules to ourselves. These rules remind us of all the "shoulds" and "should nots" and help us to shape our perceptions of ourselves relative to others. We say things like, *"No matter what happens, I will never do what my mother did."* From that point forward, we make decisions and shape our lives to be sure that we follow the rule — even if we *want* to do something, we won't do it if it was something Mom would have done.

The problem arises when one or more of our rules conflicts with something we want (or don't want) to do. For example, a young girl, we'll call her Amy, is raised in a home where her mother never worked. Mom was always there, cooking dinner, making cookies, and smiling when Amy came home from school. In Amy's Language of Rules, this is what a mom is supposed to do. When Amy turns 16, she tells her mother that she isn't going to go to college because she wants to marry her high school boyfriend and have a family. Her mother sternly says *"You have to go to college. I don't want you to end up as I did. Get an education, get a job, and make sure you have choices."* OK, now Amy has conflicting rules: "stay at home with your children and don't work," and "don't stay at home with your children and get a job."

Although they conflict, both rules are included in her Language of Rules.

Fast forward 20 years and now Amy is 36 years old, has two young children, and she's working for you. She works an early shift that is purposefully designed to let her have the best of both worlds: Amy can work and get home in time to get her kids off the bus. Amy's mother lives with her, so she really doesn't need to get home early. But she is compelled to stick to both of her rules.

Today you have a late patient and ask Amy to stay. She agrees, but her usual cheerful demeanor is gone and she grumbles through the appointment. Why? Amy's rules are conflicted. And guess what! You asked her to stay, so now it's your fault! Her Internal Conflict has become your External Conflict!

At this point, my clients usually go a little pale and ask, *"So how many of these rules are there?"* Truthfully, there are so many that there is no point in even trying to guess. You're not going to learn the rules of all of your employees, partners, patients and colleagues and then try and navigate that minefield! But you can figure out your own rules and, in the process, learn to become more effective as a leader when you're helping others to resolve their conflicts. So, let's do Activity 20-1. (I suggest you do this Activity before you read on.)

ACTIVITY 20-1. Identify Your Language of Rules		
Imagine that you are between the ages of 3 and 16. Watch a movie of those years in your mind's eye. Imagine your kitchen as you were growing up, the playground, your school, etc. As you watch this movie, ask yourself *"What rules am I learning by watching others?"* *"What rules are they teaching me verbally?"* and *"What rules am I making up on my own?"* Place a check (✓) next to any rules on the following list that you have learned from others or made for yourself. If you think of other rules that aren't on the list, write them in at the end.		
Be perfect	Obey the rules	Don't grow up
Be strong	Do the right thing	Don't think
Hurry up	Be nice	Don't be angry
Be on time	Be different	Be critical
Please people	Don't be important	Don't embarrass me
Be sad	Be friendly	Be defiant
Be angry	Be thin	Drink to unwind
Be careful	Be sexy	Be strict
Be a good boy/girl	Be rich	Run away
Be what I want you to be	Be healthy	Don't be different
Don't question your elders	Don't rock the boat	Be just like me
Be just like your sister/brother	Don't make mistakes	Be independent
Be a success	Don't fail	Ignore your problems

(Activity continues next page)

ACTIVITY 20-1. Identify Your Language of Rules *(continued)*				
Be a planner		Don't trust		OTHER RULES:
Be a good husband/wife		Don't be a kid		
Be a good mother/father		Don't play		
Suffer in silence		Don't talk to strangers		
Clean your plate		Don't talk back		
Forgive everyone but you		Don't stick up for yourself		
Stay busy		Don't say "NO"		
Make the best of it		Don't trust yourself		
Be in control		Don't ask for help		
Work/study/play hard		Don't do what you want		
Be thoughtful		Don't be close		
Take care of your family		Don't have fun		
Be home with the kids		Don't express feelings		
Play with the other kids		Don't ask for anything		
Be better than everyone		Don't break the rules		
Stay on top of things		Don't talk		
Be responsible		Don't break family tradition		
As we get older, we keep adding and subtracting rules in response to new people and circumstances. So now, look back over your entire life. What rules did you learn or add from 16–35? How about from 36–50? 51–65? Write them on your list too.				

Sometimes we create additional rules to get us through extremely stressful situations. These rules are specifically designed to solve a problem that we are dealing with at the time. When we leave the situation, we no longer need the rule, yet it stays in the back of our mind, out of our awareness like a file all the way at the back of a file cabinet. Any time we are in a situation that even remotely resembles the first one, we (consciously or unconsciously) enact the rule. Any time we think there is a chance that we might *get into* a situation like the initial one, we enact the rule. We use the rule to keep us safe and sometimes it becomes so much a part of our life that it affects much of what we do.

> **Most of the time we live our lives being influenced by rules we created long before we were old enough to understand the impact they could have on us later on.**

These rules guide and shape many of our behaviors and choices, propelling us in one direction and holding us back from another. I call these powerful, self-made rules "Guiding Rules."

Practice Spotlight

Dr. B was a member of a very successful plastic surgery practice. He liked and trusted his partners, and respected them as competent doctors. Dr. B was an Enthusiast and was the life of the practice. He would start his practice days by hanging out by the front desk, getting everyone laughing, then would go off to the nursing station and get them giggling. He and his partners had weekend barbeques with their families and played golf on many occasions. Dr. B never had a second thought when he took time off, because he knew his partners would always treat his patients with the utmost care and kindness.

After Dr. B had been practicing with his partners for about five years, he happened to run into one of his old patients at the local grocery store. He was happy to see her, but she seemed nervous so he decided to let her be. As he was about to walk away, she came up to him and told him a story about one of his partners. She claimed that, while Dr. B was out of town, Dr. G had tried to talk her into an additional surgery. Dr. B was sure there must have been some mistake and asked for more details. As his patient became a little braver, she told him a story that he knew had to be true.

He began to wonder about some of his other patients and had his scheduling coordinator make some follow-up calls. Sure enough, a significant number of his patients reported similar experiences.

Dr. B decided to ask Dr. G before jumping to any conclusions. His partner never denied it. In fact, he told Dr. B that the patients were *"fair game"* when he wasn't around. Dr. B walked out and called his attorney. It was a long and bitter breakup.

In the meantime, Dr. B was being recruited by a number of other practices, all of whom wanted his vast experience and following. He joined a practice with two other doctors, after spending thousands of dollars on attorney fees to cover any and all problems that could cause him to lose money or patients in the new practice.

Dr. B's new partners were nothing like Dr. G, and he knew he was safe with them. Yet, no matter how much they tried to recruit him for joint projects or social gatherings, Dr. B declined. He kept to himself, saw his patients, and went home. His nurse and scheduling coordinator knew something was wrong, but they just couldn't get him to talk with them. The other staff thought Dr. B was a *"mean snob"* and avoided contact with him as much as they could.

When we sat down to talk with Dr. B, he shared his story with us and as he spoke, out popped his Guiding Rule:

"After what I went through, I'll never trust anyone again."

Dr. B's story is a familiar one. People make guiding rules and often don't realize they're making them. The challenge is to recognize the rules you've made and then decide if they are working for you any more. If not, make a new rule that will trump the old one.

> After some talking, Dr. B made a new rule *"I'll meet every new person with an open heart and open eyes."* It was a good rule for him because it engaged his Analyst State of Mind in the process so that he would be free to enjoy people, knowing his Analyst would be on alert.

Here's another example:

Practice Spotlight

Dianne had been a dental hygienist for almost 20 years. She loved her patients, and they loved her. We had consulted with Dianne and her practice a couple of years earlier, and then she moved and joined a new practice in her 21st year when her husband was relocated. It was a new and innovative practice with four doctors, three of whom had a large cosmetic practice.

The next winter, Dianne went with her practice to the Chicago Dental Society's winter meeting and sat in with one of her doctors on a program about case acceptance. Her doctor liked the presentation, and told Dianne that he wanted her to start using the techniques to discuss veneers and whitening with her patients. He told her to see if there was still room in a similar lecture the next day. Dianne was horrified. She told him that she could never do anything like that. Realizing she was about to cry, she excused herself and ran ahead.

Dianne ran out of the building and called us on her cell phone. I was glad to hear from her, but she sounded upset and got right to the point. As Dianne was telling me the story, she suddenly remembered a time back in college when she had taken an English course called "Speaking in Public." Dianne thought it sounded like fun at the time, but the first time she got up in front of the class to do a presentation, her teacher was pretty tough on her. The way Dianne described it, it sounded like the teacher tried to embarrass her by correcting most of Dianne's word choices, her tone of voice, diction, volume and body language, and whatever else she could find. According to Dianne, no matter what she did, the teacher didn't like it. She walked out humiliated and dropped the class. When I asked her what she did after that, she said, *"I swore I would never make another presentation as long as I lived!"*

Dianne went on to explain that when she received her certification as a registered dental hygienist (RDH), she made a clear distinction in her mind between "education" and "case presentation" and vowed that she would just stick with education and leave the rest to the doctors. No one had ever asked her to do otherwise, until today. Her Guiding Rule was getting in her way, and she had to either change it or find another practice.

Everyone has at least one Guiding Rule, and most people have several. It's important to realize that this is a normal and natural part of life. The problem is this:

We make Guiding Rules to solve problems, and then our Guiding Rules become the source of our problems later in life.

How can we increase our success when we have rules in our heads that force us to do (and not do) behaviors that literally block our successes? Clearly, we can fight our rules, but not unless we are aware of them. The problem is, most of us follow these rules completely unaware that we are being affected by decisions we made years before.

The first step to breaking through this Internal Conflict is to make a conscious effort to identify your Guiding Rules. You can do this in conversations with a competent psychotherapist, but let's see if I can save you some time.

In Activity 20-2 you will find a list of some common Guiding Rules. Please understand, these aren't happy rules, they are strong rules that are typically made because people had to find a way to cope with a difficult situation. Follow the instructions in this activity and allow yourself to identify some of your Guiding Rules.

Are you stuck with all of your rules forever? NO! In fact,

You can change your Language of Rules to include only rules that allow you to live the life that you want to live.

Your current Language of Rules is, in some ways, running your life, causing you to make choices that you might not make if you were living according to a different set of rules. Your Language of Rules is affecting what you think, what you feel and what you do, and while some of the rules may seem logical and even desirable, here's what I need you to understand:

As long as you have these rules, you are compelled to live by them. When you decide to remove these rules from your life, you then have a choice about when you want to apply them and when you don't.

ACTIVITY 20-2. My Guiding Rules			
Think back on your life and check off the rules you have made along the way. You'll know they are part of your Language of Rules if when you see them you have some kind of response. Some may sound familiar with words you've heard yourself say dozens of times. Others might hit you like a jolt of electricity. Others will mean nothing at all. When you find the rules that fit, just place a check (✓) next to them. If you think of some along the way, write them in at the end.			
I'm not good enough		I have to be strong	
There something wrong with me		Nobody likes me	
I'll keep my mouth shut and my head down		I'll show you!	
I'll prove it to you!		I'll never amount to anything!	
I'm a loser		I'm not worthy	
I never get what I want		I'm not supposed to be successful	
I'm a born failure		I'll never make it	
I'm just average		I have to work hard my entire life	
I won't get close so I don't get hurt		I'll try harder	
I'll show you even if it kills me		I can't do anything right	
I'll run away		I won't and you can't make me	
There's nothing I can do about it		I have to take care of her/him	
It's my job to make you happy		I'm not smart enough	
I can't make it on my own		I have to make it on my own	
I'll never trust anybody		I have to keep my guard up	
I'm different		I have no choice	
I don't trust myself		It's all up to me	
I don't need anybody		I'm on my own	
I have to be tough		I have to succeed no matter what	

For example, let's say you have a rule that says, "*I have to work hard.*" On the surface, that sounds like a good rule. In fact, it sounds like a rule you'd like all of your staff and partners to adopt! So, now imagine it is Sunday morning. It's a beautiful day and your family wants you to come on a picnic. You'd like to go, but a voice in your head reminds you about the stack of unread journals in your office. *"No thanks,"* you reply, *"I have to work."* You feel proud of your strong work ethic. On the other hand, you realize that your rule forces you to work all the time, and you are missing cherished time with your family that you'll never get back. You decide to break your rule and go, but you feel guilty the whole time, thinking about the work you "should" be doing.

How do you remove a rule from your Language of Rules so that every part of you feels good about it? What do you do if one part of you thinks the rule is a good rule and doesn't *want* to break it?

The first step to eliminating Internal Conflict and freeing yourself from rules that hold you back is to consciously go through your rules and determine which ones are serving as barriers to your success (Activity 20-3).

ACTIVITY 20-3. Identifying My Success Barriers

Go back through Activities 20-1 and 20-2 and look at the rules you checked. These are the rules that you are currently living.

As you go through your two lists, take a red pen and circle any rule that you think is a barrier to your success in your practice and/or in your personal life. As you circle it, ask yourself,

"How is this rule keeping me from getting what I really want?"

The more you think about that, the more you will bring the rule into your conscious awareness. This is the first step to freedom.

Once you have identified your success barriers, you have an important decision to make:

Do I want to keep these rules?

If your answer is "yes," then that means you are not at a point in your life when you are ready or feel the need to change anything. The rules are serving you well, and you have no reason to change them. Simply be aware that your rules may be conflicting with other people's rules in your practice. For example, if you have rules like *"Don't ask for help," "I'm on my own," "Don't trust anyone,"* or *"I don't need anyone,"* then you may find it difficult to Align with and allow yourself to be connected to other members of your Team. If you have a rule that says, *"Work hard!"* and you have a partner with a rule that says, *"Play hard!"* you may be prone to conflicts in the practice.

There's no right or wrong here, it's just a fact that different Languages of Rules can conflict and if you are aware of it you will have much less stress and conflict because you'll understand the source of the conflict.

If you decide that some of your rules are blocking your success, then make a decision to change them. You can change any rule you want because you are the one who decided to take it on in the first place!

Here's the key to success with all of this: If you want to eliminate a rule from your life, it isn't enough to say *"OK, I'm not going to do that anymore."* You have to replace it with a *new* rule that will eliminate the need for that other one. For example, let's say you have a rule *"I won't rock the boat."* You've decided that this rule is blocking your success, so you circle it. Ok, well now what? You create a new rule *"I'll speak up whenever I think there is a problem."* Now the "kid" in you knows that this is the rule and will follow that instead. As you use your new rule, you find that it makes you sound like a complainer, so you change it again to *"I'll speak up whenever I think there is a problem, and I'll offer to help find a solution."* You decide this new rule works for you and you're good to go.

If you want to change any of your rules, simply write a new one that will erase the old one and commit to tweak it until it fits precisely the life you want to live. There's a space all ready for you to do this in Activity 20-4.

ACTIVITY 20-4. My New Rules	
Go back over all of the rules you circled in Activities 20-1 and 20-2. Look at each rule one at a time and ask yourself *"What new rule will I create to free me from this old rule that is blocking my success?"* List your new rules here.	

Once you have taken charge of your Language of Rules, consider helping others to do the same. Teach this to your partners and other leaders in your practice. Help them to be aware of their Language of Rules and how their respective rules might be conflicting. Invite them to talk about how their rules are keeping them from being Aligned as a Team, and encourage them to be accountable to each other with statements like, *"My rule has led me to behave this way with you, and I want to change that."* Work together to create a list of rules that will help your practice to live up to your Mission Statement and get you everything you want.[1]

EXTERNAL CONFLICT

Every Team experiences conflict among its members. While these External Conflicts are to be expected, it's important to help your Team to understand how to handle them when they occur.

Unfortunately, one of the biggest challenges we see in healthcare is that so many people are conflict averse. When people think there is the slightest possibility of a conflict, they look down, walk the other way, or pretend nothing is wrong. Because of this, little and big events occur with frequency and often repeat because no one knows that they are doing anything that is bothering someone else. Sometimes the conflict avoidance behaviors that people use actually *create* the conflict.

> ### Practice Spotlight
>
> Dr. P was a competent and experienced doctor with a tremendous sensitivity to the needs of others. His passion and warmth made him beloved by those who knew him. Those who did not know him, however, had developed an impression of Dr. P that made them want to keep him at arm's length.
>
> Dr. P generated sound and creative ideas that would have greatly improved the ability of everyone in the hospital to work more efficiently as a Team, but no one at the hospital would listen because Dr. P had a reputation for being *"rude and disruptive."*
>
> After several years, key physicians in the hospital sent a letter to Dr. P's practice stating that they were no longer willing to work with him nor would they refer patients to the practice as long as he was there. How did this happen?
>
> Here's what we discovered:
>
> Whenever there was a meeting of physicians, Dr. P would come in late, sit down, and keep his eyes closed throughout the meeting. Even if he was directly addressed, he would keep his eyes tightly shut, unwilling to make eye contact with anyone in the room.

[1] When we work with a practice, we often have Team members compare their Language of Rules. There is always a great deal of laughter and mutual accountability as they start to see that their practice is being guided, in part, by the eight-year-old kids who had made these rules so long ago.

If someone made a comment that he didn't like, he would push his chair back, fold his arms, and drop his chin down to his chest.

On the floors of the hospital, if he didn't like something someone did, he would simply stop whatever he was doing and walk away.

The hospital physicians and staff interpreted Dr. P's behaviors as anti-social and counterproductive to effective Team work. Dr. P saw it as his way of keeping the peace. You see, Dr. P was extremely conflict averse. In point of fact, he was terrified of getting into any conversation that could end in an argument. So, he would close his eyes to calm himself. Unfortunately, his efforts to avoid conflict had led everyone around him to form an opinion of him that, while completely erroneous, was disastrous to his ability to Align with the hospital, affecting his reputation, his income, and the revenues of the practice.

Most people are surprised to learn how many people are afraid of conflict. In fact, I have done speaking engagements on conflict management from Nebraska to Australia and, without exception, every time the halls are filled with people who admit to doing whatever they can to avoid conflict.

I haven't kept track of this officially, but I can tell you that a high percentage of our private group practice clients include one or more doctors and/or administrators who were conflict averse when we first met. In fact, we've had several clients who originally contacted us to serve as referees, hoping our presence would allow them to find solutions and keep them safe from erupting into something that would have been uncomfortable for them.

Practice Spotlight

One of my healthcare marketing colleagues called and begged me to go to visit one of her clients. The 12-doctor practice had been sitting on her proposed marketing campaign for three months, unable to come to a decision about whether or not to approve it. My colleague was willing to work with them, but no one would give her any feedback. In the meantime, she had a deadline to complete their project for a huge event that was pending and asked me to go facilitate their decision.

I don't mean to be disrespectful, but it was probably one of the most comical scenes I have ever witnessed. These gentlemen were considered the cream of the crop by their colleagues. Experienced neurosurgeons and orthopedic physicians, they had top credentials including board certifications and impressive fellowships. Yet all of that was useless to them on the day of our meeting. These highly skilled men felt totally lost as they walked into the room and sat down in their leather executive chairs. No one looked up or said a word.

I knew they didn't like the campaign my colleague had produced, so I asked them to talk about what they didn't like about it. They said that they *"just didn't like it."* No one would express his specific dislikes, and all they would tell me was that they wouldn't approve it as it was.

Little by little, I gently extracted opinions from each doctor. It was painful for each of them to talk about what he didn't like, and they weren't all that comfortable talking about what they did like. No two doctors agreed on what they wanted to change about the campaign. After about an hour, I called a quick break to give them a chance to stretch and check their messages.

All of a sudden it was like someone had switched actors in the scene. During the break an entirely different group appeared. They were strong, confident, straightforward, and demanding. They talked to each other about cases and gave orders to assistants with the full authority of their positions. When I called the meeting back to order, however, they slithered back into their seats and reverted back to the "other" doctors. I had visions of "Superman" dancing in my head.

The beeper goes off, and look, there in the scrubs, is it an intern? Is it a resident? NO! IT'S SUPERDOC! After Superdoc repaired the brain, he returned to his chair to resume his disguise as the meek and mild-mannered doctor, unwilling to defend his position on a logo.

There was only one solution — I had to Align the Team so that they could gain strength from each other. I stood at the front of the room and announced in my best consultant-like voice,

"Gentlemen, it occurs to me that there is one thing you all agree on: You don't like the current campaign. Is this correct?"

They all quickly agreed. They seemed relieved that there was something they could agree on. I continued.

"Let's take the opposite approach. Since all of you disapprove of what they created for you, I propose that we change your slogan from **"Changing Lives Through World Class Care"** *to* **"Messing Up Lives Through Shoddy Care."**

There was dead silence. I was sure they would get mad and that this would propel them to band together and start talking about what they really wanted so we could find the solution, but they surprised me.

Everyone in the room spontaneously erupted with laughter and deep guffaws. They just couldn't stop laughing, and we all just kept on going like that for about 10 minutes!

The laughter broke the tension; and when everyone had finally regained composure, I said, *"Doctors, you hired [Marketing Company] for a reason. They don't tell you how to repair a spinal fracture, and I'm not sure you want to tell them how to create your marketing."* We talked a little further, and in the end they all agreed to leave it to the experts.

Three months lost, and an extra consulting fee, all because they were too conflict averse to talk this through on their own. But the end result was that they felt good about reaching consensus and they got a great marketing campaign from my colleague. The initial problem (conflict aversion) remained unresolved, but they were comfortable with that. They really did not want to change.

When people are conflict averse, that doesn't mean they like everything that is happening in their practice. It only means they aren't willing to bring it to anyone's attention. *"Don't rock the boat!"* is their mantra, and they live their lives accepting what they don't like, unwilling to change. Unfortunately, that leads to a series of unresolved problems that can add up and cause misalignments that could have been avoided had the original issues been addressed and resolved.

Ironically, most of the behaviors that lead to conflict are easily changed. In fact, most people welcome the opportunity to understand the impact they are having, if it is handled properly.

There are four formulas that I have taught for many years, all of which are extremely effective, particularly for people who are uncomfortable with conflict.

The Candor Formula

This formula is a great way to tell someone else when they've done something you didn't like, or didn't do something you wanted them to do. It's a simple statement of truth that explains what someone did or didn't do, how it affected you and/or others, how you and/or others felt as a result, and what you would like them to differently in the future.

Table 20-1 lists the five steps of The Candor Formula and how to apply them. Together, the steps create a statement to be given orally or in writing.

There are a couple of strategies in using this formula that will make it go more smoothly for you.

TABLE 20-1. The Candor Formula			
Step	**Complete the Sentence With**	**Example**	**Comment**
1: ***When you***	The *precise* behavior they did or didn't do	*When you leave your unwashed coffee cup in the sink*	This really has to be precise. No generalities or descriptions as in "When you are a slob." That leaves too much room for misinterpretation. Be so specific, a stranger could act out what you are describing.
2: ***The result is***	The consequences of the behavior	*The result is that someone else has to give up their time to wash it.*	Again, be precise. No judgments, just state the facts.
3: ***And I (we, they) feel***	Emotion (s)	*And they feel mad and disgusted.*	Avoid "Feel like" — that will steer you away from emotions. Inserting an actual emotion gives power to the statement so the listener understands the full impact of his or her behaviors.
4: ***Will you***	The behavior you want instead	*Will you please wash out your cup after using it or use Styrofoam instead?*	Be specific. Say exactly what you want (rather than what you don't want).
5: ***How can I (we, they) help?***	Offer of assistance	*How can I help you to remember to do this?*	This offer to Align is because it is you who wants the change, so it is only fair that you help to make it happen. Remember, the listener was perfectly happy doing what he or she was doing!

1. If you are very emotional about the situation, then, before you use the formula write out what you intend to say. It will help you to organize your thoughts and get it out more smoothly.

2. Be very clear about stating Step 2 (the consequences). If you describe it well, very often that's as far as you have to go because listeners get to see the impact in a way that they simply never saw previously. Often as soon as you give "The result is" line, they will respond with *"Oh wow, I had no idea. I'm sorry. I won't do it again."* If that happens, stop. You've gotten what you want. Don't beat a dead horse.

3. OK, now this one is really important, so please pay attention: *Get everything out in one breath.* I'm not kidding. If you have to take a breath then that means you're saying too much. Here's an example of "too much."

When you leave your unwashed coffee cup in the sink, the result is that someone else has to give up their time to wash it, and they feel mad and disgusted because let me tell you, you do this all the time and it's not just your coffee cup, you know, you also leave your dishes and now that I think of it you leave files all over the front desk and you never bother to pick up your mail and speaking of mail, how about checking your email now and then because your inbox is embarrassing and another thing, 10 years ago you were supposed to . . .

Let's just say that at this point, they've lost your point . . . And you've lost your impact.

Help your Team to use The Candor Formula by creating **Candor Coupons** (Table 20-2). Give everyone on your Team a few coupons and let them know that you encourage them to use the coupons any time anyone on the Team does anything that they don't like or doesn't do something they want. The more you encourage the use of The Candor Formula, the more it will get used. Your Team conflicts will decrease substantially, along with the levels of resentment and negativity from unresolved problems.

TABLE 20-2. The Candor Coupon

TO:_____   FROM: _____

I need to use The Candor Formula with you. Can we meet sometime this week? I can meet you at any of these days and times, so please circle the one that will work best for you, or suggest some alternate times and put it back on my desk. Thank you!

☐ Monday   ☐ Tuesday   ☐ Wednesday   ☐ Thursday
☐ Friday   ☐ Saturday   ☐ Sunday

☐ _____a.m.   ☐ _____p.m.
☐ _____a.m.   ☐ _____p.m.
☐ _____a.m.   ☐ _____p.m.

☐ Other (please suggest alternate days/times)
_____

I'll meet you at the snack bar or else please list a place that's better for you.
_____

Of course, the first step to reducing External Conflict begins with you. Take the first step with Activity 20-5.

ACTIVITY 20-5. My Candor Formula

Think through the people on your Team. Who could use a dose of The Candor Formula? Take some time and write out one formula that you will use this week. Read it into a recording device and play it while you get dressed in the morning. When the time comes, you'll be prepared.

The Candor Formula is a great tool to help you to organize your thinking and get it out smoothly. It even works at home! If you structure it properly, most people will receive it well. But the truth is, not everyone will respond with, *"Sure, no problem, glad you said something! And may I add, you said it very eloquently."* Once in a while, depending on the topic of your request, and the person you are with, you might get an emotional reaction. When that happens, you need another formula.

The Emotions Formula

How many times have you been with a member of your Team and been faced with an emotional outburst that you didn't expect? Perhaps it was an upset partner, a scared patient, or an angry employee. You tried to calm the person down, but the more you tried, the worse it got! This is actually quite common and is a frequent complaint of front desk and collections personnel.

The Emotions Formula is a fantastic tool to de-escalate someone's emotions so that you can have a fact-based conversation. In The Language of States of Mind, you're going to get them out of Critical Parent and Natural Child, and into Analyst and Socialized Child. There are nine steps to the formula, described in Table 20-3.

The Accountability Formula

One of the biggest sources of conflict that I hear about in practices today is what is _perceived_ as the unwillingness of people to be accountable to each other. I emphasize the word "perceived" because most of the time it turns out that it isn't that people are unwilling to be accountable. They simply don't know how.

> **Accountability is about acknowledging the role you played in creating a problem.**

It doesn't mean you will take all of the responsibility (unless you think you deserve it), it only means that you state your part in the issue at hand and explain your original intentions.

	TABLE 20-3. The Emotions Formula		
Step	**What to Do**	**What You Might Say**	**Notes**
1: Hear them out	Let them talk. Listen, maintain eye contact, and do not interrupt.	Absolutely nothing	If there are others present, move to a private area.
2: Ask for more	When you're sure they're done, they're usually not done. So you are going to make sure they get it all out.	*What else?* *Tell me more?* *And then what happened?*	Avoid the words "calm down" as that will escalate everything right back up again. When you let them get it out, they'll calm down naturally.
3: Verify what you heard	Paraphrase and summarize.	*So, if I understand you correctly, you are saying that . . .* *Have I got that right or did I leave something out?*	The goal here is to make sure that they know you got it. Once they know, they'll calm down.
4: Validate their feeling(s)	Give words to the emotion(s) you hear.	*If that happened to me I might be feeling (mad, sad, scared, embarrassed). Is that how you're feeling?*	You're not saying you agree with them, only that you understand their response.
5: Give a Chip	Recognize the discomfort of the situation and acknowledge it.	*I want to thank you for trusting me enough to tell me about this. I'm sure it wasn't easy for you.*	Keep it short. You just want to give a little Chip and move on.
6: Resolve the problem	Now you're going to invite them to partner with you in finding a resolution.	*What can we do that will solve this problem?*	Don't accept their bid to try and get you to do all the thinking here. It puts you in a bad position because no matter what you suggest, they will likely find something wrong with it.
7: Confirm the problem is resolved	Double check.	*So, will that solve it for you?*	Nod your head as you say this.
8: Offer further assistance	See if there's anything else.	*Is there anything else you need?*	Shake your head as you say this.
9: Give another Chip	Same as above	*Thanks again for talking to me. I really appreciate it.*	Walk them out as you say this.

If you're going to hand out Candor Coupons, you will probably want to hand out The Accountability Formula with it. They go together.

Will you need The Accountability Formula? Well, that depends on whether you think anyone will ever need to use The Candor Formula with you. After all, you've gotten this far into The M.A.D. Formula, so you're probably doing extremely well at managing the people factor on your Team. But, hey, anyone could have a bad day. So, on the off chance that someday, somewhere you do something that someone doesn't like, or don't do something they wanted you to do, it's important to know how to respond to them so that it doesn't escalate into a major conflict and break your Alignment.

There are nine steps to The Accountability Formula. I've laid it all out for you in Table 20-4.

Commercial Interruption

OK, now I've been a really good kid about not pushing you about listening to your CD, but I've just got to say something.

Each of the three conflict formulas will work for you, but only if you've got them ready to go. When you get upset you don't have time to go look up The Candor Formula, and if someone else is upset you really can't start shuffling through pages in search of The Emotions Formula, and for goodness sake if someone is confronting you, it is really kind of rude to say

"Oh wait, I know what to say, hold on a minute I've got it here somewhere. Really, it's called The Accountability Formula and it works great, OK, just wait one more little minute . . ."

Please, if you haven't done so yet, take the CD and stick it in your car now before you run into a difficult conflict and can't get out of it. Just think of me like your grandmother — you know . . . the one who always made you stop off in the restroom *just in case.*

The Splinter Formula

Teams who have worked together for more than one year inevitably build up little (and sometimes big) resentments along the way. Aversion to conflict, coupled with the reality of 80+ patients a day and no time to cross paths, means that most people pick up little Splinters along the way and move on. Over time, the Splinters can accumulate until finally one day they implode or explode. For this reason, it's important to introduce your Team to one more formula.

The Splinter Formula allows you to clean out your Splinters and heal your wounds so you can walk together again. Once you use this formula, you will

TABLE 20-4. The Accountability Formula			
Step	**What To Do**	**What You Might Say**	**Notes**
1: Verify what you heard	Paraphrase and summarize	*So what I did that you didn't like was . . .*	It's important that you stay brief on this.
2: Validate perceptions	Confirm that you see their point of view	*I can see how you wouldn't like that.* (NOTE: Never try a shortcut and say *"I understand"* – That will lead to a whopping *"no you don't!"* and you're going to need the Emotions Formula to get out of it!)	Do not say this unless you mean it. If you need information to understand, then ask them, *"Help me understand what made this a problem for you?"* When you get it then confirm you understand.
3: Validate feelings	Confirm that you understand what they feel	*If I were in your place I'd probably be mad too.* (Again, avoid *"I understand"*)	If you can't say that honestly, ask them, *"Help me understand how you ended up feeling that way."* When you get it then confirm you understand.
4: Acknowledge the role you played	State your specific behaviors	*I should have . . .* *I wish I would have . . .* *I think if I had . . .*	Suggest an alternate scenario that would have resulted in a different ending.
5: Apologize if appropriate	Apologize for any harm you may have done	*I'm sorry for the part I played in this.*	If you perceive that it is all your responsibility then take it all.
6: Explain your intentions	Briefly explain your thought process	*I was trying to . . .* *I thought I was supposed to . . .* *I had planned on . . .*	This is not an excuse. It is an honest effort to explain how this happened and to show that you didn't intentionally cause harm.
7: Offer resolution	Invite them to partner with you in finding a resolution	*What can we do to resolve this problem?*	You can offer solutions but only after you give them a chance to go first.
8: Confirm resolution	Double check	*So, will that solve it for us?*	If not, return to the previous step.
9: Chip	Realign	*Your friendship is important to me. I'm glad you came to me.*	Good time for a hug if that's your style, otherwise a handshake or some physical connection. Touch locks in the Alignment.

be free from the past resentments and available to realign. There are four steps to using The Splinter Formula.

Step 1: Install a Success Agreement

Whenever you meet to discuss sensitive or uncomfortable issues, whether it is in a Team of 2 or 100, it is important to install a process that will ensure kindness and a commitment to completion. The Success Agreement is ideally suited for this purpose. There are six components to the formula, outlined and explained in Table 20-5.

TABLE 20-5. The Success Agreement[1]	
Agreement Component	**Explanation**
We agree to talk things through until we all believe we've been understood and that the subject is finished.	The facilitator needs to check in with people frequently to confirm that this is being upheld. Ask questions like, *"What do you understand him to be saying?"* and *"Is this finished for you?"* Don't let any subject drop unless you think it is really finished.
We agree that we will not discount or dismiss our own or others' feelings or perceptions.	Instruct the group to police these three elements. Don't allow playful teasing as someone may misinterpret teasing during a vulnerable moment.
We agree to respond to each other without belittlement or intentional shaming.	"Loss of relationship" refers to Team Alignment and friendship and does not ensure permanent job security.[2]
We agree that we will not threaten each other with bodily harm or a loss of relationship.	
We agree to refrain from gossip — everything said during this conversation will stay in this room.	Go around the room and have everyone verbally agree to this. History breaks trust, so they need to be able to look into each others' eyes and know if the person means what he or she is promising.
We agree to stay through to the end of the meeting and to follow the communication guidelines of The M.A.D. Formula.	This assumes that everyone has been trained or at least made aware of The Four Languages of The M.A.D. Formula so they can communicate effectively as a Team. Ideally, they would also have had their ACTION Plan meetings. If not, leave this component out of your agreement.

[1] Whenever we work with Teams, we install this agreement first. It allows everyone to speak freely and finish the conflicts faster without injury to the relationships on the Team. When we work with couples, we always suggest that they install a Success Agreement in their relationship. A Success Agreement allows you to disagree and get through emotionally charged conversations without threatening each other. This is critical for the successful resolution of a conflict and is a wonderful tool for a marriage. Hal and I have a Success Agreement in our marriage, and it allows both of us to talk freely about our concerns without fear that the other will threaten to leave the room or the relationship. It's very cool.

[2] It is helpful to announce to a Team that nothing that is said during a Splinter meeting will be held against them in any way after the meeting. Check your HR guidelines to be safe.

Step 2: Find the Splinters

This step requires a touch of courage. You're going to invite the other person (or your entire Team) to go over the past and clean out any and all unresolved issues that may have come up along the way. The other person(s) may deny that there is anything to be discussed, but if your intuition says there's something going on, trust yourself. Your invitation may sound something like this:

> *"We've been working together for eight years now, and I'm sure I must have stepped on your toes at some point during that time without even knowing it. These things might not have been big deals to you at the time, but they could accumulate and it could affect our working relationship. I'd like to sit down with you and talk about anything that may have happened along the way in the past years and get them all out and over with. Will you do that with me?"*

If you're not comfortable face-to-face, you can pick up a phone or send an email. The key is to get it set up. In the ideal world, you would have your meeting off site. Many people meet for breakfast or go together after work for a beverage. The important thing is that you go somewhere you will be free to talk.

If you are doing this in a group, print out the paragraph as a script and have each person in your Team read it to the person they need to talk with.

Step 3: Remove the Splinters

Now you're going to invite the other person to start talking. Don't interrupt. Tell your partner you're going to make a list of what he or she says so you don't forget. When your partner finishes you talk while he or she writes. No one is going to respond. Just get all your Splinters out. The list will look something like this (Table 20-6):

TABLE 20-6. The Splinter List	
Lorraine to June	**June to Lorraine**
Told a secret to a colleague	Never paid back $50
Didn't invite me to weekend	Went over my head to boss
Threw out my messages	Spilled coffee on my report
Walked past without saying "hi"	Forgot birthday

After the list is complete, use The Accountability Formula with each other for each Splinter until everything is cleared up.

Step 4: Say Goodbye to the Past

Take your Splinter List outside where you will be out of heavy wind, place it in a tin can, and light a ritual fire. Stand together and watch the flames and commit that once the Splinters have burned they are completely gone from your lives. Commit to move on together and never again think or speak of the Splinters on your lists.

Agree that you will use The Candor Formula for future issues so that you never have a Splinter list again.

NOTE: If you decide to do this as a full Team, I recommend that you do this after hours and ideally off site. This can be a strong Alignment activity, but you need to allow at least 10 minutes per person to see it through to the end so that no one is left hanging.

While we're on the subject, what's on *your* Splinter List? Who is on your mind as you drive home at night? Whose face is on the golf ball as you drive off the tee? Let's find out with Activity 20-6.

ACTIVITY 20-6. My Splinter List
Are you walking around with old Splinters? Go ahead and make your Splinter list so that you can organize the people you want to meet with, remove your Splinters, say goodbye to the past, realign, and start fresh! Remember, when you're ready to talk with them, explain the Splinter Formula so that they have a chance to share their Splinters too!

BOTTOM LINE

The uncomfortable parts of Team Alignment are actually the most powerful interventions and yield the most dramatic results. The key is to identify and break through Internal Conflicts that may be serving as success barriers to individuals and the Team and then to identify External Conflicts and work them through with step-by-step formulas. These formulas are simple, and they work, but they have to be memorized so that the outline is ready when and where you need them. Use your CD!

Chapter 21

Sustain and Strengthen Your Alignment

NO MATTER HOW MOTIVATED YOU ARE and no matter how Aligned your Team, there will always be moments (or entire weeks) when the forces come together and attack your practice. It begins simply enough . . .

On Monday morning you drive to work, ready to face a brand new week with new opportunities to make a difference and build your success.

As you enter your door, you find faxes strewn all over the floor, mail piled inside, and everything is hot and airless from a weekend of energy-saving thermostats.

The phones begin to ring (a reassuring sound) with patients calling in for help. Everyone needs an appointment. And they need it *today.*

One of your doctors is stuck in an airport somewhere, while another is stuck in a traffic jam. Your reception area is filling up rapidly, and three employees just called in sick.

Yep, it's gonna be a great day.

Tuesday you are still handling the spillover from Monday. At 11:03 a.m. your network goes down, and all computers are frozen. . . . Wednesday the computers are up but there is a severe leak from the floor above, and you have to close at noon. . . . Thursday you have double-duty making up for Wednesday, and as you look around at your Motivated and Aligned Team, they seem a little off. Faces are red, and voices are a little higher-pitched than usual. Normally coordinated staff members are dropping papers, instruments, pens, and clipboards. People are bumping into each other and snapping at everyone and anyone who gets in their way.

Who are these people? Where's my Team?

Your Team is experiencing a normal response to stress.

The word "stress" has many meanings, but for the purposes of this discussion, we'll use this definition:

Stress is your body's reaction to a perceived threat.

Our bodies have built-in mechanisms to protect us from threats. The moment we perceive that we are in some danger, our bodies begin the "fight or flight" mechanism in an all-out effort to help us to fight the perceived threat to our safety.

The challenge is that in the 21st century, our "threats" can range from mistakenly deleting an email to a high-level terrorist attack, and our bodies have no way of distinguishing between these stimuli without the help of our conscious minds. At the moment the perceived threat begins, our bodies go into high gear, increasing adrenalin and cortisol levels and creating a cascade of changes in neurotransmitters that subsequently changes how we view and respond to our environment and the people around us.

The perceived threats begin at the moment we are awakened from a sound sleep by a buzzing alarm or blasting music and continue all day long as each new event occurs and is perceived by our minds as a threat.

After a long day of continued stress responses, our reserves begin to dwindle and we get fatigued. If this continues over an extended period of time, we can experience what is known as **"burnout."**

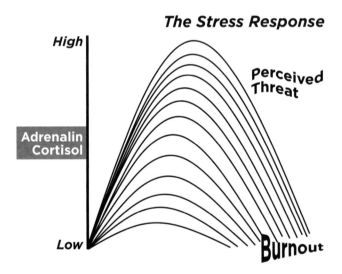

The Stress Response

Let's stop for a moment and assess your level of burnout with Activity 21-1.

ELEMENT #6: SUSTAINED ENERGY

Sustaining positive morale in the face of stress is significantly easier if your Team is already Motivated and Aligned. Here are some tried and true tips for

ACTIVITY 21-1. Determine Your Level of Burnout		
Following is a pop quiz to help you to asses your current level of burnout. For each statement below, choose "yes" or "no" by placing a check (✓) in the appropriate column.		
Question	**Yes**	**No**
Do you find yourself feeling more fatigued and less energetic?		
Do you feel less of a sense of satisfaction about your performance?		
Do you feel more cynical and disenchanted with your work and/or the members of your Team?		
Are you getting more irritable, angry, and short-tempered with the people around you?		
Are you seeing close friends and/or family members less frequently?		
Are you having more than your share of physical complaints?		
Are you having trouble getting to sleep or staying asleep?		
Do you sometimes think that you just don't have anything more to give to people?		
Count up the number of checks that you put in the "Yes" column. The more checks you have, the closer you are getting to a stress burnout.[1]		
[1] It should come as no surprise that many of the symptoms in this list mirror symptoms of hormonal imbalance and clinical depression. The more stress you experience, the more you respond at the expense of your hormones. If you gave yourself a lot of "Yes" checks, you might want to seek some professional help. Or, at the very least, take a vacation.		

avoiding and managing stress for an Aligned Team. These "stress busters" are specifically designed for use at work, but feel free to take them home with you! Some techniques can be used at the workstation, while others are ideally suited for a break room, a parked car, or even a bathroom stall!

At times of high stress, I recommend that you install "mandatory stress buster breaks." Tell all employees that they are to take two five-minute breaks per day (morning and afternoon) during which they are to choose from the list of stress busters in Table 21-1. Try it for two weeks. You'll be amazed at the difference in morale and productivity.[1] Remember, your Team includes patients, colleagues, and vendors. Consider holding a stress buster activity in your reception area and invite everyone to join in. Everyone appreciates an opportunity to laugh and relax, and that's what this is all about. The more you laugh, breath, stretch, and engage your passion, the more you increase endorphins, better known as "the natural stress reliever."

[1] I developed this idea as a result of a project I conducted at NYNEX (the phone company in New York and New England). Employee productivity increased significantly among all Teams after two weeks of initiating mandatory stress buster breaks, and was sustained throughout the six-month test period.

TABLE 21-1. Stress Busters	
In Public or Private	**In Private Only**
Play one game of solitaire or other video game.	Take a two-minute power nap.
Read for five minutes (not work or news).	Do yoga, Pilates, or other stretching.
Keep a video library of comedy sitcoms in your break room (remember to choose a variety for all generations in your practice).	Grab a Team member and "vent" about your stress with an agreement that you will "vent" for one minute each and then spend the next three minutes talking about anything that will make you laugh.
Find your spirituality and be there for a few minutes.	
Invite a Team member to play the "Glad Game" (*it's a good thing that this is happening because . . .*). The goal is to get so absurd that you both burst out laughing.	Progressive relaxation. (With eyes closed, tighten and release muscle groups from the feet to the head. Incorporate deep breathing for best results.)
Climb a few flights of stairs and then come back down.	Take a fantasy trip to some place special. (Close your eyes and imagine yourself drifting on a cloud to a special destination. Engage all of your senses to see, feel, and hear the experience.)
Have a massage.[1]	
Sing! (OK, for some that might be better done in private.)	
Deep breathing. (Inhale to the count of four, exhale to the count of four.) Warning: deep breathing for extended periods of time may cause people to be light-headed or dizzy.	Take a real trip! Get some time off, and get out of town for a couple of hours, a couple of days, or a couple of weeks. Sometimes you just have to get away.
Blow up a balloon, draw a picture of your stress, and then pop it!	NOTE: I have recorded a five-minute stress buster on the included CD that will guide you through deep breathing, progressive relaxation, and a fantasy trip. Allow me to be your guide as you bust through your stress! This recording may be used in group meetings, to end "lunch 'n' learns," to help patients de-stress, or any other time you want to relax and then reenergize your Team.
Color with markers or crayons in a coloring book.	
Have a joke-off: Five minutes back and forth without stopping.	
Keep miniature toys around the office (textured are best).	
Five minute Internet shopping spree.	
Sip water through a straw.	
Eat fruit, nuts, carrots, and celery. (Oh who am I kidding? Go grab the chocolate!!!)	
[1] I have a number of clients who contract with a massage therapist to come in several times a week to give neck and shoulder rubs to all Team members.	

There is one more thing you can do to keep your Team positive and light:

Create a "Negativity Bucket."

Put together a "Negativity Committee" and instruct them to creatively decorate a box, an aluminum can, a garbage receptacle, or an actual cleaning bucket. The more creative and outlandish the decorations, the more effective this will be. Place your Negativity Bucket in a central location (my clients usually choose the front desk). Here's how it works:

Any time any of your Team members catch another Team member displaying negativity, the offender has to put a nickel in the bucket.

I have some clients who raise the ante to a quarter and even a dollar. This game can become highly competitive as your Team members Align to see who can be the ones to stay out of the bucket.

The more elaborate the appearance of your bucket, the more you will receive inquiries from patients, colleagues, and vendors. That's when you get to explain your commitment to a positive work environment and enhance your reputation as a unique and special practice.

The fun really begins the first time one of your staff members makes the connection that patients are part of the Team.

Practice Spotlight

It was an extremely busy day at the ABC Med-Spa. Patients who were in the process of healing from plastic surgery were arriving and leaving as they intermingled with clients who were in for their spa treatments. The air was alive with activity, and we could see how the Alignment of the staff and doctors now made everything flow smoothly.

Mrs. Patient had been sitting in the "Relaxation Area" waiting for her massage just a bit longer than she thought was appropriate. She came back up to reception in her robe and slippers, towel draped around her head, looking a little out of place in the middle of all of the other clothed patients, clients, and staff members.

Susan, one of three receptionists, looked up and said, *"You look cozy in your robe, Mrs. Patient. How may I help you?"*

"Don't you get all sweet with me, my dear. I have been sitting back there waiting for Chelsea for a very long time. What's going on around here?"

"Let me check for you, Mrs. Patient. Would you like to go on back and have some juice? I'll come back just as soon as I find out what is going on," Susan said.

"I'm not going back there until you tell me what's going on. You think I'll just go back there and wait patiently but I'm not budging until you

pick up that phone and find out how long this is going to be because I spend a lot of money here and . . ."

"Excuse me just a second," Susan said smiling. She got up from her stool, walked over to the Negativity Bucket on the back table, and carried it over to the front desk. The thing was enormous, decorated with foiled wrapping paper and sparkles and little Slinkies and colorful twirly things with balls hanging off the sides and edges. She lifted it up onto the counter and said,

"Mrs. Patient, I am doing everything I know how to do to be really polite and professional, but if you succeed in getting me upset, then I'm going to have to put a dollar in our Negativity Bucket. Now I don't have a dollar, so please let me help you back to the relaxation room, and I will find Chelsea and find out what is going on for you. OK?"

Mrs. Patient burst out laughing, reached into her purse, pulled out her wallet and threw a bill into the bucket. *"I can find my way back alone. Thanks."*

The entire reception area burst into applause, and Susan did a little curtsey.[2]

CHECK IN REGULARLY

A Team will only seek to maintain Alignment to the extent that it is in the best interest of all Team members to do so. There is no great formula or magic potion to solve this. Just one simple technique:

> **Ask everyone on your Team if they are getting everything they want and need on a regular basis.**

This is such a basic concept, that it is almost a little crazy that I should have to put it in a book. But the fact is, people are often uncomfortable asking for what they want or need. Many people have rules that they *"shouldn't ask for help"* while others have rules that they should *"settle for what they get."* No matter what their rules, these people won't tell you when something isn't right. They just pull away from the Team.

I will never forget the first time I heard Hal ask a group of our client doctors if they were getting everything they wanted from us. The look on their faces was nothing short of stunned. They sat there quietly for a moment,

---

[2] I've often wondered if she would have had the courage to do that if I hadn't happened to be standing right there at the time. But it was an amazing sight to see.

then smiled and simultaneously said, *"More."* They looked at each other and the Alignment was palpable.

When you ask people if they are getting everything they want and need from you, from your Team, and from your care, you are reaffirming their trust and strengthening your Alignment. It's a powerful question, and I invite you to ask it every day to your partners, your colleagues, your staff and your patients. And don't forget to ask yourself, *Am I getting everything I want and need?*

MAINTAIN YOUR ALIGNMENT IN THE FACE OF CHANGE

To the extent that you continue to work in healthcare, you can expect ongoing, constant, never-stopping change. I consider this a very good thing. Without change, there is no need for growth or the development of new ideas. On the down side, with every change comes a demand for you to check your Team and make certain that the Alignment is firm.

I have found only one solution to this:

Bring your Team together into one room on a regular basis.

I know all of the reasons you think you can't do this, but you didn't buy this book to hear me say, *"Oh, you're busy. OK well then just forget it."* So allow me to take a moment to try to sell you on the importance of scheduling regular, well-organized Team meetings. I'll be quick.

1. People usually work alone or in small groups. When you get everyone face-to-face with the full Team, they feel the strength of your organization and become simultaneously empowered and humbled. This is true no matter how small the size of your Team.
2. When a Team stands in the same room with each other, they reestablish a sense of responsibility to the Team as a whole and to each other as individuals.
3. If the meeting is handled properly, it is an opportunity to combine visual, auditory, and kinesthetic learning elements to present new information in a powerful and rapid format.
4. It will bring the messages of previous meetings back to the front of your Team's focus.
5. It's a great opportunity to celebrate successes and offer Chips publicly.

So, how do you do this effectively so that it's worth the time? Apply The Meeting Formula.[3]

---

[3] You probably knew it was time for another formula, huh?

THE MEETING FORMULA

Step 1: Review Your Mission Statement

Is this corny and sappy? Absolutely, but do it anyway. It's important to remind your Team that you honor the Mission Statement that they created. Have fun with this by assigning a Team member (in advance) to take charge of this step. Invite them to be creative and to find new ways to honor and celebrate your Mission Statement. The more drama the better! You'll be thrilled with the results, and so will they.

Step 2: Announce the Purpose of the Meeting

Briefly explain the goal for the meeting and what they will be able to do as a result of having attended.

Step 3: Give Team Chips

List four specific examples of things you have personally witnessed your Team doing that reminded you that your Team has great Skill and Heart (two of each). Mention specific Team members.

Step 4: Disseminate Information

This is the part where you will update the Team on new information and changes to procedures or process, review information from a previous meeting, or teach something new. Deliver this in a high-energy format.[4]

Step 5: Defer or Answer

If you have time and are willing to address questions, go for it. My only caution is that this can suck the energy right out of your meeting if you get a bunch of questions that don't apply to the full Team. Answer questions that affect the Team, and defer others to Sub-Team leaders.

Step 6: 25-Second Successes

Individuals who have done something they are proud of since your last meeting have 25 seconds to tell the rest of the Team. No matter what gets announced, everyone cheers and you go to the next person. Assign someone to hold a stopwatch and announce 20 seconds to keep it moving. This is a high-energy way to end your meeting and send everyone out ready to hit the ground running.[5]

How often should you hold these meetings and who should attend? There is no concrete answer that fits for every practice. Table 21-2 gives a general

----

[4] See Chapter 26 for tips on public speaking.

[5] Don't think this is only for your employees! I've done this with a room full of doctors and it's very cool. Remember, doctors have five States of Mind too!

TABLE 21-2. Sample Meeting Schedule			
Practice Size	**Teams**	**Length of Meeting**	**Frequency**
Solo practitioner, 10 or fewer employees	Doctor and staff	30–60 mins	1 X per week
		90–120 mins	1 X per month
		3 hours	1 X per quarter
		1–2 days	1 X per year
	Doctor, staff, and patients	2 hours	1 X per year
	Doctor, staff, and vendors	30–60 mins	Varies
Multiple practitioner 10–50 employees	Doctors	2–3 hours	1 X per month
		1–2 days	1 X per year
	Doctors and full staff	30–60 mins	1 X per week
		90 mins	1 X per month
		3 hours	1 X per quarter
		1–2 days	1 X per year
	Doctors, full staff, and patients	2 hours	1 X per year
	Doctors, full staff, and vendors	30–60 mins	Varies
Multiple practitioner 50+ employees	Doctors	2–3 hours	1 X per month
		1–2 days	1 X per year
	Sub-Teams	30–60 mins	1 X per week
		90 - 120 mins	1 X per month
	Doctors and full staff	3 hours	1 X per quarter
	Doctors and full staff	1–2 days	1 X per year
	Doctors, full staff, and patients	2 hours	1 X per year
	Doctors, Sub-Teams, and vendors	30–60 mins	Varies

template for different-sized practices regarding recommended attendees, duration, and frequency, but you will have to do what works best for you and your call schedule. If you make these Alignment meetings a priority, then it's quite amazing what you can get done to make them happen.

While your ability to serve patients will always come first, I can't stress enough the importance of setting up some sort of schedule and sticking to it. Your Team needs constancy, and Alignment will dwindle if you allow too much time to come between meetings.

Practice Spotlight

It had been four years since our original training program, and since that time the practice had developed a solid reputation in the community for Five Star Service. This reputation had allowed them to build their practice enough to recruit an additional physician and 10 new employees. The challenge was that the new people didn't know the techniques that the others had learned with us, and even the veterans had begun to *"get a little lazy."* They asked us to come back for a *"quick refresher."*

We arrived the day before to observe the practice in motion. In many ways we were overwhelmingly impressed with the changes they had made. On the surface, everything looked great, but as we watched the faces of the employees, we saw that they weren't doing well. They walked from room to room looking tired and stressed. No one was smiling or laughing as they had been when we left. Something was clearly wrong. We spoke with the office manager, the clinical manager, and the administrator, and all three confirmed our hunches.

In the physician meeting that night, we discussed the changes in the practice and suggested that they were having an Alignment problem. They agreed and asked us to address this the next day. So we went back to the hotel, and I re-wrote the beginning of the workshop so that I could focus them off of their patients for a little while and onto each other.

The next day, they all filed in and sat in their separate camps. I spoke for a few minutes about the power of Team Alignment and reminded them of how much their impact as a practice depended on their willingness to bring out their individual strengths and merge their talents for a more powerful and effective result. I asked them what was in the way of that, and they launched into a great discussion. They talked about what was going well and what needed work. They agreed that they were doing an outstanding job of providing Five Star Customer Service for their patients, but that they were failing to give the same service to each other. One of their senior nurses took a deep breath and asked,

"How can we give each other Five Star Service when we have burned our bridges with so many people on our Team?"

Talk about a show-stopper! Hal and I looked around the room as 57 people all froze. I asked if anyone else felt that way, and they all nodded their heads.

Here's what came out as the discussion continued: Over the course of the four years, they had let some things slide internally. Whereas in the beginning months they had given out LOTS of Chips internally and externally, over time they had gradually dropped the technique. In the beginning they were shifting Action Types and States of Mind, and over time they'd let that go with each other as well. In the beginning they were meeting regularly to discuss challenges and celebrate victories. But as they had gotten busier, they had stopped having meetings to allow for more availability for referring doctors' patients.

Without face-to-face contact, the employees had no way of knowing what people from other departments were doing. Since the Chips had stopped, they began to assume that no one appreciated them. Each Sub-Team became resentful of the others, and they stopped trying to understand what other Sub-Teams needed from them. Perceiving that they were misunderstood and undervalued by their co-workers and the physicians, the tension just kept building. Each Sub-Team was working completely unaware of the challenges of the other Sub-Teams and so they were unable to understand how their protocols were interfering with others'. The more time had gone by, the more separate the Sub-Teams became and the more stress started to mount throughout the practice as people struggled to do their jobs effectively and not let their tensions show in front of the patients.

The doctors sat and listened to this discussion with their mouths hanging open. They had no idea this was going on. And it was such a simple fix! They all agreed to go back to what had worked so well before. The managing partner launched the initiative. He picked up the microphone and gave Chips to individuals and Sub-Teams right then and there. The energy soared while each group got to hear what they had needed to hear for over three years, "*We see how hard you work for us. We see how dedicated you are to patient care. We appreciate how much you give every single day.*" They started passing the tissues and laughing all at the same time. They agreed that they would reinstate their weekly Sub-Team and monthly Full-Team meetings; and while everyone was talking, laughing, and planning, the managing partner took us aside and said, "*I hope you know this means we're done with you.*"

I know that meetings cost you money. I also know that *not* having meetings costs you money. It's easy to calculate how much it costs you to have a meeting. There is no way to estimate how much you'll lose if you don't.

If you do nothing else listed in Table 21-2, please consider monthly meetings and an annual retreat of some sort. Every Team needs an opportunity to come together under one roof, review their commitments to achieve their mission, get rid of any Splinters they may have picked up along the way, learn some new techniques, refresh existing techniques, gain a richer understanding of each Sub-Team's needs, celebrate their successes, and make new plans for their future together. If you commit to make this happen, they will spend the rest of the time doing what you want them to do. It's a good deal. Take it.

PULLING IT ALL TOGETHER

As you can see, it takes a lot to Align a Team, and we have yet to talk about patients and other Sub-Teams! Is it worth it? I could add more Practice Spotlights and even testimonials of those who have made the effort and reaped the rewards. Instead, I suggest that you do Activity 21-2 and then decide for yourself.

ACTIVITY 21-2. Our Current Alignment Status					
Rate each Sub-Team of your practice on each of the following characteristics using the following scale: 1) Never true　2) Rarely true　3) True about half the time　4) Often true　5) Always true					
Characteristic of Alignment	1 = Never true　　2 = Rarely true 3 = 50-50　　　　4 = Often true 5 = Always true				
	1	**2**	**3**	**4**	**5**
I have diagramed my Team, identified all of our Sub-Teams, and relayed that information to my Team					
My Team doesn't make assumptions but, instead, asks clarifying questions to get to the truth of all communications					
Every member of my Team has been mapped for Action Types					
Each member of my Team has been mapped for Value Sets					
Each member of my Team has been mapped for States of Mind					
Each member of my Team gives Skill and Heart Chips on a regular basis					
Each member of my Team flexes his or her behaviors to communicate with colleagues, patients, and everyone who comes in contact with our practice					

(Activity continues next page)

Characteristic of Alignment	1 = Never true 2 = Rarely true 3 = 50-50 4 = Often true 5 = Always true				
	1	2	3	4	5
My Team effectively uses words, tone, and visual cues to express their messages in every communication					
All members of my Team trust each other					
We walk through fire and acknowledge it when we do					
I trust my full Team and each of my Sub-Teams					
Our current Mission Statement was created by 95% of my current Team					
Our Team ACTION Plan is derived from our Mission Statement					
Our Team ACTION Plan is updated minimally once a year					
All people who are working closely together find that their work styles are appropriately matched					
All Team members have worked to identify and actively choose their Language of Rules					
Doctors and staff effectively and comfortably request change from their teammates and patients (The Candor Formula)					
Doctors and staff effectively and comfortably handle each other's and patients' emotions (The Emotion Formula)					
Doctors and staff effectively and comfortably handle difficult emotions (The Emotion Formula)					
Doctors and staff are accountable to each other and to patients (The Accountability Formula)					
All Team members have resolved past resentments and said goodbye to the past (The Splinter Formula)					
We have a process for discussing sensitive or uncomfortable issues that ensures respect and a commitment to completion (The Success Agreement)					
We have an ongoing program to avoid, manage, and resolve work-related stress					
We have an ongoing process to ensure a positive and upbeat work environment					
Doctors, staff, and patients are getting what they need and want					
We meet regularly in Sub-Teams and as a full practice					

ACTIVITY 21-2. Our Current Alignment Status *(continued)*

(Activity continues next page)

ACTIVITY 21-2. Our Current Alignment Status *(continued)*					
Characteristic of Alignment	1 = Never true 2 = Rarely true 3 = 50-50 4 = Often true 5 = Always true				
	1	**2**	**3**	**4**	**5**
Our meetings are high energy and well-received by all Team members					
I tell my clients that any characteristic where they rate themselves 3 or less is an area that could use some work. Where will you begin, and when?					

BOTTOM LINE

Whether you are in a time of stress or at the top of your game, installing stress management techniques to sustain a positive environment is a cost-free intervention that will save you thousands of dollars in lost employee time due to illness and stress-induced decreases in productivity. Make a plan to hold regular meetings that are productive and energizing, and commit to assess your practice across the Six Elements of Alignment. While you don't need to apply every strategy and formula to Align your Team, you will strengthen your Team's Alignment with each piece you add, leading to a more efficient, enjoyable, and profitable practice.

Chapter 22

Align With Your Patients

THERE ARE A LOT OF happy and grateful patients in the healthcare system today, but there are also many who say they wish they had a better relationship with their doctors and better care from their doctors' staff. As I was writing this book, a friend posted a comment on my Facebook[1] wall:

> *As someone who deals with many healthcare professionals, I for one—from the patient's standpoint—hope everyone reads your book. If they learn to master the people factor for purposes of Aligning their Team, maybe they'll even master the people factor enough to actually learn to also Align with patients!!*

I have spoken with patients as they shared countless stories of kindness, compassion, and excellence. Unfortunately, I have also heard reports of inadequate or inappropriate communications, failure to build trust and rapport, and a sense of being considered *"an intrusion"* in their healthcare providers' day.

In my experience as a consultant (as well as in my roles as a private practice provider, a patient, and a caregiver), I have encountered three types of practices:

The True Patient-Oriented Practice: All doctors and staff are fully Aligned with their patients as individuals. Everyone in the practice is committed to building and sustaining ongoing trust and rapport with their patients. While maintaining excellence in clinical care, they work to ensure that their patients understand their choices and know that they have partners with whom they can discuss their needs and wants, and work through the barriers that would keep them from taking effective action for their health and appearance.

The Friendly Practice: Members of the practice focus primarily on their clinical and administrative responsibilities to the patients. While they

---

[1] In case you don't know about Facebook, it's a social networking Web site that allows you to keep your friends close via the Internet.

maintain a consistently "pleasant" and "helpful" posture, they do not attempt to connect or partner with their patients on an individual basis.

The Strictly Business Practice: Those who deliver healthcare services without making any attempt to communicate with patients beyond what is necessary to schedule, diagnose, treat, and collect fees.

It is not my place to tell you which of those three types I think you should be. I would, however, like to remind you of some key facts:

1. The therapeutic alliance has been shown in significant research findings to be a critical part of the treatment process. This alliance depends on your ability to Align with your patients.
2. Alignment has a direct relationship with trust: the more you Align with your patients, the more they will trust you; and the more they trust you, the tighter they will Align with you. The tighter they Align with you, the more they will permit you to help them.
3. The more your patients permit you to help them, the more honest they will be with you about their problems and the more they will share sensitive information that you need to diagnose and treat. The more they share information with you, the more they will feel Aligned to you.
4. The more you know about your patients and the stronger your Alignment with your patients, the less likely you are to be sued.
5. Alignment leads to happy, satisfied patients who tell all of their friends about you.
6. Misalignment leads to unhappy, dissatisfied patients who tell all of their friends about you.

Actually, it occurs to me that I'm probably preaching to the choir. If you read the last chapter and haven't sent this book to the place where all discarded and unwanted books go to meet their untimely demise, then you probably don't need to be convinced about Aligning with your patients. Perhaps you'd like some tips to make it easier, or even some ammunition to use with skeptical members of your practice. So, here you go:

In addition to following the suggestions in Chapters 18 to 21, there is one critically important step I recommend that you take with your patients.

Recruit your patients as members of your Team.

I know this idea sounds like a "rah-rah" thing, but it isn't. I'm talking about making a conscious effort to Align your patients to your Team as you would your doctors and staff.

THE IN-GROUP/OUT-GROUP EFFECT

At some point in your life, you've probably experienced the feelings that come when you are excluded from a group, either accidentally or on purpose. It is an awkward feeling that can lead you to be sad, mad, and even humiliated. When people are excluded (perceived or real), they draw conclusions about themselves and/or the people who excluded them. These conclusions then shape their perceptions and behaviors, affecting all future encounters.

> **Practice Spotlight**
>
> A woman in her late 30s or early 40s walked into a general dentistry practice and up to the front desk. There were three staff members at the desk, one of whom looked up, took the patient's name, and gave her a clipboard with forms to be completed. As the woman sat down to write, the three people at the desk began laughing and whispering. When the woman returned the clipboard, the three immediately dispersed. As soon as she walked away, they came back and started whispering and laughing again.
>
> The woman walked up to the front desk and said, *"Tell the doctor I'll come back another time,"* and walked out.
>
> I was a patient in that practice, but I was intrigued so I followed her out into the parking lot. I asked her what happened and here's (approximately) what she said to me:
>
> *"I felt like I was in the high school cafeteria all over again. I know it's stupid, but I just don't want to be where I'm not wanted."*
>
> Then she got into her car and drove away.[2]

What happened there can best be described by the sociological construct called "The In-Group/Out-Group Mentality." Simply defined, we are either members of the In-Group or we're not. If we are in, then we get to experience the benefits of membership, such as security, safety, friendship, prestige, and increased self-esteem. If we are on the outside of the group, we have none of these benefits, and may consequently experience feelings of sadness, fear, shame, and/or anger.

In response to being excluded, we develop ways of thinking that help us to ignore the discomfort we feel. These newly formed perceptions and opinions not only allow us to convince ourselves that we don't *want* to be a part of the In-Group, but lead us to tell others to avoid that group as well.

[2] True confession time: I often watch what is happening in my doctors' offices through my consultant eyes and then tell my doctors what they are doing well and what they could change for more success. Sometimes I wish I could turn it off and just "be a patient" but then there would be nothing to do but read outdated magazines. Where would be the fun in that? Plus, some of the things I see give me great examples for my trainees!

Eventually, we might create a new In-Group, the purpose of which would be to bring together people who "don't need or want" to be associated with the first In-Group.

Does this sound like high school stuff to you? It is! Remember the Jocks, the Nerds, the Geeks, the Cheerleaders, and the Hoods? We all experienced this to some degree back in our day, although increasingly we find that it has taken on a much more serious and frightening element with gang behaviors. But the In-Group/Out-Group mentality isn't exclusive to high school. It extends well into adulthood and happens in every organization. It forms a foundation for conflict between unions and management, doctors and interns, clinical and administrative staff, and so on.

I am a member of Sweet Adelines International, a group of 30,000 women worldwide who sing four-part barbershop harmony a capella[3] style. Every year, all over the world, Sweet Adelines compete in regional contests in which choruses and quartets sing and dance to achieve coveted medals and awards. The winners of those regions go on to compete in an international contest where champion choruses and quartets from all over the world convene in one location to strut their stuff in a massive convention center for four days of intense competition.

During International Convention week, Sweet Adelines take over the city, singing on street corners and shopping wherever money is to be spent. Surrounded by 10,000 of our closest friends dressed in sequins and sparkles, our mutual membership in the international organization leads us to smile widely and talk openly with strangers. There is an automatic Alignment and trust that comes from knowing we are all members of the same tribe. We are in the In-Group . . . to a point.

As it turns out, within the larger organization, there exist several levels of In-Group/Out-Group mentality. As you walk into the enormous convention center to watch the contest, there are seats reserved for "V.I.P.s" with ushers checking tickets so that "ordinary members" will not invade this elite area. Further down, there is a cordoned area where International Judges and members of the International Board of Directors and honored guests are seated. Every member knows, without having to be told, that they dare not enter that sanctified area. While 10,000 women hold hands, singing "Harmonize the World" in perfect harmony, there is no doubt that some are more IN than others.

Men have their own version of this in the Barbershop Harmony Society, which is just as big and displays its own In-Group/Out-Group behaviors.

---

[3] For further information, visit the Sweet Adelines International Web site at www.SweetAdelineIntl.org

In fact, we see this in every large group. Walk into the annual conventions of the American Medical Association and American Dental Association or any local study group, and you know immediately that there are degrees of In-Group/Out-Group throughout both organizations.

The In-Group/Out-Group can happen anywhere, and so it's important to do everything you can to make everyone on your Team a member of the In-Group, especially your patients.

So how can you make this happen?

Invite your patients into your In-Group, and make sure they know they are full-fledged members with all the associated rights and privileges!

In addition to practicing all of the steps we discussed to speak The Four Languages of the M.A.D. Formula in Section Two, the techniques to Motivate your patients to ACTION in Section Three, and the formulas to Align your Team so far in this section, there are nine additional steps you can take to build strong Alignments with your patients and avoid the In-Group/Out-Group phenomenon:

STEP 1: WELCOME THEM TO YOUR PRACTICE AND TO YOUR CARE

It seems like such an obvious thing, but most practices do not do this. They may politely say "hello," as they see the patient, but most staff members don't introduce themselves to the patients, and rarely (if ever) use the word "welcome."

Why do we see "Welcome" mats in the entry ways to a car mechanic shop, but rarely at the thresholds of our healthcare facilities?

From the moment your new patients book an appointment, welcome them to your practice. Use your name and their name. Give your new patients the names of the people in your practice who they can expect to be on their healthcare Team when they arrive for their appointment.

Send a "Welcome to Our Care" letter, and make sure it includes statements that reflect your warmth. Here's an example of a letter I prepared for a client:

WELCOME TO OUR CARE!

Dear Mr./Mrs./Ms. Patient:

It was a pleasure talking with you today. I'm delighted that you have decided to schedule an appointment with us on DAY, DATE, at TIME, and look forward to welcoming you in person to our care.

Enclosed is the information I promised you. I have no doubt that you will enjoy reading about our Team of doctors and caregivers, as well as about all the services we have available to help you to achieve your health goals.

I would encourage you to be sure to read the section on (illness, service, etc.), since that is your immediate concern.

I am also enclosing directions from your address to ours. Please feel free to contact me if you will be arriving from a different location, and I will be happy to provide you with a different set of directions.

Again, thank you for considering us for your care. We are all looking forward to learning more about you so that we can work together to help you to get what you need and get back to enjoying your life.

Respectfully yours,

Your Name,

ABC Healthcare Associates

This is one of those great ideas that clients always like and then forget to implement. Even if you don't have a brochure or packet of information, the Welcome Letter is an important gesture. So, take a moment now and do Activity 22-1:

ACTIVITY 22-1. Create Your Welcome Letter

Take a few minutes and edit the letter above to fit for your practice. Then, put it onto your letterhead and start using it immediately.

When your patient arrives at the practice, instruct all of your Team members to do whatever they can to help the patient know that they are truly welcome. That doesn't mean "treat them nicely," it means

Do things that will tell your patients that you are genuinely glad they are there.

Fake techniques won't cut it for this. In fact, the only thing that will work here is the genuine enthusiasm that comes when you are happy to see someone. Granted, that may not always be easy, particularly on difficult days or with particularly difficult patients. That's when you need to take this piece of sage advice.

If anyone on your Team is in a place where they can't genuinely welcome a patient to your care, then it's time for a stress-buster.

Practice Spotlight

In an effort to perk up the staff and increase their percentages when Motivating new patients to sign on for orthodontic treatment, I installed a new process that included taking the prospective patient and his or her parents on a tour of the practice. As they would pass the treatment area, the Treatment Coordinator would yell out, "Hey, everybody! This is (Patient's First Name)!" The entire Team, including patients-in-the-know would yell back, "Hi, (Patient's First Name)!"

This little moment thrilled children and parents, injected great energy into the treatment area, and made the doctor very happy when his number of new starts skyrocketed.

You decide what's best for you, whether it's a simple *"welcome to our practice,"* or a big brass band and ticker tape parade. Check yourself and your Team every day to make sure that everyone is welcoming patients to your Team. This is one of those things that patients may not miss, but will always remember.

STEP 2: DESIGN YOUR INTERIOR TO FIT YOUR PATIENTS

If you have a practice of all male patients, then you're probably not going to create an artistic mural of a mother nursing her newborn baby surrounded by storks and harps. By the same token, you're probably not going to choose floral prints for your chairs or stock your reception area with female-oriented magazines like *Self, O,* and *Soap Opera Digest.* Do some men like *Soap Opera Digest?* Of course! But a lot of money has been invested to determine the demographics of magazines, and it would be a smart move to choose the magazines that fit your patients' interests, as opposed to your own.

The important point is to do everything you can so that when your patients walk in and see your environment they will never think, *"Oh I am definitely in the wrong place."*

First impressions are everything they are cracked up to be, so make sure yours says "Welcome Home," and remember that "home" varies for different types of people.

When you design your practice, think in terms of The Four Languages of The M.A.D. Formula and make sure your office fits all of your patients.

Practice Spotlight

In an all-out effort to surpass their competition, the group of radiologists redesigned their office. The challenge was to cater to a wide demographic range of patients and make sure everyone in their patient pool felt comfortable in their environment. The renovation required rental of some additional space, expanding their total area to well over 10,000 square feet. It was worth the expense.

As patients entered the office space, they found a reception area with five receptionists spread out across the entire room and separated by privacy dividers. There were chairs in front of each check-in area for patient comfort. Around the perimeter and in different nooks there were chairs placed in groups of two and four. On one side of the reception area was an elaborate and organized display of 35 different magazines with topics ranging from sporting to cooking and from business to wellness.

The area was clean, simple, and functional (ideal for Type 1s) but the walls had custom molding and fine art to appeal to the Type 2s. But here's what was so spectacular: patients who were referred for female-specific testing (such as mammograms and pelvic ultrasounds) were escorted to an entirely separate area. The Women's Center had private check-in nooks and cushy chairs. The reception area was filled with candles and potpourri, little candy dishes, and spaces to plug in laptops. As patients were escorted back for testing, they were taken first to private dressing rooms that were equipped with a full-length mirror, comfortable chair, hangers, toiletries, and freshly laundered robes.

Technicians (in lavender scrubs) waited patiently outside the dressing rooms and, when the patients were ready, escorted them back through pastel-painted hallways with peaceful art back to the testing area. When testing was completed, patients were escorted to a waiting area, equipped with waterfall; freshly brewed one-cup tea, coffee, and hot cocoa; female-specific magazines; and practice brochures providing educational information about their testing as well as marketing brochures about their additional offerings in vein therapy and laser hair removal. When the radiologist had reviewed the films, the technician would come back to the waiting area to inform the patient whether more films were necessary or to escort her back to the dressing room.

The revenues of this radiology practice tripled in one year, more than paying for their renovations. But here's the key: they never changed any of their testing services, only the environment in which the tests were offered. News spread quickly and when doctors referred for testing, the patients were requesting this location!

Practice Spotlight

In less than 2,000 square feet of space, the seemingly insurmountable goal of this orthodontic practice was to create an environment that would be comfortable for all of their patients and their families, while accommodating a panoramic x-ray room, extensive files, on-site lab, office space for the practice manager and treatment coordinator, front desk, locker and storage areas, consultation room, and reception area, while, at the same time, leaving enough room for Dr. R and his eight-member Team to create beautiful, healthy smiles!

To make it even more complex, Dr. R had a large patient base that came from all over the area, representing a wide variety of demographic groups with varying treatment and communication needs.

In consideration of all of this, he had divided his treatment areas to include a space for adults and a larger treatment area for children. As his adult practice grew, he created "Adults Only" nights. His younger patients were of all ages and demographic groups, so Dr. R's very artistic wife (and office manager) worked hard to create a colorful and appealing environment that would speak to all of them, changing the art and design of the patient treatment area every month with different ceiling designs and three-dimensional mobiles.

The reception area was nothing short of spectacular. In a tiny amount of space, Dr. and Mrs. R created a play area for children, and a quiet area with comfortable seats for waiting parents and adult patients. They had a beverage machine that made cappuccino and hot cocoa, and electrical outlets for plugging in laptops. The space was warm and friendly, not too upscale for the Type 1 patients, and just upscale enough for the Type 2 crowd. It was colorful enough for the Enthusiasts, cozy enough for the Relaters, practical enough for the

Commanders, and had enough books, brochures, and videos to keep the Thinkers busy for years.

Everyone who came to Dr. R's practice felt comfortable and knew they were in the right place. It was the perfect environment for their practice and the result was a group of happy and loyal patients, productive and comfortable staff, and a practice that brought enough revenues for Dr. R to attract just the right doctor to buy him out so that he could go on and build his next mountain.

What message is your practice sending? Do Activity 22-2 and find out!

ACTIVITY 22-2. Look at Your Practice
Walk through your practice and look at it through the eyes of the first three Languages of the M.A.D. Formula. Each time you see something that you think would appeal to different Action Types, Value Sets and States of Mind, place a check (✓) in the appropriate column. In addition, place checks (✓) in the demographic columns as you find places in your practice that will appeal to each. When you are finished, look over your columns and make sure you have the right balance of check marks to fit your unique combination of patients (or the patients you are trying to attract). If not, call a Team meeting and invite input regarding how you could balance your practice design to better fit your patients.

ACTION TYPES	RELATER		ENTHUSIAST		THINKER		COMMANDER	

VALUE SETS	TYPE 1		TYPE 2					

STATES OF MIND	CRITICAL PARENT	NURTURING PARENT	ANALYST	SOCIALIZED CHILD	NATURAL CHILD

AGE COHORTS	0 – 10	11 - 18	19 – 29	30 – 50	51 – 64	65 +

GENDER	MALE	FEMALE				

STEP 3: INCLUDE YOUR PATIENT IN YOUR CONVERSATIONS

Nothing enacts the In-Group/Out-Group mentality more than talking in front of a patient about something that has nothing to do with the patient. I can't stress this enough:

Never tell stories or discuss unrelated experiences while you are working on the patient without including the patient in the telling of the story.

This is a behavior that is rampant throughout healthcare, and that causes problems ranging from misalignment of patients to mistakes in patient care.

Practice Spotlight

Dr. L was working in a teaching hospital with his Team of interns. They gathered around the patient's bed and talked over him frenetically as each intern took a turn at making diagnoses and treatment recommendations. This went on across the entire floor until finally, in the last room, a patient sat up and complained, *"Am I in your way here? I'd be happy to leave so you guys could stay and talk."*

My recommendation was to include the patient in the "teaching" aspect of rounds by inviting patient input. Patients enjoyed being included in the process and the predictable result was that the interns learned more than medicine, they learned about Aligning with patients. An added bonus was that, for some patients, joining in on the conversations led them to remember important information that they had neglected to include in their histories.

Practice Spotlight

Dr. K was conducting a gynecological exam when her assistant came into the room and said, *"I'm ordering lunch, do you want anything?"*

Dr K continued to work as the assistant read the take-out menu to the doctor and the two women discussed the benefits of chicken with broccoli over sweet and sour pork. In the meantime, the patient lay on the table, turning red in the face, and never saying a word.

Practice Spotlight

Ruth, a nurse practitioner, was giving her patient a laser treatment on her face when Jan, the office manager, came into the room. Jan came up to the patient's head and stood on the opposite side of the table from Ruth.

Jan said hello to the patient and then told Ruth about another patient who had called and cancelled her appointment for later that day. In an angry tone, Ruth said, *"I knew she was going to do that! She's done that to me three times now."*

> The two staff members got into a conversation, making fun of patients and laughing about some of the excuses they'd heard when the patient on the table suddenly lifted her arms and whacked both women simultaneously in their abdomens with the backs of her arms.
>
> The sudden movement surprised Ruth, causing her to jerk and the laser wand fell to the floor. No damage was done to the patient, Ruth, or the machine, but the possibility of what could have happened stayed with Ruth for some time.

If your Team has to interrupt during a patient's visit, I recommend that you instruct them to use **The Five Steps of a Polite Interruption**:

Step 1: Introduce yourself, making eye contact with the patient.

Step 2: Apologize for the interruption.

Step 3: Request permission to do what you need to do.

Step 4: Briefly provide necessary information or question.

Step 5: Apologize again and thank the patient for her patience.

The Five Steps will sound something like this:

Interrupter:

Hello Mrs. Patient, my name is Lisa. I am Dr. A's Scheduling Coordinator. May I interrupt your visit for just one minute to speak with Dr. A? (wait for OK)

Dr. A, Your meeting at the Chamber of Commerce has been moved up to 5:00 p.m. Do you need me to do anything for you?

Doctor:

No that will work out fine. Thank you Lisa.

Interrupter:

Thank you Doctor. Sorry again for the interruption, Mrs. Patient. Thank you for your patience.

Let's face it . . . you don't need a consultant to teach you this stuff. These are simple rules of etiquette that you and your Team members probably learned by the time you were six years old. Go ahead . . . follow the five steps and make your mothers proud.

Longer Procedures

What about when you are doing a procedure or treatment of some length with one or more people in the room along with the patient? Does everyone work quietly or do you start talking? And if you talk, do you include the patient? Table 22-1 provides some recommendations for you.

TABLE 22-1. Including Your Patient
In order to keep patients from being excluded during their visits to your practice, incorporate some or all of the following techniques.
Begin by asking the patient if he would prefer silence, conversation, or, if available, music, TV, or DVD.
If the patient prefers silence:
Ask the patient if he minds if all of you talk or if he would prefer total silence.
If the patient still requests silence, refrain from talking except for essential comments.
Of course, in the ideal world, you would never have conversations in front of a patient unless it is about the patient. That said, some patients find it enjoyable to be distracted from what is going on, so if he says it's OK for you to talk, be sure to continually include the patient in your conversation with:
• A nod of your head in his direction; • Eye contact; • An occasional yes or no question that allows the patient to respond without further conversation; • An explanation of what you are doing; and • An explanation of what you are talking about.
HINT: Remember the rule about tone and visual cues. If the patient can't see you, remember that he will respond to your tone of voice and interpret your communication largely by the sound of your words. Don't try to send "secret codes" to each other with your tone. The patient will hear it and will draw conclusions that may, or may not, be desirable.
If the patient prefers conversation, and the patient is able to talk:
Ask leading, open-ended questions that enable the patient to do most of the talking, for example: • What does a forest ranger actually do on a day-to-day basis? • What kinds of things did you do on your vacation? • What were some of your favorite memories of the wedding? • I bet there's a great story associated with that pin, will you tell us about it? • Your wardrobe is always so coordinated, what's your secret? • What do you think about the new library downtown? • What are you looking forward to when this is over?
If the patient prefers music, TV, or DVD:
Offer the patient choices and check in now and then to find out if he is happy with the entertainment choice or would like to switch to something different.

At the risk of sounding irreverent, it's easy to understand why so many doctors prefer to work when their patients are asleep. To do what you do takes a lot of focus and attention to detail and I'm sure the last thing you want to worry about is the additional task of making conversation and other niceties. If this is how you feel, then know that you can maintain Alignment and take care of your needs by saying something like:

> *"I need to give my full attention to what I am doing and I don't want you to think I'm being rude. Is that OK with you?"*

It is the rare patient who will say, "*No! I want you to talk to me!*" but if this happens, recruit a Team member to entertain and distract your patient while you focus on your patient's clinical care. Either way, you will have done what needed to be done for the patient's well-being and yours, while maintaining a strong Alignment.

STEP 4: AGREE UPON GOALS AND ROLES

By nature, the therapeutic relationship puts the patient in a vulnerable position. While some patients willingly accept that, others fight hard against it. Part of the process of Aligning with your patient is to find out what role your patient wants to play in your relationship. You can easily find that out by adding one question to your intake paperwork (Table 22-2):

TABLE 22-2. Intake Survey for Goals and Roles
Add the following question to your standard intake forms for new patients:
How much involvement do you like to have during your visits to the doctor? Do you (please check ☑ as many as fit):   ☐ Want to know the results of your testing   ☐ Want to be educated regarding your condition   ☐ Want to be educated regarding your treatment plan choices   ☐ Want to be included in consultations with other doctors or healthcare professionals   ☐ Want to sit back and leave the driving to us

Of course, you need to read the answers and discuss them with your patient to be certain you are interpreting them correctly. Remember not to assume that you are in full Alignment about what they really want until you ask them to validate your perceptions.

I always recommend that doctors or staff begin their relationships with new patients using The ACTION Formula (see Chapter 15). This will help you to understand your patient's goals and enable you to make firm statements regarding the degree to which you will be able to help them to attain their goals. This will also assure that there are no misconceptions regarding what you can, and can not deliver. Further, since The ACTION Formula allows you and your patients to talk about what they will get as a result of your treatment, it will permit you to establish strong Alignments as you focus together on how to help them get what they truly want.

STEP 5: ALWAYS ASK PERMISSION

If the goal is to Align with your patients, then it's critical that they be comfortable in your presence and that they know you have total respect for their privacy and dignity. Here are simple tactics that will allow you to send a strong message of respect:

- Knock before you enter and if you don't hear a response, knock again. If still no response, open the door slightly without looking in and call the patient's name. If still no response, enter the room.
- If you open the door and the lights are out, stand with the door open and allow the light from the hall to enter the room for a moment rather than shock the patient by throwing on all the lights. Ask the patient if he or she is ready for you to turn on the light. This is particularly important in a hospital setting. Think of how you would like to be awakened from a dead sleep, particularly if you were up all night in pain. Just because you are on your third double shot of espresso, is no reason to charge in as if they have just unlocked the doors for the 4:00 a.m. 50%-off sale the day after Thanksgiving.
- If it is the middle of the night and you are checking vitals, reread the above.
- Always ask permission to attach something to the patient, whether it is a blood pressure cup or a dentistry bib. Always ask, *"May I put this around you?"*
- Always ask before you palpate, twist, touch, inject, or pinch. *"I need to do x, y, z, are you ready?"*
- Always introduce the instruments you use, particularly if (but not only when) they are going to touch the patient's body.

And, no matter what else you are doing,

Always introduce yourself and use the patient's name when you speak.

Remember, unless patients are in immediate danger, they deserve your efforts to Align. This will create a strong relationship with your patients and allow for significantly lowered resistance to your care and recommendations. Remember, lowered resistance means less muscle tension and subsequently less pain in response to your touch. This is particularly important in dentistry where tension can exacerbate TMJ disorders, cervical issues, and headaches. Always remember, go **AT** your patients:

Ask — Treat

STEP 6: SHARE CREDIT FOR SUCCESS

I've heard two types of comments following the successful completion of a treatment, procedure, or surgery:

"You've done a great job," which gives a Chip to the patient, and

"This treatment was the right move for you," which gives a Chip to the practitioner.

Both comments are fine, but if your goal is patient Alignment, try these:

"We make a great Team!"

"Look what is possible when we stick together!"

"You worked hard for this, and I was proud to work with you."

"Congratulations to you for getting through this — we were all rooting for your recovery!"

Treatment and cure is a Team effort. The more you acknowledge that, the more the patient will feel proud of his or her accomplishment and be Aligned with you and your staff.

Practice Spotlight

On the fourth day following my hip replacement, it was time to transfer me from the hospital to a rehabilitation facility. As the ambulette driver wheeled me from my room, I saw an amazing sight.

All of the floor nurses, aids, and all available doctors and physician assistants had lined up down the hallway from outside my door all the way to the elevator. As the driver wheeled me past, everyone whooped and applauded. Wearing scrubs and enormous smiles, they touched my arm, wished me well, and let me know that we were all in this together. To this day, I am still grateful for the care and attention that Team took to make sure I knew that I wasn't alone.

STEP 7: DECIDE IF YOU REALLY WANT TO ALIGN WITH YOUR PATIENTS

If you find yourself hesitant to Align with your patients, there are two questions to ask yourself:

1. *Are my patients right for me*?
   Maybe you just aren't attracting the kind of patients with whom you can comfortably talk or Align. Perhaps you need to consider a different strategy to bring the right patients to your door. We'll cover this in Section Five.

2. *Am I right for my patients*?
   Maybe you have never been one who likes to Align with others. Perhaps you have always been a loner, operating solo and liking it. If you're comfortable with that then simply make sure that you work with a

Relater or Enthusiast so that there is someone in the room who will take care of the people-stuff for you. On the other hand, perhaps you'd really like to Align with patients, but have some personal rules that are keeping you from feeling comfortable using some of these techniques. Review Chapter 20 and create some new rules for yourself or sit down with someone you trust and work through whatever is holding you back.

STEP 8: SPEAK THEIR LANGUAGE

I have spent countless hours on my in-house coaching days watching doctors and their Teams speaking to patients and watching their patients' faces in response. I am frequently reminded of my dog when he was first learning to do all of his cute little tricks. I'd say *"Parfait, sit!"* and he would open his big, black eyes, wag his tail, stick out his tongue, and jump up and down and up and down just like popcorn popping. He would respond with such passion and joy, and I just knew he understood everything I was saying. Well, except for the small detail that he wouldn't actually sit. Finally my dog trainer explained it to me when she looked me straight in the eye and said, *"Wendy. Dogs don't speak English."*

Look at your patients. Really look at them. Do they look like they are getting what you're saying? Even if they are smiling and nodding and really look like they're with you, don't be fooled! Patients will walk out completely befuddled and ask a front desk person for interpretation before they will shame themselves by admitting that you lost them after *"Hello."*

Apart from the obvious risk-management concerns, Alignment depends on your ability to help your patient to understand what you are saying. Follow these four rules, and don't leave any out:

Rule 1: 6-Year-Old-Kid Words

We talked about this earlier but it is important enough to repeat. Make sure that everything you say would be easily understood by a 6-year-old child. This will cover you for all miscommunications.

Rule 2: Respect Cultures

Obviously, if your patient comes from a different country, it would be ideal to have someone with you who is able to translate for you. Consider also that there are people who speak English but who have different cultural rules in communication. Through Internet research, consider helping your Team to learn key Alignment behaviors from other cultures (such as bowing, whether or not to shake hands, gender rules, etc.). And of course, no matter what, always speak The Four Languages of the M.A.D. Formula.

Rule 3: Confirm That You've Been Heard

Always make sure that your patients have understood by asking them to feed back instructions. Make every effort not to sound like you are treating your adult patients as if they are children (*"Now, Mrs. Patient, what did I just say?"*). Instead, put them into the position of helping *you* by saying something like, *"Please help me make sure that I was clear. What do you understand are your choices with respect to having the surgery?"*

Do you ever ask your patients if they have any questions? If they say "no," consider adding another line like, *"Is there anything you'd ask if you could speak with someone else?"* That will help your patient to gracefully request another person to talk with, particularly if there is a gender-related illness or if your Action Type is in any way intimidating.[4]

Rule 4: Always Say "Thank You"

What do you say when you get a cookie, Billy?

How is it that we have to say "thank you" when people give us a cookie but not when people put their lives in our hands? Enough said. Consider thanking your patients for their trust in you. Remember, they could have chosen someone else.

And they still can.

STEP 9: COMMIT TO MAKE IT HAPPEN

Right now, sitting in your chair with this book in your hands, it probably makes all the sense in the world to do whatever you can to Align with your patients. Why wouldn't you want to do something that has so many benefits for your patients and for you?

Well, funny you should ask that question. There are some very good reasons not to.

The fact is that the more you Align with your patients,

- The more difficult it is to stay distant, aloof, and uninvolved;
- The more time you'll have to spend with them, some of which will be non-billable;
- The more you'll have to multitask;
- The harder it will be to give them bad news; and
- The harder it will be to say "good-bye."

---

[4] Of course, this will *never* happen to *you* because you will be pacing your patients by flexing your Action Type to theirs, but I just thought I'd mention this so you can tell *other* people about it.

On the other hand, if you do Align with your patients, you will reap the rewards of better healing, lower risks of malpractice suits, and more loyal patients who will refer more often and sing your praises to their other doctors who will also refer more often. So, here are four last things to consider:

1. Your patients want to Align with you;
2. Your patients will do better if they Align with you;
3. You will enjoy a safer and more fruitful practice if they Align with you; and
4. If you don't do it, someone else will.

So, now that you have all of the Alignment information, let's go for a walk and do Activity 22-3.

ACTIVITY 22-3. Listen to Your Practice

Take a walk around your practice and listen to the words and tones used between your patients and your Team. Look at faces. Pay attention to skin changes, volume and tone shifts, and speed of speech. If possible, stop and observe to get a kinesthetic measure of the degree to which your patients seem comfortable and connected to your Team. Take notes as you go so you know where you need to do some coaching to improve your patient Alignment.

Consider videotaping patient visits (with patient permission, of course) and then review the tapes with your Team. And above all else, ask your patients to tell you how you're doing. Explain what you think Alignment should be like and then ask them to assess you and your Team. Ask for feedback about how you could improve to build a stronger connection with them. The more you talk, the more you'll Align. Take the time now, while this is fresh in your mind.

BOTTOM LINE

Aligning your Team includes Aligning with your patients. In addition to following the steps and formulas outlined for Aligning your doctors and staff members, there are additional strategies that are particularly important when working with patients. Mastering these strategies will allow you to build strong and lasting Alignments with your patients and help you to build a stronger foundation of growth for your practice.

Chapter 23

Align With Everyone Else

OK, SO YOU'VE ALIGNED your doctors, your staff, and your patients. Who's left?

There are many people outside of your practice who can be recruited to enhance your success. It's important to make an Alignment plan for each of these groups and consider them as Sub-Teams of your practice. Let's go through them together so you can see more of your options.

SUB-TEAM #1: YOUR COMMUNITY COLLEAGUES

What makes one doctor decide to refer to another? I've asked this question to hundreds of doctors, and their answers are always similar. They refer for any and all of the following five reasons:

1. They have a strong friendship with the doctor. They like and respect him as a person and while they may or may not know much about the doctor's clinical skills, they trust his integrity and perspectives on healthcare.
2. They met the doctor at a meeting or social event and liked her, although they have little or no knowledge of the doctor professionally.
3. They have "heard good things" about the doctor from other doctors and patients who "liked" the doctor, although they have never spoken with the doctor personally.
4. They were exposed to the doctor's skills and perspectives through journal articles and association presentations and developed respect for the doctor from a distance.
5. They had personal experience with the doctor as a colleague, student or patient and continue to maintain a strong loyalty and/or affection for the doctor.

If you look carefully at this list, you will notice that all of the reasons these doctors refer to other doctors have to do with Alignment. Amazing though it may be, the take-away message of this informally collected data tells us that

100% of the time, doctors will make referrals because they, or someone they trust, likes and/or respects you!

Remember from Section Two, people like us when we speak their language. They trust us because they perceive that we are like them, or at least that we understand them. I find all of this very exciting because this means that you can increase your success exponentially when you know how to Align with your colleagues.

So, the obvious question is: What efforts are you making to Align with your colleagues at the local, state and national levels? Do you seek them out in an effort to build rapport and develop relationships? Consider these two Practice Spotlights and then I'll give you some ideas:

Practice Spotlight

The senior partner of a cosmetic dentistry practice, Dr. O is a firm believer in working as a Team. He travels frequently to teach in schools outside his state and has developed a strong reputation for skill throughout the national community. In addition, he has worked hard to develop strong Alignments with other doctors locally and it has paid off for everyone involved. He and his local colleagues have Aligned to help their mutual patients to get everything they need for their dental health and overall appearance. In his group are general dentists, as well as an endodontist, a periodontist, an orthodontist, a pediatric dentist, a plastic surgeon, and an owner of a large hair salon.

Dr. O believes it is important for people who are inter-referring to have an opportunity to see how each of their unique contributions fit into the puzzle of the overall health and well-being of each patient they've shared. Everyone in his referral group gets together monthly for lectures and case studies at one of their practices. They take turns speaking, and they bring in outside speakers to give the meeting added value. They have refreshments, and the social time gives them a chance to get to know each other on a more personal level.

Dr. O's Alignment with each of these doctors is made stronger each time they get together and the referrals into his practice keep growing every month.

Practice Spotlight

There are many medical and dental study groups that meet weekly, monthly, quarterly, and annually to review case studies, listen to guest speakers, and share best practices. One particular group of doctors took their study group to a new level by taking full advantage of the power of the In-Group/Out-Group mentality.

Selecting only members who had already displayed a high level of financial success in their practices, this exclusive club meets throughout the year in small regional groups and once a year at a five-star resort to share ideas and to be the first to hear of innovations from their vendors. They bring speakers into their local and national meetings (held at hunting lodges, camp sites and fine resorts) and use this time for lots of learning and lots of play.

The energy of their meetings is extraordinary as the best of the best exchange strategies, relay case studies, discuss new innovations, and share results they've had with their patients. The energy continues all year long as they share ideas on their private, members-only Web site. They have helped each other through slow economies and have been there for each other when difficult cases needed an extra set of eyes. They support each other as friends as well as colleagues, encouraging their entrepreneurial zest for success and ongoing quest for excellence. They work together to make legislative changes that enable them to give better care to their patients and create better earning opportunities for their industry.

I've been privileged to work with this group and the members told me that their Alignment with the other members was largely responsible for a significant portion of their success as doctors both financially and personally. Their Alignment makes their profession safer and much more enjoyable.

How can you build Alignments in your community? Here are some strategies to make it happen:

Strategy #1: Hire a Full- or Part-Time Practice Representative

A Practice Representative is an employee who is responsible for Aligning your practice with others in your community by engaging in activities that are similar to what you see from pharmaceutical and device representatives. Your Practice Representative will visit designated practices in your community on a regular schedule, providing new information and education regarding your specialty through lunch-and-learns, brochures, and spontaneous discussions. Often your Practice Representative will bring little treats for the staff and doctors, which serve as reminders and keep your name at the front of their memories. Don't underestimate the power of this position. While it sounds "touchy-feely," this is a strong marketing tool if you are looking to build your referral base.

Strategy #2: Get to Know Your Counterparts

The CEO, COO, practice administrator, and other leaders of your practice need to meet and talk with people who hold like positions in all practices where you seek Alignment. Together they can create a strong network to lend support and build greater success for your practice throughout your area. If your plan is to build national recognition as a facility of prominence, then your executive leaders need to get out there to shake some hands, build trust, and establish strong rapport with their counterparts nationwide. In addition to getting support and information, they will become increasingly adept at building relationships. This is the heart and soul of what others call "playing the political game." It doesn't have to be an uncomfortable process, as long as you know how to build strong Alignments with people.

Building trust and rapport requires the same techniques, no matter what your ultimate goals may be.

The doctors in your practice also need to get out and visit with doctors from other practices. They need to shake hands, discuss common challenges, and speak face-to-face about the best ways in which to support each other's practice.

Is everyone too busy for this? Yes, and I suggest that you do it anyway. Have your trusted staff member call the doctors and administrators whom you have targeted as potential referral sources and make appointments for you to talk to them by phone or, better, to meet them in person.

Create a small script so that you can be sure you are well-represented. The script may sound something like this:

> *"Hello, my name is (NAME), I am the (POSITION) at (PRACTICE NAME) here in (TOWN). Dr. A would like to meet Dr. B to discuss the possibility of how they might work together to help mutual patients. Dr. A would be glad to come to your office, to speak by phone, or even to meet for a quick lunch. Which would Dr. B prefer?"*

Set up the appointment and reconfirm on the day of the meeting to make sure the schedules will still allow for the meeting. If not, reschedule for a more convenient time.

WARNING: If you are the one making the initial effort to Align, then no matter what emergencies come up, do not let it happen that you reschedule more than twice. The first time is understandable. The second time is annoying. A third time is over the top, and sends a message that you will always put your needs ahead of theirs. Clearly this will ruin your attempt to establish Alignment.

Strategy #3: Provide Mutually Beneficial Learning Opportunities

Create your own mini-conference, inviting prominent doctors from your community to provide case presentations, a trusted consultant to discuss practice management issues, and a panel of patients to offer their perspectives on treatment. Hold your conference at your practice, in a hospital auditorium, or at a locally owned restaurant or hotel.

Keep your conference to no longer than three hours, including time for refreshments. Make sure that your marketing announcements boldly disclose your sponsorship of this event. Have your Practice Representative or designated staff members hand-deliver invitations to key doctors who you are looking to attract, and then do a general mailing to doctors in your area.

The doctors with whom you are most interested in forming an Alignment should be the ones you personally invite to present in your conference.

Create a Sub-Team in your practice who will be responsible for this event, and make sure they follow up with the practices to remind the doctors of the date and to encourage participation.

Strategy #4: Follow-Up When You Receive a Patient Referral

Whether you receive a patient referral from a doctor or a member of his or her Team, it is important to follow up. Without exception, all of my clients agree that the doctors with whom they are most likely to Align always:

- Send a note of thanks following a referral.
- Get permission from their patient to share diagnoses and treatment plans and then send a copy of notes and testing results to the referring doctor.
- Send the patient back to the referring doctor for follow-up.

Strategy #5: Newsletters

Create a monthly or quarterly newsletter to share important information in your specialty for patients and send copies to referring doctors. This will help your colleagues by providing them with educational information for patients and will keep your name out there. Make absolutely certain that there is no competitive information in your newsletter that would pull patients away from your colleagues.

If you really want to get the juices flowing, call one of your colleagues for a quote and include his or her name in your newsletter. This "free" advertising will make your newsletter a hot item in your community as every doctor vies to be the next to be quoted in your newsletter. It's fun to be the popular kid, and everyone likes (and needs) exposure.

Strategy #6: Make It Easy for Them

Up in your ivory tower, it's easy to forget that not everyone understands what you do or what kinds of patients need you. While you may think that what you do is ordinary, others may look at you and think you are one-of-a-kind. No matter what, if you aren't receiving referrals it may be because other doctors don't know who you want to see and/or how to recognize the symptoms that you treat. Remember,

Doctors need to know how to refer to you.

Create a small, laminated card that has the symptoms you treat, the demographics of patients who are likely to develop these symptoms, and your name and phone number. Drop these cards off with a cover letter.

If you are completely complimentary to a referring colleague and offer no competition whatsoever, then you can take a page from the pharmaceutical companies and let patients educate their doctors about the need for your services. Create a simple, tri-fold brochure written to and for patients. In simple language, describe the symptoms you treat and how to recognize if they need help. Of course, use all Four Languages of the M.A.D. Formula and remember the 20-20-60 rule. Place your name at the bottom of your brochure on the back panel, and then ask the referring colleagues to place your educational brochure in their reception areas.

Strategy #7: Gifting

I have clients who hire stretch limousines to carry their female referring doctors to lavish day spas and their male referring doctors to top-notch golf resorts. Some of my clients send elaborate gift baskets addressed to the full practices of their referring doctors at holidays, while others send trays of bagels and fruit and keep it up all year long. I've had clients who send branded coffee cups and pens. A number of my clients send their referring doctors gift certificates to elaborate restaurants, gift cards to local stores, and expensive wines. I had one client who sent a copy of my first book to all of her clients for the holidays. I thought that was really special (she said, coyly).

Is it necessary to send gifts to referring doctors and their staff? It really depends on the culture in your community, your marketing budget, and the degree to which there is competition in your community for referrals. The point is that unless you are the only provider of your specialization in your community, then you have to compete by keeping your name at the front of your colleagues' minds, and gifting is one way to make that happen.

Shouldn't it be enough to be good at what you do? The truth is that it doesn't matter if you're the absolute best at what you do — if people don't know that you appreciate and want their referrals, they are not likely to continue to send patients to you. It may sound cold and manipulative, and maybe it is. But that doesn't mean you should never send gifts. You just need to learn how to do it in a meaningful way so that it expresses your true appreciation.

Many practices send gifts to referring doctors but don't take the time to get to know them, so their gifts are generic. In some communities, that's enough. In others, the doctors who win are the ones who send out the best gifts.

In my opinion, the way around the "salesy" nature of this is to target your thank you gifts to the recipient. In other words, take time to find out the personal life DESIRES, interests, and hobbies of your referring doctors and send gifts that are customized to them. This shows your extra care and attention and the message it sends is "We'll give the same personalized attention to your patients."

The fact is that, whether you approve or not, gifting is rapidly becoming the norm in our society. Unless you excel at networking and building personal Alignments with your colleagues by using Strategies 1 through 6, then Strategy #7 is going to be a smart move for you.

Strategy #8: Keep Track

The most difficult piece of Aligning with colleagues is losing track of how long it's been since you've spoken with each other, referred to each other, or acknowledged each other's colleagueship. So, start keeping track of your Alignment and then share your record-keeping (Table 23-1) with your colleague on a quarterly or annual basis. For ease of record-keeping, I recommend that you keep a separate list for each colleague.

TABLE 23-1. Align With Your Colleagues				
COLLEAGUE: Karen Sweit, MD				
Patient Referred to Us	Patient Referred from Us	Date of Visit	Follow-Up Notes Sent	Additional Contact With Colleague
Janie Tam		1-2-09	1-3-09	Thank you note 1-3-09
	Gina Kaiz	1-5-09	1-5-09	Follow-up call 1-6-09
	Fred Kay	1-7-09	1-8-09	Follow-up call 1-10-09
Annie Benow		1-23-09	2-1-09	Thank you note 2-2-09

When you send a copy of this to your colleague, include a handwritten note from you that thanks your colleague for his or her continuing trust. Don't skimp on the handwritten part. It says a lot about you and your practice when you take the time to do this. If you don't like your handwriting, then print slowly — the effort will be well appreciated.[1]

SUB-TEAM #2: YOUR VENDORS

When your vendors are trying to get your time, attention, and money, it's easy to forget that their goal is to help you and your practice to succeed. Do they have something to gain from your success? Of course. For some vendors, the more patients you see, the more you need their product or service. For others, the more success you build the better they look for having helped you. The trick is to distinguish who can help you to serve your patients better and to increase your revenues. Alignment with your vendors can be a real win-win arrangement, if you know how to use it. Here are some tips that you may find helpful:

Step 1: Make a list of where you need RESOURCES to enable you to run your business and treat patients, and then make sure you have a vendor for each need. When possible, find ways to overlap so that you have more needs being met by fewer vendors. Your list might look something like Table 23-2.

Step 2: Designate a trusted staff member to be in charge of keeping your list up to date with vendor representative names and contact information.

Step 3: When a vendor contacts your practice, look at your list. If the services and/or products the new vendor is offering addresses one of your missing categories, invite them to educate you about how they can help you in your practice. On the other hand, if you already have that area covered, tell them about the services you are receiving from your current vendor and invite them to show you how they offer superior or different services or pricing.

Step 4: Many vendors have budgets to assist practices with training, sponsorships, treats, and more, so find out from your vendors how much they can offer you beyond their regular services and products.

Step 5: Find out from your vendors how often they think they need to speak with someone in your practice in order to best serve your practice.

Step 6: Ask your vendors to help you with a cost-benefit analysis to determine the extent to which their services and products are worth your time and money.

---

[1] As long as we're on the handwriting thing . . . right or wrong, your ability to Align with people can be hindered when they have to work hard to read your writing. M.A.D. Leadership includes clearing the path so others can succeed, so make an effort not to muddy the waters of your fabulous leadership with your handwriting.

TABLE 23-2. Align With Your Vendors			
Administrative Supplies	**Clinical Supplies**	**Support and/or Training Needs**	**Assigned Vendor**
Paper, cartridges, clipboards . . .			Chris' Supply House 888-555-3232
		Syringes, vials, 4X4s . . .	Betty Peng 888-555-5297
		Locum tenens	Associates on Call 888-555-3322
	Samples: antibiotics		Haley Gem 877-555-8787
		Patient financing	Jake Cool 800-555-6666
		Annual retreat	Wendy Lipton-Dibner ☺ 800-704-6722
	Compounding Rx		Michael Robs 877-555-9011
		Software support	Patti Lavich 800-555-1211
		Updates re: tx protocols	Donna Seegew 877-555-1720
		HR laws	Research
	DVD for tx rooms		Research

Step 7: Let your vendors know that you would like to Align with them for your mutual success, and find out how you can be of service to them in their business.

Remember, your vendors are there to help you but the key is to work together to find a process that will work for everyone.

SUB-TEAM #3: YOUR FAMILIES

In an effort to separate "work" from "home," it's easy to create a chasm that is so deep and wide you might never cross it again. There have been many studies looking at divorce rates among healthcare professionals, and the bottom line is that it's not good.

As our society changes, both men and women feel an increasing pressure to be able to "do it all," and if someone or something is going to suffer, it's usually the family. There is a lot of truth to the old song lyric,

You always hurt the one you love.

So how can you avoid the difficulty and keep your family strongly Aligned while focusing your energy on treating your patients and building a successful practice? All it takes is two steps:

Step 1: Reread This Book From the Beginning

Seriously, everything in this book applies to your family. From The Four Languages of The M.A.D. Formula to how you design your space, from Motivating people to ACTION, to The Five Steps of a Polite Introduction, from building a Mission Statement to creating a survey for goals, roles, and individual work styles, there is nothing in this book that won't enhance your relationships and your success in your family. Reread it with a different eye, and you will see a different set of techniques all within the same two covers.

Step 2: Apply the Techniques

See one, do one, teach one. You've seen this work in your practice, you've done the techniques yourself, and now it's your turn to teach. Sit down with your family and help them to understand how to apply what you've learned. Begin with a demonstration of Chips. Explain the concept of Chips, particularly the importance of giving Chips without teasing or belittlement. Go around your dinner table and invite all of your family members to say out loud one thing they did that week that was proof of their skills and one thing they did that week that was proof of their hearts. As each person speaks, that is your chance to give some Chips. Make this a ritual at your table and everyone will look forward to meals together. Each week, teach them something new from The M.A.D. Formula and enjoy the Alignment it brings to all of you.

Practice Spotlight

Hal and I were invited to dinner at the home of one of our clients. He had invited his partners and their spouses to join us so that everyone would have a chance to meet "the consultants."

It was a pleasant evening, and everyone was chatting comfortably. Someone asked us to explain what we were doing with the practice, and so I briefly summarized our initiative. When I'd finished, one of the wives put down her wine and made a comment that seemed to be more directed to her husband (the doctor) than to us,

"It's so good to hear all of this. Normally I'm totally in the dark about what's going on in the practice."

Her sarcastic tone made it clear that this was more than a passing comment, and it was an uncomfortable moment for everyone.

Her husband looked at her and said, *"I figured it would be boring to you."*

Her eyes welled up, and she replied, *"I want to share your life."*

He was genuinely surprised and said, *"I'd like that."*

THE 24/7 TEAM

An increasing number of healthcare practices are owned, managed, and staffed by married couples. As doctors and their spouses merge their talents to work together, we see a frequent outcome: While the professional alliance is financially and strategically sound, the nonstop reality of living and working together 24 hours a day, 7 days a week puts a strain on their personal relationships.

Is it possible to work together and still maintain the spark that brought you together as a couple? Is there a way to comfortably toggle from "equal" to "subordinate" as you go from home to work and back again? Is there a strategy for giving and taking direction that won't leave either of you feeling "one-down?" Is it possible to spend an evening out without talking about work? Is it possible to get past the years you've spent focusing on everything and everyone but you?

Yes! 24/7 works — when you know what to do. Here are the secrets to success:

Strategy #1: Don't assume that just because you are married you can skip the Alignment steps. Make a commitment to follow every strategy and formula in this section, not just with your employees, but with each other.

Strategy #2: Separate "Work Splinters" from "Home Splinters." It's too easy to pile them all together and feel like you are carrying an enormous load of resentments in your relationship. Discuss them separately, and keep them separate.

Strategy #3: Take two weekends a year. One that is all about work and the other that is all about personal. Spend both weekends going through The ACTION Formula, create an ACTION Plan, and make sure that you are living your lives by design, instead of by default.

Strategy #4: Apply the techniques in Sections Two and Three with each other at home as well as at the office. In fact, practice together!

Strategy #5: Consistently give each other Five Star Service (see Chapter 28).

OK, that takes care of *your* family, now what about everyone else's family in your practice? Here are some tried-and-true ideas:

SEND CHIPS TO FAMILY MEMBERS

One of the most brilliant ideas I've ever heard for Aligning families to an organization, I learned from Tom Hopkins, a famous sales trainer in the real estate world. Tom suggests that sales managers send announcements home to family members when their employees do a great job. I think that has a real application in healthcare.

Remember, most family members have no idea about what their mothers, fathers, wives, husbands, daughters, and sons actually *do,* let alone whether they are any good at it! Receiving an occasional note from an employer telling them how wonderfully their family member is doing on the job will not only help your employee to get all kinds of Chips, but it will help you to get some loyal allies who will help you when you're not around.

> Imagine it is a cold, rainy day and your staff member just hit the snooze button for the third time. Little Susie comes running in the room and says, *"Daddy, Daddy, wake up! You don't want to disappoint your boss after that great thing you did last week!"*

I'm telling you — you will have a bunch of managers out there, and you won't have to pay for their services! This is great stuff!

INVITE FAMILY MEMBERS TO PRACTICE CELEBRATIONS

Most practices do a holiday celebration and invite families. I recommend that you do something different! Have a Sub-Team party and invite families to attend. Do a quick, fun presentation to explain what is new in your practice and take questions. Then eat—preferably unhealthy carbs, and a lot of them. Comfort food is very important for Aligning people. Just ask my grandmother.

Practice Spotlight

We had worked with the practice for a year. First, we took the physicians away from their families for a weekend retreat. Then, in the interest of keeping the practice open on weekdays, we took everyone in the practice away from their families on three separate Saturdays from 9:00 a.m. to 9:00 p.m. Now it was time to Align their families with our change initiative.

On the last Saturday evening, we invited the families of physicians and staff to attend a Gala Celebration. It took careful planning to get all 90 staff and doctors and their families wined and dined but it was well worth the effort. Everyone enjoyed the opportunity to relax, eat, and be together for a few hours.

At one point in the evening, I took the microphone and thanked the families on behalf of the practice for all of the support they give day in and day out. I told them a bit about the program their family members had been through and the goals of the initiative. Then I asked them if they would like a taste of what their spouses and parents had learned, and they enthusiastically replied "*YES!*"

I taught them about Chips[2] and I gave them an opportunity right then and there to experience the power of the technique by asking the practice members to turn to their families and give them Skill and Heart Chips.

The noise in the room was deafening as over 200 people started spreading the Chips, laughing, hugging, and talking.

The rest of the evening was filled with introductions and laughter. It felt a bit like "Family Night" at school with all of the "kids" introducing their families to each other. It was a joy to watch and a fantastic experience for everyone.

Your families can benefit from being a part of your Team as much as you can benefit from having their support. Make it happen.

BRING YOUR FAMILY TO WORK DAYS

The "bring your child to work" concept has been popular in the corporate world for a very long time. Not only does it Align the family member to your practice, but it also helps to educate children regarding future possibilities for their own careers.

So why is it only children who are welcome? Invite spouses and parents too, as long as that's what your employees want. Obviously this can be difficult in practices that deal with sensitive equipment or contagions. But if your practice is safe, you might consider this as another way to Align your families.

INITIATE SUPPORT GROUPS

Another way to Align families to your practice is to Align families to each other. Consider creating support groups for spouses, teenagers, and elderly parents of your employees. That may have a combined benefit of creating an Alignment with your practice and taking some pressure off of your employees.

---

[2] Many already knew about Chips and much of the content of the program. In fact, our clients often share the M.A.D. information with their families.

Remember: your employees will only be positive and upbeat to the extent that they get good support at home. Encourage them to share their work with their families and to use the communication techniques that you've taught them 24 hours a day, 7 days a week.

When it comes right down to it, our families are our greatest source of energy and strength. They deserve at least as much attention and care as we give to everyone else. Just because they're not sick, doesn't mean they don't need your attention. Take a few moments and do Activity 23-1. It may be just what you need.

ACTIVITY 23-1. Align With Your Family

Whether you are hundreds of miles away or just in another room, right now, before you do anything else, pick up your cell phone or get out of your chair and take a walk down the hall and find someone you love.

Say the words **"I love you"** and then say **"because"** and finish the sentence by filling in the precise reasons for your love. *"I love you because you're sweet. I love you because you're gentle. I love you because you put up with me!"*

Tell someone who shares your blood, what it means to you to be a member of your family, and ask your relative what it means to him or her.

Tell the people in your family that no matter what they do, you will always be there, by their side.

Tell your daughter that you are proud of her. Tell your son that you honor him. Tell your spouse that you would get married all over again. Pet your cat and throw a ball to your dog.

Right now, drop what you are doing and find someone you love. Ask questions, laugh, and learn about each other.

Right now, tell the people you love *that* you love them and *why*. Put down this book and go. Every moment you wait is a moment you've lost forever.

Nothing is more precious than the Alignments we make with the people in our lives. Who will you Align with today?

BOTTOM LINE

In addition to your doctors, your staff, and your patients, there are Sub-Teams that need to be carefully Aligned for your practice success. Using all of the formulas in Chapters 18 through 22, and adding a few specialty techniques, you can create a dynasty of support and strength that will help you to get on top and stay there, for as long as you choose to be there.

SECTION

5

D is for
Differentiate

Chapter 24

Differentiate Your Practice

Differentiate: to distinguish a specific difference; to develop differential characteristics; to acquire a distinct and separate character; to evolve so as to lead the pack.

WHAT WERE YOUR DREAMS when you first launched your career in healthcare? Did you imagine being at the helm of a large center of excellence with a group of professionals who had superb diagnostic skills and a wide range of treatment capabilities? Perhaps you dreamed of a specialty practice with a few partners to share the load and a staff you could count on to keep your business alive. Or, perhaps you dreamed of a quiet solo practice with a steady stream of loyal patients who would bring you fresh baked pies and tease you about the days when you used to sit in their classrooms as a child.

Whatever your dreams may have been, and whatever they've become, the bottom line is that you aren't going to achieve them unless you understand some hard facts about running a practice in the 21st century:

- Today's patients demand more than your clinical excellence.
- Referring doctors expect more than diagnostics and treatment.
- Employees want more than a pay check.
- The increasing popularity of privately and publicly held group practices means decreased visibility and resources for the solo practitioner.
- Internet and other media have created a population of consumers who are empowered with knowledge and ready to hold you accountable.
- It's just not enough to be good at what you do.

The fact is that,

Unless your practice is swelling with referrals and you have little or no competition in your community, then you will continually find yourself in competition for the best patients, partners, and staff in your community.

So, how are you supposed to win, or at least stay competitive, in this fight? Assuming that you are keeping on top of your profession clinically and that you have mastered the formulas of Motivating and Aligning people, then there is only one thing left to do:

Differentiate your team in the eyes of the community.

Differentiating your practice requires you to master **The Four Strategies of Differentiation:**

Strategy #1: Define your uniqueness;

Strategy #2: Magnify your uniqueness;

Strategy #3: Do what no one else is doing; and

Strategy #4: Develop The Five-Star Attitude.

When you understand and apply The Four Strategies of Differentiation, then as the movie says, *"they will come."*

BOTTOM LINE

This section is all about helping you to master The Four Strategies of Differentiation so that you are able to bring your practice as high up the success ladder as you want to go.

Chapter 25

Define Your Uniqueness

THERE IS NO DOUBT that your practice is unique, if for no other reason than the fact that no other practice has your Team of people. The combination of talent, skills, experiences, perceptions, knowledge, and personalities on your Team combines to create a unique product that only you can offer. Translating that into words that describe your uniqueness to others is difficult, however, because it usually comes out sounding like a contrived advertisement.

Still, it's important to define your uniqueness so that you can answer questions such as:

- Why would someone choose you over your competition?
- What is it about you, your Team, your environment, your care, your services, and your products that others would call "special," "appealing," or "different?"
- Would everyone like your difference, or is your uniqueness going to appeal to a select group of people?
- How can you inform others about your uniqueness so as to better serve your community?
- How can you capitalize on your uniqueness to attract better and/or more patients?
- How can you explain your uniqueness to attract better employees and partners?
- How can you use your uniqueness to increase your revenues?

Let's find out! The process of defining your uniqueness involves attaining a variety of opinions and then assessing the information to find the "truth" of who you are. It is easy to do, and profoundly effective once you've got it all completed.

The foundation of this process stems from a concept I learned in graduate school while living on cookies, coffee, and late night runs to the library. Sitting in a quiet corner of the Duke University library, I discovered the writings of George Herbert Mead,[1] professor at the University of Chicago

---

[1] George Herbert Mead, *Mind, Self and Society,* 1934, Chicago: University of Chicago Press.

and renowned philosopher. Sociologists consider Mead to be the father of social psychology and the creator of a branch of sociology called "symbolic interactionism." As I read his work, I realized that I had found the key to unlock the door of yet another mystery regarding what makes us do what we do.

Mead wrote that individuals are best understood in the context of the group and postulated that all individuals have two visions of themselves, the "**I**" and the "**Me**." The "**I**" is how we see ourselves, and the "**Me**" is how we think others see us. Together they create the truth of who we really are. Let's look a little closer at this concept.

The "**Me**" is the socialized part of the individual and is created through interaction with others. In short, the "**Me**" is the picture we have of ourselves that is based entirely on how others see us. It is important to make a distinction here — the "**Me**" isn't necessarily how others *actually* see us, but only of how we *think* others see us. The "**Me**" is developed as we watch how others respond to us. We then interpret their responses through the haze of our own perspective, and that interpretation in turn forms a part of our perception regarding who we are as individuals.

For example, if every time I speak to an audience, they hoot and howl, applaud wildly, jump to their feet, chant my name, and scream "*Encore*!" then I might presume that I am a great public speaker. If, on the other hand, the audience responds with loud booing, hisses, heckling, and early departures, I might presume something about myself that is, well, quite frankly too awful to imagine, let alone to put in writing. But you get the point, right?

So, let's look at you. Mead would say that the interesting piece of information is how *you think* others perceive your practice. The purist researcher in me can't stop there, because at that point all of our data would be entirely subjective. We need to know how others *actually* perceive you to generate a more realistic picture of your uniqueness, and then interpret that information for our use. So, we begin by finding out:

How do those who use your services see your practice?

The second layer of the individual comes from the "**I**," the active part of the individual. Mead wrote that the "**I**" is in direct response to the "**Me**," and that it is defined by how we see ourselves when we are alone and look in the mirror after having been surrounded by people all day.[2]

---

[2] I am simplifying Mead's highly complex philosophical position.

In order to find your "**I,**" we will look at your Internal Team's perception of your practice's uniqueness by asking them:

How do you see our practice?

The combination of all of your Sub-Teams' perceptions will help us to paint a true picture of your uniqueness.

LET THE DATA COLLECTION BEGIN!

We are going to initiate a research project and find the answers to our questions. This is a simple process that will bring you a wealth of information. Don't panic! Survey research is really easy to do. Let's break it down into five specific steps:

Step 1: Create Your Surveys

Create a survey to give to everyone on your internal Team, another for your patients, and a third for your colleagues. (If you are associated with a hospital, include those colleagues you see on a regular basis.)

Your survey can be as complex or simple as you want it to be. The more complex you make it, the more information you'll get, but the more likely you will be to find yourself bogged down with data to interpret.

As a general rule, the more questions you ask, the less likely people are to respond in a timely manner, if at all. This yields data that are likely to be skewed because the people who are most likely to respond will be people who really like you and want to help, or really don't like you and want to complain. So, keep it short enough to encourage involvement and long enough to get the data you need.

Your internal survey will be distributed to all doctors, clinical and administrative staff. Your patient survey will be similar to your internal survey. Remember, this is not a "customer service" survey or a "wellness" survey. You are specifically looking to identify your uniqueness, so don't confuse your respondents by throwing in extra questions that muddy the waters.

Your colleague survey can yield the most interesting results of all. Prepare your survey to find out what you want to know. Ask about their perceptions regarding your availability, your accessibility, and other characteristics that would make you somehow different than others in your specialty. **Keep it brief!**

Following are examples of surveys you might use for your internal Team (Table 25-1), your patients (Table 25-2), and your colleagues (Table 25-3).

TABLE 25-1. Internal Survey						
Please take a few minutes to complete this brief survey and then place it in the sealed box at the front desk by Friday afternoon at 3:00 p.m. <u>Do not sign your name</u>. We want this to be anonymous so that everyone will be free to give their honest opinions. INSTRUCTIONS: For each statement listed, please rank our practice by placing a check (✓) in the column that best describes us: (1)= Never (2) = Rarely (3) = About half of the time (4) = Most of the time (5) = Always						
Characteristics of Our Practice		**1**	**2**	**3**	**4**	**5**
Our adminis-trative staff members are	Motivated to help others to succeed					
	Efficient					
	Relationship-oriented					
	Knowledgeable					
	People I can talk to					
	Sensitive to others' needs					
	People who go above and beyond					
	Skilled at managing difficult situations					
	Effective communicators					
Our clinical staff members are	Motivated to help others to succeed					
	Efficient					
	Relationship-oriented					
	Knowledgeable					
	People I can talk to					
	Sensitive to others' needs					
	People who go above and beyond					
	Skilled at managing difficult situations					
	Effective communicators					
Our doctors are	Motivated to help others to succeed					
	Efficient					
	Relationship-oriented					
	Knowledgeable					
	People I can talk to					
	Sensitive to others' needs					
	People who go above and beyond					
	Skilled at managing difficult situations					
	Effective communicators					

(Table continues next page)

TABLE 25-1. Internal Survey *(continued)*						
Characteristics of Our Practice		**1**	**2**	**3**	**4**	**5**
Our office is	Comfortable					
	Decorated the way I like it					
	Filled with interesting reading					
	Educational					
Our services are	Up to date and competitive with others					
	The right variety for our patients' needs					
	Unique					
Please place a check (✓) next to the one statement that best completes this sentence: The most unique part of our practice is: ☐ Our clinical skills ☐ The relationships we build with our patients ☐ The state-of-the-art equipment we have on site ☐ The design of our office ☐ Other_____						

Again, please don't think that these characteristics are the best or only ones you would list. Every practice is different and so every survey will be different. The idea is to list a combination of characteristics that would help patients to identify what is special about you.

TABLE 25-2. Patient Survey						
Please take a few minutes to complete this brief survey and then return it to us in the enclosed envelope by March 23rd. Please do not sign your name. We want this to be anonymous so that you will be free to give us your honest opinions. INSTRUCTIONS: For each statement listed, please rank our practice by placing a check (✓) in the column that best describes us: (1)= Never (2) = Rarely (3) = About half of the time (4) = Most of the time (5) = Always						
Characteristics of Our Practice		**1**	**2**	**3**	**4**	**5**
Your administrative personnel (practice administrator, front desk, check out, treatment coordinator, billing, and insurance) are	Motivated to help others to succeed					
	Efficient					
	Relationship-oriented					
	Knowledgeable					
	People I can talk to					
	Sensitive to others' needs					
	People who go above and beyond					
	Skilled at managing difficult situations					
	Effective communicators					

(Table continues next page)

TABLE 25-2. Patient Survey *(continued)*		1	2	3	4	5
Characteristics of Our Practice		1	2	3	4	5
Your clinical personnel (physician assistant, nurse practitioner, medical assistant, dental hygienist, chairside assistant, etc.) are	Motivated to help others to succeed					
	Efficient					
	Relationship-oriented					
	Knowledgeable					
	People I can talk to					
	Sensitive to others' needs					
	People who go above and beyond					
	Skilled at managing difficult situations					
	Effective communicators					
My doctor is	Motivated to help me to succeed					
	Efficient					
	Relationship-oriented					
	Knowledgeable					
	Someone I can talk to					
	Sensitive to my needs					
	Someone who goes above and beyond					
	Skilled at managing difficult situations					
	An effective communicator					
Your office is	Comfortable					
	Conveniently located					
	Run with an on-time schedule					
	Decorated the way I like it					
	Filled with interesting reading					
	Educational					
	Fun					
	Child-friendly					
	State-of-the-art					
	Spacious					
Your services are	Up to date and competitive with others					
	The right variety for my needs					
	Unique					

(Table continues next page)

TABLE 25-2. Patient Survey *(continued)*					
Characteristics of Our Practice	1	2	3	4	5
Please place a check (✓) next to the one statement that best completes this sentence: The most unique part of your practice is: ☐ Your clinical skills ☐ The relationships you build with your patients ☐ The state-of-the-art equipment you have on site ☐ The design of your office ☐ Other_____					

As you can imagine, it's easy to get carried away when you create your surveys, and these three surveys are only examples of the characteristics you can list. The more you think about it the more you'll want to throw in there, but try to restrain yourself. Remember, you're going to have to analyze all of the data.

TABLE 25-3. Colleague Survey					
Please take a few minutes to complete this brief survey, and then place it in the enclosed self-addressed envelope and return it to me at your earliest convenience. Please do not sign your name. We want this to be anonymous so that you will be free to give us your honest opinions. INSTRUCTIONS: For each statement listed, please rank our practice by placing a check (✓) in the column that best describes us: (1)= Never (2) = Rarely (3) = About half of the time (4) = Most of the time (5) = Always					
Characteristics of Our Practice	1	2	3	4	5
I have found your administrative personnel to be — People who go above and beyond					
Skilled at managing difficult situations					
Effective communicators					
Efficient					
Relationship-oriented					
Knowledgeable					
I have found your clinical personnel to be — People who go above and beyond					
Skilled at managing difficult situations					
Effective communicators					
Efficient					
Relationship-oriented					
Knowledgeable					

(Table continues next page)

TABLE 25-3. Colleague Survey *(continued)*		1	2	3	4	5
Your doctors are	Responsive					
	Available					
	Well-received by my patients					
	Skilled at partnering with colleagues					
	Versatile					
	Personable					
	Dependable					
I am comfortable referring my patients to you						

Please place a check (✓) next to the one statement that best completes this sentence:

The most unique part of your practice is:

☐ Your clinical skills
☐ Your responsiveness
☐ The relationships you build with your patients
☐ The state-of-the-art equipment you have on site
☐ The design of your office
☐ Other_____

Keep in mind that the goal of your research is to help you to Differentiate your practice in the community by defining what is unique about your practice through the eyes of your internal Team and those you serve. Be sure to list instructions, specify confidentiality, and provide a deadline for completion. The simpler you make this the more likely you'll be to get a response.

Step 2: Distribute Your Surveys

Getting people to respond to surveys depends, in large part, on how you distribute them to your respondents. Let's look at your three target groups and how best to assure their participation.

Internal Surveys

It seems that every time employees turn around, there is another survey coming across their path. In order to distinguish this as an important project, begin by explaining the reason for your survey. Reassure your Team that their answers will be completely confidential and give them a secure place to return their completed surveys. My favorite plan is to provide an inexpensive lock box that is flimsy enough to allow you to create a slot for people to drop in their responses. Get a small hacksaw and create a rectangular opening in the front so that people can slide their completed surveys into the box. The more effort you make to keep this private, the more honesty you will get, and you can use the same box when you survey your patients.

Remember, you need to take the survey too!

Your Patients

Distribute your patient survey to all of your patients by mail and in person. Set a goal to get a minimum of 10% of your surveys returned[3]. Make sure that you include a self-addressed, stamped envelope and a cover letter, signed by all of your doctors. Your letter might look something like this:

> *Dear Patient,*
>
> *In an effort to understand how best to serve our community, we are asking all of our patients to complete a brief survey to help us to identify what makes us unique. We recognize that your time is very valuable, and if you can spare a few minutes, we would deeply appreciate your help.*
>
> *Please follow the instructions, and then return your completed survey in the enclosed self-addressed, stamped envelope no later than March 23rd.*
>
> *If you have any questions, please don't hesitate to call our office. Thank you, in advance, for your help.*
>
> *Respectfully yours,*
>
> *The Doctors and Staff of ABC Healthcare*

Your Colleagues

Your colleague surveys will be delivered by mail with a cover letter and self-addressed, stamped envelope. For colleagues only, place a small code on the outside of each return envelope so that you can identify which people have responded. You will then check them off of your list and discard the envelope. This will maintain confidentiality and allow you to follow up later.[4]

Your colleagues' cover letter might look something like this:

> *Dear (Colleague's name),*
>
> *In an effort to understand how best to serve our community, we are asking all of our referring colleagues to complete a brief survey to help us to identify what makes us unique. We recognize that your time is*

---

[3] Survey research generally yields a response rate of 4%. Since your target group knows who you are, you can expect a higher result.

[4] In the ideal world you would code your patients' return envelopes as well, but that can be time consuming and costly.

very valuable, and if you can spare a few minutes, we would deeply appreciate your feedback.

Please return your completed survey in the enclosed self-addressed, stamped envelope no later than March 23rd.

Thank you, in advance, for your help.

Respectfully yours,

(Sign your name)

Be prepared, this will be the most difficult survey, to get respondents to complete. Your cover letter, the length of your survey and the degree to which you are respected will be some of the determining factors, but don't take it personally if you don't hear back. Be prepared to call the office and send two or three additional copies before you get your response. It's worth it!

Step 3: Informally Survey Your Vendors

Some of the most useful opinions you can get will come from people who know your practice but don't utilize any of your services. These people can give you a unique perspective since they sit further out in the stadium. Remember, they spend their time visiting other practices as well (many of whom may be your competition), so their perspective could be very valuable.

Invite them to walk around your practice and to tell you three things that they see, feel, or hear in your practice that they don't typically find in other practices. Then, just go about your business and let them "hang around." You will be amazed by the feedback you get!

Step 4: Analyze Your Data

Study the responses you receive and find the patterns that point to your uniqueness. As you view your patterns, you may find some indicators of problem areas in your practice. That is normal and to be expected. Put those areas on your to-do list to be addressed in upcoming meetings and trainings. The important thing for now is to focus on the positive and find out what makes you truly unique.

Step 5: Interpret Your Data

Once you have quantified the results of your surveys by looking at the numbers, it's time to step back and ask yourself "*What does all of this say about us?*"

Interpretations of data can be highly subjective, and while it's important to read between the lines, you also want to be careful not to imagine things that aren't there. Remember, if you torture your data enough they'll confess to anything, so make sure you stay honest with your interpretations. Show your results to others in your practice and ask them how they interpret the findings. Share your results with non-healthcare friends and see what they say. The more input you get, the closer you'll come to the truth of what you see.

Once you are confident in your interpretation, it's time to write a statement that will summarize your results. If you aren't creative with words, then recruit someone to help you. The final product will be your **Differentiation Statement.**

> **Practice Spotlight**
>
> DIFFERENTIATION STATEMENT: *We are a practice of people who have found the balance between professional and personal. We laugh and cry with our patients and educate them about how to improve their treatment results through lifestyle changes and commitment to treatment protocols. We encourage our patients to participate in their own treatment, and we stay with them and their families every step of the way.*

> **Practice Spotlight**
>
> DIFFERENTIATION STATEMENT: *We are a diagnostic facility that cares as much about our patients' experience during testing as we do about the quality of results we give to our referring colleagues. Our patients tell us that our testing rooms are more comfortable than their own bedrooms and that our staff makes everything fun and easy. Everyone who knows us knows that we do what we do because we love to do it.*

A Differentiation Statement is similar to a Vision Statement, with a unique twist. Where a Vision Statement typically describes how your practice *could* or *should* be, your Differentiation Statement will describe **what is**. This makes it an accurate and Motivational benchmark for your practice, and an extraordinarily strong marketing tool.

Your Differentiation Statement is a summary of the OPINIONS, FACTS, and FEELINGS of your respondents and is therefore a direct representation of the collective States of Mind of those you serve internally and externally. It explains what is unique (OPINIONS) about the services you offer (FACTS), and the experience of being in your care (FEELINGS). It encompasses everything you need to enact the 20-20-60 rule of Motivating people (see Chapter 15). It is, quite frankly, the perfect marketing tool.

Now that you have your data-driven Differentiation Statement, you're ready to magnify your uniqueness so that the members of your community will be able to learn about what the people who know you already know.

BOTTOM LINE

Differentiating your practice begins with defining what is unique about your Team, your services, and your office. You can accomplish this through internal and external surveys. Once you have your data compiled, analyzed, and interpreted, use the results to develop a Differentiation Statement and then get ready to capitalize on your findings!

Chapter 26

Magnify Your Uniqueness

IMAGINE YOU ARE HOLDING a magnifying glass. If you hold it at the perfect angle, it will help you to see everything more clearly. But if you hold it at the wrong angle, everything will become distorted and ugly.

What we are going to do is find the perfect angle to hold your magnifying glass to make your uniqueness more visible to the community, without making it so obvious that it loses its special quality and becomes a circus sideshow.

Practice Spotlight

After my client had completed his surveys and defined the uniqueness of his practice, he was delighted to find that his internal Team, his patients, and his referring colleagues all saw his practice as he had always envisioned it to be.

The practice was described as *"unusually caring, extraordinarily gentle, and sensitive to the needs of the environment."* I suggested that we talk about ways to magnify that for the community so that he could attract more patients and build his practice. Dr. A had a spouse who had taken a few marketing courses and was excited to handle the project on her own.

When we came back for our follow-up visit, we saw an enormous billboard on the main highway. The sign had a bigger-than-life photo of Dr. A with a big smile and the practice Differentiation Statement flowing out of his mouth in a comic-like speech bubble. It was quite a sign.

To magnify their uniqueness even further, my clients had done some redecorating at the office. From the reception area to the lab, they'd mounted colorful posters with their survey results inscribed in calligraphy.

The combined effect of the billboard and the internal signage was a bit too much. Even their most loyal patients recommended that they scale it back.

I discovered that I needed to be a little more specific when I use the word "magnify," so let me make sure that I am absolutely clear for you.

Magnifying your uniqueness has two specific goals:

Goal #1: To help your Team to understand how to do more of what makes you special; and

Goal #2: To help you to express your uniqueness to others.

Let's look at each:

GOAL #1: HELP YOUR TEAM TO UNDERSTAND HOW TO DO MORE OF WHAT MAKES YOU SPECIAL

No Team does everything perfectly 100% of the time. What we need to do is help your Team to understand what makes you unique and how to do more of that so that your strengths as a practice will appear more consistently.

> **The secret of magnifying your uniqueness is to find ways to increase your percentages so you can do what you do so well more of the time!**

Talk together as a Team (partners and staff) about your Differentiation Statement and the details of your survey results. Determine together what you would need to tweak so that you can bring out more of your great characteristics on a daily basis. Double check to make sure that you're not setting yourselves up to fail by creating too much pressure that will lead to the disappearance of some of your other unique qualities. There is a fine balance that you're looking to create. Remember,

> **You're already successful.**
> **Now you're looking to finesse your way to a higher level.**

Once you've determined what needs to be done, create an ACTION Plan equipped with the necessary RESOURCES, designated leaders, and deadlines. This should not be hard since all you're doing is creating a plan to do more of what you already do well. Here's an example:

Practice Spotlight

When they reviewed the results of their survey, the results showed that the characteristic of the Team that respondents chose most often as an indicator of the practice's uniqueness was ***"You take the time to really listen to your patients."*** Since this was the most common response, the Team determined that it was a key to defining their uniqueness.

When they looked at the actual numbers, however, they realized that, although this was the most common response, the actual percentage of respondents who had selected that characteristic was 77%. That meant 23% of the respondents hadn't selected it! They decided to go after that group and set a goal of raising their overall percentage to 87% over the course of the next year.

Everyone was excited about the goal, and so we talked about what would have to change in the practice to make it possible for them to achieve it. They discussed the logistics and discovered that there were two problems: Not enough time and not enough space. Everyone agreed that they would gladly spend more time with patients but that there were certain days when the schedule simply would not allow it.

They talked about the fact that listening to patients required that staff members stay longer in the rooms with their patients, which was fine on Tuesdays and Thursdays. But on Mondays, Wednesdays, and Fridays they couldn't afford to tie up rooms or staff members. They had to move patients through quickly.

The Team agreed that this was a critical piece of their success as a practice but it seemed impossible to increase their percentages. I asked them to think about what they would get if they were able to make it happen.

One partner said that he found it easier to talk with patients who had already been "warmed up" by his assistants.

The scheduling coordinator said that she thought they had more surgeries booked on their slower days and wondered if that was because they spent more time and worked through The ACTION Formula with those patients.

The billing and collections manager spoke up and said she thought that patients who didn't have their ACTION Formula Interviews might be the ones who went late and delinquent on their bills.

This information changed the discussion. Now we were talking about revenues. We did a chart review of the previous year and discovered a direct correlation between patients who had their ACTION Formula interview and patients who had gone ahead with surgeries and paid their bills on time. The numbers took all the opinions out of it and told us precisely what to do.

The doctors decided to give up their separate offices and move in together. This allowed them to turn the other office into an additional consultation room. They hired a part-time assistant for two busy mornings a week and the treatment coordinator agreed to work an extra afternoon to fill in. It all paid for itself.

This is internal Magnification at its finest.

GOAL #2: EXPRESS YOUR UNIQUENESS TO OTHERS

The second goal of magnifying your uniqueness is to relay the information to people externally without sounding pushy or "salesy." There are five strategies with accompanying tactics that will allow you to accomplish magnification with style and finesse: I call them **"Magnification 1X, Magnification 2X, Magnification 3X, Magnification 4X, and Magnification 5X."** As their names imply, each strategy is more powerful than the one that came before, allowing your community to get a closer look at the uniqueness of your practice.

Magnification 1X: Throw a Pebble in the Pond

The smallest pebble can create a massive impact in a pond, if you throw the pebble at just the right angle in just the right spot. Your "pebble" is going to be a well-written letter that announces the results of your study. The placement of your pebble will be subtle and powerful:

> **Send a feedback report to your patients and referring colleagues, and then send a copy to your local newspaper.**

The point of Magnification 1X is to subtly recruit others as your practice representatives. By sending your feedback reports, you will be giving people words to use when they speak about you in the community. This will be particularly powerful for those who responded to your surveys. They are self-identified as people who are willing to say what they think and when they have the right words to use, that will be a beautiful thing for your practice!

The key is to make sure that your feedback report is written factually with humility and gratitude. The more perfect your pebble, the more powerful will be your impact. It might look something like this:

Practice Spotlight

Dear Ms. Patient,

Thank you for your participation in our recent practice survey. We are grateful for the time you took to respond, and thought you might enjoy viewing the results of the survey.[1]

We sent out surveys to 2,500 active patients, 25 referring colleagues, and our internal team of 30 employees and doctors. A total of 384 people responded, yielding a response rate of 15%. Here is what the survey results showed:

77% of respondents stated that our greatest uniqueness as a practice is **the time we spend listening to our patients.**

When asked to rate our staff and doctors across specific characteristics, 92.3% of respondents gave us the highest rating possible ("Always") and an additional 7.2% of respondents rated us at "Most of the Time" for the following characteristics:

Friendly, Accurate, Knowledgeable, Caring, Gentle, Responsive, Available, Dependable, Professional, Sensitive to Others' Needs, and Skilled at Communicating With Others.

99.4% of respondents stated that our office is **Conveniently Located and Comfortable** and 96.1% rated us as "Always" being **On Time** for their appointments.

We interpret our results to mean that **our patients and colleagues find us to be a practice of people who listen to our patients and who use a unique combination of caring and expertise to help them to get what they want and need.**

We are proud of these results, but we believe that we can do better. We have created a plan for the coming year to expand our commitment to building strong relationships with the people we serve, and we look forward to receiving your feedback when we send our next survey.

Respectfully yours,

ABC Plastic Surgeons and Medical Spa

Send a copy of the letter to everyone you serve. In the ideal world, you would send word-processed letters so names appear in the salutation of the letter, but at least make sure you send personalized letters to your colleagues. You can go generic with patients and vendors if you want to save some time.

If you have an electronic newsletter, send your survey results out as an e-blast, and make sure you post the news in a prominent place on your

---

[1] This opening only works if you coded every survey. Otherwise, change your language to say, "*We recently conducted a survey of our patients and referring colleagues. Since the surveys were confidential we can't identify who responded, so we are sending the results to all of our patients with special thanks to those of you who sent us your feedback.*"

Web site. The pebble will strike the gossip mill, which will then spread your ripple throughout the community as your e-blast is forwarded to others.

Next, send a copy of your report to your local newspaper. Don't shoot for a front page story but rather send it to the "local news" desk with a simple cover letter that says, *"We thought you might be interested in this. If you have any questions, feel free to call."* You might not get in the paper immediately, and you might not get in at all, but you can be sure that people will hear about it through the grapevine. When you conduct a properly managed research survey, the data speak for themselves and the ripple effect carries the information all through your pond.

Magnification 2X: Get Branded

You may have heard about "branding," but just in case, let me offer a quick review. Branding is a technique that allows you to capture the essence of your uniqueness and display it for the world to see. Your brand sends a message to the community about who you are and what you do, and so it needs to be managed with the goal of projecting a clear and consistent message that helps others to answer one question:

Why you?

Your brand will be expressed in everything from the colors on your business card to the comfort of the chairs in your reception area. It includes the way you answer the phone, the material of your scrubs, and the service you give to your customers. Your Differentiation depends on your ability to build an effective brand and maintain it consistently. If you decide to create brochures, a Web site or to use media advertising, your brand will help you to send a consistent message and to develop more rapid name recognition in the community.[2] When you get it right, your brand tells the world,

This is why people choose us!

If you have any concerns that the brand someone creates for you isn't the right representation of your uniqueness, then ask your consultant to conduct a focus group analysis of the proposed brand. In this analysis, selected members of the community (representing the type of patients and colleagues you wish to attract) will be invited to offer their interpretations and impressions of the brand. These data will tell you what you need to know without the prejudice of your own perspective. If what they say matches your Differentiation Statement then you'll know it was accurate.

---

[2] If you are ready to begin marketing externally, consider using an experienced consultant. I've had many clients who tried to do it themselves and threw away thousands of dollars because of their inexperience. I am not an expert in marketing, but if you need help finding someone, you can email me, and I will gladly refer you to one of my trusted colleagues.

Magnification 3X: Choose Your Patients

There are many ways to help your community to find you, and in Magnification 3X you're going to set the stage that will attract the patients you want. The first step is to decide who your "target" will be. Will you serve everyone in your community or do you have a select group you'd like to serve?

Think of it as a pot and a lid. Unless you have an enormous kitchen with space to lay out every pot with its lid attached, you probably have different sizes and shapes of pots in one area and all of the various lids in another area. When you're cooking, the crazy-making task is to quickly find the lid that fits your pot before the soup boils over onto the stove. Choose any lid other than the correct one, and you won't create the strong seal you need to create the perfect soup. There is a perfect lid for every pot.

Ask the romantics in the world and they will tell you, when it comes to affairs of the heart, *"there is a lid for every pot."* I thought that was a silly myth, until I found Hal. OK, so I guess that makes me a romantic too, but I found my perfect lid, and I believe in happy endings for those who are willing to do what it takes to get them.

Now, here's the point: Just as there is a lid for every pot in your kitchen and in romance,

There is a practice that is just the right fit for every patient.

Why should patients have to be uncomfortable with another practice when they could be in your practice enjoying a perfect Alignment with your Team and getting the services they need under your excellent care?

By the same token, why should you have to treat patients who might be a better fit for your colleagues?

Some would say that you should be grateful for the opportunity to treat whoever comes to your door. I don't know what the "shoulds" are here, but I do know one thing: if you don't decide who would be your ideal patients and go after them, then you will miss a percentage of the population who would have been best served by your care.

The fact is that some people feel most fulfilled when they are treating one type of patient population while others blossom when challenged by a variety of types. Perhaps you owe it to yourself and your future patients to connect the square pegs with the square doctors. Um, well, you know what I mean. Find the patients that are right for you and help them to know that you are Dr. Right.

Activity 26-1 gives you an opportunity to stop and think about this issue so that you can identify precisely the patients that you want to serve.

ACTIVITY 26-1. My Ideal Patients			
Following is a list of characteristics of patients. It is by no means an exhaustive list, but it will give you a jump start to begin thinking about who is the lid to your pot. Place a check (✓) next to each characteristic of patient that you would like to treat. When you are finished, sit back and look at your ideal practice. HINT: Focus on one characteristic at a time. Don't start painting pictures or adding characteristics together until you're done.			
Enthusiast		Relater	
Thinker		Commander	
Value Set Type 1		Value Set Type 2	
Expresses opinions		Expresses facts	
Expresses feelings		Average to high level of Chips	
Low to average level of Chips		Self-Motivated	
Needs help getting Motivated		Difficult to Motivate	
Responds best to external Motivation		Responds best to internal Motivation	
Male		Female	
Age 0 – 12		Age 13 – 21	
Age 22 – 35		Age 36 – 50	
Age 51 – 65		Age 66 – 80	
Age 81 +		Pregnant	
Full family		Don't educate, just treat and go	
Interested in preventive treatment		Looking for education	
Spiritual orientation:		Current occupation:	
Primary language is:		Ethnicity:	
Other:		Other:	
Other:		Other:	

Now take the picture of your ideal patients, craft your marketing efforts to speak directly to those people, and Differentiate yourself as the perfect group for them.

Magnification 4X: Tell Them What They Need to Know

Just because your Team is filled with caring people who have extraordinary clinical skills, that may not be enough to bring patients to your door. You see, unless you live in a rural area where you are the only provider of your specialty for hundreds of miles, or you are a magician with a cure rate unlike anyone else's in the world,

Patients can't distinguish what makes you a better choice for them unless you tell them.

The fact is that patients simply don't know if you're really the best at what you do. They don't *really* know what your credentials mean and how your training enables you to do something better than someone else. They don't understand what makes you good, and quite frankly, neither do many of your colleagues. Mostly, they know what other people tell them about you. They know what they hear from their friends, family members, and other doctors. They know what they read in the magazines about "The Top Doctors" and in the newspapers about law suits and allegations. But they don't really know if you're right for them until they're sitting in front of you. So how do you get them there?

If you want people to understand why they should come to you, then as Ricky said to Lucy, *"You've got some 'splainin' to do."*

The "*'splainin'*" will come in your marketing. There are many ways to get the word out about your uniqueness (see Table 26-1), but whichever avenue you choose, I will offer you two pieces of marketing advice that my clients affectionately call "Wendy Wisdom":

Wendy Wisdom #1:

Remember that marketing is a communication from your practice to people whom you have never met. The goal is to Differentiate your practice from others, establish trust, build an Alignment, and then Motivate them to call you, make an appointment, and be there on time.

Because marketing is such an important communication, it needs to follow all the rules we've been discussing throughout this book. Make sure your marketing addresses The Four Languages of The M.A.D. Formula and follows the 20-20-60 rule of selling to account for all States of Mind. Check to see that Action Types and Value Sets are addressed and that your copy is sensitive to the Chips of your prospective audience. Consider the likely DESIRES of your patient population along with their probable RESOURCE and PERMISSION barriers. Be certain that your marketing speaks to your ideal patient, represents your Differentiation Statement accurately and makes a strong effort to Motivate and Align the audience to your Mission Statement.

A good marketing consultant will allow you to make a reasonable amount of suggestions or revisions, so establish in advance their definition of "reasonable" and be willing to invest a little extra cash to get them to Align with you. It is worth the investment of your time and money to find people who will customize your marketing and not place

TABLE 26-1. Avenues to Magnify Your Uniqueness		
Following is a list of some of my favorite vehicles to magnify your uniqueness and Differentiate you from your competition.		
Internal Marketing		
Educational posters showing "real" people who use services like yours	Practice brochure that lists your services and information about your practice	Patient newsletters in reception area
Welcome kit with information about you and your practice	Ongoing surveys for patient satisfaction	Using The Four languages of The M.A.D. Formula
Patient appreciation events	In-house patient seminars	The ACTION Formula Interview
Sub-Team Motivation	Patient Alignment	Sub-Team Alignment
External Marketing		
Practice representative	Doctor-to-doctor networking	External signage
Yellow Pages advertising	Print ads in newspapers and magazines	Radio and TV programmed advertising
Appearances on local radio and TV talk shows	Direct mail	Differentiation Survey
Articles in newspapers and magazines	Community event sponsorships	Web site
E-newsletters	Community education seminars	Paid Internet marketing
Business cards for all Team members	Image Management	Ongoing colleague appreciation

you into a cookie-cutter version of a project they did for your colleague in another state. You have a distinct uniqueness, and it is your marketing consultant's job to help you to magnify it so that everyone can see it clearly.

Remember, this is your practice. While your marketing consultants have the expertise to put it all together, they can't possibly know what you know about your uniqueness. Let them know in advance that you want to partner with them in the creation of your marketing so that your M.A.D. formula is properly addressed.

Wendy Wisdom #2:

Make sure that every doctor and employee in your practice understands how best to represent the image of your practice, and is accountable for doing so.

It's true what they say, *"You only get one chance to make a good first impression."* Right or wrong, I have seen many competent professionals misunderstood and even ridiculed by colleagues and patients because they simply didn't know how to manage their image. So, let's take a moment to talk about that.

Image management is defined as the way you look and act when you are around others.

Appearance and Image

Like it or not, we live in a visual world. People read your appearance and equate it with your credibility. Whatever you know, whatever your credentials, whatever your track record, if your appearance falls short of the mark, people will assume that you do too.

If your practice prides itself on a commitment to excellence and attention to detail, then your appearance must send that message. Your appearance includes your body, skin, hair, clothes, jewelry, posture and carriage, facial expression, and makeup for women.

I have seen neurosurgeons with misaligned buttons on their lab coats; dentists with chipped, yellowing teeth; and bariatric surgeons with an extra 40 pounds of weight around the middle.

I've seen administrative personnel dressed as if they were ready to go "clubbing" on a Saturday night date and clinical personnel wearing big clunky jewelry and overwhelming perfumes.[3]

I've seen scrubs that are too tight, too wrinkled, too revealing, and too frayed at the edges. I have seen ties with mustard stains, shirts with pen stains, and scrubs with blood stains. I've seen skirts that are too tight, shirts that are too low, shoes that are too old, and hair that is too colorful.

Ask yourself one question:

Is my choice of appearance damaging the image of my practice?

Take some time soon and do Activity 26-2 to make sure that your image is where it needs to be.

A friend once taught me a rule that has been of enormous help to me:

Before you go out your door each day, run quickly past your mirror. If you see anything on your body that stands out, then take it off, cover it up, gel it, or comb it.

---

[3] I strongly recommend that you create rules about perfumes. Many people are sensitive to certain perfumes and will turn their discomfort with one staff member into a negative image of your entire practice.

ACTIVITY 26-2. My Appearance

Go through your closet, locker, drawers, etc. Try things on and make a decision about whether the way you look fits the image you want to project for your practice. Look in the mirror and decide if there's anything you need to change about your facial hair or makeup. Take all clothes and accessories that you've decided don't fit the image you want and bring them to work with you on Monday. Show everyone on your team what you've decided to change about your appearance, explain why you've chosen to make this change, and then encourage them to follow suit.

What will people notice about *you* today?

Behaviors and Image

How we behave with others sends a strong message about who we are. Unfortunately, when we are preoccupied or focused on what we are doing, we often lose track of our behaviors and consequently send messages we never meant to send. This is particularly true when we are feeling anxious (scared) or frustrated (mad).

Practice Spotlight

"Don't get around him when he's doing a procedure. He'll bite your head off."

"He snaps at the floor nurses."

"No PA will work with him."

"I'm embarrassed to say he's my partner."

As I read through the pre-training comments about this physician, I wondered what he would be like when we met in person. In my fantasy, he would be cold and distant, with menacing eyes that said, *"Don't mess with me!"*

On the night of the pre-training physician dinner, we stood at the door as the surgeons arrived. As each man shook our hands, we waited to hear **his** name. Those who had arrived stood together in the room, talking and laughing. They were warm, easy, and friendly.

I was talking with a new arrival when someone slipped by me talking on his cell phone. With his back to me, I could hear him on the phone. He was soft-spoken and gentle with the person on the line. As he talked I noticed that one of his shirt tails was sticking out, his shoes were untied, and his hair was sticking straight up in back.

As I was trying to talk myself out of tying his shoelaces, his tone suddenly became loud and harsh, his words were accusatory, and his style aggressive. His language left the G-rated sphere and with that he slammed shut his phone, turned to his partner, and raged about a hospitalist who he clearly didn't like. Then, just as suddenly, he turned to me with the warmest of smiles and said, *"You must be Wendy. It's good to finally meet you."*

I felt like I had entered a moving clip of *Dr. Jekyll and Mr. Hyde.*

After the first course was completed, I brought up the concept of Differentiation and explained about image management. All eyes turned to Dr. Jekyll. We opened up the discussion and listened as the other surgeons carefully and respectfully talked to him about his behaviors and told him that they believed his behaviors were damaging their reputation as a practice.

We all waited for an explosion that never came. He sat quietly for a moment with his eyes closed. No one moved. When he opened his eyes to speak, a tear fell. He looked stunned. He said that it had never occurred to him that anything he did had any bearing on the rest of them. He honestly never made the connection. Ironically he was touched that they thought of him as a part of the Team and promised that from that day forward he would represent them honorably. And he did.

Practice Spotlight

She had been their Treatment Coordinator for 10 years. The doctors depended on Rhonda for her strong work ethic. Her case conversion rate was only 52%, but they assured us she just needed some new communication skills and she'd be great.

Rhonda handled all inquiries for plastic surgery that came in by phone or off of their Web site. I sent a mystery inquiry to the Web site and the response that came back to me was enthusiastic and inviting. The only problem was that it was filled with grammatical and spelling errors. Of course, my first thought was of image management.

When we arrived on site we found a spectacular office. The image it sent was nothing short of meticulous attention to detail, state-of-the-art technology combined with fine artistry, and a great sense of design. It was exciting. The front desk personnel were stunningly attractive, although their street clothes were a bit distracting from the image of the rest of the practice.

Then we met Rhonda. I tried to be polite, but I just couldn't take my eyes off of her breasts. They were bursting out of her tight suit like a walking brochure for breast augmentation. She followed my glance and said *"Aren't they great? Dr. T did them!"* Then she burst into a great big smile revealing cracked, yellowed teeth and enormous spaces where two teeth were missing. As she took us on a tour of the facility, she walked on spiked heels and her skirt was so short and tight that we wondered what would happen if she tried to sit or bend over.

When we mentioned Rhonda's appearance to the doctors, they said *"Oh yes, that's our Rhonda. We asked her to change but she won't."* They went on to say they were afraid to let her go before they found a replacement. It took them another year to get around to that. We'll never know what it cost them.

What can you do when Team members' behaviors are damaging your image? Here are some ideas that have worked for my clients:

1. Have a Team meeting and talk about image management. Give tips on how to adjust tone of voice, facial expression, posture, dress, etc. to send the image you want to send.
2. Use the Candor Formula. Tell the Team member what he or she is doing, how it is impacting your image, and what you'd like him or her to do differently.
3. Bring in someone from a local hair salon or an image specialist to work with your entire Team. Often this will be the spark of energy to get everyone in line with what you are trying to accomplish.
4. Consider a practice-wide uniform that will take the guesswork out of getting ready for work. Set boundaries for hair, makeup, and jewelry.
5. Form an alliance with a local barber and create onsite days for convenient haircuts.
6. Make image management a part of the job description, and document all indiscretions.
7. Consider Chips. Often I find that people dress exotically because they are seeking attention. When they get enough recognition for other things, the unwanted behaviors tone down substantially.

Image management goes beyond the four walls of your practice. Remind your doctors and staff that everywhere they go they are representing your Team. While there is pressure associated with that, there is also honor in knowing that each and every one of you are a part of something unique and special.

Wear your practice image proudly in grocery stores, bowling alleys, and supermarkets. Carry your unique image around the world to association meetings and on vacations. Remember,

You never know who will be sitting next to you in an airport or at a fast-food restaurant.

The image you send out while you are out may determine how you feel about yourself today and may dictate your net worth next year.

Magnification 5X: Give Them a Taste of Your Practice

From the finest restaurants, to discount warehouses, everywhere you go you are invited to taste the merchandise so you know what you're buying before you dive in. Why not do the same for patients who are on the market for the services you offer?

You can accomplish this easily, with a low investment of time and money, by offering free, educational seminars in your community. I think that this may be the smartest and most effective way to Differentiate your practice and attract the patients that you really want.

Providing free seminars in your community allows you to:

1. Attract patients who are predisposed to be Aligned with your perspective on healthcare.
2. Set yourself up as the guru in your specialization.
3. Market your practice without being pushy or "salesy."
4. Give back to the members of your community.
5. Magnify your uniqueness in a way that no other marketing technique will allow.
6. Give your prospective patients an opportunity to understand your perspective on some of the best avenues to improve their health and/or appearance.
7. Give your prospective patients a chance to see, hear, and feel you up close and personal.

If attracting new patients is a strong goal for you, then magnifying your uniqueness in the public eye is a fast track to success. It tells everyone in your community who you are and what makes you best suited for certain patients. It helps eliminate the confusion when patients are searching for the right doctor, and it helps you to find the right patients.

I understand that for some people public speaking sounds worse than an enema. In case you are one of those people, then I'll tell you what I have found after working with many, many doctors:

If you have an important message, and a group of people who want or need to hear it, then there is very little you can do to mess it up.

Are there things you can do to make your presentation more dynamic and powerful such that it moves people to spontaneous applause? Absolutely, and I'm going to give you some of those secrets right here. But first let me share with you something I learned early in my speaking career:

Your audience has no idea what you forgot to say, and no way of knowing that your palms are sweating.

I know surgeons who are completely comfortable doing open heart, brain, and spinal surgeries, but ask them to talk to even one patient and their hearts start pounding. If this describes you, then I'd like to suggest that you think about finding a way to become comfortable talking with people, even if you don't decide to do seminars. Activity 26-3 will help you to overcome your fear of speaking (without picturing people in their underwear).

If you find that you still have trouble overcoming your fear of speaking, look back at your Language of Rules. You may find there is a Do or Don't Rule or even a Guiding Rule lurking around that is creating a barrier to our success. When you find the rule, create a new one that will free you once and for all!

When you're ready to use this incredibly effective marketing tool, here are the Six Steps that will make you a star!

Step 1: Announce Your Seminar

First things first — what's the point of giving a party if no one comes? And "giving a party" is what you are going to do. Your seminar should be promoted and executed as you would a gala event. People like attending special, exciting events. So roll out the red carpet, and extend your invitation to everyone you want as a patient!

Which brings up an important question: Who should you invite? You are looking for the person[4] who is confused about the myriad of choices available, and who would like some help figuring out which choices are best. She wants to put her health in the hands of an expert. The problem is there are so many who claim to be experts. As a result, she has done nothing yet, except cut out advertisements in magazines about the latest "miracle drugs" and articles about "all-new solutions" and kept them in a file marked "*Healthcare Stuff*," "*Face Fixes*," "*Smile Makeovers*," or who-knows-what.

One day, she looks in the newspaper (or mailbox, or email box), and there it is — an invitation that describes a nonthreatening event. It's at *a convenient time and a convenient location, it's free, and refreshments are being served.* What has she got to lose? Except her aches, pains, fat, fatigue,

---

[4] Women are more likely to attend seminars than are men, so if you are using seminars to promote to men, you will likely use a slightly different marketing approach than the one described here.

ACTIVITY 26-3. Overcome Fear of Speaking

Make a list of everything you imagine could possibly go wrong if you spoke in front of an audience. For each thing on your list, recruit the Analyst in you to determine what you could do to avoid or recover from that problem. For example,

Possible Event	How I'll Avoid It or Quickly Recover
I'll forget my speech.	I'll use the Spaced Repetition method, record my speech onto a CD and play it two times a day for seven weeks before my event. If for some reason I forget something, I'll just check my notes and remember that the audience doesn't know what I had planned to say next and will have no idea that I missed anything.
Someone will ask a question I can't answer.	I'll take the person's contact information and promise to follow up within one week with the correct answer.
Someone will heckle me.	I'll invite the person to stay after everyone else leaves so we can talk privately.
A competitor will come and challenge my information.	I'll offer to discuss this over lunch another time, and explain that I don't think it's appropriate to get into a complex debate when these patients came for straight talk and straight answers.

OK—your turn:

Possible Event	How I'll Avoid It or Quickly Recover

sleeplessness, snoring, depression, lost libido, incontinence, gastric distress, poor eyesight, wrinkles, and/or crooked, painful, or yellowing teeth!

Don't overlook newspaper, radio, and TV spots. Depending on your marketplace and the time of year, you can get a lot of exposure for relatively little money by using these media effectively. No matter what kind of advertising you do — remember to:

1. Advertise your event four weeks in advance, once a week for the first three weeks and then every day on the week of your seminar;
2. Choose more than one advertising medium (newspaper and radio, mailed invitation and newspaper, TV and newspaper); and
3. Prepare your Team!

Whoever is answering your phones must be prepared to answer seminar inquiries with a prewritten script that gives answers to commonly asked questions such as "*What is the seminar going to cover?*" "*Can I bring a friend?*" and "*Are you trying to sell something?*" The better prepared and trained your staff is, the more likely it is that people will actually make and keep their reservations.

Step 2: Choose a Good Location

One of the most important decisions you can make is where to hold your seminars. People will judge the worthiness of your event on its location. There are two good choices, and each has merit.

Choice #1: Your practice. If you have a fabulous location and you want to show it off, this is a great way to do that. Make sure that you have plenty of comfortable chairs with room to walk around. The upside of holding your seminar at your location is obvious — you don't have to pay rental for the space; your Team is there already to answer questions, make appointments, and sell retail (if appropriate); and you can pop out between procedures to do a quick seminar.

The downside of using your location is equally important. My experience suggests that fewer people will attend a seminar that is held at a practice because they assume that you are holding the seminar to hook them into becoming patients.

Choice #2: Offsite. If your facility isn't large enough to hold at least 25 attendees comfortably, then you should have your seminar offsite. Local hotels are an option, but can be expensive. Consider a local country club, women's club, community center, public library, or an elementary school. There is often someone who would gladly make their space available to you in exchange for an opportunity to place their cards or brochures in your reception area. The upside of holding your seminar offsite is that it makes your seminar look less "salesy" and threatening and more legitimate as an educational event.

Step 3: Keep It Simple

The more complex you make your seminar the less likely it is that people will get your message. Remember that your attendees are not educated in your area of expertise and they are not looking to be trained as technicians. In fact, most of your attendees aren't looking to understand anything as much as they need someone to tell them *"this is safe and effective and it really is OK to do it!"*

Choose one subject and stick to it. The best marketing seminars use the time to help patients understand options and learn how to make safe decisions regarding their healthcare.

Do not try to sell them on any one perspective or treatment. Instead, *teach* them about one or two options. Explain the benefits of a given approach versus the lack of safety with another. Distinguish temporary solutions from permanent cures. Tell them about things you *don't* do, and tell them why you *won't* do them. Be honest and real. They will respect you and want to hear more.

If your seminar is connected to appearance changes, then be certain to include before and after photos and include personal stories about those patients (with their permission, of course).

Tell a personal story. Not about a patient but about your *response* to a patient who either did or did not get help. Let your audience see how that affected you personally. The more vulnerable you are, the faster you will help your attendees to know that you are someone who is trustworthy.

Customize your presentation to Align with all of your attendees by using all Four Languages of The M.A.D. Formula throughout your seminar and remember the 20-20-60 rule!

Your program should ultimately address the three main strategies of The M.A.D. Formula:

1. Motivate your audience to want to know the truth, to think about the benefits of getting help and to take ACTION;
2. Align with your audience by being real, speaking directly to them and answering their questions; and
3. Differentiate your practice by being the people who took the time to bring straight answers straight to the community.

Step 4: Use Visual Aids

PowerPoints are very effective presentation tools, if you use them effectively. There are some important "DO"s and "DON'T"s (see Table 26-2), but the most important is this — your slides should serve to *enhance* your point — not *make* it. The critical information should come directly from your mouth.

TABLE 26-2. The DOs and DON'Ts of PowerPoint Presentations	
DO	**DON'T**
Use animation throughout your presentation	Animate slide transitions—it makes people seasick
Allow your presentation to unfold one point at a time by using animation — your audience shouldn't see where you're going . . . only where you are and where you've been	Put all your points on the slide and then go through the list — people read ahead and miss what you're talking about
Use color and clip art to emphasize important points and bring entertainment to your presentation	Overwhelm the slides with "stuff" — busy is stressful and distracting
Line yourself up physically so you can see your presentation on your lap top without looking away from your audience	Lean on furniture, shift from one leg to the other, fold your arms, or put your hands on your hips
Use a laser pointer and remote control	Look back at the screen, walk up to the screen and point with your finger, or turn your back on your audience
Create a presentation folder with all of your slides so that you know what is coming in advance	Say things like, "let's see . . . what did my assistant put in here next?"
Plan your transition statements — specifically what you will say before and after each slide	"Wing it" — it sends a message that this is how you practice clinically

Remember that *you* are a visual aid. The facial expressions you use, the degree to which you make eye-contact with your audience, your body language and your posture all tell a story that must compliment your message. I've coached far too many doctors who, in their efforts to look "easy and comfortable" come across looking "bored." Stand tall, move around, look like you're actually enjoying being there with them and above all else, remember to smile!

Step 5: Keep It Short

Your seminar should be 45 minutes, with a 15 minute question-and-answer session at the end. Script your presentation to take your attendees on an emotional rollercoaster ride that is peppered with information, humor, and passion. It should begin with your audience politely listening and end with them sitting on the edge of their seats, Motivated to make a change in how they care for their own health and that of their loved ones.

Step 6: Invite Your Audience to Become Patients

People who attend your seminars are self-selecting as interested in your services, but they may not know you are accepting new patients.

> ## Help them to know that you would welcome the opportunity to talk with them personally to discover if you are right for each other.

At the end of your speech, invite attendees to see a Team member to learn more about your practice. If you have a new partner or associate who is looking to build his or her practice, consider offering a "complimentary five-point health check" or "complimentary consultation."

If you are going to give away gifts like pens or pads, make sure they are well-branded. If you offer elective services, have plenty of menus of your services, along with well-posted notices about the availability of financing options.

Instruct your Team not to push! The biggest mistake people make is when they try to sell at their seminars. This is a *gift* you're giving to your community. Don't mess it up by trying to sell them something. Inform them about the possibilities, and show them your heart — the rest will happen as a result of your well-scripted presentation, your tasteful, entertaining slides, and your helpful staff who is available to answer their questions after your presentation.

Practice Spotlight

Following are comments from clients who used seminars to magnify their uniqueness in the community:

We sent out fancy invitations to a list we purchased from a local women's organization. The invitations were handwritten, calligraphy-style, by one of our office staff members. Our phones started ringing immediately! K.J., MD

The first time we did it, we thought "how hard can this be?" Then we got our answer — it's only hard if you don't plan and prepare for it! The second time we used the script and trained our front desk. We had ZERO no-shows and converted 100% of our attendees to patients. This works! L.T., MD

77% of our attendees made appointments for their Surgical Eligibility Analysis before they left that night. And 100% of those people actually showed up for their appointments. What I found really interesting was that all of those who turned out to be eligible for surgery went ahead with it. H.K., MD

I do these seminars once a month in my practice. My aesthetician and I take turns talking and then we do a Q and A. We always have a lot of fun and get new patients as a result. We've even gotten some referrals from people who attended our seminar but never used our services. It's the best marketing we do. D.S., MD.[5]

I honestly believe that every specialty has something it can teach that would be a real help to the community. There is so much confusion today between all of the media outlets trying to educate the public. Why not help your community and increase your visibility at the same time?

Consider getting together with colleagues and offer a co-sponsored seminar. Helping the members of your community to understand their options is a great way to give back and could make a substantial difference for one of your attendees. It could also make a huge difference in your bottom line.

Whether you choose one Magnification technique or apply them all, the important thing is to make sure that your choices are a good fit for your practice uniqueness. No matter what you do, remember that the best results will come when you magnify your uniqueness by showing the heart of your practice along with the skills.

BOTTOM LINE

Magnifying your uniqueness means applying a combination of internal and external strategies to Differentiate your practice. The degree of Magnification you choose will depend entirely upon the extent to which you want to build your practice. The stronger the Magnification, the more complex the approach, and the greater will be your results.

---

[5] While many dentists and hygienists offer education in their local schools for children, I haven't heard of dentists offering community education seminars for adults. I think there is a huge need and opportunity to help adults to understand the health and cosmetic subtleties of good dentistry, and would encourage you to explore this avenue to help them and Differentiate your practice.

Chapter 27

Do What No One Else Is Doing

ONE OF THE BEST WAYS to Differentiate your practice is to actively find ways to do things that your competitors aren't doing and to make sure that you *don't* do the "undesirable" things that your competitors *are* doing. Of course, the trick is to find out what everyone else is doing! There are six steps to this Differentiation process:

Step 1: Recruit your Team in a plan to gather data.
Step 2: Find out what is happening in other practices through subjective research.
Step 3: Find out what is happening in other practices through objective research.
Step 4: Select what fits best for your practice.
Step 5: Motivate and Align your Team to prepare for the changes.
Step 6: Launch it!

Let's go through the steps one at a time:

STEP 1: RECRUIT YOUR TEAM IN THE PLAN

Have a lunch meeting with your Team and explain that you are launching a research project to collect data that will help you to further Differentiate your practice in the community.[1] Specifically, explain that you want to know:

1. What other practices are doing that you are not doing;
2. What other practices are doing that you would never want to do; and
3. What you are doing that no one else is doing.

Let them know that the success of this research project hangs on their willingness to participate and to collect accurate data in a timely manner.

If you have a small practice, it's all hands on deck. Larger practices can create committees to focus on different areas of research. If you prefer,

[1] It is important to decide the boundaries of your "community." In a large city, you may consider a 10-mile radius. The more unique your specialty, the wider your community will be. The more you can expand the boundaries of your research, the more ideas you'll discover to help you to Differentiate your practice.

make participation voluntary, but however you create your research Team, make sure you create a fun aspect to the project by offering incentives and rewards for participation. Launch a contest for the most interesting findings and then have your Team act as judges. The more enthusiastic your introduction of the project, the more cooperation and involvement you'll get from your Team of researchers!

Once you have your research Team, set a timeline for the project and keep a steady stream of Motivational and encouraging coaching coming their way so as to assure that everyone stays focused on the goal. Assign one person to serve as the organizer of the data so that all results are directed to one place.

STEP 2: FIND OUT WHAT IS HAPPENING IN OTHER PRACTICES THROUGH SUBJECTIVE RESEARCH

Ask your research Team to begin by keeping track of what they see when they work with or visit other healthcare practices (medical and dental). Table 27-1 provides an example of what you might suggest.

Suggest that they take notes so as to remember the details of what they experienced from other practices. Consider encouraging your Team to recruit their friends and family members to join in the research! And remember to recruit yourself in the effort by doing Activity 27-1.

ACTIVITY 27-1. Do Your Own Research
Recruit yourself to be on the research committee. Take notes of practices you work with or use for your own family. The more you participate in this effort, the more genuine you will be in leading others to do the same.

STEP 3: FIND OUT WHAT IS HAPPENING IN OTHER PRACTICES THROUGH OBJECTIVE RESEARCH

Where *subjective* research yields personal opinions, *objective* research will bring you straight facts. Together they will bring you a full and rich picture of what is going on outside your four walls.

Let's say you are an orthopedic practice that regularly refers out to your colleagues at the radiology center for diagnostic studies. It is of no consequence to you if there is an orthopedic practice across town that has their own MRI onsite. Right? Hmmmm . . .

What if you are a primary care practice with limited parking and the dentist

TABLE 27-1. Subjective Assessment of Healthcare Practices			
INSTRUCTIONS: The next time you have contact with a healthcare practice, either as a patient or in the process of working as a member of our Team, pay attention to your experience and notice the ways in which the practice seems different from ours, positively and otherwise. Here are some general areas to watch for:			
Area of Practice	**What They Do That We Don't Do**	**What We Do That They Don't Do**	**What They Do That We Should Never Do**
Phones			
Check-in			
Reception area			
Set-up and design			
Wait time			
Escort to room			
Communications with clinical staff			
Experience with doctor			
Services offered			
Onsite testing			
Attitudes of personnel			
General "feel" of the office			
Customer service			
Check-out			
Follow-up			
Other			

a few miles away starts advertising complimentary valet parking for her patients. That has nothing to do with you, right? Well . . .

Actually, these things can affect your practice because of a phenomenon that sociologists call "relative deprivation." Basically, it goes like this:

"I was perfectly happy going downtown for my MRI even though it took me all morning to get there and I had to miss my hair appointment. But then I heard that my friend Sadie's doctor has an MRI machine right there in his office! Why don't you do that?"

Or,

"I was perfectly happy parking my car two blocks away and walking to your practice until I found out that my friend Sadie's dentist has valet parking. Then I started to wonder, 'so what's up with my doctors?' What, are you guys cheap or something?"

When your patients start talking to Sadie, you don't want to flunk the comparison.

You need to be able to say things like,

"We considered an onsite diagnostic center, but then we'd have to get rid of our physical therapy department, which that other practice doesn't have. We think it's more important to have an onsite service that you will be using two to three times a week than one that you'll use maybe once a year. What do you think?"

You need ammunition to fight the "Sadie Phenomenon," and so your Team is going to put on their Sherlock gear and find out what's going on in your community. While you could easily look in directories that are offered by your association to learn the details of your community healthcare practices, they won't give you the important information to help you to Differentiate your practice from others.

The most useful data will come from what you hear about other practices and what they market to the general public.

The goal of this research project is to find out how other practices are trying to compete with you by looking at their practice marketing and talking to others who may have had experience with that practice. Because your patients will compare you to other practices outside of your specialty, I recommend that you look at all healthcare practices in your community, regardless of whether they are in your specialty area.

The extent of your data will depend entirely on the degree to which you're willing to give your Team the time and permission to do their research or hire people to be your Sherlock crew.

In addition to checking practice marketing, keep your ears open for information that will come through the grapevine of your patients, colleagues, and vendors. If patients list other doctors in their histories, consider asking about the other practice with questions like *"Where is that practice?"* or *"How many doctors have they got over there?"* or *"What do you like about their practice?"*

Similarly, ask your vendors and colleagues what they see going on in the community. If they ask you why you want to know, be honest. Tell them you are always looking for ways that you can improve your practice and would appreciate any information they are willing to share.

Table 27-2 lists the areas of research to be divided among your research Team members:

TABLE 27-2. Objective Assessment of Healthcare Providers						
INSTRUCTIONS: Make a list of what is being offered throughout your local healthcare community by observing from the outside. Fill in the following chart:						
Source	**Practice Name**	**Specialties**	**Services**	**Location**	**Size**	**Unique Offerings**
Yellow pages						
Newspaper ads						
Direct mail (coupons, invitations, and ads)						
Radio						
Television						
Web site						
Grapevine • Patients • Colleagues • Vendors						

Give your Team one month to collect the data. Have fun with this. The more you encourage them, the more information you'll get. And don't forget to participate in the research as well by doing Activity 27-2.

ACTIVITY 27-2. Use Your Connections
Now is the time to use your connections to gather information. When you attend association meetings, keep your ears open and find out what other practices are doing. Ask questions at monthly study groups and in social gatherings. Set a goal to win your practice's contest by bringing in the best information of all!

STEP 4: SELECT WHAT FITS BEST FOR YOUR PRACTICE

When all of your research is complete, it's time to compare your findings and make some decisions. Begin by bringing your Team together to report the initial results of their research.

Report the Findings

At the end of the month, bring everyone together for a lunch meeting and assign someone to be the secretary. Invite each committee to report on its findings, and to offer opinions regarding the benefits and or liabilities associated with each finding on the list.

As everyone reports their findings, your Team secretary will make three lists:

1. The Good Stuff List: What others are doing that we might want to do
2. The Scary List: What others are doing that we want to be sure we never do
3. The Unique List: What we are doing that no one else is doing

If you had a contest going, then now is the time to get out the prizes and reward your Team for a great job bringing in the data! Celebrate, give lots of Chips, and applaud the entire Team's efforts.

Sort the Data

Step back and look at the three lists and discuss them as a group. Circle every item that your Team deems worthy of consideration as something your practice should consciously choose to do, not do, or expand. Your circled items now represent a list of ACTION items to be considered for your enhanced Differentiation.

Next, divide your Team into groups (two or more people) and assign the ACTION items evenly among your groups. The next step is to develop an ACTION Plan for each item, describing the

- DESIRE (benefits to the practice if you were to add the item, or succeed in avoiding that item);
- RESOURCES (what you would need to be able to accomplish the goal); and
- PERMISSION (what might make the Team unwilling to make the necessary changes).

Give your Team one month to complete their ACTION Plans and tell them to be creative! Just as you did with your Mission Statement, instruct them to work as if money were no object, but to keep in mind that money is an object. Also, remind them that all ideas will be reviewed by the Team and then by the Executive Team for final decisions.

Review the ACTION Plans

One month later, bring your Team back together for your next lunch meeting. Invite each group to present their ACTION Plans and recommendations for the practice. Remind them that no decisions are final until your Executive Team has a chance to review their recommendations and plans. Give lots of Chips for creativity and for the efforts of each Team member in putting together the ACTION Plans.

Executive Review

Get together with your Executive Team and discuss which of your Team's recommendations you'd like to incorporate. If you need more information to make your decision, get back to the Team members or committees with your request.

STEP 5: MOTIVATE AND ALIGN YOUR TEAM TO PREPARE FOR THE CHANGES

When you've made your decisions regarding the changes you want to make in your practice, bring your Team together. review the ACTION Plans that the committees put together and invite your Team to expand upon them. The more you involve your Team in planning for the changes, the more they will be Motivated to succeed and Aligned in the plans to make it all happen.

Again, assign committees or individual Team members to make sure that all RESOURCE needs are met and that all PERMISSION barriers are resolved.

No matter how small a change may seem to you, always remember that it may impact one of your Team members more than you will ever see.

Address everyone's concerns so that there is no one sabotaging the success of your plan.

STEP 6: LAUNCH YOUR PLAN!

When you are ready to initiate the change(s) in your practice, make sure that everyone in your community hears about it.

- Send letters to your patients and colleagues to alert them about the new and exciting events happening in your practice.
- Create signage for your front desk.
- Add a flash alert on your Web site.
- Send an e-blast to your patients.
- Place informational brochures in your reception area.
- Send out a press release online.
- Send an announcement (with photos) to your local papers (particularly if your changes involve incorporating new Team members).
- Have a party and invite colleagues and patients to attend. Serve refreshments (never underestimate the power of a mini meatball) and give a small speech to announce your news.

Change is cause for celebration, so don't miss the opportunity to laugh and Align with those you serve! Remember that what you are celebrating is another uniqueness that will help to Differentiate your offerings and your Team from the average healthcare practice. Invite everyone so they can see that you never stop working to improve the care you provide to your community.

BOTTOM LINE

In our competitive healthcare arena, it is important to stop and take a close look at what others in your community are doing (and not doing) in their practices. Recruit your Team to research what is going on in the healthcare community and then use that information to take your practice to a higher level of Differentiation and success.

Chapter 28

Differentiate With Five-Star Service

WE ARE SEEING A GROWING TREND in which healthcare providers are working hard to improve not only the quality of their care, but the degree to which they provide "good" customer service. This topic is all the rage in practice management, and you can't open a journal or go to an association meeting without hearing people talk about it. Companies are being built exclusively to test it and train it, and doctors are paying thousands of dollars to get their Teams to do it. Don't waste another minute! If you hurry, you could be the first practice on your block to give that "WOW" experience to your customers.

Don't get me wrong, I think there is definitely a need to improve the service we are providing in healthcare practices, both internally and externally. But I am a little concerned about how we are interpreting the word "service."

In the past three years, my company has had a rapid increase in the number of requests for "customer service" training. We've had clients who wanted us to teach their staff how to provide warm blankets and serve water on trays with lace doilies. We've had requests for programs that would teach personnel how to gracefully walk a patient back to a room and provide menus of video and audio entertainment. I've had doctors tell me that they want their staff members to answer phones like receptionists in an upscale hotel and others who want their assistants to take histories with all the enthusiasm of the world's most famous mouse and all his goofy friends.

Let me save you some money — if you want to turn your practice into a spa-like, pampering environment, you don't need to pay a consultant. Simply send your administrator to a real spa for a day. For about $300, he or she will be able to bring back all of the cool ideas that make an environment look and feel "pampering." But be forewarned: not all of your patients will want aroma therapy, and putting a lemon in your patient's water is not going to give your practice the edge in customer service. The edge comes from the *attitude* you carry when you hand your patient the water. If you are filled with genuine concern for your patient's welfare and heartfelt appreciation for your patient's trust, you will deliver the water with a bounce in your step and a smile on your face, and the water will taste great — lemon or no lemon.

> **Customer service isn't about bringing pampering extras to your practice. It's about changing the attitude behind what you do every day. When the attitude is right, the service is naturally extraordinary.**

Practice Spotlight

Nicole worked reception and check-out for an ophthalmology practice, until she was fired for failing to follow practice guidelines. Nicole had a nasty habit of spending an extra two to three minutes with patients as they entered and left the practice. She would see their pain and take a moment to talk with them in an effort to bring some joy to their lives. She would inquire about their family members and offer *"oohs and aahs"* when they showed their holiday photos. As she completed their paperwork, Nicole would get the patients laughing so they always walked out with a smile despite their co-pay.

Nicole suffered from diabetes, so when patients were diagnosed with the same disease, she would offer them reassurance about the doctors' skills and her own success managing the lifestyle changes. Her patients adored her and were Grateful to her for reaching out and understanding their pain.

Nicole's practice administrator was not as impressed. She gave Nicole frequent warnings that she was slowing down the patient flow, creating a line of patients at check-out, and failing to follow policies regarding the separation of personal and professional behaviors.

When Nicole was fired, she applied at several physician practices until she found one that would allow her the freedom to use her instincts regarding when patients needed some extra personal attention. Since her knowledge and experience were precisely what they needed, they gave her a chance.

Nicole brought a dimension to the practice that fit perfectly with its mission. Since she arrived, she has developed an expertise in coding that helps patients and the practice to get significantly higher reimbursements. She is well-liked by the doctors and her coworkers, but no one appreciates her more than the patients.

Standing just a few feet away, you can see, hear, and feel Nicole's impact on the practice. Staff members from other Sub-Teams come into her area just to visit and say "hello." Nicole is considered by many to be the oasis amidst a stress-filled practice of hard-working professionals.

While there is sometimes a line at her check-out counter, the patients don't get impatient. The laughter and kindness in Nicole's voice assures everyone that she is there to help, while her skill and precision allow patients and doctors to be confident that their needs will be met by her fine attention to detail.

Nicole told me that she still watches over her shoulder, *"I keep waiting for someone to tell me I can't talk with patients any more."* I asked her what she would do if they told her she had to stop being playful and real with the patients and employees. She said, *"I guess I'd have to go somewhere else."*

She worries from time to time that the practice administrator will make her take down the photos she keeps of her coworkers' children. But so far, everyone is so pleased with her Five-Star Service Attitude and the impact it has had on their patients and employees, that they have learned to welcome her personal style into their professional and highly successful practice.

Five-Star Service is an Attitude.

When the Attitude is right, our behaviors are generous and contagious to others. Enthusiastic "welcomes" and polite "thank yous" come out naturally without sounding pressed or fake. The Five-Star Attitude leads us to jump up and help patients with doors and chairs and propels us to treat coworkers with kindness and respect. The Five-Star Attitude stops us from screaming patients' names across crowded reception areas and drives us to walk up politely and escort them to their rooms. The Five-Star Attitude leads doctors to take an extra moment to touch a patient's hand and to take another moment to shake the hand of a colleague. The Five-Star Attitude Motivates everyone to go beyond their job descriptions in an all-out effort to assure that no one is overlooked or taken for granted and that everyone gets more than what they expected and exactly what they need.

So, how do we get a Five-Star Service Attitude? I think it emerges as a function of two elements:

Gratitude and Vision.

When staff members are Grateful to each other, they go out of their way to be kind and to help one another to do what needs to be done.

When doctors are Grateful to their staff, they remember to give Chips and to treat everyone with respect.

When doctors and staff are Grateful for their patients' trust, they speak with respect and express their Gratitude openly.

When people have Vision, they are able to look past the Critical Parent behaviors of others and see their fear and pain, their shame and anger, and the perpetual hope of their Natural Child.

When people have Vision, they are able to see the physical and emotional discomforts of everyone on their Team (doctors, staff, patients, vendors, colleagues and families). Their Vision enables them to put aside their own discomfort and to reach out to others.

When people combine Gratitude and Vision, they combine heart with expertise and create an extraordinary healing experience.

I've seen many wonderful examples of the Five-Star Service Attitude throughout healthcare, but my favorite story comes from a personal experience.

Practice Spotlight

It was about 2:00 a.m. on the second night following my total hip replacement surgery. I had managed to get onto a bed pan and now I realized I couldn't get off. Embarrassed and mad about my helplessness, I finally broke down and rang for help.

A nondescript voice came on the intercom, *"May I help you?"*

I tried to sound pleasant, *"This isn't an emergency, but could somebody come help me please?"*

A hospital aid came in immediately. I had seen her earlier, and she explained that she had just clocked in for her second shift of the day. She was several years older than I, and as she walked in, I could see her limping. She was clearly in pain but she smiled pleasantly, handed me a towel, and in a deeply caring voice, asked how I was feeling. I told her that I couldn't get off the bedpan and she quickly came to my rescue.

While she was helping me, I asked her if she was in pain. She briefly explained that she had a persistent back problem, assured me that she was fine, and then quickly turned her attention back to me. I knew she wasn't fine and suggested that with that kind of pain maybe she should consider going home. She looked at me, smiled warmly, and said,

> *"If I go home now, then somebody else is gonna have to come in early and double up on her shift. That just wouldn't be right."*

She helped me to get comfortable and was careful not to do anything to cause more pain. She moved so gracefully through her routine that I completely forgot about being embarrassed. She took the shame out of my situation as she chatted comfortably about nothing in particular, and worked around me to change my sheets, rearrange my pillows, and get me settled back in bed.

She wasn't particularly witty or entertaining. She wasn't highly educated or even very attractive. In fact, I don't remember anything else she said that night, yet I can still see her face in my mind's eye, and I remember her more than anyone I met at that hospital. She had one of the most thankless jobs for the least amount of pay, and yet she is the one who stays with me even now.

This woman was the personification of Gratitude and Vision. She was profoundly Grateful for her job, for the hospital that treated her well and fed her family. She was Grateful for her coworkers and friends, and the health that allowed her to keep on working. She also had Vision that allowed her to see past her own pain, to the pain of others. Gratitude and Vision kept a smile on her face and kept her working through the night. Imagine if everyone in healthcare were just like her.

DEVELOPING GRATITUDE AND VISION

When the economy is drooping, along with your bank accounts, your energy, and your spirit, remember to be Grateful for your knowledge, your position, and your responsibilities.

When your patient is yelling, complaining, criticizing, and fussing, remember that he or she has a right to dignity and kindness.

When you have payroll checks to sign, remember that without your Team you would have no practice.

When you're facing a reception area filled with people and your back is hurting and your spouse is paging you because you were supposed to be home an hour ago, look past your own pain and be Grateful that all of those patients picked you to be their doctor.

When your colleagues page you in the middle of the night because you are the only one they trust to handle an emergency, be Grateful for their referrals.

When the floor nurses page you with a question about your orders, look past your resentment and use your Vision to see that the nurse was caught between his or her fear of disturbing you and fear for your patient's well-being.

When your partners are late for a meeting, your administrator is on vacation, and you have no earthly idea how to get the projector to work, be

Grateful that you have established enough credibility and trust to be elected president of the corporation. *"No one else would do it,"* you reply. And I assure you, if they didn't trust you, they would never have allowed you to take control of their money.

And what about at home?

When you have a disagreement with your spouse, look past your own discomfort and remember to be Grateful that he or she chose to marry *you* out of everyone else in the world.

When your children are leaving bikes in the driveway and causing you to have to run out in the middle of the day to speak to their teachers, move past your anger and embarrassment and remember to be Grateful that you get to *be* a parent and that the teacher cared enough to watch out for your children.

You have a lot of pressures tugging at you and a lot of balls you're juggling, and in the face of all of that it's easy to forget to be Grateful and to lose sight of your Vision. I know what I'm suggesting is not always easy. But I will promise you something:

If you will remember to be Grateful for the people in your life, to use your Vision to see their pain, and to express your Gratitude and your Vision openly . . . if you will do that, then you will master the Five-Star Attitude and create a reputation that will give you enormous pride and substantial revenues.

There is no finer way to Differentiate from the pack than to be Grateful to be a member of the pack and use Vision to see that everyone in the pack is just as frightened and hopeful as you.

Do Activities 28-1 and 28-2, and then we'll talk about how to help your Team to develop the Five-Star Attitude.

I think you've probably figured out the next step, but I'll tell it to you anyway. Take Activities 28-1 and 28-2 to your Team and invite them to do what you have done. Begin a habit of inviting your Team to mention something they are Grateful for at meetings. Start telling staff members that you are Grateful to them for the work they do. Tell patients you are Grateful to them for the trust they give you. Tell colleagues that you are Grateful to them for their referrals. And make a commitment to use your Vision and always look for the heart in everyone.

The truth is that the Five-Star Attitude can't be completely mastered until you and your Team members are Motivated and Aligned. But once you've got the M and the A, the D will naturally follow as all of you Differentiate

ACTIVITY 28-1. My Gratitude

Make a list of everything you have to be Grateful for, and what it is about that thing that makes you Grateful. The more detailed you can be, the more powerful this activity will be for you. I'll start you off. . . .

I'm Grateful For	Because
My career	
My education	
My patients	
My administrative staff	
My clinical staff	
My partners	
My colleagues	
My career	
My health	
My family	

ACTIVITY 28-2. My Vision

For the next week, make a concerted effort to see the Natural Child inside of every patient, colleague, and staff member you see. In other words, look beyond the façade of the competency and professionalism and see the hope, the joy, the fear, the sadness, the excitement, the pain, the pride, the embarrassment and the relief of those who come to you for help and work by your side. Let yourself see, hear, and feel what others won't tell you with their words. Give yourself permission to look the beyond the scrubs and the Johnny coats and see the kids that live inside of all those grownups. When you find them, just smile, touch their hand, or stand quietly. They'll understand that you understand.

your practice by delivering Five-Star Service in a way that no lemon water experience can top.

THE EIGHT COMPONENTS OF FIVE-STAR SERVICE

A while back, I was sitting at my computer creating a presentation on Five-Star Service to deliver to a private practice. It was going to be a difficult program for a troubled Team, so I wanted to make it a little fun for them. I started playing with the letters in "Five-Star" to create an acronym. Since then, I've discovered it was more than a fun idea — it was an accurate map and I teach it everywhere I go.

You know you have what it takes to be a Five-Star Service practice when you have:

Flexibility: Everyone on your Team is using The Four Languages of The M.A.D. Formula for flexibility in communications, is cross-trained for flexibility in work assignments, and is Motivated and Aligned for flexibility during times of stress.

Integrity: Your Team members are honest, they trust their instincts, and they trust each other to protect your practice and your patients by staying focused on the Team Mission Statement at all times.

Value-Commitment: Everyone shows Gratitude to each other and your patients by offering Chips and going the extra mile to use their Vision to see the pain and hope of others and to help them in whatever ways fit for each individual person.

Excellence: Every Team member has identified their DESIRE, RE-SOURCES, and PERMISSION so they are Motivated to keep changing and growing with the goal of continually improving their expertise.

Safety: All Team members utilize the Alignment formulas to keep your practice emotionally safe and they adhere to strong practice guidelines to keep all Team members and patients physically safe from harm.

Team-Orientation: No matter what, everyone remembers to enforce the "In-Group" and to help every doctor, employee, patient, colleague, vendor and family member to know they are part of the Team.

Accountability: Every member of your Team is answerable to each other, your patients, your colleagues, and themselves.

Relationship-Savvy: Everyone remembers that the stronger the relationship, the more you can accomplish with each other, your patients, and your colleagues. They consistently work to build trust and rapport and to create long-standing relationships with everyone they meet.

As you can see, The Eight Components of Five-Star Service come naturally when you apply all of the strategies and techniques of The M.A.D. Formula! Is that just a coincidence? Somehow, I don't think so.

EVERYTHING ROLLS DOWN HILL

The simple fact is that Five-Star Service starts at the top and trickles down through the ranks. If you want your staff members to give good service to your patients, you've got to give good service to your staff.

> **Practice Spotlight**
>
> The 12 doctors wanted their practice of 150 employees to improve their customer service. Highly aware of the competition in their area, they were looking for a quick fix. They gave us one day to make it happen, because there was no way they were going to shut down their practice for more than that. I had my doubts as to the probable success of the plan, but they assured me that they had a group of Motivated and Aligned employees who simply needed new skills to help them to Differentiate their practice.
>
> We sent out pre-training questionnaires, and the results portrayed a drastically different picture than what we'd been told. I called the administrator and gave him the aggregate results. I told him that I had concerns about the staff's comments, but he said that the questionnaires had been completed during a difficult week and that the doctors and staff were open to the initiative and were all looking forward to our arrival. Something didn't make sense.
>
> As we walked around the practice for our onsite evaluation, we spoke with patients and staff, watched the practice in motion, and saw in living color what most of the employees had written in their pre-training questionnaires. It was an uncomfortable environment where staff and doctors were formally polite one minute and snapping at each other the next. Everyone was rushing in and out of appointments, complaining about Team members, and doing their level best to stay out of everyone else's path. Of course, this ultimately affected the patients, who then released their frustrations on the people at check-out. There was no way that this practice was going to wholeheartedly partake in a customer service initiative given their attitudes.
>
> We spoke with the practice administrator, reminded him of the survey feedback we'd given him in our pre-training discussions, and told him what we'd seen that day. He slumped in his chair and finally confessed what he had hesitated to say previously. He told us stories about

strained relationships between the doctors and their staff. He talked about administrative and clinical managers who were impatient with staff, and about doctors who were brutal in their comments to staff and to each other. He spoke of the doctors' unwillingness to change and of his embarrassment for the part he had played in allowing it all to get this far. Now everything made sense.

We met that night with the doctors. I told them what we had witnessed and explained that they needed more than a one-day seminar to achieve the results they were seeking. They were adamant that we had to get it done in one day, so I decided to try a different approach and explained that we might be able to make it happen in one day if *they* were willing to change and follow through on the foundation we would lay. They shifted uncomfortably in their chairs but they didn't kick us out so I kept talking.

I explained that everything rolls down hill and that they were getting the result of what they were giving. I explained that they had to give great customer service to their employees if they expected their employees to change the way they were treating their patients. A few nodded their heads, while others turned shades of red and looked like they were going to explode.

After some discussion, the doctors admitted that they had been *"pretty rough on the staff"* and asked if we could *"fix it."* I thought it was a really hopeful sign that they had asked the question and so I suggested we take a different approach. Instead of presenting a *"Customer Service"* training, we would do a *"Stress Management"* program. We would tell the staff that it was a *"gift from the doctors to thank them for their hard work."* We would take everyone through a full day of communication skills and stress busters to help them to manage and resolve the tremendous stress of their work place. I instructed the doctors that they would have to sit among their staff, be thoroughly involved, enthusiastically participate in all activities, and follow through with assignments and meetings to make it all happen. They agreed, although not all were completely on board, so I playfully got into my Critical Parent and threatened them that if they didn't do their parts then we would have to come back and charge them a lot of money to make it happen. They laughed and agreed to be *"good kids."*

I stayed up all night reworking their seminar with the goals of Motivating the doctors and staff to change, Aligning them in a common mission to bring out their individual strengths, and teaching them communication skills that would enable them to give great customer service to each other — all under the guise of a "Stress Management" seminar. I really wasn't sure that it would work, but I was determined to give it my best shot.[1]

Saturday morning everyone arrived and sulked into the room. The doctors wormed their way into the crowd asking to sit next to staff members who looked understandably perplexed. By lunchtime, everyone was talking and laughing together. In the afternoon, they worked in groups, developing ACTION Plans to lessen their stress in the workplace, and their energy seemed to be building as they worked together. The doctors made a commitment to their staff that they would follow through on the plan and the staff thanked them for a great day.

When the official seminar had ended, nearly everyone stayed. Doctors and staff alike sat talking, mending fences, and making solid plans for the future. Hal and I sat down and watched. They were doing just fine without us.

This practice didn't need customer service training. They needed the opportunity and the tools to develop Vision so they could see each other's pain and hope and remember that they were Grateful for each other, their jobs, their patients, and their lives. Once that was done, the Five-Star Attitude came out naturally and they started getting compliments from patients for their "excellent customer service." Let me reiterate: I never said a single word about customer service during that seminar. What I did do was provide an opportunity for them to develop the Five-Star Attitude. Once that was done, the rest took care of itself because the doctors did their part. The staff, in turn, did everything the doctors wanted them to do and the patients got all the benefits. It all rolls down hill.[2]

ALWAYS REMEMBER

Look beyond the words of the complaining patient and see the human being who needs some Chips. Listen beyond the tension in your colleagues' voices and you will hear the request for a moment of peace. Read between the lines of your overbooked schedule and find the Gratitude for your success.

When you and your Team practice with Gratitude and Vision, you will have mastered the Five-Star Attitude and tied the bow on the package of your

---

[1] I have colleagues who tell me that I should stop this "up-all-night-changing-the-plan-at-the-last-minute" thing that I do. But if consultants aren't flexible, then all we're doing is what *we* want to do and not necessarily what is best for our clients. The end result is that our clients don't make the changes they need to make for their increased success. The fact is, if you want people to do what you want them to do, then sometimes you have to be willing to do things that you would rather not do. It all rolls down hill.

[2] Ultimately we did have to go back and work with the doctors and their leadership team to help them to make some internal changes, but the exciting part of the story is that they had become Motivated to change. I love happy endings, don't you?

uniqueness. The end result is that you'll attract more people who want to practice with you, more people who want to work for you, and more people who want to be treated by you.

You can try to make it more complicated than this, but honestly, that's all there is: Gratitude and Vision from and to everyone will Differentiate you as a practice of real professionals who practice with their heads and from their hearts. Who can resist that?

BOTTOM LINE

Five-Star Service requires an attitude of Gratitude and Vision that begins at the top and works its way down. In order to become a Five-Star Service facility, you need to develop eight specific components: Flexibility, Integrity, Value-Commitment, Excellence, Safety, Team-Orientation, Accountability, and Relationship-Savvy. The combination of these eight components with the Five-Star Attitude creates an environment where everyone associated with the practice is able to achieve their goals and the practice is Differentiated as a service-oriented facility with extraordinary people.

Now That You're M.A.D.

Chapter 29

Make It Count!

YOU AND I HAVE TRAVELED a long way together. We've been through The Four Languages of The M.A.D. Formula and gone over scores of strategies, tactics, formulas, and techniques to enable you to Motivate and Align your Team and Differentiate your practice. You worked through activities, thought about possibilities, explored your barriers, and kept on going until you got it all read.

Now it's time to act.

ACTION takes commitment, tenacity, persistence, and determination. No one understands that better than those who work in healthcare. Through new clinical discoveries and new legislation, through poor economies and challenging times, through critical traumas and catastrophic events, day after day, new problems arise and new opportunities present themselves. And you just keep on going, always looking for new ways to make a difference.

Every once in a while, you find a rare and precious moment when no one is around. In the quiet calm before the storm you stop, take a deep breath, and exhale. You think about where you've been or look ahead to where you'd like to be, and you ask yourself,

Are we doing all we could be doing to serve our patients?

This book was written for those moments. For the times when you need something else, another answer, a way to be a better leader, a better doctor, and a better partner. I am honored that you've allowed me to join you in your quest for excellence and I deeply hope you've found some ideas that will help you in your efforts to help others and get more joy from your practice.

This book was also written for the times when you put on your entrepreneurial hat and say,

Are we doing all we could be doing to increase our revenues?

Remember: if you're looking to build your profitability, the road to get there will *always* depend on your ability to Differentiate yourselves as the best at what you do, and *that* will depend on your ability to Motivate and Align all of the people involved with your practice so that everyone will consistently and passionately strive for the best. Don't leave anyone out in your efforts to get M.A.D.!

You know, they say if you read a book and get one good idea, then it was worth it. I vehemently disagree with that statement. You've invested your time and your money in this book, and I want you to have gotten lots of good ideas. But ideas by themselves won't make a difference. You've got to act on them.

If you want things to be different, you've got to do something different.

What could I possibly say to you after all you've read that would entice you to listen to the CD and start making the techniques a part of your natural repertoire? What inspirational affirmation would make you take ACTION first thing tomorrow morning to figure out your next steps? What could I write on this page that would compel you to go back and do the activities and teach everything to your Team? What parting words could I leave with you that would propel you to jump up and say,

I'm going to get M.A.D. right now!

I'm sure you have a lot on your plate with a business to run and clinical issues to address. Resting on your shoulders are the needs of your patients, your partners, your employees, your colleagues, and your family; and the thought of doing anything new must seem overwhelming, no matter how much you may want to. Where would you begin? How would you make it work? How could you get everyone on board?

OK, let's take one question at a time:

WHERE WOULD YOU BEGIN?

Start with the CD. Put it in your car, your bathroom, your home gym, your kitchen or your office. Upload it to your computer and put it onto your iPod. Put it wherever you can access it easily whenever your hands are busy but your mind is free to wander. Go ahead, do it now. I'll be right here when you get back!

Now make a decision to push "play" once or twice a day every day for the next week. Remember, don't listen to it. Just allow my voice to be with you while you're busy doing something else. Over the next few weeks, you'll incorporate The Four Languages of The M.A.D. Formula, and more.

Next, go to your calendar (wall, desk, PC, MAC, Blackberry, PDA, or whatever), and schedule a time when you will devote 15 uninterrupted minutes to get M.A.D. once a week for the next three months. Commit to those 15 minutes once a week, and if you can devote more time, go right ahead. Don't let anyone or anything take away your 15 minutes. At the end of three months, if you want to keep going, write it on your calendar and make it happen.

HOW WOULD YOU MAKE IT WORK?

During your weekly 15 minutes, do these three steps:

Step 1: Go chapter by chapter until you say, *"Oh yeah! I liked that idea."*

Step 2: Determine how you will go about installing that one idea into your practice. If it seems too complicated, simplify your thinking by writing out an ACTION Plan. What RESOURCES will you need and how will you get them? Who will you recruit to help you? Identify any PERMISSION barriers and how you'll break through them. Figure out your DESIRES by asking yourself, *"What's in it for me to do this?"* Set a deadline for the completion of the plan and remember: it's always OK to change your deadline, but don't ever give up on your goal to make it happen.

Step 3: Give yourself a Chip for having met your commitment to get M.A.D.!

Every week, sit down for 15 minutes and follow the same three steps. No matter how busy you are, you can find 15 minutes to get M.A.D., right?

Please don't try to rush it or push yourself. Just 15 minutes, once a week, and keep playing your CD. Before you know it, you'll be totally M.A.D.!

HOW WOULD YOU GET EVERYONE ON BOARD?

You get everyone on board first by modeling the behaviors. The more you incorporate the new techniques, the more they will start to ask questions like *"You seem more relaxed lately. What changed?"* or *"You're giving out all these compliments. What's that about?"* Use those opportunities to teach. Start The ACTION Formula meetings. Create your Mission Statement. Teach them the Alignment Formulas. Invite them to start researching your uniqueness and create a Differentiation Statement. Help them to discover their Gratitude and Vision.

Bring your Team on board one step at a time. The more they get it, the more the ripple effect will take over. Pretty soon everyone in your practice will be M.A.D.!

BOTTOM LINE

You've put a lot of time and attention into this book, and I hope you will turn around and use what you've read. Let it help you to make every moment you spend with another human being richer, more meaningful, and more rewarding. Life passes so quickly,

Now is the time to make it count.

Chapter 30

A Chip for You

IF WE WERE TOGETHER RIGHT NOW, I would ask you to hold out your hand and I would place in your palm a clay Chip with the Success Icon imprinted on the top.

As you held the Chip in your hand, I would remind you that in your efforts to get M.A.D., there are likely to be people along the way who will serve as homeostatic mechanisms to your change initiative, resisting or even sabotaging your efforts in the interest of maintaining the status quo.

I would warn you that no matter how positive and committed you may be, there will always be something or someone that will lead you to question your own value, your own skills, and your own heart, ultimately leading you to squash your own Chips.

I would remind you that from time to time you will be faced with difficult people who will actively try to steal your Chips.

As you closed your fingers around this Chip, I would emphasize that it takes a lot of Chips to change and so I would ask you to keep this one Chip as an extra just in case you ever need one.

I would advise that you keep this Chip somewhere close to you—in your pocket, your drawer, or anywhere where you could get to it quickly.

I would tell you that if a moment comes when you feel as if you have nothing left to give and no answers left to find, you can take out the Chip and hold it in your hand, and let it serve as a reminder that no matter what comes your way, you have the strength to handle it and there is someone out here who is rooting for you.

As we stood there together, I would invite you to hold onto that Chip for as long as you need it, and all I would ask in return is that when the time comes that you have built up your Chips so that you no longer need the one I gave you, you will pass it on to someone who needs it more.

Even though you're there and I'm here, I'm rooting for you because, although we've never met, I have no doubt that you are someone who has put your skills and heart into making this world a better a place. I know that because you took the time to read this book, and if you made it this far, we're definitely on the same Team.

I'm sorry I can't be there to hand you a Chip, but I know that the more you succeed with the techniques in this book, the more Chips you'll build, and the less you'll need my Chip.

HOWEVER, if for any reason you find yourself hesitating to apply any of the techniques in this book, then email me immediately and I'll gladly send you a real Chip to keep in your pocket for a little shot of strength.

Trust yourself, trust your Team, hold onto your Chips and get ready to enjoy the rewards of getting totally M.A.D.!

Appendices

The Origins of The M.A.D. Formula (The Inside Story)

MANY OF THE FORMULAS AND STRATEGIES of The M.A.D. Formula are based on things I learned from dozens of great minds who mentored me along the way. The rest were developed through trial and error (lots of error) over the course of an ever-evolving career and through the grace of clients who had the courage to experiment and the flexibility to allow me to test and rework techniques until I could trust them to work in every situation, every time.

My clients are often surprised by the comprehensive, eclectic nature of the formulas I've built. But with the complexity of the people with whom we live and work, how could we possibly expect simple, cookie-cutter approaches to be completely effective? There is wisdom to be gained from so many sciences and business settings, and I think we need to take it all into account and put it to good use.

People always ask me where this all began and how it came to be, so I thought I'd give you some insight into the evolution of The M.A.D. Formula. I'm hoping that it will help you to grasp more fully the magnitude and power of what you are about to install in your practice.

IN SEARCH OF ANSWERS

After 17 years of battling my family to let me do the things I wanted to do, they drew a line in the sand and told me that I had to go to college. OK, here's the truth: I had no interest in college. I wanted to be Barbra Streisand.

Then, in a stroke of manipulative genius, my mother told me I could major in music and theater if I would just go to college. So with hard memories of teachers who had written comments on report cards like, "*Wendy is bored in class*," and "*Wendy is not living up to her full potential*," I went off to college and prepared to be miserable.

As I took my seat in an auditorium with more than 100 freshman strangers for a mandatory course in Sociology 101, my mind was still in the theater class from the previous period. The only classes I really cared about were the ones where I was on the stage or learning about the stage. I sat all the way at the top of the auditorium, doodling stage lighting diagrams and waiting for the hour to start and end so I could go to choir rehearsal.

Suddenly, the door burst open, and Mr. Eugene Fappiano came bolting in with more drama than I'd ever seen in any Streisand movie. He crossed the room below us in wide strides, flailing his arms, pacing to one side of the room and then all the way back to the other, bobbing his wild head of hair, and looking all around. He halted abruptly, dead center stage, raised his pointed finger straight up to me and with an overly enthusiastic, booming bass voice he yelled out

"So! Who are you and why do you do what you do?"

I had found the teacher who knew everything I wanted to know.

Week after week, Mr. Fappiano spoke and I took avid notes. He awakened the student in me, and my zest for knowledge knew no bounds. I immersed myself in books and journals about socialization, social control, social class, the power of the group, delinquency, and the criminal justice system.

Just when I thought it couldn't get any more exciting, I was handed a little blue textbook by Alan Kerckhoff, PhD. I was highlighting so many lines that after a while I had to stop because I was coloring the entire book. I was enthralled with the findings of Dr. Kerckhoff's research, the most interesting of which revealed the secret of how my mother had gotten me to eat green, yellow, and orange JELL-O when all I'd ever wanted was red. It was nothing short of sheer genius.

I couldn't get enough. I took course after course in sociology and then went on to study under Dr. Kerckhoff in the graduate school at Duke University. I signed up for every class I could find that would help me to understand the mysteries of people and the things that Motivate us to do the things we do. I discovered social psychology and that led me to George Herbert Mead and studies of the "I" and the "Me" and the critical importance of self-esteem.

My professors at Duke instilled in me a passion for research and an obsession for perfection as I worked to learn the skills that would turn my creative thinking into science. They supported my efforts to conduct original research on self-esteem at a summer camp for overweight boys and girls and then later at an adult weight loss program at the Duke University Medical Center.

Every class led to more questions and more research as I analyzed data from the Michigan Youth and Transition Study and cross-continental studies between the United States and the United Kingdom. As I sat in the basement of the sociology building, sending punch cards through dinosaur computers and praying the vending machine wouldn't run out of cookies, I found data to support my hypotheses and more data that led me to pose still more hypotheses.

As I poured through statistical anomalies and path diagrams, I finally found answers that explained the foundations of Motivation, the factors that create group Alignment, and the key components that Differentiate some groups from others. All the while I was fortunate to have been mentored by an extraordinary group of people: Dr. Alan Kerckhoff, Dr. Dwayne Smith, Dr. Dick Campbell, Dr. Kurt Bach, Dr. Phil Costanzo, and Dr. Jay Williams.

I was presenting a paper at a professional meeting in Philadelphia when I met Barry Tuchfeld, PhD, professor of sociology at Texas Christian University (TCU) and director of The Center for Organizational Research and Evaluation Studies. He offered me a one-year grant position to evaluate a hospital, and I just couldn't resist.

I left Duke and moved to Texas, where I worked for three years as an instructor at TCU and as a project manager evaluating hospitals and organizations all over Texas. I published my findings, spoke at academic meetings, organized national symposiums, managed a staff, taught classes at night, and stayed involved with my first love by singing in a band and performing in community theater productions. It was a rich and exciting time.

While in the process of conducting a longitudinal evaluation study of a hospital-based alcoholism treatment program, we attracted the attention of the U.S. Senate. The Senate had put together a committee to determine whether alcoholism treatment should be considered for third-party reimbursement and thought that our study would shed light on their questions. The next thing I knew, I was surrounded by hospital and university attorneys, watching me with eagle eyes as I prepared my report. They double-checked my figures and edited my punctuation. We walked a fine line together as we tried to keep the data pure and the hospital's reputation untainted.

As we all walked into the hearing room of the Senate Building, I felt like I had just walked into Watergate. The only thing missing was Deep Throat. The stress of it all made my knees weak, and my stomach was doing flip-flops.

The process of preparing my data and then presenting my report to the senators at this highly political hearing took its toll on me. The good news was that our work helped the Senate committee to decide that alcoholism is a disease that could be treated in a hospital and covered by insurance. The bad news was that I was physically and emotionally exhausted and wanted to get as far from academia as I could.

Other than academia, my only career options with a masters degree in Sociology were criminal justice (not my style) and marketing. That made perfect sense! A doctorate in a discipline that was all about getting people to do what you want them to do! I began looking into PhD programs in Marketing.

Then one night, sitting in my apartment, I got a crazy idea. The more I thought about it, the more excited I got, and I stayed up all night drawing sketches and typing out ideas. When the banks opened the next morning, I walked in with my sketches and a typed proposal. They gave me a loan on the spot (ah, the good ol' days), and I promptly turned in my resignation at TCU.

Within a week I signed a lease on a slot in a new shopping strip and launched a ridiculous plan that turned out to be the best thing I could have done: I opened a New York-style, full-service spa/salon right across the street from Neiman Marcus and the ritziest salon in Fort Worth.

OK, if you really have to laugh that hard, at least put down your coffee cup so it doesn't spill on the book.

I knew nothing about how to run a spa, but I was determined to make it work. I figured things out as I went along, and when I got stuck, I made my decisions based on what science said should work.

The first few months weren't great. I couldn't get any experienced stylists or therapists to work for an unknown establishment. I went from place to place all over Fort Worth. I must have had my hair done 30 times trying to talk people into coming over but no one budged. Finally, I dragged myself into the beauty school and massage school and got graduates to come work for me. They had no clientele to offer, but at least they had state licenses. That was a good start, and I figured I could get the customers!

For my first marketing attempt, I sent out a teaser card to 10,000 households with a picture of my logo and the statement *"East of Eden Awaits You"* with our phone number on the bottom.

In no time, the phone started ringing. The only problem was that all the callers were men asking variations on the question, *"So what are ya'll, a massage parlor or somethin'?"*

OK, time for plan B.

I planned a catered grand opening with a fountain of champagne, food galore, and lots of door prizes. I sent engraved invitations to a different list of 10,000 households. This one was more expensive because I paid extra for a demographic group that was targeted for my ideal customer. I was feeling very optimistic.

On the day of the party, my employees, some friends from TCU, my mom, and I waited, trying not to touch the custom-made chocolate cake that was in the shape of my logo. As it got later and later, I took out the box of leftover invitations and in a fit of anger I threw them up in the air. As my friends picked them up, one of them came up to me and said, *"Where's the address?"*

I had neglected to include the address or the phone number on any of the invitations and evidently no one thought well enough of the invitations to call information for our number.

We ate cake for a month.

My next business coup was a ribbon-cutting ceremony courtesy of the Chamber of Commerce, equipped with invitations to all the local media. The ribbon cutting was very exciting, except the mayor showed up three days early, and we had to go ahead without the press. The newspaper did show up on the correct day, but they weren't interested in us without the mayor or the ribbon. Nevertheless, it was a very nice ribbon.

I sat with an empty book and a team of 12 employees who got more disillusioned and cranky by the day. In an effort to keep their spirits up, I started to hold classes. I taught them about Motivation and self-esteem and the differences in people's Value Sets and how demographics affected people's decisions. I told them about my research in Motivation, and we role played different ways to talk with different types of people. I taught them about Gratitude and Vision and how to build trust and rapport. We had a great time, and they became increasingly eager for the success I promised them.

Then, one day, the phone rang. Everyone ran to the front desk to answer it at the same time, and in a scene worthy of a slapstick routine, I slipped under all of them and grabbed the phone. We were all laughing and hushing each other up as I picked up the phone, and the background noise led the caller to say, *"Wow, you sound busy."*

OK, I'm not really proud of this, but in that moment, with all of those faces looking at me with those hopeful, desperate eyes, I simply couldn't help myself. I seized the moment, opened my mouth, and lied.

"Yes, we are very busy today, but how can I help you?"

My employees looked at me like I had completely lost my mind, and maybe I had.

The woman on the phone said, *"Well that's just great! Is there any possibility you could fit me in today?"*

I don't know what came over me. It was like some evil twin jumped in and took over. I stood there looking at my employees and looked down at our empty book, and looked back up at them and felt the weight of the world on my shoulders. I took a deep breath and lied again.

"Oh, I'm so sorry, we're totally booked for the next three weeks. I'll be happy to put you on a waiting list, and I'll call you just the minute something opens up. Would that work for you?"

You should have seen their expressions. They looked like they were torn between laughing out loud and jumping over the desk to strangle me. No one moved, and no one said a word. And then the woman on the other line said something I will never forget.

"Well if y'all are that busy, you must be really good!" She went on to give me her name and number, and I promised to call her the moment something opened up. Which I planned would happen in about 10 minutes.

That afternoon the phone started ringing. I mean a lot. It was amazing. Suddenly everyone in town had heard of us and wanted an appointment. By the end of the week, we had a full schedule, and we never looked back.

That first caller turned out to be one of my best clients and strongest referral sources. About a year later, I took her to lunch to thank her for all of her referrals and finally broke down and confessed the truth of the first day she'd called. I was so embarrassed and apologized profusely. Marti looked at me with her big, brown eyes and said, *"I'm really glad you did."* As it turned out, she had called her friends asking if they had been able to get an appointment at "the new spa" and that's what started the ball rolling. Of course, getting them there was only the first step. We had to *keep* them there, and then Motivate them to want all of our services and products and to tell all their friends!

WOW, THIS ACTUALLY WORKS!

Marti's friends were great, but it wasn't enough. We had to go out and get more people. Understand, it wasn't a matter of convincing people to want our services. Everyone in the area wanted the services we were offering. It's just that they were all going to different places to get the services, and I needed some of them to *switch* and come to us. That meant we had to break through established relationships and loyalties and create a brand that was so appealing, people would have to come to check it out. Then, once they were there, we had to do all of the right things to keep them there. It was a difficult task at best.

I searched for the answers to what made us unique and started asking our existing customers for input. The most frequent answers were that our clients felt "at home" with us and that we were offering all services in one location. We also got a significant number of comments about our environment. We didn't look like the spas they were used to. I had created a lush garden oasis in the middle of a concrete desert. I had green plants everywhere, a waterfall, and two doves named Adam and Eve. Of course, if you know anything about doves, you'll understand when I tell you that it wasn't long before Adam and Eve laid eggs and I needed another cage for (yep, you guessed it) Cain and Abel. OK, it all sounds very corny, but it was really gorgeous, and there was nothing like it anywhere in the Metroplex.

Since I had Differentiated the spa with a brand that was totally unique, I had to educate the community to help them to understand what it meant when we said, *"East of Eden: Your one-stop oasis for total personal care."* Through trial and error, I finally found the formulas that would work.

Clearly, direct mail marketing had too much bad history, so I switched to newspaper advertising. The ads I wrote were all based on the science of Motivation, Alignment, and Differentiation, and they worked. Each ad was targeted to a different type of client, speaking directly to that group's needs and wants and purposefully written to appeal to the sociological and social psychological concerns of each target group.

My favorite ad still hangs framed in my office today. I hired a professional photographer to create a collage of photographs of me wearing different outfits, hairstyles, and makeup against five different stage sets. My Team worked all day and night rearranging my hair, my sets, and my face and together we built an amazingly powerful ad. The phones started ringing and kept on ringing with precisely the type of clientele I wanted to attract.

No one was more surprised than I to find that my theories actually worked in the real world. Inside of one year, I had built a successful business. OK, this is no time to be modest. The truth is, I broke industry standards for retail sales, and my service sales were growing every day.

The best success of all came on the day when two of Neiman Marcus' top stylists came to me and asked for a position on my staff. In that moment, I knew we had arrived.

Over the course of three years, I Motivated people, Aligned my Team of employees and customers, and Differentiated my spa from the massive competition that was right across the street and throughout the Metroplex. It was my private playground, my social psychological laboratory, my pride and joy, and it taught me more with every day.

Where I had initially sat alone staring at 2,000 square feet of empty work stations, now I had nail technicians, massage and skin care therapists, a magnificent receptionist, and a group of experienced stylists who had brought their clientele from their previous salons. By my second year, I had a staff turnover of 0% (very rare in the industry), a waiting list for appointments, and a loyal clientele. I cut my marketing budget way back, since 95% of my clients came by referrals.

Each month when I walked into the Chamber of Commerce meetings, everyone knew who I was. I began to do speaking engagements on image management, leadership, and sales technique throughout the community and held steadfast to my belief that if you Motivate, Align, and Differentiate, you will succeed.

I had found a lot of answers in my spa, but I still had more questions. So after three years, I sold my business and went full speed ahead into a training program in Transactional Analysis and Gestalt Psychology.[1] There I found many more pieces to the puzzle of what makes people willing and able to change, along with a language that allowed me to explain some of the amazing results I'd had in my sales at the spa. Most importantly, it was there I learned about the internal forces that propel us forward and hold us back.

When I got my certification as a psychotherapist, I was faced with a new marketing challenge: to build my private practice. Hal helped me by introducing me to doctors and involving me as a co-therapist in one of his groups. It wasn't enough, so I decided to reach out to the community and offered free seminars on sales training and stress management for sales organizations in Fort Worth. The seminars allowed me to meet a lot of people.

My seminars took attendees through The ACTION Formula (although I hadn't named it that as of yet). I led them through a process of identifying their short- and long-term goals (DESIRES), I gave them techniques so they'd be able to improve their revenues (RESOURCES), and I helped them to identify and break through personal barriers that were causing their "slumps" and leading them to block their own success (PERMISSION).

While these seminars did yield clients for my therapy calendar, the unanticipated result was that I began to get requests for consulting work. Soon I was teaching leadership seminars for sales managers and training workshops for sales professionals. As my clients' revenues exploded, I realized I had an opportunity to pull together everything I knew and loved. I could teach my formulas and make a difference for people, and I could do

---

[1] That's when I met Hal, my husband, my business partner, my best friend, my hero, and the most clinically comprehensive, skilled, and perceptive doctor I have ever had the privilege of knowing.

it all on a great big stage with an audience! Wow! I had come full circle.

For the first time in years, I thought back on the teacher's comment *"Wendy isn't living up to her full potential,"* and realized that she had been right. Now I was ready to make that happen. I launched my career as a consultant, author, speaker and trainer and never looked back.

In 1992 my mother was diagnosed with lung cancer. I went home to help her and ended up moving back home for the duration of her illness. At first I took small consulting assignments, but I couldn't bring myself to leave her alone for extended periods. I took on a consulting job for a major weight loss company and ended up managing one of their local storefront locations as a pilot study to see if my formulas would work in that environment. There I worked with the staff and clients, giving seminars, helping them to increase the number of clients who signed on for the program and to increase the number of clients who made it to their weight reduction goal. Over the course of a year, I installed a series of strategies that quadrupled the number of starts, and more than doubled the likelihood of those clients to get to goal and maintain their loss for more than one year. I left them when my mother's illness progressed and spent the next year sleeping on the floor of hospital rooms.

In the hospitals, I was always amazed by how hectic it was during the day and how incredibly peaceful it was at night. When my mother would fall asleep, I would walk the halls, talking with doctors, nurses, and other hospital personnel and learning about the challenges they faced.

In 1994 my Mom passed away and I had to generate the energy to go back to work and build my client list all over again. Many of my contacts were long gone to other companies and in those days we didn't have the power of the Internet that we have available today to track people. I decided to spend some time getting back my rhythm and accepted a contractual position with a large seminar company that provided one-day public programs.

My experience there was nothing short of extraordinary. As I traveled around the world, I learned more and more about the challenges of the workplace and found more ways to apply my formulas. The contacts I made allowed me to build my business back up, and after three years, I resumed my private consulting.

MORE QUESTIONS!

As I worked in more and more organizations, I found certain patterns of behavior that just couldn't be explained by our social influences or the things we learned growing up. These behaviors just seemed to happen for no good reason, except that they happened consistently in patterns.

I found the answer in the work of neuropsychology. There I found different models of the four personality or behavioral types and, from that, created the Action Types I teach and use today.

My life was perfect. I was traveling, teaching, consulting, researching, standing on stages and entertaining my audiences, making a real difference in the lives of my clients, and in love with a warm and brilliant man. Then we took the cruise that I told you about in the beginning of this book (see Author's Note).

Now I'll tell you what I didn't tell you earlier:

When Gary invited me to do the first speaking engagement for his doctor clients, I was really nervous. It was one thing to talk to thousands of executives and their employees, but this audience was going to be all *doctors*! Like the rest of our society, I was raised to hold doctors in high esteem and to place them on a higher plane than the rest of us mere mortals. I totally trusted my formulas to work with "normal" people, but I wasn't sure that they would fit for doctors. Doctors were, well, *different.*

I got up on stage and went into high gear. I spoke from my heart and told them what I thought would be helpful to them as leaders. As I spoke, I felt them lean in to me, and when I finished my presentation, they gave me a warm and enthusiastic ovation. I stepped down off the platform and walked over to see Gary and Hal when suddenly a swarm of doctors surrounded me asking question after question. I stood back a bit and took a very close look at them. They were different ages from varying specialties, but all of them shared the same air of hope and excitement, and I could see the frustration and desperation in their eyes. Ironically, they reminded me of my employees back in the beginning days at the spa, eager for something new that would build their success.

In that moment I realized that doctors were just normal people with normal fears and normal dreams. But they had one problem that normal people didn't have — their patients and employees didn't *want* them to be normal. These people wanted their doctors to be superhuman heroes who knew how to surpass their own needs; think clearly in emergencies; and always, always, always know precisely what to do and how to do it. At the same time, doctors were supposed to be warm and sensitive, interpersonally adept, and empathetically supportive. It seemed like an impossibly oxymoronic existence. Doctors had to spend their lives avoiding connections while somehow connecting, and all the while staying on top of the latest clinical research, running a successful business, and never allowing themselves to fall off their pedestals. I suddenly saw the tremendous pressure that defined their roles.

I turned to Hal and said, *"Honey, we have to heal the people who heal the people."* With tears in his eyes, he said, *"Let's go."*

As you can see, it was a long series of twists and turns that led me to bring The M.A.D. Formula to healthcare. I wouldn't trade one moment or go back and make one decision differently. Each experience taught me something that made it possible for the next answer to unfold. Each step logically led to the next and I still use everything I learned along the way. I can't wait to find out what I've yet to learn. It's waiting for me in the next practice we visit.

No- and Low-Cost Rewards for Your Employees

Compensation is what you give people for doing the job they were hired to do. Recognition celebrates the individual uniqueness that each of your Team members brings to your practice every day.

BRING ENERGY AND JOY into your practice and keep your staff guessing what you'll do next! Here are some great ideas to reward your Team for a job well done and to keep the atmosphere positive and energized.

- Hold contests to generate activity.
- Celebrate important events.
- Announce a special dress code (crazy shirt day, Hawaiian Day, Suspender Friday).
- Have a surprise picnic in the parking lot.
- Make buttons out of employee baby pictures and have them wear each other's and try to figure out who's who.
- Call an employee into your office just to thank him or her — don't discuss any other issue.
- Post a thank you note on a workstation.
- Volunteer to do someone's least desirable work task for one day.
- Wash an employee's car in the parking lot during lunch.
- Give out recognition awards for good attitudes.
- Name awards after outstanding employees.
- Have an awards ceremony and then have the employee pass the award on the next week to another employee (and so on . . .).
- Create a Success Wall with photos of outstanding achievers.
- Make a photo collage about a successful project that shows the people who worked on it, its stages of development, and its completion.
- Create a Family History wall, and have everyone bring in pictures and stories about their families.

**Celebrate the ordinary and the extraordinary,
who they are and what they do, and help everyone to
feel excited and energized every day!**

- Bring an employee a lunch that you made personally.
- Have a pizza delivered to an employee's home for dinner with "great job today" on the card.
- Cover a workstation with balloons.
- Buy a little something for an employee's child.
- Tape a candy bar to a piece of work that is halfway done with a note that says "you're halfway there!"
- Rent a cool car and give it to an employee to drive for a weekend.
- Create a "GOOD TRY" booklet to recognize those whose innovations or ideas didn't achieve their full potential. Be sure to include what was learned during the project so that this information can benefit others.
- Give an employee a round of golf.
- Give movie tickets for a local theater.
- Invite employees and their spouses to your home for a special celebration and recognize them in front of everyone.
- Repeat a positive remark you heard about an individual as soon as you see him or her.
- Use charts and posters to show how well an employee or Team is performing.
- Write a letter of praise to recognize specific contributions and accomplishments—send a copy to the spouse!
- Send birthday cards.
- Send information about an accomplishment to a trade publication and the home newspapers. Get the employee's picture printed.
- Write and publish a personal ad or publicity article in the local newspaper praising an employee for a job well done.
- Create special tokens or coins that can be redeemed for a future favor.
- Write "thank you" on a piece of fruit.
- Provide an extra break.
- Give a two-hour lunch.
- Pay for dessert.
- Give spontaneous time off for specific accomplishments and arrange to have the employee's work done.
- At a meeting, tape gift certificates to the bottom of chairs.
- Arrange a fishing day for an entire work Team.

**If you do nothing else, make sure to give out
Skill and Heart Chips all day long!
People do more when they know you've noticed!**

Appendix III

Role Playing (The Fun Way)

ROLE PLAYING?!?! UGH!

Yeah, I know. There are many people who are averse to the idea of role playing, and who can blame them? Why would anyone want to be embarrassed by having to perform in front of their peers? Nobody wants to fail, particularly when others are watching and judging! So let me tell you two things up front:

1. The style of role playing that I recommend does not require anyone to perform in front of a group; and
2. Everyone is permitted (and encouraged) to use written scripts or "cheat sheets."

The goal is to give everyone a chance to get comfortable with the techniques in an atmosphere where it is OK to make mistakes.

If we were instructing people to use a software program on a computer, we could show them how to do it and give them the manual. They could then learn on their own, studying and practicing until they could run it perfectly. Learning how to work with *people* is entirely different because, unlike computers, no two people are alike. When you and your Team are learning how to get M.A.D., you have to understand the strategies and learn the techniques, and then you need to take it a step further. You have to develop a comfort level applying the techniques with all different types of people in all different situations *and* make the techniques fit you personally so that the techniques don't come across as sterile or rote.

When you use M.A.D. techniques, they need to come out like natural conversations between people.

The successful application of M.A.D. Leadership requires comfort and familiarity with the techniques and the willingness to allow your natural self to come through. In order to master that, you have to

1. Study the techniques so that the steps are completely familiar; and

2. Practice the techniques with different types of people in a safe environment until you have reached a level of personal comfort.

I've seen training programs that failed because the trainees were unwilling to incorporate new techniques into their daily routines. This makes perfect sense to me. The fact is that most people are afraid to use new techniques until they are confident in their skill. They don't want to take the chance of failing with "real" patients, so they just don't use the techniques at all. For these people, the only answer is to give them the opportunity to practice the techniques in a safe, nonjudgmental environment and give them lots of Chips when they do. People need an opportunity to stumble and fall, pick themselves up again, laugh it off, and keep going until they get the techniques mastered. And that's what we're going to create.

INSTRUCTIONS

Role Plays?!?! Those are so boring!!

I have experimented with many ways to conduct role plays over the years and have found a way that is fun and effective. The fastest avenue to create comfort and success is by providing an experience that is fast, fun, and powerful. Participants shouldn't have to think about anything other than applying the newly learned strategies. Everything must be planned for them so they can just step in and use the techniques in a stepwise fashion that allows them to begin with training wheels and then fly on their own. If you make it fun, and give them everything they need to succeed, you will have a great training outcome.

GET READY

While there are many techniques in M.A.D. Leadership that can be role played, we are going to focus here on selected techniques for Motivation (The ACTION Formula Interview, Inviting Patients to ACTION and Handling Objections) and Alignment (The CANDOR Formula, The EMOTIONS Formula, The ACCOUNTABILITY Formula, and The SPLINTER Formula). I recommend that everyone review those chapters (14, 15, 16 and 20) and use the CD so that the techniques come easily and naturally.[1] Make sure that everyone involved has written copies of each formula so that they can use their notes to help them through the process in the beginning. Over time, invite them to take off their training wheels and soar!

The more noise you have around you during role play activities, the more likely you are to let things come out naturally. In a quiet area, people hear the sound of their own voice and others' and that makes them self-conscious.

[1] You may want go back to Chapter 3 and review how to use Spaced Repetition to quickly learn.

They begin to censor and alter their wonderful styles to sound more like the others they hear, and that's not always such a great thing! Creating distractions during practice sessions will enable you and your Team to use these techniques during the most hectic days in your practice while encouraging everyone to use their natural style.

SET IT UP

Get your Team together and pair them in Teams of two[2] — tell them to choose who is "A" and who is "B." They will switch later so that "A" will become "B" and "B" will become "A."

Everyone needs to have a chance to play both sides of each formula. Instruct them to move their chairs together or to sit on the floor somewhere in the room. Make an effort to keep everyone together in the same room for distraction and accessibility in case there are questions.

ROLE PLAYING THE MOTIVATION FORMULAS

Person A is going to conduct The ACTION Formula interview. The goal is to become comfortable asking the questions and filling out The M.A.D. Chart so that it is complete. Remind everyone that their completed M.A.D. Chart must tell the story of the patient's DESIRES, RESOURCES, and PERMISSIONS, and must indicate the patient's Value Set, Action Type, and favorite State of Mind. Encourage Person A to read the interview questions, to take his or her time, and not to worry about being perfect. When your Person A's are comfortable with The ACTION Formula interview, invite them to move on to the scripting for Inviting Patients to ACTION. At that point, they will hear some objections from Person B and will need to refer to the language from the scripting for Handling Patient Objections.

Person B is going to play the patient and will receive one of the completed M.A.D. Charts that are included in Appendix IV—X.[3] Person B's job is to act out the role of the patient (including body language, words, and tone of voice) in a way that best portrays the patient that is described in the provided M.A.D. Charts. This is Person B's big chance to be a star! The better the role is acted out, the easier it will be for Person A to guess the Value Set, Action Type, and favorite State of Mind, and to identify the full set of DESIRES, RESOURCES, and PERMISSIONS. Be sure to remind your Person B's that these M.A.D. Charts reflect real patients from real practices!

---

[2] Orthodontists — I have included some family role plays for you on the Motivation formulas, so in those scenarios you will need to create groups of two, three, and four.

[3] Each Appendix includes sample M.A.D. Charts for different specialties in medicine and dentistry. If your specialty isn't specifically represented, please chose the one that is closest to you or change them to fit just right for your practice.

Tell Person B that he or she has the more difficult job! The goal is to be as true to the character as possible. That means he or she has to understand The Languages of The M.A.D. Formula so that each is portrayed correctly. Although Person B will receive completed M.A.D. Charts with patient responses written in, encourage Person B to elaborate and expand. Encourage all of your Person B's to be creative and to fill in the gaps with their own additional words. The most important thing is to help Person A to succeed, so instruct Person B to be supportive rather than to try to trick Person A. Remind everyone that Person B will have to be Person A when they switch positions! When it is time to role play the scripting for Inviting Patients to Action, Person B will throw an objection or two at Person A. Again, don't be too difficult here. The goal is to help Person A to do a great job and be comfortable with the language and flow of the technique.

Time It

The ACTION Formula interview should take less than six minutes. When you first begin role playing, give them 20 minutes to work through it. After a few rounds, cut back to 15, then 10, and then create prizes for the first Team to finish!

Round Robin

Have your Team members move around the room to create new pairs. You can use the provided M.A.D. Charts over and over again by switching them throughout your Team, or create some of your own!

Advanced Role Playing

Once you've incorporated The M.A.D. Formula into your practice, you'll begin to have real data that you can use for your role plays. Take the information from your patient M.A.D. Charts, and run role plays from those. I recommend that you role play once a month as part of your staff meetings to keep the techniques fresh.

ROLE PLAYING THE ALIGNMENT FORMULAS

Person A is going to initiate the role play by reading The CANDOR Formula. You will find sample topics to use for this formula in APPENDIX XI.

Person B is going to respond to Person A with The ACCOUNTABILITY Formula and will have to be creative regarding what words he or she chooses in filling in the missing information.

Next, switch Person A and Person B. The new Person A is going to complain about something (sample complaints are in APPENDIX XI) and Person B is going to respond by using The EMOTIONS Formula.

When that is done, instruct Persons A and B to read The SPLINTER Formula to each other so they can become accustomed to hearing themselves speaking the words out loud. There is no role play for this formula per se. We simply want everyone to develop familiarity and comfort with the process.

Make sure that everyone has an opportunity to use each of the four formulas, and be sure to encourage laughter and lots of Chips along the way.

TO ENSURE SUCCESS FOR ALL ROLE PLAYING
Make the experience
FUN and NONTHREATENING.

Role Plays!!! Yiiiipppppppeeeeeee!!!!

Bring prizes and reward those who actively participate, regardless of whether their results are perfect. Give out the prizes while they are working. Interruptions are very effective because it helps to prepare the participants for application in the real world. Chip everyone for their willingness to take risks, to try new things, and to stretch their perspectives.

One more thing: if you practice with your Team, they will take this seriously. It's good for them to see you struggle with remembering the questions and then to see you laugh at yourself as you grow to master the techniques. It is important to be a good role model, so get a jump start and start listening to your CD right away. Remember, if you want them to do what you want them to do, you have to do it too. After all, that's what being a M.A.D. Leader is all about.

Appendix IV

M.A.D. Charts for Motivation Formula Role Plays: Family Practice

Patient One You are a stay-at-home mom with three young children and a husband.											
T1	T2	R	E	T	C	CP	NP	A	SC	NC	CHIPS
PD I have these horrible headaches and lights make it worse.						D1 Increased energy					*List Date of Chip*
D2 Get more done around the house						D3 More energy to spend with family					
D4 Happier family						D5 More fun at home					
D6 Less stress						BD Get a good night's sleep					
R My schedule is ruled by my family, and I can't take medications that would keep me from being able to care for them.											
P Truthfully, my headaches have been a great excuse to say "no" to the things I don't want to do.											

Patient Two You are a manager at a factory.											
T1	**T2**	**R**	**E**	**T**	**C**	**CP**	**NP**	**A**	**SC**	**NC**	**CHIPS**
PD Annual physical, renew cholesterol and BP meds						**D1** I'd like to be in better shape.					*List Date of Chip*
D2 The guys would stop ribbing me.						**D3** I'd get more credibility on the floor.					
D4 Maybe I'd get a promotion.						**D5** I'd make more money.					
D6 I'd get a new house for my wife.						**BD** I'd make her happy and proud of me.					
R I don't have time for exercise.											
P Do you really think an old dog can learn new tricks?											

Patient Three You are a 48-year-old attorney.											
T1	**T2**	**R**	**E**	**T**	**C**	**CP**	**NP**	**A**	**SC**	**NC**	**CHIPS**
PD I want this cough to stop.						**D1** I'd be able to get some sleep.					*List Date of Chip*
D2 I'd be able to focus more on my work.						**D3** I could tackle anything that comes my way.					
D4 I'd walk into court and show the DA what great attorneys do.						**D5** I'd make a name for myself.					
D6 Maybe I'd get known better downtown.						**BD** I'd run for mayor.					
R I can't stay home and do bed rest.											
P I don't want anything that makes me groggy, I have to stay sharp.											

Patient Four You are a newly licensed real estate broker.										
T1	T2	R	E	T	C	CP	NP	A	SC	NC	CHIPS
PD I have pain in my knee, especially in cold weather.						**D1** I need to get around.					*List Date of Chip*
D2 I'd be able to walk up and down stairs .						**D3** I could show houses better.					
D4 I'd make more sales.						**D5** I'd make more money.					
D6 I could help my kids with their college fund.						**BD** I'd show my kids that I am still strong and active.					
R I can't take aspirin-related meds.										
P What if I feel better and then I can't sell anything?!										

Patient Five You are a 63-year-old builder who is separated from his wife.										
T1	T2	R	E	T	C	CP	NP	A	SC	NC	CHIPS
PD I'd feel like I did when I was 33.						**D1** I'd have more energy.					*List Date of Chip*
D2 I'd be able to run from job to job and still have something left at the end of the day.						**D3** I'd feel better about myself.					
D4 Maybe I'd put myself out there again.						**D5** Maybe I'd meet some new friends.					
D6 I'd get my groove back.						**BD** I'd try to get my wife back.					
R Money is an issue.										
P Nope.										

	**Patient Six** **You are an elementary school teacher.**

T1	T2	R	E	T	C	CP	NP	A	SC	NC	CHIPS
colspan="6"	**PD** I wish the dizziness would stop—it's happening every day at school	colspan="5"	**D1** I could stop being scared and snapping at the kids.	*List Date of Chip*
colspan="6"	**D2** I could put my focus on them where it belongs.	colspan="5"	**D3** I'd be a better teacher.	
colspan="6"	**D4** I could make a real difference for my kids.	colspan="5"	**D5** I could look forward to work every day.	
colspan="6"	**D6** I'd know I was really good at this.	colspan="5"	**BD** I'd be proud of me.	
	**R** I had trouble getting here today. It's hard to take time off from school.	
	**P** I'm scared of finding out I have some kind of tumor or something.	

	**Patient Seven** **You are an executive assistant at a large technology corporation.**

T1	T2	R	E	T	C	CP	NP	A	SC	NC	CHIPS
colspan="6"	**PD** I feel great, and I want to keep it that way.	colspan="5"	**D1** Do you know how many sharks are out there—I have to stay on top of my game.	*List Date of Chip*
colspan="6"	**D2** I could show my boss how invaluable I am.	colspan="5"	**D3** He would start taking me on the road with him.	
colspan="6"	**D4** I could have the opportunity to travel around the world.	colspan="5"	**D5** I'd meet new people, learn new things—it would be an amazing experience.	
colspan="6"	**D6** I'd put it all on my resumé.	colspan="5"	**BD** I'd go after his job!	
	**R** Money is always an issue.	
	**P** I'm not big on drugs. Do I have to take drugs?	

	**Patient Eight** **You are a 52-year-old dog trainer.**
T1	**T2**	**R**	**E**	**T**	**C**	**CP**	**NP**	**A**	**SC**	**NC**	**CHIPS**

PD My allergies are driving me nuts.	**D1** I could stop sneezing on all my dogs.	*List Date of Chip*
D2 I'd stop scaring them half to death.	**D3** They'd get their commands faster.	
D4 That would make me look pretty good.	**D5** I'd build my business.	
D6 I could put my kid through law school.	**BD** I'd know I was a good mom.	

R	I can't take anything that would make me drowsy. I work with some skittish dogs, and I have to keep my guard up.
P	I heard allergies can be psychological. Do you think I'm crazy?

M.A.D. Charts for Motivation Formula Role Plays: Plastic Surgery and Aesthetics

Patient One You are a stay-at-home mom with three young children and a husband.											
T1	**T2**	**R**	**E**	**T**	**C**	**CP**	**NP**	**A**	**SC**	**NC**	**CHIPS**
PD I hate my nose—it slants to the right and I've had enough of it.						**D1** It wouldn't make my life different—but I'd feel different.					*List Date of Chip*
D2 I'd have more confidence.						**D3** I've always wanted to open a dance school.					
D4 I could have my own business.						**D5** My kids are getting to the point when they don't need me here all the time—it's my turn.					
D6 I'd have a little pocket money, and a great feeling of accomplishment.						**BD** I'd finally feel good about myself as a woman.					
R I can't be down too long—I have to take care of the kids.										
P Just because I have a new nose, what if I haven't got what it takes to launch a business?										

						Patient Two You are a manager at a factory.					
T1	**T2**	**R**	**E**	**T**	**C**	**CP**	**NP**	**A**	**SC**	**NC**	**CHIPS**
PD I have a sagging double chin and "love handles."						D1 I'd like to be in better shape.					*List Date of Chip*
D2 The guys would stop ribbing me.						D3 I'd get more credibility on the floor.					
D4 Maybe I'd get a promotion.						D5 I'd make more money.					
D6 I'd get a new house for my wife.						BD I'd make her happy and proud of me.					
R I don't have time for exercise.											
P Honestly—I'm a sissy when it comes to pain.											

						Patient Three You are a 48-year-old attorney.					
T1	**T2**	**R**	**E**	**T**	**C**	**CP**	**NP**	**A**	**SC**	**NC**	**CHIPS**
PD I look old.						D1 I'd look young and alive.					*List Date of Chip*
D2 I'd get more of the better cases.						D3 I'd make a name for myself.					
D4 I'd make partner.						D5 I'd make more money.					
D6 I'd have more security.						BD I'd know I'd made it.					
R I can't be out of the office more than one week.											
P I keep thinking this is frivolous and vain.											

	**Patient Four** **You are a newly licensed real estate broker.**
T1	**T2**	**R**	**E**	**T**	**C**	**CP**	**NP**	**A**	**SC**	**NC**	**CHIPS**

Patient Four
You are a newly licensed real estate broker.

T1	T2	R	E	T	C	CP	NP	A	SC	NC	CHIPS
PD My eyelids are wrinkled.						D1 I wouldn't have to hold them up to put my makeup on!					*List Date of Chip*
D2 I wouldn't look so old.						D3 I'd have more confidence.					
D4 I could show houses better.						D5 I'd make more sales.					
D6 I'd make more money.						BD I'd show my kids that I am NOT getting old.					
R I'm allergic to adhesive tape.											
P What if I feel better and then I can't sell anything?!											

Patient Five
You are a 63-year-old builder who is separated from his wife.

T1	T2	R	E	T	C	CP	NP	A	SC	NC	CHIPS
PD I lost 150 pounds, and now I need to get my skin fixed.						D1 I'd look a lot better.					*List Date of Chip*
D2 I'd feel like I did when I was younger.						D3 I'd feel better about myself.					
D4 Maybe I'd put myself out there again.						D5 Maybe I'd meet some new friends.					
D6 I'd get my groove back.						BD I'd try to get my wife back.					
R I can't take a lot of time off from the job site.											
P The weight thing was for health—the insurance thing says that the skin folds are a medical issue but the truth is, I just can't stand how it looks. Is that ok?											

											CHIPS
Patient Six **You are an elementary school teacher.**											
T1	T2	R	E	T	C	CP	NP	A	SC	NC	CHIPS
PD I'd like to increase my breast size.						D1 I would feel better about myself.					*List Date of Chip*
D2 I could be more outgoing.						D3 I'd be more confident.					
D4 I'd be a better teacher.						D5 I could make a real difference for my kids.					
D6 I'd know I was really good at this.						BD I'd be proud.					
R I had trouble getting here today. It's hard to take time off from school.											
P I'm scared of breast cancer. What if this gives me breast cancer?											

											CHIPS
Patient Seven **You are an executive assistant at a large technology corporation.**											
T1	T2	R	E	T	C	CP	NP	A	SC	NC	CHIPS
PD I want to reduce the size of my breasts.						D1 I wouldn't get so many backaches.					*List Date of Chip*
D2 I could show my boss how invaluable I am.						D3 He would start taking me on the road with him.					
D4 I could have the opportunity to travel around the world.						D5 I'd meet new people, learn new things—it would be an amazing experience.					
D6 I'd put it all on my resumé.						BD I'd go after his job!					
R Money is an issue.											
P What if I don't look OK when it's done?											

Patient Eight **You are a 65-year-old rancher.**											
T1	T2	R	E	T	C	CP	NP	A	SC	NC	CHIPS

PD I want to remove moles and correct uneven brows.	**D1** I'd look better.	*List Date of Chip*
D2 I've put everyone else first my whole life. It's about time I did something just for me.	**D3** I'd feel better.	
D4 I might go on a vacation.	**D5** You never know who you're going to meet.	
D6 I might start a second life.	**BD** I'd know I wasn't too old to have a good time.	
R I'm always in the sun.		
P Do you think it's stupid for someone my age to care how he looks?		

M.A.D. Charts for Motivation Formula Role Plays: Orthopedics and Neurology

Patient One											
You are a stay-at-home mom with three young children and a husband.											
T1	**T2**	**R**	**E**	**T**	**C**	**CP**	**NP**	**A**	**SC**	**NC**	**CHIPS**
PD I can't stand the pain in my hip any more.						**D1** I could get more done.					*List Date of Chip*
D2 I'd get more sleep and have more energy.						**D3** I've always wanted to open a dance school.					
D4 I could have my own business.						**D5** My kids are getting to the point when they don't need me here all the time. It's my turn.					
D6 I'd have a little pocket money, and a great feeling of accomplishment.						**BD** I'd finally feel good about myself as a woman.					
R I can't be down too long—I have to take care of the kids.											
P Everyone tells me I'm too young, but I think quality of life is important. Don't you?											

Patient Two You are a manager at a factory.											
T1	T2	R	E	T	C	CP	NP	A	SC	NC	CHIPS
PD My knee is shot. Too much running I guess.						**D1** I'd like to be in better shape.					*List Date of Chip*
D2 The guys would stop ribbing me.						**D3** I'd get more credibility on the floor.					
D4 Maybe I'd get a promotion.						**D5** I'd make more money.					
D6 I'd get a new house for my wife.						**BD** I'd make her happy and proud of me.					
R I don't have time for exercise.											
P Honestly—I'm a sissy when it comes to pain.											

Patient Three You are a 48-year-old attorney.											
T1	T2	R	E	T	C	CP	NP	A	SC	NC	CHIPS
PD My shoulder is killing me. First it aches, then it's sharp. I've done the rehab, and it's just not working.						**D1** I need to be on top of my game—can't have this pain anymore.					*List Date of Chip*
D2 I'd get more of the better cases.						**D3** I'd make a name for myself.					
D4 I'd make partner.						**D5** I'd make more money.					
D6 I'd have more security.						**BD** I'd know I'd made it.					
R I can't be out of the office more than one week.											
P I keep thinking I'm a failure because I couldn't rehab this.											

T1	T2	R	E	T	C	CP	NP	A	SC	NC	CHIPS

Patient Four
You are a newly licensed real estate broker.

PD I've been getting dizzy a lot, and my regular doctor said I should see a neurologist.	**D1** If the dizziness were gone, I wouldn't have to be afraid to drive.
D2 I'm a realtor—I have to drive my clients around.	**D3** I'd make more appointments.
D4 I could show houses better.	**D5** I'd make more sales.
D6 I'd make more money.	**BD** I'd show my kids that I am NOT getting old.

List Date of Chip (CHIPS column)

R I need to understand what is happening to me.

P What if I have a brain tumor? I don't want to find out I have a brain tumor.

Patient Five
You are a 63-year-old builder who is separated from his wife.

T1	T2	R	E	T	C	CP	NP	A	SC	NC	CHIPS

PD I've been active my whole life, and I can't do anything because of these knees.	**D1** I'd go skiing, get back to running and paddle ball, and have a life.
D2 I'd feel like I did when I was younger.	**D3** I'd feel better about myself.
D4 Maybe I'd put myself out there again.	**D5** Maybe I'd meet some new friends.
D6 I'd get my groove back.	**BD** I'd try to get my wife back.

List Date of Chip

R I can't take a lot of time off from the job site.

P I'm not great with pain, and I don't do pain pills.

	**Patient Six** **You are an elementary school teacher.**
T1	T2	R	E	T	C	CP	NP	A	SC	NC	CHIPS
colspan="6"	PD I have constant tingling and numbness in my hands.	colspan="5"	D1 I could hold the chalk and help the kids with their projects.	*List Date of Chip*
colspan="6"	D2 I could stop being scared all the time.	colspan="5"	D3 I'd be more confident.	
colspan="6"	D4 I'd be a better teacher.	colspan="5"	D5 I could make a real difference for my kids.	
colspan="6"	D6 I'd know I was really good at this.	colspan="5"	BD I'd be proud.	
	R I had trouble getting here today. It's hard to take time off from school.	
	P I'm scared of surgery and don't want to wear a brace thing.	

	**Patient Seven** **You are an executive assistant at a large technology corporation.**
T1	T2	R	E	T	C	CP	NP	A	SC	NC	CHIPS
colspan="6"	PD I keep getting shooting pains down my legs. I've tried everything, and they just won't stop.	colspan="5"	D1 I could get back to being me.	*List Date of Chip*
colspan="6"	D2 I could show my boss how invaluable I am.	colspan="5"	D3 He would start taking me on the road with him.	
colspan="6"	D4 I could have the opportunity to travel around the world.	colspan="5"	D5 I'd meet new people, learn new things. It would be an amazing experience.	
colspan="6"	D6 I'd put it all on my resumé.	colspan="5"	BD I'd go after his job!	
	R Money is an issue.	
	P I have enough pain. I don't want more from whatever you do.	

Patient Eight You are a 65-year-old rancher.										
T1	T2	R	E	T	C	CP	NP	A	SC	NC	CHIPS

PD When I wake up in the mornings, I can't feel my hands, and my arms are all numb.	**D1** I could live my life again.	*List Date of Chip*
D2 I'd play catch with my grandkids.	**D3** I might sell the ranch.	
D4 I might go on a vacation.	**D5** You never know who you're going to meet	
D6 I might start a second life.	**BD** I'd know I wasn't too old to have a good time.	

R I don't have anyone at home to take care of me after surgery.

P Do you think it's stupid for someone my age to start over again?

Appendix VII

M.A.D. Charts for Motivation Formula Role Plays: Bariatric Medicine and Surgery

Patient One											
You are a stay-at-home mom with three young children and a husband.											
T1	**T2**	**R**	**E**	**T**	**C**	**CP**	**NP**	**A**	**SC**	**NC**	**CHIPS**
PD I'd be a size 14.						**D1** I'd have more confidence.					*List Date of Chip*
D2 I've always thought maybe I could do some modeling, but I got pregnant, and the rest is history. Now that the kids are in school, it's time to find out! Not the super-model thing — just, you know, a regular person, even a little oversized is OK. It would still be modeling.						**D3** Well, if someone actually hired me to do some modeling, I could make a little extra money.					
D4 I'd open my own modeling agency.						**D5** I'd be able to give lots of girls the chance that I never had.					
D6 I'd feel like I really made a difference in someone's life.						**BD** I'd finally feel worthy.					
R I have to cook for the kids and my husband, and I really don't want to have to do something special just for me.											
P I don't know what it would do to my marriage after all these years.											

	**Patient Two** **You are the owner of a dry cleaning store.**
T1	**T2**	**R**	**E**	**T**	**C**	**CP**	**NP**	**A**	**SC**	**NC**	**CHIPS**

Patient Two
You are the owner of a dry cleaning store.

T1	T2	R	E	T	C	CP	NP	A	SC	NC	CHIPS
PD I'd wear size 36 pants.						D1 I wouldn't be embarrassed when customers come into the shop.					*List Date of Chip*
D2 I would smile more at the customers.						D3 Our customers would refer more customers.					
D4 My wife would be happy.						D5 I'd take her on a vacation.					
D6 We'd be like when we were first married.						BD I'd be proud.					
R I don't have time for exercise.											
P Honestly—I'm pretty lazy.											

Patient Three
You are a 48-year-old attorney.

T1	T2	R	E	T	C	CP	NP	A	SC	NC	CHIPS
PD I can't exercise any more. I've tried every diet. I've got to get this weight off.						D1 I'd feel young and alive.					*List Date of Chip*
D2 I'd get more of the better cases.						D3 I'd make a name for myself.					
D4 I'd make partner.						D5 I'd make more money.					
D6 I'd have more security						BD I'd know I'd made it.					
R My hours are long so I don't know when I could get here. How often do you need to see me?											
P I keep thinking this is frivolous and vain.											

T1	**T2**	**R**	**E**	**T**	**C**	**CP**	**NP**	**A**	**SC**	**NC**	**CHIPS**

Patient Four
You are a newly licensed real estate broker.

T1	T2	R	E	T	C	CP	NP	A	SC	NC	CHIPS
PD I can't even get clothes to fit me any more. I can barely take a shower without help.						**D1** I'd smile all over the place.					*List Date of Chip*
D2 Well the first thing I would do is cut my hair really short and go blonde.						**D3** Well, of course I'd have to redo my wardrobe.					
D4 I'd go out and find a daddy for my daughter.						**D5** We'd have fun.					
D6 I would have a real family.						**BD** I wouldn't feel so alone.					
R I'm allergic to a lot of foods.											
P What if I look great and no one wants me?											

Patient Five
You are a 63-year-old builder who is separated from his wife.

T1	T2	R	E	T	C	CP	NP	A	SC	NC	CHIPS
PD I want to get back to a 34 waist and stop having to deal with my diabetes.						**D1** I'd feel a lot better— I'm exhausted all the time.					*List Date of Chip*
D2 I'd fit into an airplane seat without the extension belt.						**D3** I'd feel better about myself.					
D4 Maybe I'd put myself out there again.						**D5** Maybe I'd meet some new friends.					
D6 I'd get my groove back.						**BD** I'd try to get my wife back.					
R I can't take a lot of time off from the job site.											
P The weight thing is for health, but I have to tell you—I'm sick of this life.											

											CHIPS

Patient Six
You are an elementary school teacher.

T1	T2	R	E	T	C	CP	NP	A	SC	NC	CHIPS
PD I want to be a size 14 and not have to worry about my blood pressure.						D1 I wouldn't dread looking in the mirror every morning.					*List Date of Chip*
D2 I could wear regular clothes.						D3 My self-confidence would go up.					
D4 I'd probably be a better teacher.						D5 I'd go back for my PhD.					
D6 I'd teach at the university level.						BD I'd finally be doing what I always said I'd do.					
R I had trouble getting here today. It's hard to take time off from school.											
P I'm not sure I'd know what to do if I was actually attractive.											

Patient Seven
You are an executive assistant at a large technology corporation.

T1	T2	R	E	T	C	CP	NP	A	SC	NC	CHIPS
PD I want to be a size 16, and I want to be able to tie my own sneakers.						D1 I'd be able to get up a flight of stairs without huffing.					*List Date of Chip*
D2 I could go to the gym with my friends and not be embarrassed.						D3 I'd meet some new people.					
D4 I'd get more confidence.						D5 I'd go to school and get my MBA.					
D6 I'd quit my job.						BD I'd open a company right across the street and take all my boss's customers.					
R Money is an issue.											
P Truthfully, my boss comes on to me now, and it's a little uncomfortable. I'm a little worried that if I look better he might get worse.											

	**Patient Eight** **You are in retail sales.**

T1	T2	R	E	T	C	CP	NP	A	SC	NC	CHIPS
colspan="6"	**PD** I want to be a size 10.	colspan="5"	**D1** I'd enjoy my summers.	*List Date of Chip*
colspan="6"	**D2** I'd go to the beach.	colspan="5"	**D3** I'd go out and meet people.	
colspan="6"	**D4** I'd find someone and fall in love.	colspan="5"	**D5** I'd build a home, adopt some kids, and do the whole white picket fence thing.	
colspan="6"	**D6** I'd decorate the house for Christmas. I haven't done that for years.	colspan="5"	**BD** I'd finally have a real home.	
	**R** I already have diabetes and high blood pressure. Am I healthy enough to get healthy?
	**P** Do you think it's stupid for someone my age to care how I look?

Appendix VIII

M.A.D. Charts for Motivation Formula Role Plays: Cosmetic Dentistry

Patient One You are a stay-at-home mom with three young children and a husband.											
T1	**T2**	**R**	**E**	**T**	**C**	**CP**	**NP**	**A**	**SC**	**NC**	**CHIPS**
PD I hate my teeth. They cross over on the bottom, and they look awful.						**D1** It wouldn't make my life different—but I'd feel different.					*List Date of Chip*
D2 I'd have more confidence.						**D3** I've always wanted to open a dance school.					
D4 I could have my own business.						**D5** My kids are getting to the point when they don't need me here all the time. It's my turn.					
D6 I'd have a little pocket money, and a great feeling of accomplishment.						**BD** I'd finally feel good about myself as a woman.					
R I can't be here a lot—I have to take care of the kids.											
P Just because I have a new smile, what if I haven't got what it takes to launch a business?											

Patient Two **You are a manager at a factory.**										
T1	T2	R	E	T	C	CP	NP	A	SC	NC	**CHIPS**

PD I smoked for 30 years and now I quit. Time to make my teeth look better.	**D1** I'd look younger.	*List Date of Chip*
D2 The guys would stop ribbing me.	**D3** I'd get more credibility on the floor.	
D4 Maybe I'd get a promotion.	**D5** Make more money.	
D6 I'd get a new house for my wife.	**BD** I'd make her happy and proud of me.	
R It depends on what it all costs.		
P Honestly—I'm a sissy when it comes to pain.		

Patient Three **You are a 48-year-old attorney.**										
T1	T2	R	E	T	C	CP	NP	A	SC	NC	**CHIPS**

PD I want to get rid of these old fillings, and I've got these cracks in my front teeth.	**D1** I'd look young and successful.	*List Date of Chip*
D2 I'd get more of the better cases.	**D3** I'd make a name for myself.	
D4 I'd make partner.	**D5** I'd make more money.	
D6 I'd have more security.	**BD** I'd know I'd made it.	
R Scheduling can be tough during the day.		
P I keep thinking this is frivolous and vain.		

Patient Four
You are a newly licensed real estate broker.

T1	T2	R	E	T	C	CP	NP	A	SC	NC	CHIPS
PD My teeth are cracked and yellow, and they are sensitive to hot and cold.						D1 I could smile without being self-conscious and drink a cup of tea without seeing stars.					*List Date of Chip*
D2 I wouldn't feel so old.						D3 I'd have more confidence.					
D4 I could show houses better.						D5 I'd make more sales.					
D6 I'd make more money.						BD I'd show my kids that I can SO do this realtor thing.					
R I have back problems so I can't sit in a chair for too long.											
P What if I have a better smile and then I can't sell anything?!											

Patient Five
You are a 63-year-old builder who is separated from his wife.

T1	T2	R	E	T	C	CP	NP	A	SC	NC	CHIPS
PD I lost these teeth over the last few years, and I look twice my age.						D1 I'd look a lot better.					*List Date of Chip*
D2 I'd feel like I did when I was younger.						D3 I'd feel better about myself.					
D4 Maybe I'd put myself out there again.						D5 Maybe I'd meet some new friends.					
D6 I'd get my groove back.						BD I'd try to get my wife back.					
R I can't take a lot of time off from the job site.											
P What if after all this my wife doesn't want me back?											

	**Patient Six** **You are an elementary school teacher.**
T1	**T2**	**R**	**E**	**T**	**C**	**CP**	**NP**	**A**	**SC**	**NC**	**CHIPS**
colspan="6"	**PD** I can't compete with those commercials. I always thought I had a nice smile, but now I feel like I'm ugly compared with those models on TV and in the magazines. I tried the teeth whitening stuff but it didn't do anything for me.	colspan="5"	**D1** I would feel better about myself.	*List Date of Chip*
colspan="6"	**D2** I could be more outgoing.	colspan="5"	**D3** I'd be more confident.	
colspan="6"	**D4** I'd be a better teacher.	colspan="5"	**D5** I could make a real difference for my kids.	
colspan="6"	**D6** I'd know I was really good at this.	colspan="5"	**BD** I'd be proud.	
	**R** I had trouble getting here today. It's hard to take time off from school.	
	**P** I'm embarrassed about all of this.	

	**Patient Seven** **You are an executive assistant at a large technology corporation.**
T1	**T2**	**R**	**E**	**T**	**C**	**CP**	**NP**	**A**	**SC**	**NC**	**CHIPS**
colspan="6"	**PD** They told me I have TMJ from an uneven bite, and so as long as we have to fix that I thought maybe you could make my smile look better?	colspan="5"	**D1** I wouldn't get so many headaches and I'd also look a lot better.	*List Date of Chip*
colspan="6"	**D2** I could show my boss how invaluable I am.	colspan="5"	**D3** He would start taking me on the road with him.	
colspan="6"	**D4** I could have the opportunity to travel around the world.	colspan="5"	**D5** I'd meet new people, learn new things. It would be an amazing experience.	
colspan="6"	**D6** I'd put it all on my resume.	colspan="5"	**BD** I'd go after his job!	
	**R** Money is an issue.	
	**P** I don't want to look like I have a fake smile.	

	**Patient Eight** **You are a 65-year-old rancher.**

T1	T2	R	E	T	C	CP	NP	A	SC	NC	CHIPS
PD I'm sick and tired of these dentures. There's got to be a better way.						D1 I'd look better, and I could stop messing with these things.					*List Date of Chip*
D2 I've put everyone else first my whole life. It's about time I did something just for me.						D3 I'd feel better.					
D4 I might go on a vacation.						D5 I might sell my ranch.					
D6 I might start a second life.						BD I'd know I wasn't too old to have a good time.					
R I drove two hours to get here, so I'd like you to figure out a way to do whatever you need to do in one or two visits.											
P Do you think it's stupid for someone my age to do this?											

M.A.D. Charts for Motivation Formula Role Plays: General Dentistry

Patient One You are a stay-at-home mom with three young children and a husband.											
T1	**T2**	**R**	**E**	**T**	**C**	**CP**	**NP**	**A**	**SC**	**NC**	**CHIPS**
PD I am constantly in pain—I tried the sensitivity toothpaste, and it just doesn't work for me.						**D1** It wouldn't make my life different—but I'd feel different.					*List Date of Chip*
D2 I'd have more confidence.						**D3** I've always wanted to open a dance school.					
D4 I could have my own business.						**D5** My kids are getting to the point when they don't need me here all the time. It's my turn.					
D6 I'd have a little pocket money and a great feeling of accomplishment.						**BD** I'd finally feel good about myself as a woman.					
R I can't be here a lot—I have to take care of the kids.											
P Just because I have a new smile, what if I haven't got what it takes to launch a business?											

Patient Two
You are a manager at a factory.

T1	T2	R	E	T	C	CP	NP	A	SC	NC	CHIPS
PD I bleed every time I brush my teeth.						D1 My gums are always red and swollen, and the guys are always ribbing me about it.					*List Date of Chip*
D2 I might smile more often.						D3 I'd get more credibility on the floor.					
D4 Maybe I'd get a promotion.						D5 I'd make more money.					
D6 I'd get a new house for my wife.						BD I'd make her happy and proud of me.					
R It depends on what it all costs.											
P Honestly—I'm a sissy when it comes to pain.											

Patient Three
You are a 48-year-old attorney.

T1	T2	R	E	T	C	CP	NP	A	SC	NC	CHIPS
PD I think I have a cavity or crack or something. It hurts when I breathe or chew or drink.						D1 I could stop thinking about my mouth.					*List Date of Chip*
D2 I'd concentrate more on my clients.						D3 I'd make a name for myself.					
D4 I'd make partner.						D5 I'd make more money.					
D6 I'd have more security.						BD I'd know I'd made it.					
R Scheduling can be tough during the day.											
P I'm a little claustrophobic.											

	**Patient Four** **You are a newly licensed real estate broker.**

T1	T2	R	E	T	C	CP	NP	A	SC	NC	CHIPS
colspan="6"	**PD** My teeth are cracked and yellow, and they are sensitive to hot and cold.	colspan="5"	**D1** I could smile without being self-conscious and drink a cup of tea without seeing stars.	*List Date of Chip*
colspan="6"	**D2** I wouldn't feel so old.	colspan="5"	**D3** I'd have more confidence.	
colspan="6"	**D4** I could show houses better.	colspan="5"	**D5** I'd make more sales.	
colspan="6"	**D6** I'd make more money.	colspan="5"	**BD** I'd show my kids that I can SO do this realtor thing.	
	**R** I have back problems so I can't sit in a chair for too long.	
	**P** What if I have a great smile and then I can't sell anything?!	

	**Patient Five** **You are a 63-year-old builder who is separated from his wife.**

T1	T2	R	E	T	C	CP	NP	A	SC	NC	CHIPS
colspan="6"	**PD** I broke my crown.	colspan="5"	**D1** I could chew on that side again.	*List Date of Chip*
colspan="6"	**D2** I'd feel a lot better—it's kind of sensitive.	colspan="5"	**D3** I could get back to business.	
colspan="6"	**D4** I'd make some money— maybe do some socializing.	colspan="5"	**D5** Maybe I'd meet some new friends.	
colspan="6"	**D6** I'd get my groove back.	colspan="5"	**BD** I'd try to get my wife back.	
	**R** I can't take a lot of time off from the job site.	
	**P** I hate to admit it, but I really hate needles.	

Patient Six
You are an elementary school teacher.

T1	T2	R	E	T	C	CP	NP	A	SC	NC	CHIPS

PD I can't compete with those commercials. I always thought I had a nice smile, but now I feel like I'm ugly compared with those models on TV and in the magazines. I tried the teeth whitening stuff but it didn't do anything for me.	**D1** I would feel better about myself.
D2 I could be more outgoing.	**D3** I'd be more confident.
D4 I'd be a better teacher.	**D5** I could make a real difference for my kids.
D6 I'd know I was really good at this.	**BD** I'd be proud.

List Date of Chip

R I had trouble getting here today. It's hard to take time off from school.
P I'm embarrassed about all of this.

Patient Seven
You are an executive assistant at a large technology corporation.

T1	T2	R	E	T	C	CP	NP	A	SC	NC	CHIPS

PD I have really bad headaches and someone said it might be TMJ.	**D1** I wouldn't get so many headaches.
D2 I could do better at work and at home.	**D3** I want my boss to take me with him on the road.
D4 I could travel.	**D5** I'd meet new people, learn new things, it would be an amazing experience.
D6 I'd put it all on my resumé.	**BD** I'd go after his job!

List Date of Chip

R Money is an issue.
P I'd be self-conscious wearing a contraption at night.

											Patient Eight **You are a 65-year-old rancher.**

T1	T2	R	E	T	C	CP	NP	A	SC	NC	CHIPS
											List Date of Chip

PD I'm sick and tired of these dentures. There's got to be a better way.

D1 I'd look better and I could stop messing with these things.

D2 I've put everyone first my whole life. It's about time I did something just for me.

D3 I'd feel better.

D4 I might go on a vacation.

D5 I might sell my ranch.

D6 I might start a second life.

BD I'd know I wasn't too old to have a good time.

R I drove two hours to get here, so I'd like you to figure out a way to do whatever you need to do in one or two visits

P Do you think it's stupid for someone my age to do this?

M.A.D. Charts for Motivation Formula Role Plays: Orthodontics

IN THESE ROLE PLAYS, Person B could be an adult family member of the child patient (Person C), Person B could be the child patient, or Person B could be the adult patient (adult profiles are at the very end of this section). To make things more interesting, combine profiles to create families of mother, father, grandparent, child, etc., and instruct Person A to ask everyone in the family The ACTION Formula questions! When you work through the Inviting Patients to ACTION strategies, use the Parent and Adult M.A.D. charts (as opposed to the child charts) since adults are always the financial decision makers.

T1	T2	R	E	T	C	CP	NP	A	SC	NC	CHIPS

Parent One
You are a 63-year-old builder who is separated from his wife.

PD He's the one who wants this. I think it is complete nonsense.
D1 Well, maybe he'd stop being alone so much.

D2 I'd like to see him happy—maybe get into sports more, be more confident.
D3 I'd always hoped he'd come to work with me, but I think he just needs a chance to be happy.

D4 Well, if he doesn't work with me, maybe I'll just retire and go have some fun.
D5 Maybe I'd meet some new friends.

D6 I'd get my groove back.
BD I'd try to get my wife back.

R I can't take a lot of time off from the job site to take him here.

P I feel kind of stupid spending money on this when other people can't even pay their rent.

List Date of Chip

Parent Two
You are a manager at a factory.

PD I want whatever is right for her.
D1 If my daughter is happy, I'm happy.

D2 I would stop worrying about her.
D3 I'd get her mother off my back.

D4 I could stop feeling guilty like I'm not doing enough for my family.
D5 I could focus on work.

D6 I'd get a new house for my wife.
BD I'd make my family happy.

R It depends on what it all costs.

P I don't want to have to deal with her fussing when she doesn't like the braces.

List Date of Chip

	**Parent Three** **You are a 48-year-old attorney.**

T1	T2	R	E	T	C	CP	NP	A	SC	NC	CHIPS
colspan="6"	PD Her front teeth are crooked, and the bottom ones are overlapping.	colspan="5" D1 I want her to have the things I never had.	*List Date of Chip*
colspan="6"	D2 I'd have a happy kid.	colspan="5" D3 The kids would stop teasing her in school.	
colspan="6"	D4 She could be more successful in school.	colspan="5" D5 She'd get into a good college.	
colspan="6"	D6 I'd feel like I was a good mother.	colspan="5" BD I'd get her grandmother off my back.	
	R Scheduling can be tough during the day.	
	P It has to be OK with her or we don't do it.	

	**Parent Four** **You are a medical doctor.**

T1	T2	R	E	T	C	CP	NP	A	SC	NC	CHIPS
colspan="6"	PD I want her to have straight teeth.	colspan="5" D1 She is self-conscious, and all of that causes a lot of problems for her and for me.	*List Date of Chip*
colspan="6"	D2 I want to be proud of her.	colspan="5" D3 I'd feel like I helped her to be successful.	
colspan="6"	D4 I could focus on my practice.	colspan="5" D5 I'd be a better doctor.	
colspan="6"	D6 I'd make more money.	colspan="5" BD I'd be a good provider for my family.	
	R She'd have to coordinate appointments with her mother.	
	P I don't want her to think this is because I want it for her. It has to be her decision.	

	**Parent Five** **You are a stay-at-home mom with three young children and a husband.**

T1	T2	R	E	T	C	CP	NP	A	SC	NC	CHIPS
colspan="6"	colspan="5"	*List Date of Chip*
colspan="6"	**PD** I want her teeth to be straight.	colspan="5"	**D1** I'd be able to stop worrying about her.	
colspan="6"	**D2** I'd be so proud of her, I'd buy her all new clothes.	colspan="5"	**D3** I'd get excited about showing her off at church.	
colspan="6"	**D4** I could finally show up that Julie Tomato—she thinks her daughter is the only pretty girl ever to be born in this town.	colspan="5"	**D5** I could hold my head up high with those snobs.	
colspan="6"	**D6** She'd be more popular.	colspan="5"	**BD** I'd know I was a good mother.	
R		My schedule is ruled by all three of my children's schedules, and I don't know if I could always be with her for her appointments.
P		I'm afraid her older sister may get jealous—this one is really the prettier of the two, and they are in constant competition as it is.

	**Parent Six** **You are an elementary school teacher.**

T1	T2	R	E	T	C	CP	NP	A	SC	NC	CHIPS
colspan="6"	**PD** She can't close her teeth together to bite and she's always getting teased about the way she talks.	colspan="5"	**D1** I could stop worrying about her so much.	*List Date of Chip*
colspan="6"	**D2** I see her at school, and I can't help but watch her and want to rescue her from the bullies.	colspan="5"	**D3** I could pay more attention to my own students	
colspan="6"	**D4** I'd be a better teacher.	colspan="5"	**D5** I could make a real difference for my kids.	
colspan="6"	**D6** I'd know I was really good at being a teacher and a parent.	colspan="5"	**BD** I'd be proud.	
R		I had trouble getting here today. It's hard to take time off from school.
P		I'm embarrassed that I waited so long to bring her here.

	**Parent Seven** **You are an executive assistant at a large technology corporation.**
T1	T2	R	E	T	C	CP	NP	A	SC	NC	CHIPS

PD She came home crying the other day because the kids were teasing her. She's got such a pretty face until she smiles. We've got to get that fixed before she gets too far into high school and it really affects her life.	**D1** My life wouldn't be different at all—but her life would be totally different.	*List Date of Chip*
D2 She would be more confident.	**D3** She'd make more friends and have more fun.	
D4 She'd probably do better in school if she wasn't self-conscious.	**D5** She'd get into a great college and have a fabulous life!	
D6 I'd feel great knowing that she was happy.	**BD** I would know that I did the right thing for her.	
R Money is issue.		
P I don't want her to hate me thinking I *made* her wear braces.		

	**Parent Eight** **You are a 65-year-old rancher.**
T1	T2	R	E	T	C	CP	NP	A	SC	NC	CHIPS

PD This is my grandkid—his parents want him to have braces. I think he looks just fine.	**D1** I'm already proud of him. I couldn't be any more proud of him.	*List Date of Chip*
D2 I suppose he'd be happier.	**D3** His parents worry about him all the time, and I have to listen to it.	
D4 I can't have people talking about my grandkid as if there's something wrong with him.	**D5** So, I suppose they could see the great kid he is and stop looking at his teeth.	
D6 He'd probably have an easier time in school.	**BD** I'd be happy for him. I love the kid.	
R I drove two hours to get here, so his parents will have to figure out how to get him here for appointments.		
P If it were up to me, I'd leave it alone.		

Patient One: Child **You are in the eighth grade.**										
T1	**T2**	**R**	**E**	**T**	**C**	**CP**	**NP**	**A**	**SC**	**NC**	**CHIPS**

PD I want my teeth to be even— I used to suck my thumb.	**D1** I wouldn't look so stupid.	*List Date of Chip*
D2 I might smile more often.	**D3** I'd feel better about me.	
D4 I might audition for the school play.	**D5** I could get the starring role.	
D6 I could make new friends.	**BD** I could show Dad that I should be an actress and he would stop trying to talk me into being interested in science.	
R I don't want it to hurt.		
P Would I still be me if my teeth look different?		

Patient Two: Child **You are a junior in high school.**										
T1	**T2**	**R**	**E**	**T**	**C**	**CP**	**NP**	**A**	**SC**	**NC**	**CHIPS**

PD I want to look normal.	**D1** I wouldn't look so stupid.	*List Date of Chip*
D2 I might smile more often.	**D3** I'd be more confident.	
D4 I would probably volunteer more at school to do projects and answer questions.	**D5** I would get better grades.	
D6 I could get into a better college—maybe move out of state.	**BD** I could get away from my family and be on my own.	
R I don't want Mom and Dad to have to work another job to pay for this.		
P I don't want to upset Mom and Dad.		

Patient Three: Child
You just finished high school last year.

T1	T2	R	E	T	C	CP	NP	A	SC	NC	CHIPS
PD I've always been really self-conscious about my teeth. I just want them to be straight.						D1 I'd feel a lot better about smiling.					*List Date of Chip*
D2 I know looks aren't everything but it would be nice to talk to someone without them looking grossed out when I smile.						D3 I think I'd have a whole lot more fun because I wouldn't be self-conscious around people.					
D4 I would probably do better in job interviews.						D5 I'd get a really good job.					
D6 I've never had the guts to ask a girl out on a date. I went to my senior dance with a group of kids. I'd like to go ahead and ask my neighbor's daughter to a movie.						BD I'd look normal.					
R I've got a bum neck—I used to wear a back brace—so I don't know if this will hurt it.											
P I don't want one of those head gear things—I just couldn't stand it.											

Patient Four: Child
You are a freshman in high school.

T1	T2	R	E	T	C	CP	NP	A	SC	NC	CHIPS
PD Whenever I talk, I do thith whitheling thing, and I can't thtop it. I tried thpeech therapy but they thed it'th cauthe my teeth don't line up right.						D1 I jussssstht want to talk like a normal perthon.					*List Date of Chip*
D2 I could do better in thkool.						D3 I could get a job on the radio and do a talk thow.					
D4 I would thtop worrying about my future and know I'd be OK.						D5 My mom would thtop crying all the time.					
D6 I'd be able to thow everyone that I'm jutht as good as my thithter.						BD I'd feel good about my thelf.					
R My fokthz don't have a lot of money.											
P What if thith doethin't fikth how I talk??											

Patient Five: Child You are age 12.											
T1	T2	R	E	T	C	CP	NP	A	SC	NC	CHIPS
PD	I would look just like my sister.					D1	I'd be pretty.				*List Date of Chip*
D2	Maybe I'd get to go to some of the parties and stuff.					D3	I don't even know what happens at those parties, but I'd like to get invited just once.				
D4	I wouldn't feel like I was so different from everyone else.					D5	I'd fit in better.				
D6	I wouldn't be alone all the time.					BD	I'd be happy.				
R	I don't know if my Mom can afford this.										
P	Will it hurt?										

Patient Six: Child You are age 10.											
T1	T2	R	E	T	C	CP	NP	A	SC	NC	CHIPS
PD	My Mom promised that I could get my teeth fixed when I turned 10. So here we are.					D1	I look stupid, and I want to look normal.				*List Date of Chip*
D2	I wouldn't look like an alien.					D3	I'd get to do more stuff with the other kids.				
D4	I'd have more fun.					D5	I wouldn't just be sitting around after school.				
D6	I'd have some friends.					BD	I'd be just like everyone else.				
R	I'd have to come after school.										
P	Am I gonna look even more stupid with whatever you do to me until it's all fixed?										

T1	T2	R	E	T	C	CP	NP	A	SC	NC	CHIPS
	**Patient Seven: Child** **You are age nine.**	

T1	T2	R	E	T	C	CP	NP	A	SC	NC	CHIPS
PD My dentist told me that I have to get these fixed now before I get any older.						D1 I'd have a healthy smile.					*List Date of Chip*
D2 To tell you the truth—I didn't think there was anything wrong with my smile. But my Mom and Dad said I have to do this.						D3 Well I guess it would make them happy.					
D4 When they're happy we do fun stuff.						D5 Maybe we could finally go to Epcot Center.					
D6 It would be fun to go with them there. I could see all the science stuff up close.						BD Maybe we could even go to NASA!					
R I'm very good at following instructions if you just tell me what to do but I can't do anything extra until I've done my homework.											
P I don't want any of those colored things — just silver.											

T1	T2	R	E	T	C	CP	NP	A	SC	NC	CHIPS
	**Patient Eight: Child** **You are age 16.**	

T1	T2	R	E	T	C	CP	NP	A	SC	NC	CHIPS
PD I decided I want to be a trial lawyer, and no one is going to listen to me unless I get this fixed.						D1 I took a speech class last semester, and they just laughed at me. I won't let that happen again.					*List Date of Chip*
D2 I'd be on the debate team.						D3 I'd go for early admission.					
D4 I'd go to Harvard.						D5 I'd get the best summer internships.					
D6 I'd get into Harvard Law.						BD I'd show those kids I'm not stupid.					
R I can do anything.											
P Just do it fast because I have to get onto that debate team next year.											

	**Patient Nine: Adult** **You are a stay-at-home mom with three young children and a husband.**
T1	T2	R	E	T	C	CP	NP	A	SC	NC	CHIPS

PD I hate my teeth. They cross over on the bottom, and they look awful.   **D1** It wouldn't make my life different—but I'd feel different.   *List Date of Chip*

D2 I'd have more confidence.   **D3** I've always wanted to open a dance school.

D4 I could have my own business.   **D5** My kids are getting to the point when they don't need me here all the time. It's my turn.

D6 I'd have a little pocket money and a great feeling of accomplishment.   **BD** I'd finally feel good about myself as a woman.

R I can't be here a lot—I have to take care of the kids.

P Just because I have a new smile, what if I haven't got what it takes to launch a business?

	**Patient Ten: Adult** **You are a manager at a factory.**
T1	T2	R	E	T	C	CP	NP	A	SC	NC	CHIPS

PD It always bugged me about my crooked teeth. I just turned 50, and it's time to fix it.   **D1** I'd look younger.   *List Date of Chip*

D2 The guys would stop ribbing me.   **D3** I'd get more credibility on the floor.

D4 Maybe I'd get a promotion.   **D5** I'd make more money.

D6 I'd get a new house for my wife.   **BD** I'd make her happy and proud of me.

R It depends on what it all costs.

P Honestly—I'm a sissy when it comes to pain.

											CHIPS
T1	**T2**	**R**	**E**	**T**	**C**	**CP**	**NP**	**A**	**SC**	**NC**	

Patient 11: Adult
You are a 48-year-old attorney.

											CHIPS
T1	**T2**	**R**	**E**	**T**	**C**	**CP**	**NP**	**A**	**SC**	**NC**	

PD I need to get these teeth straight so I can look more professional.

D1 I'd look young and successful.

D2 I'd get more of the better cases.

D3 I'd make a name for myself.

D4 I'd make partner.

D5 I'd make more money.

D6 I'd have more security.

BD I'd know I'd made it.

List Date of Chip

R Scheduling can be tough during the day.

P I keep thinking this is frivolous and vain.

Patient 12: Adult
You are a newly licensed real estate broker.

											CHIPS
T1	**T2**	**R**	**E**	**T**	**C**	**CP**	**NP**	**A**	**SC**	**NC**	

PD I need to have a great smile.

D1 I could smile without being self-conscious.

D2 I wouldn't feel so old.

D3 I'd have more confidence.

D4 I could show houses better.

D5 I'd make more sales.

D6 I'd make more money.

BD I'd show my kids that I am NOT getting old!

List Date of Chip

R I have back problems so I can't sit in a chair for too long.

P What if I have a better smile and then I can't sell anything?!

	**Patient 13: Adult** **You are a 63-year-old builder who is separated from his wife.**
T1	T2	R	E	T	C	CP	NP	A	SC	NC	CHIPS

PD	I was in an accident a long time ago and lost some teeth, and now I have all these spaces in front. I look twice my age.	D1	I'd look a lot better.	*List Date of Chip*
D2	I'd feel like I did when I was younger.	D3	I'd feel better about myself.	
D4	Maybe I'd put myself out there again.	D5	Maybe I'd meet some new friends.	
D6	I'd get my groove back.	BD	I'd try to get my wife back.	
R	I can't take a lot of time off from the job site.			
P	What will people think of a guy my age wearing braces?			

	**Patient 14: Adult** **You are an elementary school teacher.**
T1	T2	R	E	T	C	CP	NP	A	SC	NC	CHIPS

PD	I can't compete with those commercials. I always thought I had a nice smile, but now I feel like I'm ugly compared with those models on TV and in the magazines.	D1	I would feel better about myself.	*List Date of Chip*
D2	I could be more outgoing.	D3	I'd be more confident.	
D4	I'd be a better teacher.	D5	I could make a real difference for my kids.	
D6	I'd know I was really good at this.	BD	I'd be proud.	
R	I had trouble getting here today. It's hard to take time off from school.			
P	I'm embarrassed about all of this.			

	**Patient 15: Adult** **You are an executive assistant at a large technology corporation.**

T1	T2	R	E	T	C	CP	NP	A	SC	NC	CHIPS
colspan="6"	**PD** They told me I have TMJ because my alignment is off. Time to get it fixed.	colspan="5"	**D1** I wouldn't get so many headaches, and I'd also look a lot better	*List Date of Chip*
colspan="6"	**D2** I could show my boss how invaluable I am.	colspan="5"	**D3** He would start taking me in the road with him.	
colspan="6"	**D4** I could have the opportunity to travel around the world.	colspan="5"	**D5** I'd meet new people, learn new things. It would be an amazing experience.	
colspan="6"	**D6** I'd put it all on my resumé.	colspan="5"	**BD** I'd go after his job!	
	**R** Money is an issue.
	**P** I'm scared about whether I would look OK while we do this.

	**Patient 16: Adult** **You are a 65-year-old rancher.**

T1	T2	R	E	T	C	CP	NP	A	SC	NC	CHIPS
colspan="6"	**PD** I'm sick and tired of how I look when I smile.	colspan="5"	**D1** I'd look better.	*List Date of Chip*
colspan="6"	**D2** I've put everyone else first my whole life. It's about time I did something just for me.	colspan="5"	**D3** I'd feel better.	
colspan="6"	**D4** I might go on a vacation.	colspan="5"	**D5** I might sell my ranch.	
colspan="6"	**D6** I might start a second life.	colspan="5"	**BD** I'd know I wasn't too old to have a good time.	
	**R** I drove two hours to get here, so I'd like you to figure out a way to do whatever you need to do in one or two visits.
	**P** Do you think it's stupid for someone my age to do this?

Appendix XI

Alignment Formula Role Plays: All Practices

THE CANDOR FORMULA

GIVE PERSON A one of the following topics. Instruct him or her to use the topic as the first step of The CANDOR Formula and then to complete the final steps of the Formula with anything they like. Encourage creativity!

- When you interrupt my thinking . . .
- When you talk to me while I'm on the phone . . .
- When you are late for your appointment . . .
- When you belittle me in front of patients . . .
- When you overbook my schedule . . .
- When you don't return my page . . .
- When you don't do what you said you would do . . .
- When you don't return my phone call . . .
- When you don't return a patient's phone call . . .
- When you leave your food in the refrigerator for more than 2 days . . .
- When you don't enter complete information in the patient's record . . .
- When you don't do your dictation . . .
- When you talk to me in an angry tone . . .
- When you use sarcasm with me . . .
- When you don't iron your scrubs . . .
- When you don't come in on time . . .
- When you disappear without telling anyone where you're going . . .
- When you accuse me without questioning me . . .
- When you take up two parking spaces . . .
- When you don't return the money you borrow . . .
- When you don't refer patients to us . . .
- When you raise your voice to a patient . . .
- When you whisper in front of a patient . . .
- When you rush through a patient appointment . . .

- When you don't clean up after yourself . . .
- When you don't prepare the room properly . . .
- When you write quickly without printing . . .
- When you read a magazine at the front desk . . .
- When you talk on your cell phone in front of a patient . . .
- When you discuss your personal relationships in front of a patient . . .

THE ACCOUNTABILITY FORMULA

Role playing this formula means that Person B will follow the steps in The ACCOUNTABILITY Formula and respond to the statements given by Person A when he or she uses The CANDOR Formula. This role play requires Person B's to imagine what they might say if they were really in that situation. Encourage everyone to use their imaginations and to allow themselves to "go with the flow."

THE EMOTIONS FORMULA

In this Role Play, Person B will take a topic and give the story to Person A with all of the drama and pathos he or she can muster! Person A will walk through The EMOTION Formula, and Person B needs to pay attention carefully to his or her response to Person A so that the de-escalation of emotions comes naturally.

- I was billed for a service I didn't receive! . . .
- I've been waiting for 45 minutes! . . .
- I've been waiting three days for someone to return my phone call! . . .
- My insurance said they won't pay for this! . . .
- Don't you dare come near me with that! . . .
- My husband was treated rudely by your receptionist! . . .
- I was treated rudely by a doctor in your practice! . . .
- The noise in here is making me crazy! . . .
- Nobody cares I'm here! . . .
- I keep getting the run-around about my test results! . . .
- You changed my appointment and messed up my entire day! . . .
- I can't take time off for a test! . . .
- You left me alone in this room and no one came in for an hour! . . .
- You made me see a different doctor than the one I'm used to! . . .
- That lady was so rude she made me cry! . . .
- That doctor came and went so fast I never had time to ask my questions! . . .
- My husband had questions about my case and no one would listen to him! . . .
- I heard you folks talking about me outside in the hall and someone called me a bad name! . . .

- That doctor acts like he is king of the mountain. Who does he think he is? . . .
- I have never been so humiliated in all my life! . . .
- I can't have surgery! I have things to do and . . .
- You told my daughter my test results without my permission! . . .
- Don't treat me like an idiot! I wasn't born yesterday! . . .
- I don't want this pill, I hate taking pills and I won't take it! . . .
- I hate needles! Get away from me with that thing! . . .
- I need an appointment today, and I don't care if you're all booked up! . . .
- I sent in my check last week and it isn't my fault you didn't get it! . . .
- You better do something about the mess around here—it's disgusting!. . . .
- Those two were talking about their dates, and my daughter overheard them! . . .
- I'm leaving this practice! Give me my records now! . . .
- I couldn't find a parking space, and it's pouring down rain! . . .
- What do you MEAN you can't find my record!. . . .
- You're hurting me! That's too tight! Take it off take it off! . . .
- I'm claustrophobic! Get me out of here now! . . .
- I'm not putting that gown on! Who knows who else has worn it! . . .
- That thing is COLD! Don't you care about your patients at all? . . .
- Did I say you could use my first name? How about some respect! . . .
- I am NOT going to wait ONE MORE MINUTE! . . .
- I'm not paying this bill! It's ridiculous! . . .
- I was here first! I was here first! . . .
- Of COURSE my insurance will cover it! You just didn't try hard enough . . .

THE SPLINTER FORMULA

This one is easy. Simply practice using the formula with each other so that it becomes comfortable. Encourage everyone to move away from the actual script and deliver the spirit of the formula in his or her own words.

Remember to give lots of Chips throughout these role plays!

FAST TRACK TO M.A.D.ness CD TRACKS

Step up to greater success with Professional Impact Programs

Professional Impact

Inspiring Action with Knowledge, Skills and Insights

Speaking Engagements - Executive Consulting –Training Workshops

Contact Wendy to discuss how she and her Team can help you and your Team to **Get M.A.D.!**

Email: **Wendy@Pro-Impact.com**

Phone: **1-800-70-IMPACT (800-704-6722)**

Website: **www.PRO-IMPACT.com**

All Professional Impact programs are customized to your specific needs to enable you to **M**otivate, **A**lign and **D**ifferentiate your practice.

Spread the M.A.D.ness!